This book was created by Nicolas de Rabaudy, gastronomy columnist.
Translated from French by Lingorama (USA) : Frank Debonair,
Meredith Rogers and Bailey Pepper
www.lingorama.us

Library of Congress Control Number: 2016955878

ISBN: 9781419725180

©2015 Éditions de La Martinière, an imprint of EDLM
for the original and English edition
Published in 2016 by Abrams, an imprint of ABRAMS

Printed and bound in October 2016
10 9 8 7 6 5 4 3 2 1

**ABRAMS** The Art of books
115 West 18th Street, New York, NY 10011
www.abramsbooks.com

ABRAMS

ERIC BEAUMARD

With the participation of Thierry Hamon

Photographs: Fabrice Leseigneur

# THE WINES OF MY LIFE

ABRAMS New York

# Foreword

**W**hen I met Eric Beaumard for the first time, his reputation had preceded him, and I wondered who was the man behind the legend. I can honestly say that the character lives up to his fame, and the words he often repeats truly sum up his personality: "If your eyes shine when you talk about wine, my heart just opens wide."

Eric is a passionate, inspiring, spontaneous man, loyal and generous. He has traveled the world using for his only map and tourist guide the names of vineyards and winemakers. The latter overtime have become his friends. Eric never leaves anyone indifferent. He is endearing and knows how to ignite a special relationship with anyone, which allows him to discover new bottles all the time and suggest them to our patrons according to their dishes.

Charismatic, eloquent, bright-eyed, and always elegant, Eric leads the restaurant Le Cinq as would an opera-ballet director. His work demands precision, because of repetitions and emotions. Emotions are always present, as each guest lives a magical moment, in awe as soon as the conversation starts rolling. Then, the show begins. Eric is inexhaustible. He is an open encyclopedia of oenophilia. He has the intelligence of scholars without their pretension.

His exceptional career is an inspiration for the younger generations. Much of it is contained in this book: passing on this love of wine, so dear to him, and revealing to both novices and experts of this elixir what was the singular path that led him to succeed.

We are very proud at the Four Seasons Hotel George V that Eric Beaumard counts among our greatest talents.

**José Silva**
*Regional Vice President*
*CEO of Four Seasons Hotel George V*

# Foreword

.....................

I met Eric over 10 years ago at The Georges V in Paris. We immediately connected when I went to the V for dinner. His passion for wines was mesmerizing. I could listen to him talk about wine endlessly.

Shortly after that we started having memorable wine tastings in the "Cave" of the V. We drank some legendary wines together. Very quickly, a strong friendship developed between us. What a pleasure to drink great wines with somebody who enjoys and knows so much about all wines. In 2008 we decided to go visit the Chateaux in Bordeaux. Eric organized the 3-day trip with lunch and dinner every day with the Owners of the most amazing Chateaus of Bordeaux. I was in heaven. Not only did we drink amazing wines but Eric knew everything about each Chateau since the origin of it and about all the regions of Bordeaux. He is a real walking and talking encyclopedia of wine. This was one of the most memorable trips I've ever had. I was on cloud nine and I didn't' want to come down to earth.

Then in Oct 2012, Eric came to visit me in Napa, where I have a vineyard, and we did the harvest together. We had a lot of fun and once again I could experience his profound knowledge and passion for wine during the entire process from the harvest, to the sorting of the grapes, then the fermentation. Then he came back in the spring of 2014 to do the final blending of the same 2012 vintage which was my first vintage. It was so special to have Eric do the blending with us and give us his notes and recommendations for the final blend. He has an unbelievable nose and can capture all the nuances of each parcel that we were tasting one after the other. He was really instrumental in the making of a great wine for my first vintage that we harvested together! Throughout all the experiences together Eric could not have been more gracious, more helpful, more joyful. A true friend.

Maurice Marciano
*Marciano Estate*

# Foreword

T he year was 2001 and I was visiting Bordeaux with my wife Deborah, Harlan Estate's winemaker Bob Levy and estate director Don Weaver. As part of our full immersion into the phenomenon that is VinExpo, one evening we had the extremely good fortune to dine at Château Latour, as guests of Florence Rogers and Frédéric Engerer. The night was sultry and following some animated conversation and canapés on the terrace overlooking the Gironde estuary, we retired to the loveliest of dining rooms and were introduced to the other honored guest of the evening…Eric Beaumard.

We sat to the large round table, beautifully appointed with bone china, fine silver, and an encouragingly vast array of (yet unfilled) crystal stemware. Beginning with the welcoming glass of Champagne and continuing through to the dessert wine, our host Monsieur Engerer – as is his modus operandi – solicited from each of us our best hypothesis as to what we were drinking.

A few of our best guesses came close but more often were wide of the mark. Eric, on the other hand, modestly – without pretense but also lacking any self-doubt – correctly identified the appellation, producer and vintage of each of the several wines that were so generously poured that evening. He could offer with similar ease, an anecdote about the chateau's proprietor or arcane details of the growing season.

Our small California contingent discovered that evening what much of Europe and the civilized world already knew: Eric Beaumard is not only a gifted taster brimming with an immense reservoir of wine knowledge, but also a man of great charm and humor.

I recount this story because it so aptly set the tone for all of my subsequent encounters with Eric, be they in the grand cavern beneath Georges V, in the elegant environs of Le Cinq, or in the cellars and sitting rooms of some of the best addresses in the wine world. Yet it is unlikely that I could offer a portrayal of him that would not be readily apparent to all who know him or even meet him in passing: his warm demeanor and engaging personality, his optimistic outlook, the ready, infectious laughter identify him as an instant collaborator.

We view our approach to winegrowing as a pure expression of the art of Man & Nature: a form of art taking our audience on a journey, where through anticipation and contemplation, our patrons can aspire to capture a glimpse of the sublime. We strive to provide opportunities and experiences that enrich the lives of the curious, the appreciative and the discerning.

I believe that these are the same principles that have shaped and guided Eric's life and chosen profession. He has dedicated himself to engaging passion and intellect for the sheer joy of elevating the human experience. Moreover, Eric has invested the time, logged the miles, and walked the rows of vines that infuse his knowledge with special truths and insights.

As a willing mentor to an entire generation of sommeliers, he is creating a legacy of scholarly, passionate enjoyment of wine and cuisine. And amid the bastion of French wine, he is a champion of the best of California as an appellation worthy of serious consideration.

This world needs more Eric Beaumards.


**H. William Harlan**
*Harlan Estate*
*Oakville, California*

# Table of Contents

Portrait of Eric Beaumard by Nicolas de Rabaudy 11

*Champagne* Wines 30

*Loire Valley* Wines 72

*Burgundy* Wines 124

*Bordeaux* Wines 214

*Rhone Valley* Wines 348

*Other Vineyards in France* 418

Wines from *Europe & the World* 448

*Eaux de Vie, Liqueurs, Ciders and Beer* 532

Acknowledgments 572

Index of Domains 574

Bibliography 575

La Cave

# Eric Beaumard

## B RUMMEL OF THE DIVINE BOTTLE
## PROMISING STARTS

He should have been a chef. As a teenager, he had the sacred fire, the taste of good things at his table, while living with his parents in Brittany, in Fougeres.

As a child, he lived a happy pious existence (he was a soloist at church on Sundays). In the countryside, he spent his time during each season between a father, inseminator by trade, who led him from farm to farm, and an inveterate grandfather hunter, whom he followed through the fields. Germaine, his paternal grandmother, a farmer in Chemillé, a genuine cordon bleu, educated his palate and helped form his taste buds. No one could produce a creamy rice pudding like she could. The plate preceded the glass, which is in the order of everyday foods. The Sunday roast chicken farm was not yet conducive to a strong – liquid – marriage. It would come – especially given his father Louis's particular fondness for the wines of Burgundy and the everyday red wines from nearby Anjou.

Coming out of college, he was directed towards a cook apprenticeship. In Roc'Land, a restaurant in the village of Tremblay, between Ferns and Pontorson, he performed serious work. The young apprentice shared an attic with Spartan comfort and spotty heating with his peers, in exchange for unimaginable schedules by today's standards. One evening, the chefs, for a "laugh," torched his moped! A friend gave him a hand to fix it. To celebrate his graduation in 1979, his grandfather opened a Coteaux du Layon 1971 from Robin in Faye of Anjou. His first glass of wine! For, until then, Eric could not bear the idea of drinking wine …

A few years later, with his Certificate of Professional Aptitude (CAP) as a cook – his only state diploma – Eric was introduced to the game of saucepans at the Saint-Sauveur Hostel in Rennes, three forks in the Michelin, owned by chef Durand, formerly from Lasserre in Paris. There, he learned to cut meat, to clean fish and shellfish, and to draft dishes and menus. He was appointed sous-chef in this good traditional Breton restaurant where everything was homemade. He felt in his element performing the movements, in contact with the stoves. The brotherhood amid the boys of the brigade added something more after work hours. This position awarded him his first chef hat and, somehow, his only one.

**Another life**

In December 1981, the first drama in his life occurred. Eric and Bertrand, his brother, lost their mother after a long illness. From then on, their father devoted all his time to his sons. All of a sudden, the course of his life accelerated. On the afternoon of March 18th, 1982, during a break between the two shifts, Eric went to visit a friend – Clement Tumoine – at the Pontchaillou Hospital, in Rennes. The latter was in intensive care, and Eric could only see him through a bay window. The sight upset him, and on his way back, he stopped to swap his Cromwell helmet, the famous English brand, for a French standard one. Late that night, after a good day, he went home on his motorcycle. While crossing Rennes, coming out of nowhere in a bend he spotted two cars blocking the entire road in front of him. He tried to slip through in between them. The impact with the vehicle on the right propelled him a distance of 18 meters. His entire right side was hit. He crashed back on his head, his helmet miraculously saving his life. But there was still a price. His right arm was shattered, his aorta affected, his right leg badly damaged, with open fractures. Half-conscious in the ambulance, which arrived quickly, he heard an emergency technician saying, "There is a risk of gangrene." At Pontchaillou where he was taken, two teams took turns in the operating room, each operating seven and half hours in a row. A specialist for the gravely wounded was flown in from Nantes by emergency helicopter. The report was serious: three double fractures, 368 stitches, his right arm, though dead, was saved, his right leg reinforced with metal plates that would have to remain his entire life. When he woke up, his first memory was of his father who covered his mouth when he saw a body with tubes everywhere, unrecognizable, that was supposed to be his son's. The right-hander became left-handed. The nightmare softened with a glow of happiness. It was in this hospital room of suffering that he met Marie, herself a road victim, who would become his wife and the mother of their three children: Margot, Lisa and Baptist. Marie, with a friend also seriously injured, had taken on the habit every week of visiting newcomers. She was the first person who entered Eric's room. It was love at first sight.

In 1984, he showed up at Olivier Roellinger's, the famous cook of Brittany, at the House of Bricourt in Cancale. He spent four months in the kitchen, trying to rebuild his shattered dream. He invented devices to open oysters and scallops with one hand and beat his proficient colleagues in the process. But his atrophied right arm no longer felt the heat. Completely insensate, he could not help burning himself on the edge of the stove. He was forced to give up. His life as a cook came to a stop there, in the shadow of the mad-about-spices Corsican chef. For Eric, this was a double setback. A dog's life!

**First steps in the world of wine**

During the hiatus, he began appreciating wines through the magazine "La Revue du Vin de France." The June 1984 issue was devoted to the 1983 vintage in Burgundy and authored by Michel Bettane. "The headline: 'Discovery of a new winemaker in Meursault… Jean-François Coche-Dury!' I had no idea that I would meet him and become his fervent admirer." In the meantime, he decided with Marie to undertake his first foray into the wine world. He charged ahead with resolve focusing on the Bordeaux region and, specifically, Saint-Emilion – and not just any place, but Ausone. Nothing less! Again, it was through his father's relationships that he was received by Alain Vauthier. It was a revelation, a delight, which, for him, opened up a previously unknown universe. The pathway to wineries unraveled before his eyes. Then they continued their journey in the Medoc, and, if ignored by the great chateaux, they toured them and, maps in hand, tried to understand the importance of ridges of graves, the influence of brooks, pine forests and marshes. Back home, thanks to Roellinger, he found a job in the cellars of the Cellier Saint Germain, in Rennes, with Jean-Pierre Lecluse. The position came without compensation, but the boss gave him many books on wine, his first ones, which he literally devoured, including the famous "The Taste of Wine," by Émile Peynaud.

Not long after, Eric moved to Paris with only his adult disability allowance and a letter of recommendation from Lecluse for the director of the sommeliers of France. This was January 1985. He met Jean Frambourg at the headquarters of the Association of the Sommeliers of Paris, located in René Boulanger Street. He was the then-elected president of the sommeliers of France. A humanist agent, a transmitter coupled with a big-hearted companion. "John allowed me to attend the Thursday afternoon tastings. The speakers were Georges Lepré, Philippe Bourguignon, and Jean-Luc Colles. And in the audience, you could recognize Philippe Faure-Brac, Hervé Bizeul, Didier Bordas, Didier Bureau, and David Ridgway, already well situated at the Tour d'Argent. And I landed in there."

In the aftermath, Frambourg sent him to introduce himself at the Plaza Athénée, at the starred restaurant La Régence. The restaurant manager received and informed him that there was no place for him! Two steps behind the manager, helpless, the second Maitre d'hotel had nothing to say. His name was Patrice Jeanne. In spring 2000, Eric would recruit him as number two at Le Cinq on the recommendation of Roxane Debuisson, the queen of Paris gourmets.

In June 1986, Beaumard drove back to Paris, following up on a classified ad in a newspaper, which he read front to back. He was hired at L'Ecluse, a wine bar in Bordeaux owned by journalist Georges Bardawil, one of the innovators of serving wine by the glass. The rough formula is that the glasses are offered with slices of foie gras and cheese. The white and red Bordeaux from Pierre Costes and Denis Dubourdieu, an ace of winemaking, played a handsome part in these specialized Parisian bistros.

Beaumard wanted more and better. Back to square one in Brittany. In autumn 1986, Marie encouraged him to pursue this time a CAP in accountancy, for which Eric studied diligently. Was this the right path? During training sessions in Beaune, he studied with Professor Max Leglise, Jean Siegrist of the National Institute for Agricultural Research (INRA) and even Michel Feuillat (the king of tannins in Burgundy). During these sessions, he befriended a giant whom he had met several times before: Christian Péchoutre, who, moreover, would become his best man. Between 1985 and 1987, he completed three adult training sessions in Beaune and two at the wine high school of Davayé near Macon. In 1987, he reached again for the third time the final for the title of best sommelier (that year, upon seeing him enter the examination room, some candidates chose to quit). He won the regional title again.

### The title of hope

In June 1987, he won the final for the best young sommelier of France, winning the Ruinart Trophy, that took place at Vinexpo in Bordeaux. A title coveted by all the professionals of the divine bottle. This time, his career had been launched. Meanwhile, dispirited, he called his wife from a phone booth on the Croisette to inform her of his failure. She reassured him: "Raymond Garcia has called again. There is a vacancy at La Poularde, a restaurant in the Loire." Eric handed the owner his recommendation letter signed by Raymond Garcia, his professional sponsor. Although his wife Monique had some reservations, the main owner, Gilles Étéocle, a good humanist, decided to give him a chance. Eric burst out crying. Apprehensive at the beginning, he proposed to his bosses that he work on trial for two weeks without pay. If he could manage, he would get hired! He was up to the task. Better yet, he undertook to restore the restaurant's emblem and usher it to the summit of high-end gastronomy. The relationship between Étéocle and the Breton with his dangling arm was a familial one. These two had found each other. The chef was moved and flabbergasted by the mastery of this sommelier able to tie his own shoelaces and his tie with only one hand. He transcended his disability. "When he introduced himself to me, I didn't even see his destroyed arm," said Gilles Étéocle, a chef, best worker of France, and winner of the Taittinger prize. "I felt in him such a motivation, such a strong desire to be part of our restaurant that I gave him right away the job of sommelier of La Poularde." This move radically transformed the daily life of the hotel-restaurant in Montrond-les-Bains. What a bright idea for the patrons inspired by the communicative passion and energy of this new deacon of wine! "Boss, does my arm bother you?" asked Beaumard on his first day at La Poularde. "Not at all; for me, your disability doesn't exist. You've overcome it and turned it into an asset with the customers." Well spotted, dear Étéocle. Eric had already compiled a large address book filled with the best professionals of the pipette: Beaumard developed his nose and palate during competitions and countless visits to domains and tasting salons. He dragged the chef to train him in the vineyards of Burgundy and Alsace. Ah! The visits to the Amazons Faller at the Domaine Weinbach, where they received such warm welcome. And those lunches orchestrated by their cook, the best pike of his life, legendary baeckeofes, all shared on the large oak table in the kitchen between Colette (who passed away in February 2015) and her daughters, Catherine and Laurence (who left us abruptly in 2014).

**Sommelier at last**

The oenophile members in the region very quickly took note of the address. Given an opportunity in the Loire, people showed up for primarily the jewels of the cellar. The Beaumard effect moved at full speed.

Among the pearls he found upon arrival was a fine collection of three legendary vintages from Marcel Guigal. Since the early 1970s, Étéocle's father had bought these wines 240 necks at a time! In 1987, he still had 96 bottles of Mouline 1978. A dream. In the Grands Crus of Guigal alone, there were nearly 2,500 bottles, to which there had to be added: 300 bottles of Pétrus, 60 magnums

of Dom Pérignon 1975, 60 pink Cristal and some bottles of Domaine de la Romanée-Conti, as many as in La Tour d'Argent. And way more than in Maxim's, which Pierre Cardin took over in 1982, rushing to auction two cases of Mouton Rothschild 1945.

In the vineyards, Eric initiated valuable relationships in order to obtain rare and legendary vintages. The Breton with gifted taste buds became passionate about wines from the island of Madeira, "the wine that never dies," after meeting, thanks to a Belgian friend and lover of great wines, a couple from Antwerp, the first importers in Europe of the great Madeira vintages. They possessed nearly 160 vintages for sale! Unrivaled in the world. They stocked La Poularde with Sercial 1910, Boal 1922, with half-bottles of Terrantez 1955 and Malvasia 1900. Rare bottles, decanted in carafes, were displayed in a tailored wardrobe in a corner of the dining room, near the old liquors of Chartreuse of Tarragona. And whenever he could, Eric headed back to the vineyards. Thus, he found himself in 1990, along with Marie and Margot, then one year old, at Chateau Soutard, grand cru of Saint-Émilion, for the harvest alongside a wonderful family of Catalan gypsies. His meeting with François de Ligneris would have long-term benefits. The man was born a teacher, combined with a sardonic sense of humor. Robert, the former maitre d'hotel and sommelier quit La Poularde to work for the Zannier family (now friends of Eric). Beaumard was promoted as the first head sommelier in the history of the restaurant. His presence became more prominent and he began to exercise control over the room. God, all these great wines being paraded on tables! Especially since the 50-seat shift at night and 90 to 100 on Sunday afternoon were legendary. Meanwhile, he was able to get a young woman hired to help him at La Poularde: she would be his first sommelier. Joelle Marti joined the small team of Montrond. She remained loyal to him. Even today, they stay in touch although she has a very important position in London. Their friendship remains intact.

**Consuming passion**

In 1992, he put together oenological evenings for 50 seats. The members, all regulars at La Poularde, granted him unfailing allegiance. In 2015, some of them, like the Ferrante family, the Pierre, as well as several couples of friends from the Loire, are now clients of Le Cinq, as they do not go to Paris without going back to "their sommelier."

In 1992, he finished second in a feat impossible to organize or even to conceive of today, the contest of the world's best sommelier in French wines, organized by the Sopexa Group. The competitions took place over three days. All candidates had to perform all the tests; the logistics were daunting. Everything took place within the Grand Hotel in Paris. At the time, someone with whom he would one day be crossing paths again worked in the kitchen, the Breton Christian Le Squer. The competition was very popular. Olivier Poussier had won the previous session in 1990. Since then, every two years, Eric's assistant would switch, and a newcomer would occupy the function now beginning to be sought after. In early 1993, a young Brestois with a strong character – he went to school in French Guiana – made his appearance. Philippe Emmanuelli would be Eric's assistant: outstanding, tough, while simultaneously developing his own brand of knowledge. The afternoons at La Poularde resembled European finals. A passionate emulation. During this time, clients shipped bottles from around the world to him while on business travels, travels of discovery, or holidays.

In November 1994, he accepted an invitation from his great friend, Christian Stevanin, requesting his presence to sponsor his sommelier section in Dinard. One of the youths was urged by his friends to compliment him about a vintage of his own. After the reading, the teacher said to Beaumard "I'm thinking of him for the Spring training in Montrond. You two are made for each other." Readier than ever, Eric won the coveted title of Best Sommelier of Europe, the Ruinart Trophy, in 1994. The coronation took place in Reims in the Gallo-Roman chalk cellars of the Maison Ruinart, under the patronage of Count Roland de Calonne d'Avesnes, president of the ancestral house founded in 1729. He would be the great promoter and defender of wine cellars as he was of old stones. Back in Montrond, he was celebrated as the winner of the European Cup. Hubert de Billy, the iconic boss of the Champagne Pol Roger, showed up with a magnum of the flagship vintage, Sir Winston Churchill, and all the regulars of La Poularde were invited to a memorable banquet.

## A friend for life

In spring 1995, a young native Breton sommelier arrived in Montrond for a two-month stay. His name was Thierry Hamon. Regarding their relationship, one could echo the words of Montaigne describing his friendship with La Boétie: "because it was him, because it was me." Hamon took over from Emmanuelli without losing contact with the public.

Several months later, a friend of Eric's, Giuseppe Vaccarini (1978 world's best sommelier), would introduce a young colt with a substantial prize list. He was Europe's best student chef in 1993: Enrico Bernardo was about to debut at La Poularde, shouldered from the start by Thierry Hamon. What a fate! What a flair also to add Enrico to the team! He started by learning the basics of life at La Poularde before taking over Thierry's duties, who got an assigment for two years in England at the famous Manoir aux Quat'Saisons near Oxford, working for Raymond Blanc, the famous starred chef. Not a single week would go by without Eric, who was on duty at the shop before the evening shift, talking to Thierry at the Manor. Michèle was the exceptional receptionist at La Poularde. A born hostess, endowed with a rare kindness and a boundless devotion to Eric, she helped him research records and decrees. The Internet and the "fairy" Google were not born yet. Nevertheless, she managed to perform magic. A great lady of the hospitality industry.

It was actually the entire staff of La Poularde who was behind Eric to support him: the butlers, Bernard Pillard and Dominique Guitard, the cooks, Bernard Barret the grill-master, Philippe Sailly the second and the fish leader, Eric Sadot the grand debonair entremetier, Christian Point the pastry chef, and the stainless Mr. Dubois, 40, head of the pantry at La Poularde and absolute fan of Eric. Meanwhile, the Milanese Enrico, crazy about food and worldly wines, passed through Troisgros in the kitchen and the brothers Mons from Roanne, famous cheesemongers, would stand out very quickly and start to take part in competitions. Without a doubt, La Poularde was the birthplace of great talents for sommeliers. Enrico and Thierry would reteam for the opening of Le Cinq.

## Going global

While engaged in his adventure, Eric had been preparing for another sizeable one, the 1998 competition of best sommelier in the world to be held in Vienna, Austria. Between 1995 and 1998, he toured the world during his vacations with Marie and sometimes the children, in order to survey all the vineyards which hitherto had been unknown to him:

Argentina and the Province of Mendoza, Chile and the Colchagua valley, California, South Africa and the Cape province, Australia from Perth to Coonawarra... After each trip, he enriched his knowledge in oenology, in the history of vineyards, in climatology, in the study of underwater currents, in the French, European, World legislations, in grape varieties through wine territories and their worldwide synonyms. He tackled all beverages, alcoholic or not. Eric explains, "At that time, if I participated in the global competition, I had to know all the great vineyards, old and new, on the planet. It was a requirement, a form of ethics, because the wine world was undergoing a revival and particularly all "new" country producers." From his end, Edward not to be undone. He incarnated the "gentleman farmer" in all his nobility. He would become Beaumard's benefactor, the "well-dressed" sponsor of the candidate in Vienna and, in particular, he took care of the Richelieu. For Beaumard noticed at once the Church's of Edward. For our sommelier, this was an unattainable goal (they were worth in the neighborhood of 900 francs). Edward was going to handle it. At the time, he had an office in London. "I told him my dream and asked about his willingness to acquire me a pair, for a fee. He agreed on one condition: to be my sponsor for the competition!" As he said, "In Reims, we sponsored Formula One for their tire equipment, so from now on, I'll take care of your "hides" when you come back to the stall!" And this was how for several years he helped Beaumard on this ground and allowed him to work every day in Montrond in Church's Consul. "Edward doesn't know, but I still have the pair he wore the day of the contest in Vienna and the first one he gave me. And they still... walk!"

Wearing his English shoes, he completed and honed what was likely the most peculiar uniform in the annals of sommeliers. He left nothing to chance. His gray striped trousers, his logs and satin-lined jackets were made to measure by an old stephanois tailor who visited him once a year. Since the accident, it was out of the question to buy ready-to-wear garments. The scars from the accident forced him to resort to custom clothing. His shirts were ordered from the branch of a great English shirt-maker in Dinan. These were shirts with French cuffs. The shirt front was lined with honeycomb, whereas the buttonholes designed so that one could screw tiny pearl or onyx buttons. The starched collars had to be mounted on Chinese collars and then screwed in the front and back. For Beaumard to slip on this bright armor required the assistance of a young clerk. During the important evenings, Thierry became responsible for knotting his white bow tie. There only remained the black apron, cut from a wrinkle-free and light material, to gird around his waist. Descending the stairs leading to the lounge where the patient guests waited took on a Downton Abbey-like quality as when Lord Grantham was getting ready for dinner.

Both Eric and Edward knew about elegance. The dressed-up evenings, the flattering cuts, the padded-shouldered jackets that fit perfectly, the Windsor knotted ties, the alpaca, the English flannel and the perfect suits that one kept for a lifetime. Self-care reflected on everyone. Brummel was reincarnated in these two friends of the divine bottle.

Eric never forgot the Champenois's timely and generous engagement. Dressed like a lord. So British. "He is for me a model of a man," said Edward de Nazelle about him. "We have a wonderful complicity, common tastes in suits, in moccasins. I love the way he talks about wine. He made me discover wines, domains, blindfolded. I love it. He won me over in Montrond-les-Bains when he created with two revelers his association of Wines Lovers: the MWW for Mad Wines-Waiters."

For the one who was to win the world sommelier title, the payoff was huge, because the winner's picture was profiled in magazines around the world. He embodied his country. He was the universal lord of wine. Not a trifle. When the results arrived, it was the German Marcus Del Monego who stood on the top step. Eric came in second. 1998 Vice-World's Best Sommelier. Ah! La Poularde, how many memories of meals, parties, treats, of bottles priced at rates never seen before and that will never be seen again. In 1999, before Eric's departure, the 1985 Henri Jayer Richebourg cost 800 francs on the menu! They had to find customers in Saint-Etienne, Clermont-Ferrand, Roanne, and even further.

## A springboard

His friend Edward was present again when the time came to advise the leaders of the future George V. The legendary palace was owned by HRH Prince Alwaleed Bin Talal Bin Abdulaziz Alsaud, from Saudi Arabia. The general management of the hotel was entrusted to Didier Le Calvez. Beaumard appeared for the first time before Le Calvez in February 1999, in the temporary offices of the George V, rue Pierre Charron, for the choice of sommelier and restaurant manager.

In May 1999, he was hired as a consultant to create the cellars of the George V. The palace was set to reopen, with among its assets a unique florist who went on to revolutionize floral art in the great hotels around the world.

A chef, Philippe Legendre, was hired. Philippe was a three-star chef who hailed from Vendée, and was in 1996 considered the best worker of France (MOF) while at the helm of Taillevent where Jean-Claude Vrinat, the very demanding owner – together with Claude Terrail of La Tour d'argent, (himself, one of the last great restaurant owners in Paris) – appreciated the level of his talent and devotion. This last reference was related to the George V because it was Claude Terrail's father who created the George V, the first to occupy the CEO function from the opening in 1928 until the US crisis ruined the New York banker originators of the project in 1931.

**Between you and me, Paris!**

Eric started by focusing on the cellar of the Four Seasons Hotel George V, which was almost empty. In May 1999, Didier Le Calvez (now president and CEO of the Bristol Paris), who came from the Pierre, the mythical palace in New York, arrived at the Four Seasons in Paris as general manager. A native of Auray Breton, he had the strong presence of big bosses, a sharp look, broad shoulders, and a singular experience of habits and customs of great luxury hotels. For the new barely-out-of-the-ground George V, he was the right man – the deus ex machina who enlivened the 1928 art deco-inspired building, redesigned by Pierre-Yves Rochon, by taking into account the strict international hotel standards established by the founder of the Canadian group, Isadore Sharp.

Two months before the opening, Le Calvez and Beaumard discussed at length the organization of Le Cinq and the restoration of the palace. Exposed to American culture, and American at heart, Le Calvez did not want a cathedral service, a stuffy Mass of food and wine where the solemnity iced the guests. No heavy-handed rituals, but a quality relaxed atmosphere, French style, devoid of formality: a restaurant accessible to all gourmets. This marked the beginning of a warm relationship, punctuated by creativity, rigor, and parties. In private, the impressive leader turned into a jolly fellow. It was in these moments that Le Calvez discovered the great taster and sommelier in action, his unique palate, how he experienced wines, was able to speak volubly about them, and expressed an endless desire to share his impressions. Beaumard, the sommelier, was an obvious lecturer, a man whose very demeanor and gestures exuded generosity. He was a lord driven by the modesty of a young oenophile. Didier Le Calvez realized that Beaumard had erased his disability forever. This was the miracle of the wounded Breton. He lived his drama well.

Soon enough, Beaumard became aware of the scope of the very customized position created for him. There was nothing like it throughout the Four Seasons group. He joined the select club of sommelier restaurant managers among whom was Philippe Bourguignon, Best Sommelier of France, at the Laurent. He has since become its irreplaceable general manager. At the opposite end, Le Calvez's expectations were high. True, at first he did ask the director of Le Cinq for some Pinot Noirs from Oregon. But soon, he let go of this wine to serve some of the masterpieces from Burgundy and then Bordeaux. It was under his leadership that Eric piled up in the cellars of George V grand Bordeaux vineyards – vintages 1995, 1998, 1999 – in huge quantities.

Responsible for the budgets of the grand hotel, the late Chief Financial Officer, Michel Lefèvre, a ruthless controller of spending, never tampered with the wine purchases – up to 500,000 euros in the first months following the opening of the palace. Over the years, the responsibility for purchasing wine would be redirected, in part from le Calvez – forever on the lookout for new talent – to Enrico Bernardo, in whom he bestowed a great deal of confidence. He supervised everything, and, if needed, took a stance.

In 2005, Beaumard and Le Calvez and their spouses went to the Romanée-Conti – a dream-come-true for the general manager of the George V. Aubert de Villaine; and Bernard Noblet welcomed them. After the wine tasting on drums, they were ushered – a rare privilege – to the deepest vaults of Conti. Among the rare wines they were going to taste, without telling them, Mr. Noblet blindly served a grand Echezeaux 1953. The birth year of Didier Le Calvez. Unbelievable. "The wine carried notes of dried porcini mushrooms, sweet spices, with a remarkable finesse." Three hours immersed in the cellars of the most famous Grand Cru of the timeless Burgundy, in the soul of the wine with a "ballerina body" (Bernard Burtschy). In 2009, Didier Le Calvez began to acquire plots of land in the region of Puisseguin Saint-Emilion, which would give birth to Château Clarisse – the name of one of his daughters. Today, the domain owns eleven hectares conducted in biodynamic, under the vigilance of the consulting oenologist, Stéphane Derenoncourt. "Ultimately, Didier had become a true wine lover. Its production is among the best in the region." In 2015, Didier Le Calvez, general manager and chairman of the Bristol (with its showcase three-star Epicure restaurant run by Eric Fréchon ), was elected best hotel manager in the world – a title never before bestowed upon a Frenchman.

## Launch the ship George V

With his friend, expert on Burgundy wines Dominique Rézette, he built in record time a first stock of Burgundy. In the Bordeaux region, Raymond Garcia opened the doors of his reserve to build lines of great wines. His friend Jacques Diebolt from Cramant in Champagne

granted him an incredible access to some Jamet and Chave. The Perret supplied him with several vintages. Within weeks, he had purchased nearly 7,000 bottles for the high-end market. In November 1999, the time for the departure of Beaumard had come. He had to say goodbye to the Montrond house, which had come to accept him as he was and had enabled him to become what he was, a worthy sommelier.

Étéocle was in tears. He never recovered. Others would succeed Beaumard, beginning with the remarkable Richard Bernard, but his were big shoes to fill.

For others, it was a rupture. Maurice, his stepfather, put the finishing touches on the house that Beaumard had built in a private park on the edge of the village. A delightful house where the winery was located at the center and the kitchen designed according to his physical handicap. The living and dining room with its fireplace modeled after an antique store occupied a prominent place. At the beginning, Marie and the children remained in Montrond, while Eric went back and forth to Paris every week. He was first housed in Christopher Lambert's apartment, a few steps from the George V. Then Roxane Debuisson made a studio available for him in her building. She was the Madonna of cooks, pastry chefs, and sommeliers. Roxane was the guest of the best tables in Paris. She would be the first patron of Le Cinq on the opening day! And for the following eight years, the most faithful one, receiving at her table the entire elite of Paris, of the arts and letters, and also political and state personalities. In September 2000, the whole Beaumard family moved to Paris to a house in the twelfth arrondissement. The adventure took a new direction. Unknown to Paris, Beaumard had to prove himself to Chef Legendre, who knew nothing about this provincial man and about sommeliers in general – and especially given that at the time, Jean-Claude Vrinat was the only one to deal with the wines at the Taillevent. There was no sommelier on the floor. Fast and furious, Legendre and Beaumard formed a hell of a team at Le Cinq. It would be a blessed marriage for the first four years. Initially, the lanky Legendre recovered from the infernal pace at the Taillevent. He pushed himself to the limits. When leaving Lamennais Street in the eighth arrondissement, he was depleted, gasping, "a living dead," underscored Beaumard. The excitement of the challenge at Le Cinq, the creativity in the kitchen, and the presence of Beaumard, vice world's best sommelier, gave the chef, who only had to cross the Champs Elysées, a second wind. The launch of le Cinq, the stately dining room with Doric columns that opened onto a spacious and light courtyard garden, owed much to the mutual agreement sealed in June 1999 between Legendre and Beaumard. These two went on to forge a strong and lasting bond. Even before the opening in spring 2000, they met every day, shared a glass or a plate, and talked about gastronomy, about simple, coarse or fancy meals – with a focus on a harmony between food and wine, the Kingdom of the former head sommelier of Montrond. The firepower of the George V rested in the fact that the wine list was accessible from any point of sales in the hotel. Whether you were in an apartment, the bar, the gallery, or taking part in a worldly reception, the choice of wines from Le Cinq was available. Two years after their opening, the cellars matched the finest houses in Paris, such as the Ritz, Taillevent, the Plaza Athénée, and La Tour d'Argent. These dream vials had a price: Beaumard was already far beyond the ones in Montrond. The purchase prices were as well.

**Sommelier of the palace**

As soon as the dedicated Bacchus machine was launched, the director of Le Cinq secured from Le Calvez the management of the cellars, at will, with purchases of wine straight from the vineyards, without intermediaries, as well as two days of travel per month in the vineyards, taking with him young sommeliers each time, paying for their expenses regardless of the destination (from Champagne to South Africa!). All these advantages were reaffirmed by the successive general managers of the palace. The wine and spirits list was signed by Beaumard. He had all the space to develop it. At the same time, the brigade made up of two woman sommeliers at the beginning, one being Virginia Morvan (purchasing manager at Lavinia for 10 years), would be strengthened by the arrival of Thierry Hamon (who from November to December lent a hand to Richard Bernard, recruited by Eric at Troisgros to replace him in Montrond) and a few months later, the Milanese Enrico Bernardo. The latter in turn threw himself into the conquest of titles, with the kind support of Eric Beaumard. The entire brigade planned on helping Enrico in his preparations. He would win Europe's best sommelier in 2002 and the world's best sommelier in Athens in 2004, where a large part of the brigade, colleagues of the dining room and kitchen, came to support him alongside his family, parents, and oldest sister, who had been supporting him for years. In the front row of the audience, Eric Beaumard was the first to stand to help Enrico unhook the Italian flag at the foot of the stage while warmly congratulating him with tears in his eyes.

The succeeding months and years saw a unique situation in the annals of the restoration and the sommelier world, as within the same restaurant, two of the best sommeliers in the world – one awarded gold, the other silver – worked side by side. An incredible outpouring of energy prevailed at le Cinq. Sometimes there were sparks, but what great examples for the brigade's younger members. In 2006, Enrico embarked on personal projects with the success that we know: Il Vino Paris, Il Vino Courchevel, and then the Champagne & Wine shop in the district of Saint-Germain-des-Prés, and, more lately, the restaurant Goust near the Paris Opera.

Young people flocked to work alongside Beaumard at Le Cinq: Pierre Colin, head sommelier in the Rhone Valley; Fabien Bruguera, head sommelier in the Périgord; Sébastien Allano, head sommelier at the Four Seasons in Hong Kong; Koen Massechelein, director of restoration at the Shangri-La in Abu Dhabi; Vincent Debergé, head sommelier and director at the Beau Rivage in Geneva; Arnaud Kunz, head sommelier in Auvergne, and Edmond Gasser, sommelier in Munich. The list of these sommeliers, all having in common their rite of passage at Le Cinq Five in the wake of Eric Beaumard, elected by his peers sommelier of the year 2012 by the magazine Le Chef, is long. In hindsight, Beaumard confesses: "The sommelier profession can provide a remarkable social mobility. Wine brings men together, and the great lovers of fine wines need to have partners, tasting companions, who share their views and impressions. This is what we call a communion." In an effort to convince his audience that usually followed him, he organized wine tastings. Beaumard's tour de force resided in the fact that he never changed. He was the same man as at La Poularde. He talked about wines, always courteous, affable, unlike the cellar preachers who inflicted their knowledge who inflict their knowledge with haughty posturing, if not outright contempt. Another aspect distinguished him from many of his colleagues. The Breton would never stand for becoming no more than an office-sommelier who relied exclusively on wine maps and prices for proof of quality A. He occupied the turf. As for bureaucratic formalities, which a place like the George V engendered, he relied on his second sommeliers and the full investment of the purchasing and finance service of the hotel which brought him an unwavering support.

Always eager to learn more, to taste better, he learned a lot through the to-ing and fro-ing of great wines experienced at the hands of ardent wine lovers who opened their cellars with their hidden thousand treasures.

The moral was that Beaumard succeeded in replicating at the scale of the George V what he had achieved in the Loire. Some of his fans booked their suites at Le Cinq only after having had confirmation that the sommelier would be there to greet them.

People came for him, to get swallowed up in his recommendations – such as yours truly, one French patron who – since 2006 – has not only had more than 400 meals at le Cinq but has had dishes created for him by the Chef that are based on the wines he had chosen and vice versa. Alas, for this patron, the running experience resulted in a complete osmosis! Unique in every way!

**Planet Wine**

His appreciation for human relationships amplified quickly over time. An alchemy had come to life. A current flowed between the experts and the sommelier. He travelled, met clients in Caracas, and participated in the harvest in the domain of a fan in the Napa Valley. "I'm here to highlight the wines. In Los Angeles, I commented on wines made by my powerful host. That seemed normal to me. I like to teach, explain my feelings, share my impressions with winemakers and the cellar masters. Each instance is exciting." While harvesting in St. Helena in the Napa Valley in 2012, the owner of the vineyard – who owned a rare collection of chateau Lafleur Pomerol - uncorked eleven older vintages in his honor. A great moment in the life of a sommelier. Considering that there were Lafleur 1949, 1950, 1970, 1975, 1978, 1979, 1982, 1983, 1988, 1989, and 1990, it was a fabulous oenophile moment. In Crimea, Beaumard visited Massandra with customer-friends of Le Cinq. That day, the gates of the oldest vaults of the cellar were open so that they could taste wines more than a century old: some Muscats, pinot gris, vinified in sweet wines. What a vineyard! The cellars dated back to the tsar Nicolas II. They were preserved during the Revolution on Lenin's orders, then moved to St. Petersburg – Leningrad at the time – during World War II by Stalin, only to return later to their place of birth. Since the opening of Le Cinq in 1999, the wine culture intensified thanks to the complicity of successive CEOs who understood that Beaumard combined tradition and profitability. Following the departure in 2008 of Didier Le Calvez and a short interim by Mauro Governato (now general manager of the Hotel de Russie in Rome), men of great value who had taken turns contributing to the thriving art form:

– Christopher W. Norton (Four Seasons Executive Vice President, Global Product and Operations) based in Toronto. It was he who appointed Eric, during his presidency at George V Four Seasons, to becoming the advisor for the promotion of wine in Europe, Africa, and the Middle East.

– Christian Clerc (senior vice president of Four Seasons, in charge of operations for EMEA: Europe, Middle East, and Africa) based in Dubai.

– Since 2014, José Silva (Regional Vice President and General Manager of the Four Seasons Hotel George V), grand hotel manager, previously general manager of the Four Seasons Hotel des Bergues in Geneva, where he was responsible for the Four Seasons group takeover as well as all the subsequent renovations.

For Le Cinq, as always, Eric had a master art cabinetmaker in cognac design and build the four utensils chests in the room that shelter the invention of Grimod de la Reynière before the revolution. They were plated with satinwood inlay, displaying at the center the cameo biscuit of Limoges, emblem of Le Cinq, and covered with a polished dark green granite tray. The angles were made of ebony. Once again, these pieces of art were approved without an eyebrow being raised. The same requirement was applied to the cellars in 1928 during their conception. The lockers were built out of Iroko for an amount that alone exceeded the cellars' inventories in many of the large houses.

They contain today almost 45,000 bottles for annual sales exceeding 60,000 necks. From this number, we must subtract the 23,000 bottles of champagne that are served annually within the palace. At Le Cinq, some of these wines are served by the glass by a sommelier team, who rotates three Champagnes, four white, four red, four sweet, and four oxidative wines. With each change of dishes, of menu, some of them are modified to better cohere with new dishes. The change of seasons, and, more recently, in the management of the kitchen, brought these innovations forward. Indeed, recruited by José Silva, it is now Christian Le Squer who runs the kitchens of George V. At Le Cinq, the bottles of all the vineyards are uncorked and allow to express themselves in glasses without discriminating rank or goal. As Eric recalls: "One day, Edmond Vatan Chavignol confessed to me that there were no small wines, only small winemakers, because the wine was not to blame."

At le cinq, I met a charismatic sommelier-manager, happy to serve customers – many of whom became his friend over time. As a man who did good in a protected world made of sharing and good taste: oenophilia is humanism.

## Nicolas de Rabaudy

DIEBOLT-VALLOIS

P 32

VEUVE CLICQUOT PONSARDIN

P 38

SALON

P 46

DOM PÉRIGNON

P 53

KRUG

P 62

# Wines of

~

# Champagne

# Diebolt-Vallois

*Passion Flower: the Reward*

# T

## HE CHAMPAGNE REGION,
## LAND OF THE KINGS OF FRANCE

since Clovis, harbors many surprises for wine lovers. Here, the great and historical trading houses (they account for nearly 70% of the champagne production) sometimes make us forget the wealth of a creative, committed, and family-based viticulture. Luckily, for several decades, a good number of winemakers have been opening new horizons and discoveries to wine lovers. These new additions with their identities fertilize the landscape of Champagne and its champagnes.

As a sommelier, I have had the opportunity to meet some of these Champagne characters. I am thinking of Marie-Noëlle Ledru, in Ambonnay; the Moncuit family and Rudolph Peters, with two domains in Mesnil-sur-Oger; and of the Lilbert family as well, in Cramant. Still on the Côte des Blancs, in Avize, what I recall most is Olivier Bonville and his family. In this wine region, another name markedly stands out Anselme Selosse's, whose exemplary work started the vocations of many Champagne winemakers, concerned with their land and its peculiarities.

In a different style, Jacques Diebolt represents their archetype. First by the size of his vineyard (almost 9 hectares of chardonnay), then by his main and unique terroir, in Cramant (600 hectares in all in Grand Cru), the first village ranked 100% Grand Cru when you arrive on the Côte des Blancs from Epernay, with its hillsides facing south, offering a flattering aromatic expression without losing a great capacity for aging. A terroir that gives Chardonnays tension and a broad flavor.

The chalk subsoil is unique and can be found up to 20 meters deep! A great force in addition to a cool climate. This geological sponge has the ability to retain the wine's acidity and ensures that the delicate bubbles and the pleasant gustatory sensations prevail.

The Diebolt-Vallois – Jacques is now assisted by his children, Isabelle and Arnaud – live at the end of a small street strangely called "New." They are actually two families long established in the region. On the one hand, the Diebolts settled in Cramant in the late nineteenth century; on the other, the Vallois have resided in Cuis since the fifteenth century. In 1978, Jacques Diebolt and his wife, Nadia, born Vallois, combined their land and entwined their origins. They own deep cellars carved into the chalk at more than

15 meters deep. The fact that the stone was hand cut gives the cool and silent place the impression of being in a sanctuary.

Our Jacques's temperament makes him speak his mind. His wines retain the imprint of breeding added to great wines, as evidenced today by his Passion Flower vintage, whose *champenoise* rooms ensure that malolactic fermentation is avoided. This is the transformation of malic into lactic acid by means of anaerobic bacteria.)

In other words, this is a grand *blanc de blancs*, ideal for starting a meal. This is one of the reasons why it is always stocked in the champagne basin at Le Cinq!

Champagnes and desserts belong in the category of customary, even classic, partnerships. Suffice it to read the menu pages at the end of Noel Normand's book "The Fifth Republic in the Kitchen" to be converted. Not a single dessert without a great champagne vintage. Most of the time, these pairings had resulted in tragedies. But procedure has prevailed…

Since Christian Le Squer's arrival, however, a small miracle has occurred at Le Cinq. A great pastry harmony was born! A yeast-flavored dessert, virtually without sugar, prepared with a steam-based meringue, wrapped in a veil of white chocolate, with soft powdered almonds, served alongside an ice cream made with baker's and cream-based yeast. As soon as we savored this dessert, we thought about Jacques's Prestige. Prestige, with its delicate and subtle harmony, which allows both aromas to come to life without compromising the champagne's bubbles.

CHAMPAGNE
Diebolt-Vallois

# MEMORIES

The Diebolts belong to those winemakers whose demands start in the vineyard with cropping choices and controlled yields. Jacques cares for his wines until the end; for example, once he came with his wicker basket to the George V with some "sample" bottles, wrapped in straw, to pop them on the fly, in the cellar of the hotel... That evening, he had prepared some 1955 and 1961 vintages!

These wines made us experience intense bouquets of honey, dried pears, mignonettes, and wax. The fine evanescent bubbles anchored this nectar in a bed of full-bodied and persistently creamy sensations. Then the bouquet was amplified with notes of fresh black truffles and cultivated mushrooms. All of which blended deliciously with the black-truffled toasts.

Sometime later, in one of our private rooms, we dished up the true descendants of Grimod La Reynière: small game birds, "long bills," and other delights worthy of *My Father's Glory*. At the end of this journey, Jacques prepared us a 1947 Cramant, while these small prohibited birds, plump and golden, sizzling in porcelain pots, lay ahead... Nobody knows if Heaven offers those delights, but these minutes of ecstasy (greedy and rare) impregnated the paneling of the Louis XIII lounge.

For those who still would doubt the ability of champagnes to age, I am offering another memory of a "vertical" tasting (that is, to go back through time across increasingly old vintages), which I had the privilege of sharing with Pierre Arditi (without a doubt, a great wine enthusiast) and Thierry and his family, at Jacques's. All were happy to welcome us. On this occasion, we started on high notes in the cellar with 1953 and 1947 bottles, which Jacques uncorked on the fly, with toasted brioches, layered with generous slices of *foie gras* from a half-cooked goose. These wines had never moved from their resting place in the depths of the cellar, dug into the limestone. There they were, lying in their lees, on slats. Of course, these bottles are unique, and their evolution varies from one to the next. This time, they were truly alive, with their golden, bright, and intense color; a brioche and honey nose; and with their rare intensity.

Still, in the depths of the cellars, 1979, 1985, and 1990 vintages took turns! All displayed obviously more lightness and delicacy. Especially the superb 1985. A turning point in the champagne adaptation to consumer tastes came about with the famous 1999 Passion Flower. Very taut. The fruit-dazzling 2002 has an incredible aromatic tension. In these wines, we can infer Jacques's desire not to forget about the past and his father. Be that as it may, what a man, this Jacques! So endearing as he struggles like hell to preserve the family home in this region as posh as our golden triangle!

Pierre, Thierry, and I then began to go back up, leaving behind this seraglio, this paradise, where each imprisoned glass contains some truth. In the dining room, a delectable scent of Champagne hotpot presaged a good time to come. Which proved to be right! Particularly when many Côte de Beaune necks from the grand crus of Puligny-Montrachet and Vosne-Romanée joined the round of champagnes.

What a lunch! We drove back to Paris – with a driver! – well lubricated… and duly happy. I remember that during the trip back at one point I turned to Thierry, who was talking, to ask him to lower his voice because I heard Peter conversing on the phone. Thierry listened for a moment and, smiling, leaned towards me in the front seat and said, "He's not on the phone, he's reciting the second act of Sacha Guitry's *Faisons un Rêve*." We gave him all our attention. A few minutes later, Peter finished this famous monologue from the French repertory and said, "See, I'm not yet toasted! I still remember the lines!" It goes without saying that we cheered wildly.

This man, just like Jacques Diebolt, has always impressed and inspired me. And passion is the lifeblood of my life.

CHAMPAGNE
Diebolt-Vallois

# The Wines

Our character Jacques, a genuine thread in the Champagne winemaking culture, kept in his cellars something to remind us what were – and still are – the Champagne wines of the immediate postwar period. How many times did he uncork on the fly some 1947, 1953 (his first vintage made with his grandfather), some 1955, and his sublime 1959! I could barely keep count. My memory has recorded the slightest details, his vintages remaining of a rare precision. The yield has only been 4,500 kilograms per acre.

The wines originating from them give us now *Blancs de Blancs* of an extreme fullness. Jacques and his children, with their generosity, help to implant in our memories these testimonies of the past. His Prestige vintage consists of three blended vintages, aged in casks, to smooth and preserve the style of the house.

## Passion Flower vintage

As Jacques says, *"The alcoholic fermentation is done in barrels. No malolactic fermentation as my father and my grandfather conceived it, neither filtration nor collage: anything that can strain the wine is avoided in order to retain the terroir's full expression. Aging of a wine is in Burgundian barrels. It is a champagne made according to old tradition."* The first Passion Flower was born with the 1995 vintage.

2008. *To date, it is still not yet on the market but jealously sealed at the domain. However, when it comes out, it should be not missed. It is straightforward, incredible, taut, long, and full. It will certainly become one of the greatest achievements of the last twenty years.*

2004. *After ten years of aging, the wine reveals its restraint, though it falls in line with its predecessor's profile.*

2002. *A stunning bottle without heaviness and very fruity just like the 2000! In terms of matching dishes, I am thinking of a langoustines filo pasta, with a lemon juice and a 2002 Passion Flower.*

2000. *Fine nose, elegant, white flower notes. Powerful wine, very nice balance, and a good lingering finish. A great success.*

1996. *Both rich and concentrated. Endowed with a beautiful freshness, with citrus notes. Great fine bubbles.*

# Veuve Clicquot Ponsardin

*Once upon a time...*

# I

T ALL STARTED
WITH A COUNT.

Indeed, I would not have known Clicquot well without my friend the count Edouard de Nazelle, the last in a long line to serve this great house. He occupies a prominent place in my professional life since, all along, he has helped, supported and encouraged me. It all started one winter evening in 1995, at La Poularde. I still remember his table, the No. 5, near the dome, his back to the French windows. He was having dinner with Mr. Merle, the sales representative for the department of the Loire. I dare say, it was love at first sight. His immediate charisma, kindness, and energy seduced me. From that moment, we always remained in touch, and we became, over the years and shared bottles, inseparable. During our careers, some of our friends opened windows onto new horizons. Edouard opened quite a few for me.

Among the meetings that he organized, I will never forget the meal in Cancale in July 1998, at Roellinger's with my wife Marie. We chose this emblematic place because it was there that in 1984, while I was working in the kitchen despite my disability, that Olivier took me aside and, given the difficulties that my arm caused me, suggested to me, "Eric, why don't you try wine?" handing me a book on wine regions by Guy Renvoisé (a then key figure in the brokerage of great wines and the creation and management of wine lists for fine restaurants).

Consequently, this is where we decided to celebrate my silver medal, for the title of vice world champion of sommeliers, won a month before on June 7th in Vienna, Austria. Edouard introduced me to Karen H., who was back then in charge of the transition between the old and the new George V. During lunch, after a *Saint-pierre retour des Indes*, the classic Roellinger's John Dory dish, accompanied by an exceptional 1988 Chablis, grand cru Clos de Raveneau, Edouard said to his friend: "If you are looking for someone to handle the cellar of the George V, Eric is the man!"

Sometime later, shortly after the World Cup final – which France won – I was called into the temporary offices of the George V for a first meeting with Didier Le Calvez. Soon after, on his initiative, I started – first as a consultant – to purchase what would soon constitute "our cellar." On December 16th, 1999, we opened the George V; the Clicquot champagnes were of course ubiquitous. On the evening of December 31st, at midnight, whoever remained behind – most of them now work in other places, except for Martial Meneghini, our unwavering technical director – gathered to celebrate the new year around a bucket of champagne in the suite offering the best view of Paris. Thierry and I stepped onto the shoulder of the terrace where, before the glittering Eiffel Tower, we toasted to this new adventure.

But let's come back to Clicquot. To better understand this champagne house, I suggest that you immerse yourself in Fabienne Moreau's novel, "In the Secrets of Madame Clicquot," published by Plon in 2013. For sure, the story of Barbe-Nicole Ponsardin, the widow of François Clicquot at age 27, though somewhat fictionalized, contains all the authentic elements of a well-fulfilled life. Born in 1777, during the reign of Louis XVI, she died in 1866 during that of Napoleon III! The image we have of her is of an austere woman, as portrayed in a famous painting by Leon Cogniet. The painter was able of capturing all the determination of the character she needed to retain the champagne house inherited from her husband. At 27, she became one of the first businesswomen of her time and during the following years, was nicknamed the "great lady of Champagne." A famous anecdote characterized her: after the battle of Waterloo, the Russians and English invaded Champagne and ransacked her cellars. The widow Clicquot reassured her staff, saying, "Let them drink! They will pay more for the next bottles." Cleverly, she became responsible for the development of a riddling table, which gives a perfectly clear wine, freed from its lees.

After her death, her well-planned succession allowed her champagne enterprise to continue to grow, transcending all the vicissitudes of history – whose conflicts did not spare the Champagne region. Traces of machine-gun fire are still visible on the façade, garden side, of the Hotel du Marc in Reims, the private residence of the Clicquot brand. The year of the brand's bicentenary in 1972 saw the creation of La Grande Dame vintage 1962. What a beautiful tribute to this master woman. The recollection of that year reminds me of the magnum born soon after in 1964, precisely having been just tasted at the Hotel du Marc. I will come back to it. There, old bottles could be preserved thanks to the successive cellar masters. Including Dominique Demarville, only ten of them have held the chief cellars position since the creation of the brand in… 1772. This continuity has permitted them to refine the style of the wines

# CHAMPAGNE
## Veuve Clicquot Ponsardin

and to offer, above all today, batches called Private Cellar both in vintage and in rosé – one of my vinous sins and one of our regulars at Le Cinq.

M EMORIES
Memories? Where to begin? What to choose? For over twenty years, Edouard and I have lived so many incredible moments. I must repeat what an exceptional communicator he is. I can still see the chef's face at La Poularde, opening his newspaper one day. Our friend appeared in an insert carrying crates of champagne from the trunk of the Clicquotmobile (a 1960 Bentley S2 Continental Flying Spur that Edouard's father, Count Philippe, had purchased and got repainted in Cliquot yellow and aubergine) to the foot of the Great Wall of China!

So, with Edouard anything was possible. For example, during one of our first meetings with the Mad Wines-Waiters of the World (MWW) in the early 2000s, in Anjou, we met again in a hot-air balloon over the vineyards of the Aubance and its castles. All of a sudden, Edouard recognized in the distance an unmistakable silhouette, the castle of the Dukes of Brissac located in Brissac. He immediately told the pilot to fly towards the site. Once above the huge abode, known for being the highest castle in France (seven floors), Edouard said, "In the hall of the guards, there is a portrait of Barbe-Nicole Ponsardin, the widow Clicquot, with her great-granddaughter lying at her feet, by Leon Cogniet. Her great-great-granddaughter married the 11th Duke of Brissac in 1894." And that is how at 600 meters high, right above the castle, we opened a bottle of 1990 Grande Dame in tribute to the illustrious ancestors. There was also in the gondola an important lady of the sommelier world, Michèle Chantôme, to toast with us. She was an outstanding organizer of all sommelier competitions in the era of "Ruinart" and the godmother of MWW. After this appetizer, I remember this unprecedented event – still within the framework of the MWW – at the Hôtel du Marc. I must insert here a brief aside to share with you the evening outfits we wore for dinners. They were the most unlikely: evening dress or tuxedo, with white socks and black diving fins. In other words: penguin suits! One evening in May 1996, we had Mr. Francis Ford Coppola as guest of honor, accompanied by his wife and children, as well as their chef and their sommelier. We greeted him proudly below an arch of fishing rods and awarded him a "Palme d'Or"… a gold swim fin (in French, "palme" can also refer to a swim or diving fin; this pun was the brainchild of Eric Boschman). To celebrate his prize, we clinked glasses with a 1985 Grande Dame. Then we moved into the dining room, which back then, and still now, was very highly regarded at the Hôtel du Marc.

The appetizers consisted of terrine of duck *foie gras* accompanied by champagne gelatin cubes. The selected wine was a 1988 Veuve Clicquot Rich Reserve (released in 1995), which we discovered for the first time. A dry champagne with a nice balance that worked very well with the smoothness of the *foie gras*. Edouard exhibited all his communication skills to describe it. Then followed roasted langoustine tails with fresh mango chutney and spices. This was accompanied by a 1994 Sauvignon Blanc Cloudy Bay, very exotic and in complete harmony with the marine delicacy of langoustines and chutney. (This famous vineyard, Domain Cloudy Bay, located in the Wairau Valley in Marlborough, New Zealand, and established in 1985, was added in the early 1990s to the Clicquot house, as was Domain Cape Mentelle, located in Margaret River in Western Australia.)

Next came the main course: a veal fillet with a fricassee of morels, served with an exceptional 1976 Veuve Clicquot Rosé magnum popped for the occasion. The complexity of aromas and the subtlety of the bubbles in relation to the wine's momentum melted voluptuously with the dish. During dessert, we were able to savor a semi-dry Veuve Clicquot, served in a chilled carafe as was customary in large houses, with strawberries in juice, chopped icy mint, and a corolla of pink biscuits from Reims. A rare harmony since this type of service is becoming scarce, though entirely successful. After all these recollections, I am noticing how many more memories could be ascribed to the "Count." Some other time…

# CHAMPAGNE
## Veuve Clicquot Ponsardin

# The Wines

The style of the Clicquot wines is decidedly marked by Pinots. The wines, born around the Reims Montagne and the Côte des Blancs, are often vinous, powerful, and structured. As a matter of fact, Veuve Clicquot Ponsardin is one of the finest and oldest houses in the development of great champagne rosés. Here are some tasting notes taken during an exceptional lunch with Edouard, Thierry, Cyril Brun, the nose of the house (whom Edouard had also recruited), and myself.

## Tasting at the Hotel du Marc, Winter 2014

**Vintage 2002.** *Vivid and intense color and bubbles. The opened nose is floral and fruity. Light toasted notes. The palate gives creamy bubbles, the balance evolves into a beautiful fullness, a richness with a final leaning towards minerality. A great success.*

**1990 Rosé.** *Intense padparacha sapphire hue. The bubbles are very fine. Concentrated nose, kirsched, notes of tangerine zest and macerated wild strawberries. A lot of elegance. The palate is generous, spicy, with white pepper touches, structured, and with creamy bubbles. A wine that would agree wonderfully with scallops a la plancha, with yuzu.*

**Private Cellar 1979 Rosé.** *A great wine for wine lovers. And what wine! As I glanced around the table, I noticed that this wine was the most "tasted" among the guests! This is a sure sign.*

**Private Cellar 1989 White.** *Intense golden color, fine and very discreet bubbles. Wide nose, slightly generous, confit recalling frangipane, Bourbon vanilla and Lorraine plum jam. Very wide palate, spherical, slightly concave, a mineral peak in the finish. Overall, a generous champagne to serve with, for example, a poached chicken with an Albufera sauce.*

# CHAMPAGNE
## Veuve Clicquot Ponsardin

**1982 Private Cellar White.** *Wine with an intense golden yellow. Generous nose, powerful, complex, reminiscent of candied chestnut, sweet almond, and plum. Full-bodied mouth, light lack of tone. The finish is creamy and evokes an apple pie. The whole is coherent, though a tad heavy.*

**1964 Magnum.** *Very intense golden color, visual presence of bubbles almost imperceptible. Nose of incredible magnitude, grilled and salty. Lots of released energy, slightly smoked after aeration. Generous and concentrated mouth reminding me of a 1947 magnum tasted two months before. A wine with a surprising freshness, with still much-alive bubbles despite the lack of visual. A bottle having particularly well aged*

*over time that may be served with a great cigar (not to be served too cold) such as a Partagas salmon, of which one of its assets is to be enjoyable from the first third.*

*This tasting was followed by a fantastic lunch at the Hotel du Marc. We started off with some cheese puffs from the county served with 2004 Veuve Clicquot La Grande Dame; then, at the table, a very delicate appetizer of Saint-Jacques scallops in yuzu butter, in duet with a 1989 Private Cellar and a 1990 Private Cellar Rosé. A dish made of sweetbreads in chestnut shells came with a new duo: a 1979 and 1982 Private Cellar Rosé. Without visiting the pastry house, we went back to the lounge where a 1964 Veuve Clicquot magnum waited for us.*

# Salon

*Signed with an S*

# E

UGÈNE-AIMÉ
SALON'S STORY

of the establishment of the Salon house is every epicureans dream. Initially, nothing could have predicted his success. The man came from a corner Champagne unfavorable to fortunes. Later on, he made it, first as a second-hand merchant, then in the fur business, and finally in real estate. Our man loved life, and in the early years of the twentieth century, life in Paris was at Maxim's! Like any annuitant of his time, he had a table in this den of pleasure… with the *demi-monde*, as they were called then.

Plus, he loved champagne so much that he decided one day to have his own! A rare sign of success and knowledge of how to live life. He contacted one of his cousins and put him in charge of finding the best of the best: Côte des Blancs, Chardonnay, and Mesnil-sur-Oger. And since he wanted to go a step further, he decided that he would produce his champagne only when the quality of the vintage would allow it and that only he would consume it, with his family. He ran his house until his death in 1943. A distant nephew took the business over for a while; then two different companies managed the brand alternatively. In 1988, Bernard de Nonancourt, the boss of Laurent-Perrier, took the brand over not only with the charisma of his tall stature but above all with the greatness of his soul and spirit.

The first Salon vintage dates back to 1921. Up until 2013, only thirty-three vintages were produced, for the will of the founder, beyond his heirs and successive owners, has always been respected. One can easily imagine the effect "these" bottles generated, with their old-fashioned appearance, when he had them served at his table at Maxim's.

The Salon exception is also not having multiplied. Because when a Salon does not happen, the grapes grow on another stem. Here there is only one grape, chardonnay, unique in Champagne. And, above all, in Mesnil-sur-Oger, the most monastic of all terroirs.

Since 1997, a friend, Didier Depond, has run Salon. Before Bernard de Nonancourt assigned him to manage the brand, Didier had held a wide range of positions at Laurent-Perrier. Didier belongs to those sensitive, epicurean, refined types of men. One that not only does not let anything go by, "as I often say in duty," but who also is able to keep the spirit of Salon, designed primarily for the avid gourmets of elegant tables. I called on him on several occasions for client friends and organized visits so they could understand Salon. Most of the time, the terroir associated with its grape – its varieties - dictates its style. To get the best understanding, there is nothing like a visit on location, a meeting with those who transcend these wines. This is especially true in Champagne where man intervenes at every stage, including the second fermentation, which gives this unique wine life.

Salon is for me also a friendship with a client: a giant blond who confirms the theory that Vikings discovered America. Though American, he is originally from Norway. He is an inveterate bon-vivant, who only drinks Salon wherever he is – as soon as a place stores it in its vaults – no matter where on earth, which he crisscrosses constantly. When you get to know him, you understand why we conceded Normandy to his ancestors… To get a little peace!

The fact that his flight schedule drops this exceptional man at regular intervals in Paris, hence at the George V, has allowed me to taste his champagne often. Moreover, each of his visits continues in areas where gunslingers reside, such as our friend Louis, who is located in a cut-throat type of street, but where a roguish spirit, Paris's spirit, still lives on. These late suppers test my constitution, because our man has an appetite worthy of his build, and to keep up with him is not easy! For him, the evening starts with Salon!

## MEMORIES

As you can see, I have been fortunate to appreciate Salon regularly at the George V. However, like all great wines, the best time to appreciate it is with food. Indeed, when we taste wines in restaurants, after opening them, we do not seek their pleasure but their hypothetical problems. Tasting sessions at the wine growers improve the conditions, even if we have to spit out the wine for good behavior's sake!

So it was during a lunch that I tasted one of the most remarkable Salons that I can remember. It was in 2010, at the Chateau Latour; our host, Frédéric Engerer, to spice the tasting during our lunch, served the wine blind. The

CHAMPAGNE
Salon

magnum poured before the appetizers conveyed a great aromatic complexity, dried fruit, mignonette, as much honey as chalk, carving olfactory trails deep in our memory. A rich aromatic bouquet tells a great wine. The still fizzling bubbles were light, the fresh palate had a very good and complex length. The white label of this magnum informed us that it was a 1976 Salon. What a freshness, as much in the nose as the energy in the mouth! Unusual in the context of this very unique vintage, and saved by avoiding the malolactic fermentation, which allowed these Chardonnays to retain some acidity. Lunch was going to be one of a kind!

Following this memory of an aperitif, let's move on to a sublime entrée. This time we are in 2006, with Alain Dutournier, Aubert de Villaine, Jean-François Moueix, and Jacques Thorel (then chef-owner of the Auberge Bretonne, in La Roche-Bernard). The latter had brought us "horseshoe" size oysters from Riec-sur-Belon. These shells – rare, iodine, fleshy, dense, with delicate nutty notes – were accompanied by an already beautiful 1988 Salon (the recent tasting showed me its ability to mature).

In this imaginary meal, I need a dish. I am choosing without hesitation among my memories a dish that for a long time was emblematic of Le Cinq: the Bresse chicken and blue Brittany lobster luted in casserole from Chef Legendre. In this meeting, the land and sea rubbed shoulders, deliciously unified. We often called on the effervescence of a great champagne to accompany them. Echoing these 1982 Salons, we poured them until 2008 with this dish. This matured vintage remains for me the model of opulence and extreme tension; Belemnite chalk notes played a large part in the freshness of the palate, and the fine and light bubbles created a perfect synergy among the firm and squashy flesh.

And no one can blame me if, unlike formal dinners given at the Élysée Palace, I object at this stage of the meal to having a dessert, having no particular agreements with this final stage.

CHAMPAGNE
Salon

# The Wine

A confidential wine, with, however, an international celebrity. It belongs among dream wines. Its style and power seduce the wine lover. There are the "Krugists" but there are also some "Salonists." The recent 1997 and 1999 vintages seem a little more consensual, but without affecting the 1996. What righteousness! A paragon of tension.

# Tasting at Salon with Thierry, October 2013
Didier greeted us.

**2002 Salon.** *Pale gold color. Discreet bubbles, still tight nose. Wide mouth, full-bodied. Fine bubbles, beautiful finish, long and tender. An impression of seashells in the palate's finish. As is often with Salon, we must learn to wait at least four to five years.*

**1999 Salon.** *Intense and concentrated color, a bit rich. Wide and open mouth. The overall taste is still withdrawn. At this stage of evolution, it does not introduce itself in the best light.*

**1997 Salon.** *I have always believed in this Salon vintage. Today, the complexity and delicacy of the nose warm my forebodings. Bergamot and verbena notes mark the nose. A racy and subtle bouquet. Elegance and tension reveal hazelnut notes in the palate. The finish is long, taut. A great champagne worth marrying with belons, to serve with a good rye bread and sea salted butter. Bliss! The evening where it was the most difficult to assess it was undoubtedly at a Paris sommeliers gala dinner in the Salon Vendôme at the George V, which the elite sommeliers attended. In my position of power, as host to my colleagues, I was obliged to describe the first wine served during the evening. It was a 1997 Salon. Everyone present was a friend, though some were former opponents in national or international competitions.*

even low (3 to 5 grams, depending on the acidity), especially when the vintage is bright. The nose is fresh, chalky, fruity, with citrus notes, young lemon and dry floral. Overall, in the mouth, even if still rigorous, it gives full panoply to this exceptional cuvée. To be enjoyed with a beautiful sole meunière.

**1995 Salon.** *A little more pronounced color. Open and amazing nose. Fine, ripe fruit, quince, apple jelly, opening a fresh ample palate. A very nice balance. The bubbles are dynamic and support the wine. A classic finish, fresh and tender.*

**1988 Salon.** *The first bottle was disgorged in the morning, not metered, slightly tired. The second bottle, opened at the right moment, matched my memories, the optimal Mesnil, a harsh climate vintage offering the best of this great terroir. Deep mineral and spicy notes. A champagne for amateurs. The palate is the perfect reflection of the scales expressed in the nose. A chiseled and sharp style, dynamic and slender. To be consumed with a Beluga caviar or a Royal Osetra.*

**1996 Salon.** *The first was disgorged in the morning. Hence, no dosage. Well, in a word, it was alive! Very bright! In comparison, the 1996 opened at the right time was much more harmonious. The proof, if it were needed, of the importance of* liqueur de tirage,

CHAMPAGNE
Salon

# Dom Pérignon

*Famous and coveted*

# D

OM PÉRIGNON
(1638-1715, LIKE THE SUN KING)
belongs to the "father-founders" of champagne. The life story of this cellar master monk of the Benedictine Abbey of Hautvillers (from 1668 to 1715), whose name is now linked to this wine, is well known and kept up with fervor in the same abbey where he once lived. Robert Massin has also made this great man the subject of a charming book, "Dom Pérignon: a History of Champagne" (Berg International, 2014). Among his many achievements, there is one still being used today. He was the first to couple different terroirs, to understand them and interpret their different grape varieties according to their communal origins and to translate their interactions, as would a composer before his partition create a symphony without the need of the band. Dom Pérignon perfected as well the techniques of pressing and clarification of wines.

From the beginning of the eighteenth century, this wine that naturally stimulates had a general appeal to the British (some of them would also claim authorship for the development of the method of preparation). The latter remain to this day among the largest consumers of the champagne effervescence. Because of their interest in champagne, they contributed to its reputation and improvement. The famous geographer and historian, Roger Dion (1896-1981), in his "History of Grapevine and Wine in France: From its Origins to the 19th Century" (Clavreuil, 1959), already had specified it when he mentioned the importance of trade routes for the development of and qualitative interest in vineyards and therefore wines. These have always evolved based on these criteria. Here in Champagne, everything was put to work to create what became an incredible success. Such as the use of this bark from Portugal, which revolutionized the wine world and contributed to the birth of the champagne cork.

Between Dom Pérignon's early ventures and today, centuries of research, trials, discoveries, commercial developments, and conflicts also, have spanned Champagne and champagne.

This region and its wines matter heavily in the life of a sommelier. It is above all pluralistic, diversified in the types of properties, between powerful trading houses (for the record, one must not forget that trading houses account for 80% of the champagne market in terms of production and also

## CHAMPAGNE
Dom Pérignon

own 10% of the vineyards of Champagne), cooperative groups and independent family domains (often related to large houses too). Yet all are united under a strong and regulatory professional counsel. An exception in the approach to how a sommelier interacts with his wine was born from this plurality.

We sommeliers have to be the prescribers of independent growers, located in the heart of human-size family vineyards, who work the land inherited from their ancestors, pioneers of abandoned plots or fallow terroirs. This philosophy, which I share and always defend fervently, sometimes leads some professionals to deprecate certain wines produced in large quantity, whether from Bordeaux or Champagne. This is unfortunate, and I like to think that we must remain open and celebrate the talent of men who have the responsibility to present our wines around the world, beyond the size of domains or the number of bottles resulting, as long as the result is coherent and enriches the world of wine positively. If there is a house incarnating this bickering between us "wine folks," it is the one we call "The Big House": Moët & Chandon (1200 hectares ownership of vineyards, all over Champagne). At the heart of this ring stands one of the icons of Champagne, recognizable worldwide: Dom Pérignon.

The name appeared for the first time in the early 1930s. A special cuvée 1921 Dom Pérignon was created for the American market by the Comte de Vogüe (manager of Moët & Chandon). Since then, Dom Pérignon has grown, along with its successive cellar masters, and in 1990, Richard Geoffroy became the creator of this legendary wine. In twenty years, he was able to hone Dom Pérignon's image, bringing it back to the world of gastronomy from which it had been somewhat neglected in favor of other markets.

Richard is an extraordinary man, impressive for his clarity and concision, with a precise vision of the wine world, its markets, consumers, and their expectations. He is clear, precise, tense, passionate, bright, highbrow, and pragmatic. This fits well with his wine. He and his team have managed to solve the complex equation of creating a great wine in large quantity. It does not matter much how many bottles bear the coat of arms of Dom Pérignon, everyone knows that it is possible to savor it wherever in the world, provided it be well preserved and served. What is less known is the extraordinary feat achieved to assemble the supplies involved in the creation of this wine.

CHAMPAGNE
Dom Pérignon

The parcels of the immense vineyard owned by the parent company are first rate and spread over the whole region, in sixteen of the seventeen towns classified Grand Cru. The structure of the wine is roughly 50% Chardonnay and 50% Pinot Noir. Here, as elsewhere, the quality of wine results from the grapes that get into the cellars. Without them, nothing is possible. Hence, a careful monitoring of each batch.

On this basis, Richard Geoffroy's mission was to reposition the brand, already among the most well known in the world, though rarely in terms of quality, and more generally in terms of luxury without spontaneous correlation to content. After years of labor, he won his bet, and the name of the illustrious creator of the most famous wine in the world was henceforth inseparable from that of the brand. Dom Pérignon is Richard Geoffroy, and vice versa.

Richard and his team's incredible gift has been to create for each vintage (bear in mind that since 1921, only thirty-nine vintages of Dom Pérignon have seen the light) a wine that would unanimously be enjoyed by the largest number of amateurs around the world. In the wine universe, I do not see another example of this level of excellence in quality. As my friend Jean-Marie Curien says, "It's a challenge to creativity, a quest for the absolute for his team and himself."

Impressive, because even if the very image of the bottle and its label, copied a thousand times, is known to all, no one knows the secret of the making or the aging time on slats. The style of the wine rests also on the choices made during winemaking, which sometimes lead wines towards difficult phases, during tastings of young vintages, stressed with taut noses, yellow lemon notes, and unkind chalk.

So I recommend to potential critics to taste wines fifteen or twenty years of age. You'll notice that there are few examples of great champagnes that maintain such freshness for as long.

# M

## EMORIES

In the course of 2006, two wine journalist friends, one being Jean-Marie Curien (author of the famous "Curien Guide to Champagne"), and I found ourselves guests of Richard Geoffroy at the chateau de Saran. For the occasion, both Marie and Thierry were able to accompany me. The estate occupies a strategic position in the Côte des Blancs, straddling Chouilly and Cramant.

To be invited to Saran is a rare privilege. Everything is done to make the visit unforgettable, from the greeting upon arrival to the spacious bedrooms (the one where General de Gaulle slept was given to us, unmistakable with its long bed) overlooking the vineyard which stretches out of sight, not to mention the quality of the table, upon which famous agreements were orchestrated. Here, the art of receiving, as practiced in France during the nineteenth century and until the middle of the twentieth century, has not been lost. To give an idea of what may have been the service in a house of this style, Robert Altman's film "Gosford Park" offers a great example.

The stage was set. After being "refreshed" according to tradition, we all met in the grand lounge where delicate Parmesan tiles waited for us, next to a bottle of 1998 Dom Pérignon. A good omen for the evening. I had no fear, knowing our host's epicurean qualities, regarding his commitment to the consistent search for harmony between dishes and wines… of Champagne.

At table, every dish was of rare precision, as much in form as in the cooking or the correctness of seasonings. The best evidence was that, on several occasions, the conversations went silent. It is always the greatest compliment one can pay to a dish, to its creator: complete silence!

As a preamble, while dipping salt-free focaccia in olive oils of Trapani, Sicily, we compared the last three Dom Pérignon vintages: 1998, 1996, 1995. What a starter!

The first entry was a remembrance of Richard's passion for Japan: Aquitaine caviar and Japanese sticky rice, with which we continued with a 1998 vintage. A bold marriage in appearance but exposing a duality between the cloudy white rice and the anthracite grains. The wine with bright, refreshing bubbles, with curled notes, provided a rounded full mouth. The sturgeon

## CHAMPAGNE
### Dom Pérignon

beads rolled in the mouth, its flavor enhanced by the soft rice. The wine brought energy and finesse to the agreement.

A smooth foie gras followed, with beet caramel and a binomial Tetsuya salad served with a 1990 Dom Pérignon Rosé. An understanding of colors, tangy delicacy of the dish, and finesse and density of the wine.

Always in a spirit of purity and lightness, we continued with a pigeon broth with spices. The filets were melting. Time was beginning to wind up: a 1976 Dom Pérignon Œnothèque Vintage. Exceptional.

Another great memory of this evening would have to be the dessert. Although it is true that protocol demands that we serve great champagnes with desserts at state dinners, it is known that the ensuing agreement is often appalling, as the book by Joel Normand, former head of the Élysée, "The Fifth Republic in the Kitchen" (the round Table 2000) confesses. Well, that night was an exception. Our host invited us to enjoy, out of sheer indulgence, a warm white-peach tart; then we focused on an ice cream with black truffles, without sugar. There, Richard gestured to pour an "off program" wine, a 1959 Dom Pérignon Vintage! Not too cool. Disgorged for the occasion, so no dosage. The complementarity of the two elements was sublime. A tertiary bouquet, where the strain of mushroom notes mingled with the ones of mocha, came to meet the scents of truffle. The suave and gray cream with a fine "black diamond" brunoise transcended this exceptional vintage. Magical!

# The Wines

Over the last thirty years, I have been following the evolution of Dom Pérignon. I have kept the memories of shifts in the early 1990s of 1970 and 1975 magnum vintages, which were sumptuous.

## Tasting in January 2014

*In the old library of the Abbey of Hautvillers (of which only a wing has miraculously survived, adjacent to the village church). At the invitation of Richard Geoffroy. It was the first time I went inside this historic place, where one can still feel the presence of the monks who contributed to the reputation of this site for nearly eight hundred years. It was also a precious moment that we shared with Thierry Hamon alongside the master of the house.*

**2004 Dom Pérignon.** *Open, fresh. Still slightly reduced. A nose with minty touch, lime notes. The palate is full, tense, with lots of energy. Slight note of bitterness on the finish. Too young at this stage. It does not fully express its potential, given that the style is airy and delicate. Let's not forget that here malolactic fermentation is always performed. Richard insists on the fact that the "late malo" are the lactic deviant agents in wines, generating aromas of rancid butter, fatal to the bouquet, in a reductive sense.*

**2003.** *Golden color, rich sweet almond (marzipan) nose. Candied fruit (lemon, citron) note. The palate is surprisingly by its scale. Somewhat singular for a Dom Pérignon. Very nice savor. Light bitterness. But its generosity is well integrated. A technical challenge for this complex vintage, the one that Richard is proudest of, because of the involvement, the effort, the confidence of the teams and their hierarchy. He took risks, beneficial to the wine.*

**2002.** *Golden color. Rich, buttery nose, like most of the 2002 champagnes. Mirabelle notes blend with white flowers. Wide and creamy palate. A bit soft but the finish yields tension, the Dom Pérignon signature. The professionals acclaimed this vintage, for which the date of the harvest was very important. Many of them waited too long to cut the grapes and suffered from an over-ripeness difficult to offset in the wines' balance.*

**1996.** *Disgorged in 2008. Intense golden color. Complex nose, rich and delicate, intensely toasted. Slight citrus note. Remarkable. Structured palate, square and rich, mineral and seashells. Tight and confident finish. Still very taut. A great wine for meals. Ideal with fish or raw shellfish, and flat oysters. A gastronomic wine with a mindset pure and brisk*

## CHAMPAGNE
## Dom Pérignon

in the processing of raw fish in Japanese cuisine.

1990 (enoteca). *Intense golden color. Fresh and mineral nose, as Riesling can be on shale. Wide palate, full, subtle. In the finish, the wine remains opulent and fleshy. Ready to enjoy it in its fullness, for me, it reaches its peak. A wine deserving of a venison filet with porcini mushrooms.*

1982 (enoteca). *Golden, intense color. The nose reminds me of honey, white pepper, and dry floral. The wine is very wide, round and generous (despite its low dosage) on the palate. A mature and lasting vintage.*

1970 (enoteca). *Golden hue, intense. Discreet bubbles. The nose reveals candied citrus, beeswax. Accomplished mouth. As Richard himself says, "It is in line with the 2004 style."*

1966 Magnum. *Golden color. Good presence of a collar of bubbles. Very bright. Sappy nose, powerful, fine, and complex. Unbelievable. The palate displays a tasting structure and a permanence worthy of a great white wine. The retro-olfaction is grilled and honey. One of the greatest champagnes that can be enjoyed in this vintage. Given the size of the bottle and the fact that we're only three around the long table, I believe more members of Richard's team will relish these wines after we leave. They deserve it!*

2003 Dom Pérignon Rosé. *Sustained color, intense pink (a turning point for Dom Pérignon). Fine and energetic bubbles. Dense nose, full and fresh, very fruity (small red fruits, wild strawberry), spicy, some licorice notes and Maltese oranges. Wide and tight mouth with a creamy bubble. A racy wine. The Chambertin of Champagne.*

1993 (enoteca). *To the eye, the wine appears flourished with bright orange reflections. Very fine bubble. Open nose, zesty, intensely fruity, candied black currants, saffron, breathy. Frangipane and marzipan notes. Taut and full mouth, recalling macerated flavored fruits and bitter almonds. Crisp finish, and lots of elegance.*

1966. *This vintage was the fourth Dom Pérignon rosé, the first being the 1959. Bright orange color. Discrete bubbles. Open nose, complex and singular. Sage, tea plant, and dried porcini mushrooms. Notes of roots, parsnips, golden ball turnips. Roasted coffee fragrance. Ample and full mouth, yet still an intense mid-palate compared to the nose's maturity. The whole is however remarkable. Very surprising. Reminiscent of an old Vosne-Romanée pinot. It must be sublime with a poached Albufera pullet of Landes with winter roots.*

# Krug

*Men and... a Woman!*

# L

LIFE IS
ALWAYS TOO SHORT.
This is a clear fact. But whatever our allotted time, there are
people who, more than others, by their presence, passion, and
vision of enterprise, stand out. This is the case with Margareth
Henriquez. The beautiful South American woman understood very quickly
when she took over the reins of the Krug House the philosophy of Joseph
Krug, the founder. The idea of this visionary man: "Never negotiate with
mediocrity but aim for excellence without compromise." I share this message
and every day try to apply it at Le Cinq. Which is not easy, far from it!

At Krug's, time takes on a hereditary dimension. The organization is
incredible. This range of reserve wines, up to 250 different batches stored
deep in cellars, is worthy of the most complete swatches. Monet did not
overlook this array in the garden of Giverny. This complexity is an important point that is at the core of my choice, together with Chef Briffard, for an
end-of-year champagne in order to prepare an appetizer and an entree. The
Grande Cuvée often wins our vote.

Long before that, my meeting with Krug occurred at La Poularde in 1987,
thanks to a dusty and unlikely lot of 1973 magnum vintage, with square
rings, the classic bottles. The old design. A fantastic memory. A kind of
meteoric taste where the intensity was well above the codes of the time.
It was with this type of bottle that I understood how great champagnes age.
I often decided on my purchases based on my feelings for the quality of the
wines and also on the emotions winemakers provoked in me, listening to
their passions, their convictions.

At the core of the many memories binding me to Krug, I forget neither
Olivier Krug, nor his father Henry and uncle Rémi. They personally welcomed me during my first visits to their institution in Reims. The tastings
in their dark wood offices almost always took on a religious aura. We stood
in the holiness of the Saints. No one asked about the origin of what we
sipped; Rémi would otherwise take upon himself to set the rule-breaker back
on the right path. Different times… And then one day, I met Margareth
(Maggie for her inner circle), who, for me, epitomizes a "grand dame" of
Champagne. Here was a brown-haired woman, tall, elegant, self-important,
who entered into a house run by men. Before, only one woman of the family

had been involved with the business: Jeanne Krug (Olivier Krug's great-grandmother), in the years after the war, a tough period. When Maggie arrived, the 2009 global economic crisis affected the environment. With determination and tenacity, this exceptional woman who talks briskly managed to bring back into the light this secret house, sheltered from time, behind its high walls and iron gates, over which the spirit of a family has always reigned. She fires on all cylinders and wonderfully manages a team of young talents.

Note that the officials at the Clos du Mesnil, like those at the Ambonnay, are young women of strong will. One is blonde, Julie Carvil (Clos du Mesnil only plants Chardonnay), responsible for the house's great *blanc de blancs*; the other, brunette (Ambonnay is 100% Pinot Noir), presides over the destiny of Krug's great *blanc de noirs*. A coincidence or a sign? Both, like the rest of the team, are overseen by the irreplaceable Eric Lebel, head of wines. Surrounding herself with connoisseurs, Maggie became aware of the talent of this great cellar master, on whom the smooth running of the house relies, as does the choice of the "harvesting" day, as he himself mentions during this time. Through the Grande Cuvée developed on the basis of the 2004 harvest, we understand the culture of tension, of the finesse of pedigree that the house wants to preserve. These ideals could be transferred as well to Eric Lebel's first passion, namely, beautiful machines, those on the speed track (thinking of the one in Reims) that many inhabitants visit. Besides, in a house where one must take one's time, it is a good thing to "dash" behind the wheel. Another value of time, other emotions.

As we would say about a racing stable, it is reassuring, as is the case today, to see this house in top shape. And who knows if this would have happened without the firepower of the Great House (meaning: LVMH, whose group Krug joined in 1999). I am well placed to know that beyond divisions, conflicts, and objectives, to belong to a business with significant resources can be a catalyst both to realize projects and to preserve them too. And I must confess that if I had access in recent years to Krug's maze – the cellars, tanks, and vines – it was thanks to Eric and Maggie. It is fascinating to be able to discover the creative processes behind this unique Grande Cuvée.

What a privilege as well to be able to compare the developments of this wine through the years, to meet those who have custody of these vine gar-

CHAMPAGNE
Krug

dens: Clos du Mesnil and Ambonnay. What a delight to be able, as at the end of September 2013, a few days before the harvest, to try the Pinot on vine before enjoying a 1996 Ambonnay, standing in the vineyard! Mesmerizing, and, let us say, I actually felt an extension, a common thread between the bays and the vibrant expression of the terroir.

EMORIES

Several years after the opening of the George V, in 2003, we were able to have access, via Olivier Krug and Eric Lebel, to a beautiful *vertical* of Krug Vintage, with both bottles and magnums – an ideal choice for Le Cinq and the hotel. This large order, which I had developed with Enrico Bernardo, got delivered in an unusual way. For the occasion, Olivier pulled out of the garage the old Krugmobile (a 1979 Rolls-Royce Silver Shadow II) that he had just driven back from Italy, where it was being repaired. This rare model had been acquired by his uncle and dressed in the family's colors, the numbers duly plastered on the doors. As we say here, "Great House, no hesitation!" It was the only time that crates of wine were delivered through the revolving door usually reserved for residents and not through the suppliers' entrance.

This *amuse bouche* reminds me of good times tasting old vintages from this house. To prove my loyalty to Krug, I am imagining first some Bresse pullets in half-mourning (truffle-braised), in bladder, and poached by Bernard Barret, the head roaster in Montrond-les-Bains, who in 1989 I served with magnums of 1973 Krug Vintage. There was then a complicity between the tasty flesh, steeped in the scent of truffles, the cooking broth, topped with a champagne sauce, and the richness, the maturity, of this 1973 vintage, which demanded a kind of reflection, the momenTt being so ecstatic.

Not long ago, after a tasting in September 2013 with Maggie and Thierry, we had the privilege of sharing a meal in Henry Krug's former mansion, which adjoins the cellar of the house. The simply furnished dining room, with fresh and lively tones, opened onto an interior French garden, in the shade. We could choose at leisure the wines we wanted to "review" to accompany the dishes the chef had prepared. To begin with, for an aperitif, I chose a 1996 Clos d'Ambonnay. It was exemplary, not heavy, a genuine revelation.

The entrée, consisting of a carpaccio of St. Jacques scallops, was accompanied well by a 1998 Clos du Mesnil; then the confit lamb shanks, cooked in juice, called for a 2006 Krug Rosé, which we confronted with the 1996 Vintage. I must admit that the rosé offered a palette, as much in nose as in its mouth structure, structure that was in perfect agreement with the dish.

It was a new ambiance. We chatted about these beautiful dishes and rare bottles, revealing themselves with finesse – often, as they were being opened – at the temperature most suitable for each given bottle. A lunch branding these moments… If only they could be enjoyed forever.

CHAMPAGNE
Krug

# The Wines

In the Krug palette, there is a vintage, the Grande Cuvée, that first must be considered as "the" first Krug Prestige vintage because here it is not an "entry-level" wine. In many homes, this wine corresponds to the most prestigious vintage. According to Johann Krug, the founder, "a house should develop two vintages of the same level." No second place! Everything should be perfect. This choice of the founder of the dynasty, preserved today as yesterday, is the result of the incredible work that goes into both selection and anticipation. Each year, the Grande Cuvée, translates into a collection of nearly 60% of wine of the year with a 40% of reserve wines. The latter will be used with a rare expertise, among over 200 reserve wines. These are a treasured secret, kept for ten to twenty years, and without the malolactic fermentation being triggered or desired! When tasting clear wines, with each sample, one must identify its typical or atypical characteristics. Because each could someday contribute to the development of the Grande Cuvée based on its characteristics.

At Krug, painstaking work is performed regarding the plots during the harvest and vinification. Each Krug "supplier" can be invited to taste the clear wine of his plot, something rare in Champagne given the diversity of supply.

These wines are vinified in barrels only during the time of alcoholic fermentation. This time, as a matter of fact, is the only time when they "see" wood in their lives. Preferably pieces from several wines. The age of parked barrels varies between twenty to twenty-five years. The oldest one during our visit in May 2010 was from 1964! The proportion of new barrels here is even lower since no fermented wine in new barrels is retained and sent straight to the market. These champagne barrels offer a unique capacity: 205 liters. The reason is simple. A "vintage" at the time of the pressing will produce 2,050 liters of juice, hence ten champagne barrels. At Krug, nearly 5,300 of these barrels are used annually. To be ready at the appropriate time, the barrels are sprinkled from July on in order to rehydrate the staves and make the barrels waterproof again.

It is important during the creation of the Grande Cuvée that the vintage be smoothed so the "style" of the wine is preserved. Those are therefore clear white wines originating from the three major varieties (Chardonnay, Pinot Noir, and Pinot Meunier), issued from a multitude of terroirs, from which each batch may contribute all or in part to the balance of the "Draw" of the Grande Cuvée. Once the important choice made, the cellar master can proceed to manipulate them, to trigger the second fermentation. Then the slow aging of the champagne on slats will begin, for nearly eight years before being disgorged. Then it will yet remain for nearly another year before being "dressed" and spread around the world.

Once the bottles of Krug hit the market, it is possible to identify their content through the Idea Code, a principle and a system set up under Maggie's leadership. A code on the back of the bottle, easy to decrypt and scan with a smartphone, gives access to an online database allowing one to find out the blend dates of the Grande Cuvée being savored…

## CHAMPAGNE
### Krug

# September 2013 Tasting

*Strange to acknowledge that the Grande Cuvée developed with the harvest of this 2013 vintage will be marketed in 2020-2022!*

**2005 Base Grande Cuvée.** *Too young, sensual, great potential. We will come back when opened for discussion.*

**2004.** *Concentrated, bright, fruity, remarkable wide mouth, without heaviness. This wine reflects the true character of Eric Lebel.*

**2003.** *This is the complete opposite of a hot year. Hence, the importance of reserve wines in the blend. They are added to maintain the balance in the wine, like bass and treble adjustments during a music recording. This is the signature of the cellar master. Here, the fruit is thin, rich without excess. Eric understood the vintage and was able to draw the necessary freshness from reserve wines. A balanced wine, for an atypical year.*

**2001.** *Remarkable wine. Beautiful expression, nice balance. Having reached maturity. Large and long pastry and brioche notes, gentle spices giving an impression of yellow Chartreuse from Tarragona.*

**2000.** *Delicate, fine, an easy wine! The style before Eric Lebel.*

**2000 Vintage.** *Pale yellow color. Intense lemon note, wide palate, slightly minty, with dry fern notes, lots of flexibility. The blend consists of 40% Chardonnay as in 1981.*

**1998.** *Very young pale yellow color. Intense citrus nose (like citron), fresh marzipan, and sweet almond. The attack gives a lot of scope. The mouth finish has great power, a compressed finish with a nice savory touch. A big "muscular" wine.*

**1996.** *Intense golden color. Nose marked by mature and evolved notes, such as toasted brioche aromas, a pastry and lemony nose. A fleshy, pulpy mouth, full-bodied with a certain harshness in the finish.*

**1998 Clos du Mesnil.** *This famous Clos du Mesnil-sur-Oger (1.85 hectare) has been growing vines since 1698 and, as an ancient carved stone embedded in the wall indicates, was acquired in 1971 by Maison Krug. In 1979 was the first vintage of this wine, which Henry created. Pale light color. Lots of depth. Very fine bubbles, thin lemony nose, monastic. Wide and compressed mouth, both pure and lingering on. One of the 1998 greatest whites, savored in this vintage champagne.*

**2000.** *Pale yellow color, fruity nose, elegant, flattering, full and supple palate without* weakness. Easy access to the mouth with a lacy finish. Needs another three years.

1996 Clos d'Ambonnay. *Like all the Ambonnay wines, it has a pale yellow color with a slightly gray touch. Fruity and intense nose, reminiscent of wild strawberry and candied orange. Wide mouth, sappy and very concentrated.*

1998. *The pale yellow color is slightly stained (which induces a light contact between the skins of the Pinot and the juice before pressing), and more sustained. A closed nose, very compressed*

and deep, too young. You can infer a touch of white pepper in the nose. A sublime champagne after an hour of aeration. The mouth is in tune with the nose. Tremendous balance. Must wait at least another ten years.

2006 Base Krug Rosé. *Here is a pink champagne that I really like. Here again, a major turn in the house style from its past. The pale pink color is not as prominent as before. A spicy nose, with a light touch of citrus, reminiscent of tangerine. The mouth remains frisky without softness.*

# CHAMPAGNE
## Krug

P 74 DOMAINE LUNEAU-PAPIN

P 81 CLOS ROUGEARD

P 86 DOMAINE LUCIEN AND GILLES CROCHET

P 90 DOMAINE FRANÇOIS COTAT

P 96 DOMAINE EDMOND AND ANNE VATAN

P 102 DOMAINE BENJAMIN AND DIDIER DAGUENEAU

P 109 DOMAINE FRANÇOIS CHIDAINE

P 116 DOMAINE CLOS NAUDIN

# Wines of the
~
# Loire Valley

# Domaine Luneau-Papin

*One Pierre after the Next*

# W

E ARE AT THE
GATES OF BRITTANY,
steps from the estuary of the Loire, near the sea where
there is this oceanic climate, bordering swamps and hills
with complex soils, blending gneiss, granite, mica, and
serpentinite. We are in the Nantes country. The *Gros Plant* and "various"
Muscadets share this vast appellation that today stretches over a region of
nearly 9,000 hectares. For the record, I remember a time – not so long ago –
when I was studying for competitions, that the *appellation d'origine contrôlée*
(AOC) for the Muscadet covered over 15,000 hectares. It was through the
white wines of this region that many Bretons made their debut. A journey
which could sometimes turn out to be challenging.

Personally, I did not have the good fortune of being initiated with one of
the wines made in the hills of the Goulaine marshes belonging to the
Luneau-Papin family, otherwise my first opinions would certainly have
been… better! In any case, sommeliers generally agree that the Muscadet is
a lovely, light, somewhat nervous wine. You may say that this depends also
on where one is born. More precisely, Pierre, his son Pierre-Marie, and both
their lively wives, work alongside big names in the Nantes region to enhance
the names of the Maine-and-Loire and, particularly, Muscadet wines. Congratulations! They are continuing their illustrious grandfather's work, who
ran the domain until he was 83 years old and whose charisma left a strong
durable impression on Pierre-Marie. The latter arrived at the domain almost
ten years ago. With his wife, they make the ninth generation of winemakers.
The current domain is the result of his parents' alliance: the Luneau (from
Landreau) with the Papin (in La Chapelle-Heulin).

Everything contributes to the development of a reputation if you do your
job with passion and take into account the most details possible, starting with
the selection of rootstocks, soil tillage, and their composition. For example,
the so-called "serpentinite" plot, the latest Luneau acquisition, offers a 360°
panorama of the marshes at the foot of the hills, where a narrowing between
the two forms two butterfly wings. During a visit in winter 2014, with Nicolas Charrière and Thierry, hosted by Pierre-Marie and Marie, his wife, we
marveled at the vineyard from the heights of the Butte de la Roche. On that
morning, a light fog snaked in the marshes, sprinkling here and there

flooded groves, willows, and clumps of reeds. Further up, on the other side, piercing through the mist, the Renaissance castle of Goulaine reminded us of a tragic episode in France's history. It is among the few to have survived the wars of Vendée and the only one still in the hands of the Goulaine family. Time… From this point of view, the Luneau-Papin family, relatively speaking, is in a way the "grandparents of Muscadet," as represented by the Médeville family at the Château Gilette. They are known for the quality of their creamy heads in Sauternes, which are stored in large containers for nearly a decade before bottling.

Certain vintages can remain in underground tanks for up to thirty-six months and sometimes even longer! It all depends on the quality and evolution of each vintage. This winemaking method creates Muscadet wines both wide and taut, with a genuine ability to age. At the moment, we are offering the 2004 Excelsior vintage. After being kept for ten years, its freshness is exemplary. I must say that it is sufficiently rare to be noteworthy. Multiple parameters make this "eternal youth" possible, starting with reasonable degrees of alcohol and marked acidity. The absence of wood in the making process plays a part too.

## MEMORIES

After much wandering through the vineyards and a tasting session, dizzying as much by the diversity of vintages as the longevity of which these wines are capable, our stomachs were ready. A beautiful solid oak table, covered with a heavy linen tablecloth, embroidered with the family's initials, as once were found in trousseaus, waited for us. An Austrian crystal manufacturer had signed the glassware. The faience was from Gien, and utensils were out from their padded boxes for the occasion. Spring vegetable horns of plenty, with soft bright green fans, stood as ornaments on the table and seemed sprayed with a dew of arachnids.

We began with a bed of drained oysters in three varieties, some flat, with a nutty flavor, delicious, served with a 2012 *Gros Plant*. It is the perfect wine: iodized, powerful, with a nice freshness that invigorates the taste buds. One should know that pairing with oysters is not so simple. "The Oyster Lunch,"

## LOIRE VALLEY
### Domaine Luneau-Papin

the famous painting by Jean François de Troy, painted in 1735 and on display at the Musée Condé in Chantilly, praises the shell and its association with Champagne wines. Bear in mind also that the iodine and saline power of oysters overcome champagnes, dominates them. With this *Gros Plant*, though, no such thing. It has enough feedback to sustain its presence in the mouth, creating a beautiful osmosis with the flesh of the shellfish. And then the divine, still-warm rye bread, with a crispy crust, from the village baker Le Pain Virgule, spread generously with salted butter from Maison Beille-vaire, truly united hearts.

We continued with a tasting of exceptional early vegetables from Olivier Durand, a market gardener located in the Landes-Blanches in the town of Sorinières, not far away. I had never bitten with as much pleasure into a young turnip, just rinsed under cold water, tender and sweet, such as these first slightly spicy radishes, perfectly crunchy, and tiny sandy carrots with sugary… All in perfect agreement with a 2008 Muscadet grown on this serpentinite soil, with aromas of almonds, slightly minty.

The dish was made of scallops Saint-Jacques just sliced raw and seasoned with a dash of oil, a kaffir from Olivier Roellinger, a fleur de sel from Guérande, a quarter spin of a pepper mill, with peppers from around the world, and a bergamot zest. A dream, served with a 2005 Muscadet Excelsior with a golden color, a fruity and deep nose, and a remarkable concentration in the palate.

Several fresh goat cheeses, a Curé Nantais of good quality, and a creamy sheep briquette agreed perfectly with a dashing and impetuous 2010 L d'Or Muscadet.

Time flew by – too fast for our liking – but we had time to discover a tempting specialty: the Nantes cake made by Franck Dépérier, *Meilleur Ouvrier* of France, a baker in Nantes. A kind of short soft sponge biscuit harmoniously combining almonds, sugar, and butter, generously soaked in old rum from the Caribbean, a reminder of the time when the city of the Dukes of Brittany counted as one of the major ports of shipowners. An exquisite and welcome sweetness after tasting more than fifteen wines and vintages of great Muscadet!

# LOIRE VALLEY
## Domaine Luneau-Papin

# The Wines

Two large appellation areas share the Nantes vineyards. For the Gros Plant, the Folle Blanche (the noble grape of Armagnac!) has been used by controlling its great generosity (hence its name "Gros Plant"). For the Muscadet, the Burgundy melon is originally from an ancient crossbreed between Pinot Noir and white Gouais. Along with these two varieties, many other rewarding types of lovely regional appellations have to be included.

## Pierre de Terre Vintage

*Altered serpentinite soil (of magmatic origins more than 500 million years old), at a place called* La Butte de la Roche, *in the village of Loroux-Bottereau. This wine is fed and made with fermented lees for a year to eighteen months depending on the vintage.*

**2012.** *Muscadet-Sèvre-and-Maine. Vineyard taken over in 2008. Pale color. Fine nose, open, delicate, floral (sage), and minty. Ample and tense mouth. It's all there,* *but needs time for everything to fall into place. Great potential.*

**2010.** *Pale color. Open nose, lemony, fresh, damp stone, white fruit. Refined, round mouth, quite buttery. Wider than long. Very pleasant.*

**2009.** *Golden color. Nose open, rich, solar, somewhat expected. Rich and pulpy palate. Not bad for a hot year.*

## The Excelsior Vintage

*This is the famous Goulaine vintage. Very old Burgundy melon vines (75 years) on a plot in La Chapelle-Heulin. The bedrock is made of micaschist, facing south. Here, vintages remain on their lees in underground* *tanks for nearly thirty-six months before their bottling.*

**2010.** *Diaphanous color. Straight nose, floral, expressive, pear. Full-bodied, dense, close, intense, low presence of gas. Needs to age.*

*2009. Pale golden color. Thin fresh nose for 2009. What surprises me most with this great vintage is its ability to retain a good balance, enough freshness in hot years. It is even refreshing while ripe. The Luneau launched it on the market in early 2014.*

*2007. Dazzling color as always with these Burgundy melons. Open nose, fruity. Notes of roots. Fresh mouth, relatively light. I'm fond of it.*

## The L d'Or Vintage

*This granite terroir is located on the slopes upstream of the Goulaine River. The vines are 45 years old, on average. The wines are aged from nine to eleven months on lees in vats. No racking here.*

*2010. Open nose, fruity floral, advanced fermentation. Light fizziness, which brings out honeysuckle notes. In the mouth, it cuts through. Much tension can be detected. Medium amplitude, precise and chiseled acidity. A whiff of bitter lemon zest reminiscent of grapefruit. A typical vintage for the appellation.*

*2005. Honey and lees nose, slightly fermented, a touch of smoke. Opulent buttery mouth, concentrated, with dimensions, beautiful bitterness in the finish. A great wine with a meal.*

*2004. Dry floral nose, lightly minted, tertiary, and white fruit. A mature nose. The palate is beautiful, velvety, and very meaty. An unusual volume for a Muscadet with nonetheless a saline note to the finish. This is a quintessential food wine.*

*2005 Golden color. White fruit nose, very ripe. Dry flattering floral. Very round mouth, buttery, propolis notes. Very ripe vintage.*

*2003. Beeswax nose. White fruit notes. The mouth is relatively broad but ends with a nice freshness. A well-mastered vintage.*

*1989. A lemon and wax nose. One can smell aromas of root vegetables in broth. A ripe palate, broad, which retains a great tension. Defies the preconceived notion that Muscadet wines cannot age!*

# LOIRE VALLEY
## Domaine Luneau-Papin

# Clos Rougeard

*We are Born Honest Here*

O NE EVENING IN 1994, AT LA POULARDE, two characters dressed like investigators from the TV series *la Brigade du Tigre* accompanied a third party who, I would later learn, turned out to be an eminent Parisian surgeon. I recognized Charly (died in December 2015) and Nady Foucault at once. We had met three years before at a wine tasting for people in the business. They were on their way to Guigal for a tasting and had stopped at the Montrond-les-Bains Casino. They had just pocketed a jackpot and only had to cross the street to come for dinner. I remember that they had ordered a 1978 Marcel Guignal côte-rôtie, La Mouline, with truffled pockets. From that time on, I started to go to Chacé to taste in their cellars and subsequently counted on a plot in their field. The Foucault family, now in its ninth generation of winemakers, has managed to preserve the work of their elders. They have maintained the Burgundy tradition of the vineyards and the concept of vintages through parcelled land, as did their father, Raymond, and before that, their grandfather, Henry, who did the same.

Their domain stretches over 9 hectares of Cabernet Franc and 1 hectare of Chenin. The Foucaults do not claim any particular label. There, people are born honest. Without pretense. But with an ethic based on respect for vineyards – the soil – which they inherited and are required to preserve in order to pass them on. Consequently, they do not use fertilizer or herbicide, only occasionally some manure. For treatments, they have recourse only to sulfur and copper. To damage the soil and the wines is out of the question. Thus, next to the Village vintage, several parcelled vintages have always existed in the domain:

– The Bourg is located on a limestone plateau overlooking the Loire. There are no more than 30 centimeters of topsoil before hitting the tuffeau, the first layer of freestone.

– The Poyeux rests on a clay and limestone soil made of silicon-clay and limestone sand. A terroir full of subtlety. For me, it is the best terroir for Cabernet Franc, a terroir also known as Breton. In the seventeenth century, Cardinal Richelieu entrusted Father Breton, steward of his lands, officiating at Fontevraud, with the mission of replanting the Cabernet region. Breton purchased thousands of Cabernet Franc plants from Guyenne and replanted them around the Abbey Saint-Nicolas of Bourgueil. Since then, this variety has been called locally "Breton." – The Saumur Brézée is the white wine of the domain located on a clay and limestone soil, which has a more pronounced clay presence. Le Chenin grows along the hillside, facing southeast, slightly sloping. Depending on the vintage, the Foucaults produce – though extremely rarely – a sweet Chenin, which takes the appellation of Coteaux-de-Saumur.

During my last visit, Nady showed us his new cellar. The setting was strangely reminiscent of a disused factory in an American TV series. I wondered what we were going to do in this place. Nady grabbed a heavy bunch of keys and opened several locks before a heavy gray creaking metal door swung open. And then, fear and trembling! We entered into what appeared to have been actually an old factory, nothing but concrete such as the warehouses sheltering submarines in Lorient. Solid construction. Our host saw our dismay and, after explaining that the harvest receptions and the pressing took place on the ground floor, he led us towards a first basement, where the macerations took place, then to a second one, where wines ready for shipping are stored and where the labeling room is located, and finally to the third basement. The real reason why the Foucaults have remained on this site lies in this latter basement, an ancient cellar where, for decades, they have handled bottles of sparkling Saumur! There is nothing but parallel rows, one after the next, crossed by narrow corridors, the whole feeling like a maze of alleys with secret pathways.

This cellar can appear somewhat oversized for the domain. Yet, as Nady explained to us, these walkways allow them to keep the barrels in a single row without having to stack them constantly during racking. This arrangement also helps the crus to sedimentize gently without distressing them. For a long time, casks came from Chateau Latour where Nady and her brother used to go to get wine casks in which to store their crops. This is because at the domain, they do not exceed 20% in new barrels per year, knowing that the wines must age in barrels for about twenty-four months.

# MEMORIES

After a long ascent, we got back to the surface, to Nady's. Anne, his wife (the daughter of Edmond Vatan), waited for us. Since our last visit, a beautiful Maltese Bichon had replaced the famous rabbit Pint. That day, we started lunch with a *blanc de blancs* champagne 1995 Anselme Selosse, served with a giant *gougère*. This 1995 vintage showed its age, not to mention the minerality of Avize. It has a golden color, dried fruit notes, slightly honeyed and waxy. Full and sapid palate with fine evolving complex aromas, such as nuts, toasted almonds, and the bread bin. The vintages from Selosse are remarkable wines, like the 1982 we savored at Jean Gautreau's in 2010, which had a light golden color, a complex nose in the image of a great white Burgundy, with honey notes and touches of grilled exotic fruits. It was quite full-bodied with a remarkable freshness and notes of nuts, toasted almonds, and the bread bin. No more excuses, I have to get myself there one of these days!

To begin with, Anne had prepared a tuna salad with avocado and romaine. Very refreshing. She poured a 2012 Clos de la Néore (Anne's 3rd vintage), which was surprisingly fruity and surprised Anne: "It's funny, it smells like a Cabernet." Indeed, it was extremely rare that in the marl of Chavignol, the aromatic varietal character would be so prominent. Being the case, the breadth and richness of the Néore loudly conquered the mouth, and the tone of the 2012 was downright refreshing. She then served us a gargantuan roasted prime rib, with Charlotte potatoes and a few cloves of garlic, thyme and rosemary. For his part, Nady had prepared several bottles from the estate, of which the most memorable was a 1990 Poyeux. However, the most difficult wine to identify was the following: it had a golden color, topaz, intense – and from there it could be guessed, could reveal itself. It was a very old Chenin. From when? Nady did not make us wait any longer. It was a 1947 Saumur Breze. Simply dazzling.

Our visits to Nady and Anne's have always been an opportunity to share rich convivial and warm moments. I love the mood that they created in their abode.

LOIRE VALLEY
Clos Rougeard

# A vertical of Saumur-Champigny, Les Poyeux Vintage

In February 2013, at the domain of Nady, with Nicolas and Thierry Charrière.

**2012.** *Purple-red color, rather clear. Frank nose, tangy and full-bodied finish. Sensation of extraction. Soft palate, medium length, refined and timid tannin. A gourmet wine, flattering, ready to be enjoyed.*

**2011.** *Intense color, bright. Delicate and subtle nose, slightly spicy fruitiness. Racy, refined, and taut palate. Typical delicacy of Poyeux. Light and present tannin, supported by a refreshing acidity. Overall, rather tonic.*

**2010.** *Deep ruby color, opaque and intense. Closed nose, complete with black fruit notes. Full-bodied, sappy with a generous tension. Great length. A beautiful achievement. A balanced wine. Will last twenty years.*

**2009.** *Color with lots of depth, dark, intense, with a purple reflection. Open nose, black fruit, spicy, stewed fruits. Beautiful rich nose with a soft touch. Real full-bodied, sunny, very powerful. Very long lingering. A concentrated wine.*

**2008.** *Dark ruby color, shiny. Open nose, fine, fresh and complex. Floral aroma reminiscent of iris, fruity tang, light wood, and leather notes. Tannic attack in the mouth. Medium range. Finish structured with graphite aromas. A Poyeux worth waiting for. A harmonious production, a bit harsh after the 2009.*

**2006.** *Medium intensity ruby color. Fruity open nose, fine, expressive, and slightly woody. The palate is soft and flattering, generous at this stage. A supple wine. Round tannin, low acidity. Can be savored straight away and with great pleasure.*

**2003.** *A vibrant hue with light orange highlights. Open nose, very attractive, with licorice, vanilla, stewed black fruit, intense and warm, and a touch of fig. Fleshy, round, and concentrated attack. Rich generosity. An extrovert Poyeux.*

**1997.** *Garnet color, slightly sophisticated nuance. Nose open, earthy, medium intensity, truffled and kirsched. Supple and full-bodied. Very seductive. With a tender finish. A nice length. Surprising for a complicated year. Nice overall.*

**1990.** *"The" reference, propelling the Poyeux to the firmament of the greatest terroirs of Cabernet Franc in the Val de Loire. Still dense, dark and luscious color. Deep nose, fruity, spicy, full-bodied and racy. Reminiscent of black cherries and blackberries. The palate is full, long and elegant. Its fullness is unbelievable. The signature of a grand terroir. Rare sensation to find oneself in the presence of a great wine from the Côte de Nuits that reveals its refinement.*

# Domaine Lucien and Gilles Crochet

## A Great Benchmark

**W**HEN I FIRST LEARNED ABOUT DOMAIN CROCHET, it was still called Domain Picard Crochet, after Lucien's stepfather. Then I met Picard, the father, at La Poularde with his grandson, Gilles. He was thin, on the skinny side. A youngster, like me. He used to come with his grandparents. Gilles still remembers the famous Joannès Randoing's crawfish casserole. He confessed to me recently that, back then, he was impressed by the somewhat disabled sommelier, who opened bottles with one hand.

My first visit to Lucien Crochet's was in July 1989. Lucien and his wife greeted me. I discovered again Gilles's wines in 1995, thanks to Didier Dagueneau who suggested that I go to taste them. Then visits became more sporadic. In the mid 2000s, Gilles was surprised that I resumed them. During this time, sommeliers, including Thierry, would attend each year the Wine Show of the Loire Valley to taste his wines. Loving to add to my travels winemakers that I do not visit often, I decided to mend the issue.

During the 2004 winter when I went to see him, Gilles imagined, seeing my get-up, that I had become a lawyer. My clothes and, most importantly, my Andy Warhol moccasins from Berluti, captivated his attention more than my words. Among Gilles's great passions, excluding wines, were the creations of great French, English, and Italian bootmakers. Together, we would wander off on foot through the vineyards of Chêne Marchand. Though with different shoes. The Domaine Crochet stretches over 36 hectares. The best vineyards are located on caillotte terroirs. Outstanding terroirs for the Sauvignon, which can face the sun, but giving Sancerre a beautiful aging capacity. The Crochets have two strings to their bow: their Sauvignon Blanc and Pinot Noir. A feature they share with Vincent Pinard and his son in Bué and the Vacheron cousins in Sancerre (incidentally, one of the cousins is passionate about moccasins and oxfords…).

Gilles's kindness is combined with exceptional craftsmanship. He runs his 36 hectares with a master hand, very seriously. He manages to produce wines, both white and red, that are quite remarkable. However, as his colleagues already mentioned, he is always on the lookout for the Pinot Noir of the Côte de Nuits. I remember a lunch in February 2014, during which his wife had grilled a nice prime rib. Gilles made us taste blindly several

Pinot Noirs, both from his domain and from one of his great friends, Christophe Roumier. One of the great names of Chambolle-Musigny. We then had, side by side, a 2007 Bonnes-Mares grand cru vintage (as Gilles said, referring to this wine, "You'll spend your life feeling it.") and a 2005 red Sancerre Prestige from Gilles, and then a 1989 Bonnes-Mares grand cru and a 1990 red Sancerre. On paper, everything seems obvious, but in glasses, things were not so simple!

## LOIRE VALLEY
## Domaine Lucien and Gilles Crochet

# Tasting in February 2014

*Vertical of Chêne Marchand cuvée. The Crochets own 5.5 hectares of the 32 that make up the cru.*

**2012.** *Pale color, open nose, fresh and tender. Reminiscent of green tangerine, splendid and dashing. Full-bodied, rich and fresh. Lingering. It is a complete and balanced wine, a success.*

**2011.** *Pale color, nose already open, flattering. Soft and floral. On the palate, a medium length. This vintage is very accessible without complexity, frank and straight.*

**2010.** *Pale golden color. Open nose, straightforward, intense. Recalling truffles and gooseberries. Crispy mouth, nice finish, mineral and salt-forming, refreshing. Remarkable with gravlax salmon that we tasted at Gilles's last time.*

**2009.** *Intense golden color, full-bodied, voluptuous, spherical, powerful and generous, supported by a contained acidity. Consistent overall. I can imagine it with sweetbreads and mushrooms.*

**2008.** *Pale yellow color. Sharp nose, fruity, slightly spicy. With pear and ripe starfruit notes. Medium-bodied, firm and taut, a discreet roundness. We tasted it at Gilles's with a fresh goat cheese tagliatelle and raw cream.*

**2006.** *Rich and sunny vintage. When the Cabernet is slightly overripe, this caillotte terroir, after a few years in bottle, releases into the wine aromas of truffles. Try it with a risotto with white truffle; it's wonderful! A spherical wine. Full-bodied. With a concentrated finish. Beautiful acidity, refreshing, recalling a Menton lemon peel.*

# Domaine François Cotat

*Tender Monts Damnés*

THERE EXISTS TODAY TWO COTAT DOMAINS: that of François and that of his cousin Pascal. But I first visited the domain of their fathers. It was in 1993, with Philippe Emanuelli, at the time my second at La Poularde. During my visit, while battling the two brothers, I was able to order incredible vintages: 1969, 1971, 1973, and 1975. Some dry Monts-Damnés and semi-dry Grandes-Côtes, whose freshness surprised more than one customer in Montrond-les-Bains. When the two brothers retired, Paul left his vineyards to François, and Francis left his to his son Pascal. François had an early start with his father since he was already lending him a hand in 1979. Although he vinified his own wine in 1985, it was not until 1998 that he took over his father's vineyards. He has been managing since then 4 hectares of the finest parcels in Chavignol. My relationships with the Cotat would suffer during the transition. I was preparing for a world contest and was then about to move to Paris. It was only during the 2000s that I went back to the domain. The first observation that I would like to make after having much enjoyed these wines is that the quantity granted to us has not changed from one generation to another.

The other aspect that has not changed concerns the aging of the wines. It still takes place in half barrels. The wines are neither filtered nor stuck during winter. The cold is allowed in to speed the tartar. At the Cotats', the intervention is rather performed on the vine. And indeed, it is special:

– The Grande Côte: a clay and limestone soil with a Kimmeridgian marl. I remember 2001 magnums of Sancerre, La Grande Côte, with a soft peak that worked wonderfully with a roasted lobster and Maltese oranges and grapefruit.

– The Culs de Beaujeu: a beautiful plot belonging to François where the slope reaches up to 45%. This is one of the most beautiful parts of the Chavignol crus. Its exposure faces east, while the southeast is composed of a marl-calcareous soil. On the surface, you can find the famous "caillottes," a fossilized gravel.

– The Monts Damnés is a hill aptly named because of its daunting slope and its southern exposure. Soils are pretty identical to the previous ones.

– The Caillottes is a parcel that was integrated into the domain in the mid 2000s. The soil is made more out of limestone. I remember a dinner party when we served a 2007 Sancerre Caillottes with semi-dry *crottins* of Chavignol to four hundred guests at the Paris sommeliers gala taking place at the George V in 2011. A great harmony and a first for a gala, this vintage celebrates the Paris sommelier association's centenary. It took over a century for a Chavignol Sancerre to be served at a sommelier gala.

– The Special Cuvée. This cuvée saw its latest vintage with the 1998. François renamed it Cuvée Paul, in honor of his father. The subtlety of this wine stems from the fact that sometimes, some barrels do not complete all their fermentable sugars, which results in the presence of several grams of residual sugar in the wine. Hence the need for this cuvée.

# LOIRE VALLEY
## Domaine François Cotat

APPELLATION **SANCERRE** CONTRÔLÉE

2011

*Les Monts Damnés*

Mise en
Bouteille
à la Propriété

Ni Collé
Ni Filtré

FRANÇOIS COTAT

VIGNERON À **CHAVIGNOL** (CHER)

PRODUIT DE FRANCE

# Tasting in January 2014

While waiting for François who had gone to find glasses, we looked at some pictures in the cellar. One in particular moved us: Paul Cotat (whom we knew was fragile) with his violin alongside a soloist of the Paris Opera. There was also one of him with his son in the magical hills that were making us feel so alive.

When I asked François the secret of his winemaking, he replied: "It's the terroir. I do nothing except monitor the timing of the grapes." Because at François's, there is no yeast added for fermentation, no settling, fining, or filtration. With him, everything looks simple, obvious.

He is the heir to a heritage, which he preserves simply. François is the archetype of kindness, someone tender, in the most noble sense. He added: "Today, motivations are not the same. The choice of clones is important. Some allow a more qualitative production, others not. While still others produce more mineral wines than Franc vines."

In a word, nothing is lost for those who want to defend the colors of these great Sauvignon terroirs.

**2012 Sancerre Caillottes.** *Pale brilliant color. Fresh nose, sharp, fruity, floral, a touch of lemon. Semi-bodied, fairly taut, very expressive and well balanced, quite refreshing.*

**2012 Sancerre Les Monts Damnés.** *The Monts Damnés is raised for eight months in barrels of 600 liters for 7 to 8 years. The nose is closed, concentrated. The palate is still somewhat muted at this point, straight, slightly saline, lingering, and wide. A very balanced wine to keep. A grand Chavignol that will get some heart over time.*

**2012 Sancerre La Grande Côte.** *Located on the south coast of Amigny, the grape is cut a week after the Monts Damnés. Which gives a truly mature Chavignol. The citrus notes mingle with those of citronella and sweets. Lots of amplitude in the mouth and a long finish. Powerful overall. To revisit in ten years.*

**2011 Sancerre Les Monts Damnés.** *The 2011s have, in general, a lower acidity, which makes for a softer profile, pleasing, full and spherical. Ready to be enjoyed.*

## LOIRE VALLEY
## Domaine François Cotat

**2010 Sancerre Les Monts Damnés.**
*Pale and luminous color. Nose open,*
*straight, intense and floral. A vegetal*
*touch reminiscent of a broken hazel*
*branch. On the palate, we find again*
*the tension of the 2012s, devoid of*
*magnitude. Nevertheless, a very nice*
*flavor, squarer. Very nice length.*
*A serious Chavignol.*

**2008 Sancerre Caillottes.** *Tasted*
*in February 2015 at Giuseppe Lo*
*Cassale's, Saint-Nicolas Street in the*
*20th arrondissement of Paris. Bright*
*pale yellow color. Open nose, internal,*
*fruity, thin. A dominant black currant*
*leaf, lilac, lime, and hints of mint.*
*A good tension in the mouth, vigorous,*
*fluid.*

# Domaine Edmond and Anne Vatan

*The Wisdom of Chavignol*

I N 1996,
WHILE PERUSING
an article in a professional journal describing Alain Ducasse's arrival at Poincaré Avenue, I noticed a picture of Gérard Margeon surrounded by great wines, such as the Hermitage-Cathelin of Gérard Chave, the château-de-Pibarnon of Count of Saint-Victor, and, in between, a bottle with a green collar that intrigued me. I wanted to find out more, but taken up by my travels and competitions, I could not go to Chavignol. Never mind, Thierry made an appointment and went there with our apprentice at the time (presently, a wine merchant in Lyon) Tristan Ringenbach.

The reception, the tasting, and Edmond's words inspired him. When he inquired about placing an order for La Poularde, Edmond led him to understand that he would like to first meet Eric Beaumard. Intrigued and even more interested, in the following months I managed to free my schedule and go to Chavignol with Thierry. We tasted the 1996 vintage together with Edmond. And quite a few more…

There has never been a year without my having visited Edmond. Each time, he opens a 1996 bottle after sampling from the new vintage. When I went back to ask if he could allocate us wines for the opening of the George V, he asked, "Since I'm only giving you forty-eight bottles, who else is going to be on the wine list with me?" Hearing me name Vincent Pinard of Bué, he said:" If Vincent is on the list, then all is well." Afterwards, Edmond never failed to send us a shipment, even with Anne, who took over in 2008. We always serve wines from Vincent Pinard and his sons, Florent and Clément, and we visit them each year with the same punctuality.

When I met Edmond, I did not know yet how close he was to Didier Dagueneau. I learned on the following visit that Edmond was indeed his spiritual father, the one with whom he conferred and sought advice, one of the few to whom he listened and certainly one of the men he respected the most in the world.

For Edmond, everything happens in the vineyard. Once the grapes are in, things take their own course. No convoluted winemaking. It's all about mastering the maturing process. Pressing with a Vaslin, a traditional press model, has the effect of keeping more fine sediments, unlike pneumatic presses, which leave no or little sediment. Here, the lees are vital to feed the wine in glazed-concrete tanks where fermentation progresses. Then, all that is required is sieving lightly (with a strainer, kind of a Chinons steel) and bottling.

## M EMORIES

At Didier's initiative, in 2003, we organized with Marie and the children a sally to Chavignol. The youngest two, Lisa and Baptiste, were taken with Didier, with his disheveled hair and Santa beard, as if back from the North Pole with his sled dogs – a character from a tale, a legend with intense laughing eyes. We came to visit Didier's new fad: the goat stables. He had the original idea to set up a goat farm in the school of Chavignol. Each three-starred chef in France had to buy a goat. Beautiful Chamois goats. The children were delighted to see these forty goats grazing on the slopes of Chavignol, along with Didier and Edmond. Then the urge arose to have lunch at Edmond's with Didier.

Edmond arrived, carrying a bottle of 2000 Sancerre rosé from his domain into the comfortable and cozy dining room with timeless décor. The color was not very pronounced. It expressed notes of macerated fruits. A powerful, dense wine, far from the idyllic picture of a Sancerre rosé, and so much the better! He served it fresh with county *gougères* just out of the oven.

At the table, eating a divine *blanquette* of veal cheek, he opened a 1990 Clos-la-Néore to celebrate this moment with Didier. A learning experience. Nothing obscured the intensity of the soil, neither wood (there is none) nor over-ripeness. Solely the terroir of the Néore.

After that followed a selection of *crottins*, slightly bluish and semi-dry, the way I like it, with a 1985 Clos-la-Néore, which was of an incredible freshness. What vitality!

Ms. Vatan had baked an apple pie, perfectly golden, made with winter apples, picked before fully ripe, with time to mature on the shelves and concentrated until just the right time for cooking in a buttered pastry. What bliss!

## LOIRE VALLEY
### Domaine Edmond and Anne Vatan

It was the only time I got to have lunch in the company of these two characters in Sauvignon, so different, yet sharing the same aspirations. They were made for each other.

Speaking of which, I had a friend who was irrevocably impacted by his meeting with Edmond. This was Roland Marchetti, one of my most loyal fans. Always present in the audience during my contests. He even came with his wife to Vienna, Austria, in 1998. Having tasted regularly the Clos-la-Néore at La Poularde, Roland found himself in Sancerre during one of his business trips. From there, he contacted me to make an appointment with Edmond. I called right away the sage of Chavignol to confirm a tentative meeting for Roland with him the same afternoon. I described my friend and explained his commitment to the Néore. Meanwhile, I could not get back to Roland, who was already on his way. An hour later, the two men crossed paths in Chavignol. Edmond was emerging from one of his many cellars, and Roland, having abandoned his car at the entrance of the village, was walking in search of some clue to locate the Vatan home. Although they had never met, they recognized each other immediately. A unwavering friendship was born out of this first visit. It cannot be otherwise when one meets a man who exudes such wisdom.

## LOIRE VALLEY
### Domaine Edmond and Anne Vatan

# Tasting of Clos-la-Néore with Anne, in 2015, in Chavignol

with Florent Martin and Maxime Salembié, one of our senior chefs.

The Clos-la-Néore is a 80-acre parcel located in the Monts Damnés, which Edmond's grandfather acquired in 1859. In 1935, Edmund had his first harvest experience at the age of six with his grandfather. Since then, he has changed nothing or almost nothing.

2014. *Sample retrieved from a tank. Color already clear, bright pale yellow. Dense nose, peak reduction. Almond and white fruit notes. Wide mouth, sappy. Nice length, and great potential.*

2013. *Pale yellow color, medium intensity. Taut and fresh nose. It "sauvignonne" as Anne Vatan likes to say. A black currant flower note. Savory mouth, with dimensions, and a reasonable degree. Nice balance. An accessible wine with a remarkable energy. Even if it's not a great year, it needs more time. A refreshing Clos-la-Néore.*

2012. *Intense yellow color, rich nose, exotic fruit and candied citrus notes. Full-bodied and powerful, a tad warm, 14°. Very long finish. It must settle down.*

2008. *Anne's first vintage. The year Edmond turned 79, Didier enticed her to take over. Until then, Anne's only passion was for the world of art and archeology. She has hardly done anything to the vintage. The nose is very rich, recalling candied lemons. The mouth is still closed. Maybe a little too warm.*

1996. *Tasting with Edmond at his home. This is the archetype of a Néore after fifteen years. Huge density, opulent nose, well built. Boxwood and preserved lemon mingle wonderfully. The mouth is of an unparalleled density, you do not feel its alcoholic strength. A vintage concentrated by the wind. Because that was the vintage we first enjoyed together, since then, with each visit, he always has a bottle at hand.*

1990. *Real wide, with depth, not affected by aging or selected yeasts (here, only indigenous yeasts are involved in the smooth process of fermentation; selected yeasts often tend to standardize the bouquet). Ripe plum aromas, pipped-yellow fruit, light frangipane notes.*

1985. *Strong verbena tea, lemon grass, some energy, no residues or sensation of the acidity that is present.*

# Domaine Benjamin and Didier Dagueneau

*Two Names for the Sauvignon*

# T

O HAVE KNOWN DIDIER
BETWEEN 1988 AND 2008
will all my life be a huge part of my heart. We shared great
moments, and sometimes we remained distant for long
periods. But for others in his circle, was it any different?
He remains one of the most complete men that I have ever come across.
He never made concessions to his nature. He was often described as tor-
mented, anarchist, or provocative, and it was true. But he was a great antic-
ipator, a soil defender, a destroyer of stupidity, an outstanding winemaker,
a scholarly poet, a lover of the great outdoors, and a dreamer. Consider the
label of his Asteroid vintage. It mimics the image of the "Little Prince" by
Saint-Exupéry, but in Didier's version, he flies off drawn by sled dogs.

In just over two decades, he accomplished a feat: becoming the locomotive
of an appellation – which, as a whole, preferred to take another train – and
turning Saint-Andelain, a village in the Nièvre, into a famous place. All this
with his bad imitation of Janis Joplin's guitarist, from the Flower Power era.
His jokes were well known, even legendary. He renamed the end of his
street, "Ernesto Che Guevara," and some nights, when one of his sled dogs
started barking, the whole pack echoed in chorus. Didier, amateur world
champion of sled dog racing, bred Alaskan malamutes. From the heights of
the village where his house was located, the nightly din carried far away.
When we stayed over to sleep, we could sometimes enjoy these canine choirs.

Among the first to follow him was Philippe Bourguignon, then Olivier
Poussier, Philippe Charlopin, Eric Bordelet, and Marc Kreydenweiss. It was
through Marc that I met Didier. We struck up a friendship right away, and
we went to see him with Marie in Andlau quite a few times. When I left the
Loire valley, we lost touch. Which was not right. I had to do something about
it. Didier also had the ability to win over winegrowers, wine lovers, and
sommeliers across generations. After the 1980s generation, it was the turn
of young talents, such as Antoine Petrus, who fell under the spell of the man
from Saint-Andelain. So many other names could be mentioned. He knew
how to bring together men and women who shared his convictions about
wine by creating the Tradespeople Union. His thread was the humanistic
approach of Henri Jayer. His first contacts were Marc Kreydenweiss, Pascal
Delbeck, the Foucault brothers, François Chidaine, Eric Bordelet, Charles

Joguet, Marc Pagès, and Jean-Marc Boillot. The Union would take shape in 1989, during a meal at Alain Passard's, where Eric Bordelet worked. Rainer Zierock, an agrarian philosopher and specialist of wine genetics, rallied with these founders. On the gastronomic front, a friend of Didier, Didier Clément, perfectionist chef and wine lover, was in charge of the feast for them.

This organization outlasted him, like his domain, now taken over with enthusiasm and charisma by his children, Charlotte and Louis-Benjamin, who could count on the support of the whole Didier team and now reap the seeds sown by their father. It takes time for vines to grow deep roots. It's Benjamin's turn to carry forward the work of the previous generation. As for the cellar created twenty years ago, it still represents innovative modernism. Benjamin inherited his father's obsessive cleanliness towards the vats and cellar. Yet, as he points out, nothing was simple: "When my father wanted to age the wines in half- barrels, nobody had any. No cooper was producing them. Yet he found several of them still able to manufacture them." For the record, there are still half-barrels from his great-grandfather, used at the place of those who bought them, such as Edmond Vatan. In the early 1990s, in collaboration with several winemakers, Didier created the famous "cigar" drum inspired by the "pipes" of Porto. More elongated and wider than those used in Burgundy and Bordeaux, they allow a better mingling of wines with fine lees.

# MEMORIES

In late 2007, Thierry and I went to visit Didier. A couple of enthusiastic foody friends, fine wines, and English sedans, accompanied us. After the tasting, we had dinner together at his home. Simple products but of rare quality. He opened incredible bottles from his cellar, which brimmed over with them and still does. We laughed and talked a lot. On that evening, he appeared to me calmer, more composed than I had ever seen him before. He seemed resigned and more peaceful. His words, though less frequent, carried more weight. I was eager to see more of his evolution. Thanks to his children, this is today the case.

## LOIRE VALLEY
## Domaine Benjamin and Didier Dagueneau

## Tasting at the Domain in 2014, with Benjamin

Marc Le Gallic and Victor Petiot, two of our sommeliers, are with me.

In a cellar tour, we tasted all the 2013 vintages: the Buisson-Renard, the white fumé of Pouilly, the thoroughbred, the Monts Damnés Sancerre, and the famous Asteroid (a cuvée producing, in general, 150 bottles of 50 centiliters).

## A vertical of the Silex vintage, the white fumé of Pouilly

*Area of the lot: 11 hectares. Clay-limestone soils with flint on the mound. More marl on the slopes. In fact, the entire area, even if nothing states it, is organic.*

*2012. A reference vintage. Ample, rich, always a varietal touch reminiscent of gooseberry. Generous mouth without softness, very good length.*

*2011. All the power of flints, without the tense character of 2012. Medium length, but the whole is consistent. Absent varietal notes. Already enjoyable due to its flexibility.*

*2010. Golden color, with silvery reflection. Closed nose, deep, introverted. Tight mouth, sappy, long, slightly spicy, exotic note, fresh without over-ripeness. A classic, in the austere style.*

*2007. Golden color, straight nose with white peach and pear notes, fine. Perfect mouth, with a fresh and long finish.*

*2005. Pale gold color. Fine nose, straight, square, still closed, a little solemn. Mouth straight, introverted, a classic without exaltation, but strong. Long finish. Still too young, but very good potential.*

*2002. "The" bottle! Intense yellow straw color. Open nose, expressive and fine. Nice complexity reminiscent of lime, peppermint, and ripe starfruit. Sensual mouth, full, buttery. Long and saline finish, with a few varietal notes in the back. Perfect. A great flint.*

*1985. Almost 30 years. Didier's first Silex vintage. A great emotional moment. Bright golden color. Fruity nose, exotic, zest of orange peel, bitter, menthol, a flake of flint, mineral. A glowing mouth. The wood has completely melted, no oxidation, long lingering. A success.*

## LOIRE VALLEY
# Domaine Benjamin and Didier Dagueneau

# Domaine François Chidaine

*Montlouis, the Life and Joy*

# I

T IS THROUGH
DIDIER DAGUENEAU

that I met François in the 1990s. Like Eric Bordelet, he would become one of the spiritual sons of Didier, who had told me, "You must go and see him. He's a good guy." Back then, I worked with other winemakers in Montlouis: Jacky Blot at the Domaine de la Taille aux Loups, and Olivier Delétang at the eponymous domain. From my first visit, I liked the winemaker, his speech both firm and placid, and all that it entailed: sensitive wines in his image. They would always get included in the wine list at La Poularde, and also at the George V.

François began in 1989, when he purchased 3 hectares from his parents and acquired an additional 1.5. By 1998, his domain had reached 10 hectares. In 2006, his property gained a new impetus when he was able to complete the acquisition of Domaine du Clos Baudoin, a property owned for nearly a century by the princes Poniatowski. With this purchase, he increased his vineyard by another 10 hectares, reaching 35 hectares in total: 20 hectares of Montlouis, 10 of Vouvray, and 5 of Touraine.

In all my tours between Saumur and Vouvray-Montlouis, I always made sure to pay a visit to François. Two years ago, upon leaving Nady Foucault in Chacé, where I had just finished a tasting with Florent Martin (second sommelier at Le Cinq) and Thierry, we realized that we had time to call on Husseau, the hamlet where François's domain is located, via the departmental 947, along the Loire. I like this river that connects me to my roots by one of its tributaries, the Layon, from where my grandfather Beaumard came. This is the central axis of France's wine culture – which, since 2000, has been added to the World Heritage by UNESCO. So, yes, "our" Loire valley, its wine heritage as architectural, has always had an important place in my life.

So we were driving quietly that morning. We had hardly gone a few kilometers when we came upon a charming small village. Thierry stopped the sedan near the church. "Mr. Beaumard, Candes-Saint-Martin, does that remind you of something?" A moment of reflection. "You're right. Let's stop here." When we reached the porch of the college, we noticed that it was closed. Suddenly, from out of a limestone building nearby, a small ageless lady approached us. "Do you want to visit? It's closed. But ok, I can let you in." We must have made a good impression. Carrying a keychain worthy of

# LOIRE VALLEY
## Domaine François Chidaine

a Renaissance castle, she unlocked the door, leaving the keychain hanging on a nail near the gate. "When you leave, don't forget to close it behind you, because of the cats." Thank you, madam; goodbye, madam.

Without further ado, we entered this historic place: the fortified collegiate church of Saint-Martin. This is where the cenotaph of Bishop Saint Martin had been lain. History tells us that Martin died at Candes in late autumn, November 8, 397, precisely, on a bed of ashes, as dying holy men do.

A dispute erupted between Poitou and Touraine and led to the latter removing his body and relocating it to Tours via the river where he was buried on November 11. It was this legend that brought us here. I am going to tell you the lullaby of the sommeliers, the story sommeliers are told to lull them in their youth. St. Martin, who had a donkey, journeyed through Touraine to reach the Abbey of Marmoutier. He crossed a vineyard, which at the time were not trimmed. They grew in vines and produced small acid grapes, from which the monks extracted a little sour wine. Approaching the walls of the abbey, the holy man took a break. He tethered his donkey to a pole that supported a vine. He thanked the Lord for having reached his destination without complication, drank some water from his gourd and, tired, lay down to rest. The air was mild, the sun pleasant. The saint fell asleep. But not the donkey! Always hungry, the animal grazed on as much vine as its rope. It was when it got to the very last leaf that Martin awoke and noticed the damage. From the vigorous vines, only stumps remained. Sheepishly, he went to the abbey and confessed his donkey's sin to the monks. When the time came for the harvest, the monks of Marmoutier could not believe their eyes. From the very vines that the donkey had muched on, they now reaped large, juicy and sweet grapes which produced the best wine that they had ever drunk. Since then, the vines get trimmed short, and we have grown accustomed to calling donkeys... Martin!

A beautiful legend. However, a detail caught our attention upon leaving the church. We contemplated this porch, both striking and original. Inside this porch, a design of complex veins plasters a column in the center. On each side of the studded-oak portal, statues were framed by pillars, at the foot of which were carved grapes, vines, framing faces, and... a donkey's head. Beyond the legend, we owe this holy man the name of one of our royal dynasties: the Capetians. Hugues (circa 940-996), first of the Capetian line, took the name of Capet because he was abbot of St. Martin of Tours, where was kept half of the holy man's coat: the capa.

These pages of history inspiring us, we felt ready to ride the horses parked close by to the Capetian war cry: "Montjoie! St Denis!" We simply closed the heavy creaking door in the echoing empty nave. All was quiet. A veil of mist enveloped the village, not a peep. We were ready to go home to François.

Arriving on time – something pretty rare – we began by visiting his new winery. It was built on three levels, on the other side of the road from where the old cellar was located and still in business. The storage of materials and the labeling room were located on the first floor. On the two floors below, everything was designed so that pumps proved unnecessary as all mechanisms relied solely on gravity. The wine is never brutalized by pumping. The entire domain relies on biodynamic farming: plowing and scratching the soil, manual harvest, no chemical input in the soils.

# Tasting, February 19, 2013

2010 Sparkling Vouvray (32 months on slats). *Light color, leaning towards light saline nose, pleasant. This is a non-dosé Brut. On the palate, fine bubbles with great aromas of fresh apple and pear. Precise finish. A great success.*

Sparkling Montlouis (12 months on slats). *Disgorged January 6th, 2014. Darker, denser color. The nose is more feminine and accessible than the Vouvray. On the palate, the pear aroma prevails throughout the length. Stronger bubbles.*

2012 Montlouis Clos du Breuil. *This is an historic clos from François's debut. The vines are on average 50 years old. Clay and flint soil. Pale color, discreet nose. Fine wide mouth, a lot of body, minty notes in the finish. Refreshing.*

2012 Vouvray Les Argiles. *Calcareous clay soil. Discreet nose, set back. Tense mouth, slightly chalky finish. Very sapid, higher acidity, more tension than in the Montlouis.*

2012 Vouvray Clos Baudoin. *Domain of 2.7 hectares surrounded by walls. The Chenins are on average 70 years old. One of François's major wines. Limestone-clay soil on chalky freestones. It faces south and is well drained. The estate once belonged to Prince Philippe Poniatowski. Discreet nose, fine, white fruit. Beautiful amplitude, full-bodied and long at the same time, powerful. This a complete and balanced wine.*

2011 The Montlouis Choisilles. Choisilles *means small black flints. Already open nose, sappy, medium amplitude. The 2011 remains somewhat simpler in the mouth than the 2012. François's wines are aged normally for ten months in half barrels.*

## LOIRE VALLEY
### Domaine François Chidaine

**2011 Montlouis Les Bournais Franc de Pied.** *First vintage of Franc de Pied. Clay and limestone marl terroir. Intense color. Open nose. Wide mouth, full-bodied, slightly mellow. At the back, rather frangipane and white fruit.*

**2010 Montlouis Les Bournais.** *Straight nose, closed, elegant. Mouth wide, deep and intense. A woody note, with pear and dry floral notes. Perfect now.*

**2011 Montlouis Clos Habert.** *Soft clay with silex terroir (12 grams of residual sugar). A tender Montlouis. Discreet nose, thin. Supple palate without heaviness, refined finish, and, overall, because of its lack of acidity, slightly weighty.*

**2010 Montlouis Moelleux.** *Very smooth nose. Mellow attack in the mouth and a very nice finish, elegant, through which peach aromas appear. Nice balance.*

**2009 Montlouis Les Lys.** *70 grams of residual sugar. The acidity pierced through first in the nose, then the sweetness blossomed. Very ample mouth, with yellow fruit notes. A wider rather than longer wine.*

# Domaine Clos Naudin

*Harmony on the Way to Chenin*

# T

**HE LOIRE VALLEY
IS STEEPED IN *BELLES LETTRES.***

All along its course, great literary authors were born while some of the most amazing castles of France were erected. This river knows how to be discreet or invasive according to the seasons, reflecting the peculiar Loire soul, at once sweet and warm, devoid of torpor, fresh, sometimes even frisky. In its own image, the river gives birth to multifaceted wines, always elegant.

If my first visit to a winemaker took place in Saint-Émilion with Alain Vauthier in the spring of 1985, the second was the same year, in Vouvray, with Philippe Foreau and his father, André. Philippe had taken over the domain two years before. I can still experience the lemony scent of magnolias in bloom in front of their home. Meeting him, I felt my growing passion for wine and the matching of food and wine.

The knowledge of pairings between wine and food is Philippe's signature. In thirty years of wandering through the vineyards of the world, I have never found a winemaker who masters and distills with so much precision the delicate art of unveiling alliances between grape juices and the treasures of village markets. With Philippe, these agreements are always on the route to Chenin. As a matter of fact, had he chosen a different career path, he would have made a great chef, very sensitive and refined. By the same token, he has such an incredible nose that he could have made it in the perfume business in Grasse.

When I listen to him, even today, he combines the poetry of Charles Joguet with the science of Professor Jacques Puisais and the verve of the hilarious Raymond Garcia. A lot of strength and fragility emanate from them all. The wines of the Loire – so delicate and profound – are as fragile as they are infinitely diverse.

The wines of Vouvray perfectly illustrate this concept, the taste spectrum being so wide. I can still see myself at La Poularde in Montrond, in the late 1980s, serving a duck *foie gras* in cloth with a fine quince jelly and a mellow 1976 sparkling Vouvray Clos Naudin, which Raymond Garcia led me to discover at Jean Luc Hatet's, the famous restaurant owner of Le Chancelier in Montbazon (then, two Michelin stars). This memory confirms the wealth of Chenin Blancs on the soils of Vouvray. Some of their expressions are unclassifiable, incredible. Philippe is a virtuoso with this palette, just as with his semi-dry quiet dry or semi-dry rather sweet… Ah! Paul Préboist in *Le Grand Restaurant*…

Vouvray is a 2,100-hectare vineyard, of which the vast majority is vinified into sparkling Vouvray (2.5 bar pressure) or mousseux Vouvray (5.5 bar pressure). They are developed using the so-called "traditional" method, that is to say, the champagne method. The vast majority is planted on the plateau, with a limestone subsoil. The top layer is made of clay with different compositions (of firm or delicate texture). In places, the limestone sticks out (Aubuis), whereas in others, there is a significant presence of flint (Perruches). The grape variety is unique: Chenin Blanc. It matures later than the Sauvignon, two weeks later. It allows the wines to retain a subtle freshness. Philippe owns 12 hectares of vines. Even if the domain does not form a clos, all the plots are very homogeneous. They are located mainly in the Croix-Buisée on a *perruche* lot, a silty-clay terroir.

These beautiful plots do not prevent Philippe from wandering towards other crus, even as far as going to another area of Chenin: in Anjou. It was during one of his walks, in summer 2014, that he met a young winemaker in Savennières, Thibaud Boudignon, with whom I got acquainted in recent years. During our last interview, he mentioned it to me. Thibaud lives at the foot of one of the great vineyards of Savennières: the Roche aux Moines. This is where they met. The younger recognized the elder, and they began to talk, sympathized, and soon found themselves sharing glasses of Chenin.

Thibaud bought several vineyards at auction, including a clos in La Possonnière, which he operates, as well as a plot that is being planted further down from the clos. He vinified some beautiful 2013s, and his 2014s represent themselves very well. These wines have a lot of tension and salinity. Difficult features to find in Savennières. His wines reflect him: introverted, reserved, righteous, but not without power. Our man was a French champion professional judoka. Nonetheless, he found his way to the Chenin Blanc and the banks of the Loire. No doubt, when the time comes, he will go up to Vouvray, to Philippe's, where young people make their first strides in the field: Vincent, his son, the fourth Foreau generation, is all Chenin.

# LOIRE VALLEY
## Domaine Clos Naudin

# MEMORIES

It was in the 1990s. I was still at La Poularde. Raymond Garcia had organized a dinner party with Charles Joquet, his wife, Philippe Foreau, and myself. For an appetizer, we had a seared duck *foie gras* with a 1983 white Domaine-de-Trévallon of an incredible freshness. Blessed is he who might come upon it in Les Baux-de-Provence. Then a pullet with morels along with a 1970 Vega-Sicilia Unico. It was the first time I tasted this wine in this vintage. It seemed to me back then as the greatest 1970, and still today, when I come across it, I continue to think so.

A decantered wine showed up at dessert time. The wine, poured into glasses with solemnity, had a brewed black tea color. The nose was pronounced, with aromas of bitter orange jam, camphor, buckwheat honey, currants, amber, and sweet spices. The mouth had an incredible length. After several minutes of deliberation, the entire table opined that it was a Spanish wine, the type from Malaga, except for one person: Philippe Foreau. After a minute, he spoke, "No, I see here a wine coming from a botrytized harvest, an old Sauternes, probably from the turn of the century." Everyone, including myself, chuckled, and we would not let it go. It could not be anything but a Malaga! Nonetheless, Raymond remained quiet and peered at Philippe incredulously. He had found the bottle: Chateau d'Arches, 1906!

Here lies the strength of a great taster, an expert who can maintain his position, defend, and explain it to an audience that openly contradicts him.

# Tasting in February 2014, at Philippe Foreau's

With Victor Petiot, Marc Le Gallic, from the sommelier team, and Marc Plantevin, intern.

**2007 Sparkling Vouvray, reserves Bulle de Vouvray.** *This is an anecdotal production by Philippe Foreau. Yet, it is the flagship wine of the Appellattion d'origine contrôlée (AOC). Outstanding alternative to champagne, with excellent value. Shelled nose, with mushrooms. Great quality bubbles, creamy, rather wide.*
*Pairings: skewers of frogs' legs with herbs and heads of roasted Paris mushrooms.*

**2012 Vouvray dry.** *Pale and clear color. Fine and open nose. Slender mouth, very good length, with a pear and white fruit retro-olfaction. The mouth has a good amplitude, buttery (6 grams of residual sugar). Clay soil with flints.*
*Pairings: Scampi in maki, wrapped in sorrel leaves, over a brunoise of dry confit lyokan with the half-cooked, poached tails and young radish sprouts.*

**2010 Vouvray dry.** *Floral nose, open, sensitive. Lemon note bringing freshness. Medium range. Lots of tone. Plums and pipped-white fruit notes, savory finish (13.2 ° and 6 grams of acidity).*
*Pairings: Poached spider crab, served cold with green dill and lemon mayonnaise.*

**2009 Vouvray dry.** *Almond note, yellow fruit, acacia honey. The taste is fuller, the acidity lower, a saline touch in the finish, almost like a Chablis, sensual. About it Philippe says, "This wine is like a Preuses."*
*Pairings: A carpaccio of scallops Saint-Jacques of Erquy, with a bergamot lemon zest and Scampi oil.*

**2008 Vouvray semi-dry.** *Intense golden color. Open frangipane nose, and candied quince. Ample attack in mouth, full-bodied, a good length without softness. Outstanding balance (13° and 25 grams of sugar hardly noticeable).*
*Pairings: Langoustine tails with ginger and lime.*

**2007 Vouvray semi-dry.** *Spicy nose, verbena, slightly smoky from a stone gun. Creamy mouth (18 grams of residual sugar).*
*Pairings: Ideal with roasted lobster in saffron beurre blanc and icy-sanded carrots in lobster juice.*

# LOIRE VALLEY
## Domaine Clos Naudin

2005 Vouvray semi-dry. *Rich golden color. Sweet nose. Verbena notes, lots of elegance. Very wide mouth, without heaviness. Well-adjusted sugar, beautiful tone. Nice acidity. Remarkable length.*
*Pairings: Golden sweetbreads of a farm-fed calf, with broad beans in lemon grass and fresh almonds. A charming dish, with substance.*

2010 Vouvray mellow. *Dense color but not too evolved. Generous concentrated nose, with a peak of vanilla and fresh almonds. Incredibly full-bodied and balanced mouth. Typical of Philippe's wines.*
*Pairings: A lobe of roasted goose foie gras, with deglaciated nectarines in white balsamic.*

2003 Vouvray mellow Reserve. *Intense yellow golden color. Candied nose recalling yellow fruit jelly. 160 grams residual sugar. We are moving to another stage of concentration. Very nice finish.*
*Pairings: In the course of the afternoon, under a gazebo, with freshly baked madeleines in orange blossom with bits of candied quince.*

2009 Vouvray mellow Reserve. *Golden color. The nose is open with an unutterable Parfait of Menton lemon, elegant. Considerable wide mouth. Consistent overall. 145 grams of residual sugar. The grand bottle of wine tasting.*
*Pairings: Soufflé with strawberries, and peppermint ice cream.*

2011 Vouvray mellow Goutte d'Or. *Here, we reach 220 grams of residual sugar. Despite the density of liquor, a full wine, with a high acidity. Very powerful. The Chenin is here botrytized and raisined. Extreme concentration: the essence of Chenin. A meditative wine, sensual.*
*Pairings: A Corsican clementine sorbet with tiny chunks of candied peel.*

1989 Vouvray mellow 4th Sorting. *Virginia tobacco nose, vanilla, dates. Enough acid in the mouth, which structures the wine. Yellow fruit compote, apricot, honey lime, and incense. A timeless wine.*
*Pairings: The dish Saint-Pierre retour des Indes, recipe of Olivier Roellinger.*

# LOIRE VALLEY
## Domaine Clos Naudin

# Several timeless wines

Tasted during a visit with Thierry in February 2010

**1947 Vouvray mellow Reserve** *(with original cork). Mirabelle nose, pips, honey, light touch of porcini powder. The palate is delicate; the wine consumed its sugar, gentian finish. The nose is beautiful, but the mouth seems to have died.*
*Pairings: Parsnip and tuberous chervil in a porcini broth and chips of raw foie gras.*

**1947 Vouvray mellow Reserve** *(repackaged). Still hints of honey, roasted, greengage balsamic nose. The palate is crisp and sharp. We are on a Perrruches terrain, no mushroom notes in this bottle. The finish is still vivid and beautiful. Light bitterness. Complex candied quince.*
*Pairings: Lace almond tuiles with bitter orange.*

**1921 Vouvray.** *Black tea color. Although tired with slightly deviant nose, we taste hints of nougat, of confiture de vieux garcon ("old boy jam"), prunes, old Camut Calvados. Still a vibrant acidity. The mouth has consumed parts of its sugar. The wine seems more fragile, but retains delicacy and elegance.*
*Pairings: A soft and sweet Torpedo type of cigar.*

DOMAINE
VINCENT DAUVISSAT P 126

DOMAINE
FRANÇOIS RAVENEAU P 133

DOMAINE MICHEL AND
JEAN-BAPTISTE
BOUZEREAU P 141

DOMAINE ROULOT P 150

DOMAINE JEAN-
FRANÇOIS COCHE-DURY P 158

DOMAINE
JEAN-MARC BOILLOT P 165

DOMAINE
DAVID DUBAND P 172

DOMAINE
GEORGES NOËLLAT P 179

DOMAINE MÉO-CAMUZET P 186

DOMAINE
DE LA ROMANÉE-CONTI P 194

CHÂTEAU THIVIN P 206

# Burgundy

~

# Wines

# Domaine Vincent Dauvissat

*The Ascent of the Serein*

# J ANUARY 1985
## WAS THE FIRST TIME

I ventured into the department of Yonne to discover the vine-yards of Chablis. The river Serein, whose hills on either bank have been planted with Chardonnay since the dawn of civiliza-tion, ran through the village. But that January remains famous for the cold wave which broke over the country. In Chablis, the temperature dropped to - 28°C. I was with other young people as part of a seminar organized by the Interprofessional Committee of Burgundy wines. When we went down into René Dauvissat's cellar, we all thought the temperature was awfully good: 10°C! Apart from this rather frosty memory, the rest glow with the warmth of sharp wines, both crisp and palatable – a description from my earlier days as a cook. My next visit to the domain took place shortly after my arrival at La Poularde, and the visits continued on an annual basis. Nothing could derail them. Every year, between late January and early February, I orga-nized a visit to the Dauvissat. Nothing could postpone it either. This ritual pertained to an annual need to breathe the air of the vineyards. A visceral need. A way for me to recharge my batteries with passion, even though Vincent would have preferred that we come in the spring, "when the wine wakes up."

Talking with Vincent is always informative. He speaks with simple words about deep things. This is not a given – especially in the world of sommeliers where it is often the reverse. He is very sensitive, his feelings accurate. The terroirs express his precise labor in the vineyards, which finds its way into the wines. As he himself says, "Reality is the terroir." In the 1980s, he learned from his father to respect vine cycles based on traditions, monitoring and time – elements that his father had, in fact, inherited from his own father (a grandfather that Vincent shares with his cousins, the Raveneau brothers).

So, in January 1998, during a tasting in his cellar, he showed me a huge *Exogyra* or *Ostrea virgula* (small comma-shaped fossilized oyster) that he had dug out from his vineyard of Grand Cru Chablis Les Preuses, which has a limestone Kimmeridgian marl soil. When he handed it over, the shell slipped from his hands and crashed on the stone floor. A bouquet was released recalling the warm stone, chalk on blackboard, reminiscent of his early 1983 Preuses, which he then served. My memory recorded impressions of acacia

honey, verbena, hot stone, and an amplitude combined with a tension in the mouth providing an impressive balance.

Lately, his children, Étienne and Ghislain, have become part of the domain. That is very good news. His daughter takes care of logistics, and his son follows his father's footsteps in the vineyards and the cellar. A beautiful transition is underway. As a seasoned mountaineer, Vincent understands the importance of guaranteeing a new lead if he wants to continue the climb and surpass himself over and over again. As he says, "Ghislain and Étiennette complement each other well. They are at an age where their sensors are awake. A well-executed apprenticeship can be decisive." Vincent knows what he is talking about since he took over the estate from his father in 1989, even though, initially, he was not even considering becoming a winemaker. A lover of nature and space, he became a shepherd in the Alps. It was then that his passion for mountaineering came to life. When his brother declined to run the family estate, Vincent came back... with a herd of goats! And for several years, he juggled wine productions with goat cheese. Let it be known that the two go rather well together.

# MEMORIES

Wine tastings at Vincent's are always precious moments, because, in our personal cellars, his wines are both under-represented and demanding to be given time. A lot of time.

Thus, the first time we tasted his 1992 Clos was in 1996 during the second gathering of the MWW at Gerard Basset, in Winchester. God knows how many bottles from around the world, and among the most sought after, we opened on that night. Personally, I had brought – among others – this 1992 magnum. Of all the wines we tasted, this one remained for me the most memorable, even though it was clear that we did not benefit from its full potential.

Just a few weeks ago at home, Marie and I had Thierry and Nicolas for lunch. In memory of the gala in which they were involved, they brought a bottle of Vincent's 1992 Clos. This bottle came from a crate that we purchased in 2013 via Edmond, one of our young sommeliers. One day, the latter called us from a place where I do not often go, just one of these temples of consumption brimming over with products from around the world, usually of low quality, implying overpricing. He was standing in front of some bottles from Vincent's cellar, which were being kept in an air-conditioned wine closet, something rare in these sorts of places. There were both Clos and Forest from 1990 and 1992, whose price tags with only two digits made them very acceptable. They seemed to be in good shape. He inquired of the clerk about the number of bottles and their condition. He was able to check them out one by one in the cool closet where they were stored. He learned they were part of a lot from a bulk purchase. The friendly clerk knew nothing about the winemaker and only had memorized the age of the vintage in order to display a few bottles. I dispatched a squad to the site right away – the brigade of the George V, which acquired all the worthy bottles.

It was one of these bottles that the four of us savored with a European seabass from the Raz de Sein baked in a lemon scent. The Clos had developed an incredible complexity. The color still retained an intense and luminous golden glow. The nose offered a range of honey and spices, with fabulous candied citrus. The mouth was clean, opulent, lingering. The finish was straight and sapid. As often in this case, we talked little. Only once it had been intensely enjoyed did the conversation resume. The same applied to food. The first sign of appreciation when tasting is silence.

# BURGUNDY
## Domaine Vincent Dauvissat

# Tasting at Vincent Dauvissat, in February 2012

I was accompanied by one of our sommeliers,
Edmond Gasser; one of our senior chefs,
Sébastien Vigreux and two of our clerks,
Anaïs Lemonnier and David Riehm.

# Vertical of Chablis 1ˢᵗ Cru La Forest

At the Dauvissat's, regarding the work in the vineyards, organic and biodynamic farming is not required: it is obvious. As for the work in the cellars, Vincent uses Burgundian parts and casks, typical barrels for Chablis, with a capacity of 132 liters. Vincent believes that the Chablis Chardonnay needs more contact with the ambient air. This is why the elders designed this barrel. The choices of our ancestors always have good reasons behind them.

**2012.** *A clay marl soil. Wine is ample. At this point, this 2012 is still closed but already very elegant and precise. The marl brings its structure into one's mouth – the maturity of the vines, minerality, as well as the lemon peel retro-olfaction. The overall impression is one of harmony and density; it is a wine that should be enjoyed again in five years.*

**2011.** *This Forest offers progressive notes ranging from lemon rind to fennel. The nose is slightly open, rich. The ample mouth is both quite tender and complex. Ripe apple, almonds, a touch of fresh mint, with a beautiful vivacity in the finish. Ready to be enjoyed now.*

**2010.** *Discreet and concentrated nose. Ripe fruit notes. The mouth is full, with a bitter orange peel finish. A solar vintage. At this stage, the wine is very introverted. Needs to age.*

**2009.** *Golden color, fruity nose, white fruit, marzipan. Mature notes, slightly solar. It is opulent, massive, fleshy on the palate. We can still notice the minerality of the Forest, which brings balance with dill notes. It deserves great succulent dishes.*

**2008.** *Golden color. Open nose, dry floral, and dried lime. A hint of gunstone. Average amplitude in the mouth, some sparks and tension, tasting of salt, reminding a bit of green orange. Very refreshing.*

# Extended tasting during the same morning

**2012. Grand Cru Chablis Les Clos.**

*This is the most opulent cru. It gives complex wines. This one is closed at this time, complete. The mouth is very opulent. Mile almonds and vanilla sensation. The palate is very round, intense, with a lingering finish. A great Chablis wine.*

**2012. Grand Cru Chablis Les Preuses.**

*A terroir coating a clay and limestone bedrock with bluish-green kimmeridgian marl. Vincent cultivates one hectare. If we compare it to the Clos, it appears more tense. The nose is closed, though complex. By mid-mouth, we taste its salinity, its firm corseted structure, salifying. A wine with a lot of energy, very refreshing. Without a doubt, the best terroir of the property.*

*One of Vincent's specialties at the end of tasting sessions is to fetch an old vintage and to serve it blind. As a matter of fact, this is easy for him to do; the bottles have no label. Among other difficulties of the exercise is to find it in the cellar, which does not exceed 8-9°C. It is a remarkable opportunity to see how well the wines age. This time, the chosen cru was introduced as follows: Light cool color. Beautiful glow. Nose of well-ripened white fruits, frangipane, a touch of stone, licorice. A wide mouth, nice rounded power. All these observations point me towards the Clos. It had aged remarkably. The color was misleading, still very bright. I thought of a 1992 Clos. It was a 1989 Grand Cru Chablis Les Clos, with an impressive youth. Vincent has often surprised us in these cellar tastings, with bottles of premier cru Séchet or Vaillons in the fullness of their maturity.*

# Domaine François Raveneau

*A Thunderous Clos*

# I T WAS IN 1990, THROUGH MR. CUSSAC

It was in 1990, through Mr. Cussac – restaurant owner at the Saint-Michel Abbey (two Michelin stars at the time) in Tonnerre, where Marie and I had gone for dinner – that I met the Raveneau family and got exposed to their wines. Chablis was indeed located halfway between Auxerre and Tonnerre, 170 kilometers south of Paris, from where we were traveling to drive back to Montrond-les-Bains.

As I found out over my visits to their cellars, the sons of François Raveneau, Jean-Marie and Bernard, have no interest in the latest hue and cry and technological fads. Just like their cousin, Vincent Dauvissat, they are attached to tradition and a certain image of their terroirs. They cultivate almost 8 hectares consisting of lots of three Grands Crus – Blanchot, Les Clos, and Valmur – and several *premier crus* – Montée de Tonnerre, Chapelot, Butteaux, Forêts, and Montmains and Vaillons.

The Raveneaus are among the last to still harvest by hand. At present, 95% of the harvest in Chablis is performed by machine, including certain Grand Crus. This situation is the result of several factors: labor shortages as well as the domains having difficulty meeting the drastic standards which are increasingly at odds with the reality of viticulture.

The wines are aged in casks of 132 liters, the same way their father practiced. They rest in casks for 18 months. During the tastings in the cellars, one must always weigh every word. The Raveneaus are taciturn. Words must have meaning. There is no room there for those who "talk, talk, and talk until they have something to say," as Sacha Guitry said. And for those who would risk it, the tasting would shorten quickly, and upcoming visits would be compromised.

# BURGUNDY
## Domaine François Raveneau

Chablis Grand
Clos
APPELLATION CHABLIS GRAND CRU
13% Vol
PRODUIT DE FRANCE
Mis en bouteilles à la propriété
750 ml
DOMAINE FRANÇOIS RAVENEAU À CHABLIS - FRANCE

# MEMORIES

The finest bottles of the Raveneau family that I tasted were at Philippe Bourguignon's. The two are very close with each other. Friends for over thirty years. Talking about them awakens a spring-scented memory near Nemours. That Sunday, we had chosen to go by train to visit Philippe's region. Accompanying Marie and myself were Jacques Dupont, his wife, their youngest daughter and Thierry. Prudently thinking that the return trip would not be too steady, we proactively decided to leave the horses asleep under the hood in the garage, choosing the rails as a safer mode of travel.

Philippe and Michele, his wife, waited for us at the train station. From there, following roads lined with wheat fields and scattered clumps of trees spared by grain growers, we reached their mansion, lovingly furnished with happiness. Outside, the azure sky promised to remain. Having taken note, Philippe had set up a beautiful country table in the garden, overlooking the surrounding countryside. On a side table, still-warm toast, wisely preserved in the folds of a large linen napkin, waited to be soon generously slathered with a delicious pâté. Next to that, rippled shavings of Iberian ham and pink radishes with sea salt were ready to be devoured.

An impressive 1990 magnum Krug Vintage, in a beading and fogging silver bucket, waited only for its cork to fly off before refreshing our palates with its delicate effervescence.

The first shock occurred when Philippe offered me this great champagne in a unique glass. I had never seen one like it before. Was it the glass I had been dreaming of? For years, when we served great vintages or older vintages of champagne at Le Cinq, we used standard white wine glasses rather than the traditional champagne flutes. The one I was holding had a balanced shape. To describe it: the thin leg rested on a base broad enough to give it a solid foundation. The base of the slightly sanded parison created chimneys, highlighting the effervescence of the champagne and the finesse of bubbles (as is so rarely the case). The width of the glass promoted a large surface releasing the wine's aromas, whereas a classic flute makes this aromatic opening impossible. The narrowness of the lip allowed the taster to enjoy this wealth of aromas. Accustomed to this glass, Philippe had poured a suitable amount; in a word, he held the hand without going above the shoulder of the

## BURGUNDY
### Domaine François Raveneau

glass. Both the eye and the nose were in bliss. As for the mouth, the wine set in these conditions found an uplifting accomplishment. With this glass, it was not only a 1990 Krug that we discovered but a unique great white wine whose aromas and complexity revealed themselves to us. Upon my return to the George V, we contacted the creator of the glass, James Darsonville. Since then, they have been crowning our champagne trolley.

To the table Michele brought two large dishes of Burgundy snails in garlic butter. They were the fruit of patient harvesting in the surrounding thickets and brambles, after a fine spring rain. For this very French treat, he opened a magnum of 2001 Chablis Grand Cru Les Clos from the Raveneau brothers. A wine of an incredible freshness, which could teach a thing or two to Beaunois wines of the same age.

We were happy and were considering the wine pairing when Jacques Dupont put an end to it, "With garlic snails, nothing like the bubbles of a great Crémant." Right away, Philippe went down to the cellar and came back up a few minutes later. "Having no Crémant, I think this wine could challenge it." It was a 2000 Bollinger Grande Année. A great success. Of course, as always, Jacques was right. Garlic butter can be dreadful with wines. The bubbles, however, managed to overcome this obstacle.

Then from the kitchen came poultry gently roasted in an old cast-iron stove. These buxom and solid farmyard fowls were golden to perfection, their skin crisp and fragrant, their flesh soft and juicy, the rich juice with onions splendid. A large earthenware dish brimmed over with new potatoes and ceps (porcini mushrooms). For this appetizing course, our host had prepared two fully mature wines: 1986 Château Mouton Rothschild and 1986 Château Latour.

Silky mature wines, which opposed their respective evolutions and were extremely rewarding. There, too, the fire of commentaries spread without interruption. When we came to the wine pairing, Jacques let out, while fully delighting in a crispy wing, "Whatever you say, nothing beats a large and delicate fruity Gamay with roasted poultry." Again, Philippe descended into the depths of his house. He resurfaced with a magnum of the Côte-de-Brouilly 2009 Zechariah vintage of the Château Thivin. The bottles of the two previous great lords had been – as indicated by the level in the carafe – highly enjoyed. We were ready to discover this new pairing. Again, it was a success.

Later in the afternoon, Philippe took us into his library to enjoy a drop of a 1965 yellow Tarragona poured into cut and colored Bohemian crystal glasses dating from the nineteenth century. A gift from Roxanne Debuisson, the great friend of the cooks, sommeliers and pastry chefs of Paris. We raised our glasses to her, surrounded by one of the most impressive collections of ancient books dedicated to wine.

From the late afternoon to the early evening, we only took one step. Instead of heading back to Nemours to catch the evening train, we agreed that it was wiser to get a bite at home. With some groceries and crispy fresh salad, a nice farmer Saint-Nectaire and large slices of a crusty country loaf, we savored a few bottles, including a remarkable 1983 Grand Cru Chablis Les Clos from the Raveneaus – a testament to the extraordinary aging potential of the two brothers' wines.

When time came to go to bed, we were happy to return to our rooms. In the darkness of the night, I could not help thinking back to the library down the hall, a genuine Aladdin's cave. I got up very slowly – taking care not to wake up Marie – and groped my way towards the room. The light was on! Thierry had gotten there before me. He was engrossed in a book by Paul Léautaud. As for me, I reviewed the leather spines of rare bound books before landing at the reading table with a rare copy of the *Atlas of Wineries of France* by Louis Larmat.

That night, we slept little but dreamt much.

# Tasting at the Raveneau brothers' in February 2014

In my company are two of our young sommeliers, Florent Martin and Marc Le Gallic. The 2012s are all enjoyed from the cask. These have one of the longest maturation processes of the entire appellation.

**2012 Chablis.** *A gourmet wine, fat, with a nice roundness. Not marked by any trace of maturation whatsoever.*

**2012 Chablis 1ˢᵗ Cru Forêts** *(0.5 ha). Fresh nose of citrus. A balanced wine with a bitter note in the finish, chiseled.*

**2012 Chablis 1ˢᵗ Cru Montmains** *(0.3 ha). A tense wine, lemony notes, pretty nervous with a balanced mid-palate and a savory finish.*

**2012 Chablis 1ˢᵗ Cru Vaillons** *(0.4 ha). Mouth has a lemony roundness, marked by light bitterness in the finish. A straight wine.*

**2012 Chablis 1ˢᵗ Cru Butteaux** *(1.5 ha in the domain). It's a pretty tense vintage, fine, racy. The palate offers a nice roundness, balanced by the acids. A success.*

**2012 Chablis Grand Cru Blanchot** *(0.6 ha). Completely elegant, with a feminine note. The attack is supple, well balanced. Lots of finesse.*

**2012 Chablis Grand Cru Valmur** *(0.75 ha). This terroir reveals a somewhat more square structure. The wine is long and austere. Close to the stone. The mouth has a beautiful roundness thanks to the orientation of the plot on the hillside. Very bitter end in the finish and a salty touch.*

**2012 Chablis Grand Cru Les Clos 2012** *(0.5 ha). Deep Kimmeridgian marl terroir. This wine combines the qualities of the previous two. Both the amplitude, the richness, and a lot of elegance.*

# Vertical of Montée de Tonnerre during the extension of the 2012 tasting on casks.

**2012** *(3.15 ha). This is the historical cru of the domain. The Raveneaus possess a significant part of it. Very large plot. Its density is what is expected of a Chablis grand cru. A deep wine, lingering.*

**2011.** *The wine is currently much more flexible. The activities did rapidly degrade during the harvest. A kinder profile. Already has pollen aromas, sweet almond. The palate is fairly well balanced.*

**2010.** *The wine possesses the 2012 structure, but without the flesh. Extremely closed at this stage. Fine, deep but mute. A good acidity supports the structure in mouth. This is a vintage in which the wine is very long and stricter. A wine to keep and a magnificent bottle in ten years.*

**2009.** *The nose is solar. The aromas evolve into butyric notes, white fruit stewed. On the palate, the wine is very round, spherical, without aggressiveness. The acid support comes from minerals. The finish in the mouth reminiscent of verbena.*

**2008.** *Pale brilliant color. Fine nose, discreetly floral and fruity (white fruits). Licorice, still restrained. Quite flexible mouth, medium intensity, pleasant finish. A balanced wine, elegant, beautiful intensity. Wait three more years.*

# Domaine Michel and Jean-Baptiste Bouzereau

*Partage démultiplié à la Paulée*

# T
## HE BOUZEREAUS
## SETTLED

down a long time ago. There are several branches of the family in Meursault. That is why it is always important to specify the first name to find one's way when visiting the domain. I will always remember in the old days, before GPS, when still a young sommelier, I stopped to ask some old people my way, as I was late for a meeting with a winemaker of Puligny-Montrachet. In the village, at least three persons had the same last name but all with a different first name and residing in as many properties. Five minutes later, I walked away as they became entangled in the family trees of the town, the family's alliances, the contested vine inheritance, and the rents at the end of leases… Failing to answer my question, these venerable elders, certainly childhood friends, must have parted feeling angry.

We are talking about "Michel" Bouzereau here. He and his ancestors have been cultivating vines in Meursault for seven generations. For the last four generations, their only activity has been with the vines. Before that, the elders had to hold complementary businesses as was then customary in many vineyards. The crops were uncertain, likewise the revenues. As years went by, through his work, Michel enlarged the vineyard inherited from his father. Jean-Baptiste joined the domain twenty years later. He learned the trade for ten years with him, and together they acquired some prestigious plots. In 1999, Michel left to Jean-Baptiste the task of managing with the same passion the 10.5 hectares family estate. In 2008, always looking for ways to improve the quality of his wines, Jean-Baptiste decided to build a new structure, and, since the 2009 harvest, the new winery has been in operation. But during my last visit, during the 2014 winter, we came across Michel at the wheel of his Straddle, early in the morning, on his way to one of his favorite tasks. He is one of those tireless people, always at work and caring. Jean-Baptiste's wines reflect his ethics. Accessible without softness, they have an ability to be enjoyed at a young stage, without flaw. Of course, I have a weakness for his Meursaults 1st Cru Perrières, planted next to the Clos de la Ferrière, half of which is over 60 years old. I remember the fire I sensed in the 1992 Meursaults during one of my first visits in 1998.

# BURGUNDY
## Domaine Michel and Jean-Baptiste Bouzereau

# M

EMORIES

My visits to Jean-Baptiste have increased over the years, becoming, as with other domains, a twice-a-year affair. They became especially rewarding as of a specific date, in terms of Jean-Baptiste or Jean-Marc Roulot: an invitation to the famous Paulée of Meursault which Dominique Rézette always arranged. This is a unique culinary event. A kind of modern-times symposium during which nearly seven hundred guests gather according to vintages, enthusiasts flocking from all continents, most armed with delightful wines. This joust is held every year at noon, on the Monday following the charity auction for the Hospices de Beaune, which takes place every third Sunday of November. This is the largest annual wine auction in the world. The meal has taken place in the cellars of the Château de Meursault since 1923. Burgundy, including the rotating Saint Vincent and the Paulée of Meursault, has maintained this unifying, collegial and friendly spirit. The 2012 session, chaired by Patrick de Carolis from the Institute, saw that Dominique Rézette, Thierry and I were invited, along with Jean-Baptiste and Sylvie, his wife. To our left, the Roulot family; to our right, that of Charles Ballot, from the Domaine Ballot-Millot. The principle behind the lunch is simple: a large caterer from Beaune takes care of the (many) dishes, served by a large dining brigade, and the winemakers select the wines for their guests. This is when things can get out of control, because, within minutes, someone always spots a friend at a nearby table, who is then invited over to taste a "great wine." All this is happening in a festive and happy setting, based on sharing and friendship. During the meal, the famous "Joyeux Bourguignons" entertain the audience with their songs, and several *bancs bourguignon* come at regular intervals to warm up the room. During and between the courses, anthology bottles circulate one after the next, each bringing its own experience and rarity. Singing takes over, as does laughter. People reunite here and there, calling each other across the room…

Between 1:30 pm and 4 pm, we had tasted, over the first three dishes that made up the meal, no fewer than 55 white wines. There were gems: a 2005 Meursault 1ˢᵗ Cru Perrières from Charles Ballot, a sublime 2007 Meursault 1ˢᵗ Cru Perrières from Jean-Baptiste, a remarkable 2005 Meursault 1ˢᵗ Cru Les Charmes from the same man. There was also a 2005 Meursault from

Xavier Monneau, very nice and fine. A delightful, jovial man, whom we visit from time to time to share a bucket of champagne.

A frenzy of great whites arrived in groups:

– 2006 Meursault Les Tessons, Clos de Mon Plaisir from Jean-Marc Roulot
– 2001 Magnum of Meursault 1st Cru Les Charmes from Charles Ballot
– 1996 Meursault Poruzots from Michel Jobard
– 1997 Meursault-Charmes from Jean-Baptiste
– 1998 Meursault 1st Cru Genévrières from the Jobards
– 1990 Meursault Les Tessons, Clos de Mon Plaisir from Jean-Marc Roulot

Then began to appear in waves the ambassadors of illustrious vintages:

– 2009 Meursault 1st Cru Charmes from the Comtes Lafon
– 2008 Corton-Charlemagne from Domaine de la Vougeraie
– 2009 Bienvenues-Bâtard-Montrachet from the Ramonet family
– 2004 Chevalier-Montrachet from Marc Colin passed through (a huge powerful wine beginning to blossom)

There was also an iconoclastic 2002 Château-Rayas blanc (of an unheard of youth, superb) brought by a friend who passed within reach of a glass. Jean-François Coche-Dury moved towards us with his 1999 Meursault 1st Cru Perrières, catching my eye between two nods and saying in his Burgundian accent: "So, Eric, fancy tasting my Perrières?" What a wine! Within the nose, one found immediately its birth. The Coche family implants an incredible charisma in their wines. His son came back around an hour later with a 1990 magnum of Corton-Charlemagne, "Eric, Dad wants you to taste the Charlemagne."

Around 4:30 pm, the meat course was served. The ballet of red wines began with a 2006 Gevrey-Chambertin 1st Cru en Champs from Denis Mortet and a 2009 Gevrey-Chambertin Les Evocelles of Domaine de la Vougeraie, plus an incongruous 2003 red magnum of Château Haut-Brion, from an American amateur, came tickling my taste buds with all its power. And since anything is possible during La Paulée, the wine that I was offered next was… a 2003 *mondeuse* from Michel Grisard. The Savoyard held its rank with a high pass.

Then there was a still harsh 1994 Château Latour, followed by a 2007 Vosne-Romanée 1st Cru Cros Parentoux from Jean Nicolas, and a beautiful 2002 Echezeaux Grand Cru from Alberic Bichot. A man for whom I have great respect.

# BURGUNDY
## Domaine Michel et Jean-Baptiste Bouzereau

The cheese without much taste came, above all with a large slice of country bread, an essential support for any exercise of this magnitude. Time for the appearance of the great ones: a 1975 Puligny-Montrachet 1st Cru Combettes from Jean Latour Labille, simply sublime with notes of propolis and bitter orange, and a rare 1978 Meursault 1st Cru Perrières from Guy Roulot (intense emotional moment).

An impressive 1997 double magnum of Sassicaia in the hands of a giant with a Slavic accent stopped at us. The Viking passed along to me greetings from a Norwegian friend and rewarded us with a few glasses of this great Tuscan. It was still, nonetheless, overtaken by a 1976 Magnum Vega Sicilia Unico that happened to be near. The best wine of this vintage I have tasted along with a Châteauneuf-du-Pape of Mount Olivet that we serve at Le Cinq. After such a wine, one could not imagine being able to surpass it. Until Eric Rousseau allowed us to enjoy his 1983 magnum Chambertin. What freshness! What delicacy!

Dessert had long been forgotten, albeit for the 1987 Porto Taylor's Quinta de Vargellas. I shared a small glass with Thierry.

Around 6:00 pm, the spirits and old marcs started to go around. A liquor looking like a gossamer emerald thread was poured into a clean glass made for this purpose. Only one man could keep a bottle of this label: Georges Dos Santos, aka "Jojo" (he looks strangely similar to Francis Blanche in *Les Tontons Flingueurs*...). This buccaneer is a well-known wine store owner in the Vieux Lyon, a specialist in *Tintin*, and a true wellspring of science when it comes to Port, Madeira, and rare wines; he is acknowledged as such world-over. He had just served us a 1900 Benedictine, of which, to this day, I retain a vivid memory. He came back later with an 1818 Cognac from the cellars of the Hôtel de Paris.

Stretching outside helped invigorate us, especially with the wintry weather already prevailing. Our conversations took us from one cellar to the next (four cellars of domains had remained opened for the occasion, in order to receive those among the participants of La Paulée eager – and still able – to taste the latest vintages in cask) until we reached Jean-Baptist's home. The beautiful Sylvie, his wife, was waiting for us. She had had time to set up in the living room a solid snack to warm us after this chilly walk.

To refresh our palates, Jean-Baptist popped, without warning, the corks of a 2002 champagne Gimonnet *blanc de blancs* and a 1996 Dom Ruinart rosé.

We were able to embark, in all serenity, on a journey through France, through the Loire Valley and Alsace (2009 Riesling Sommerberg from Jean Boxler), to the Rhône with a 2007 *côte-rôtie* from Jean-Paul Jamet (which I managed somehow to identify blindly), without forgetting a few bottles from domains located here and there.

Around midnight, it was the turn of the Chartreuse. It was the MOF Sommelier Vintage of this timeless liqueur that accompanied our very last discussions around the fireplace where a crackling fire rekindled the flame of our thoughts.

Before going back to our room, we went out for a breath of fresh morning air. A cotton-like fog enveloped the streets. Silence prevailed, immense, soothing. For a while, we smoked this wonderful tobacco that Thierry imported from Oxford, he in a pipe of Sébilo Morta, and I holding an old heather from Courrieu's. Then we retired to close our eyes. A few hours later, we had breakfast with the Bouzereaus.

At 10:30 am, notebook in hand, I was with Thierry in Jean-Baptist's cellar to taste from the cask his latest vintage. Around 1:00 pm, we took the train for Paris. At 5:00 pm, we were dressed for dinner service at Le Cinq.

As a friend often says to me: "What fortitude!"

# BURGUNDY
## Domaine Michel et Jean-Baptiste Bouzereau

# The Wines

The Meursault 1st Cru Les Genévrières (clay and limestone soil) belongs to the first vineyards that Michel's father bought: a plot of Genévrières below, 12 ouvrées (hence 0.5 hectare).

# Vertical of Meursault 1st Cru Les Genévrières

It took place at Jean-Baptiste Bouzereau's in 2013

**2011.** *Light pale yellow color. The nose is fine, discreet. Wide mouth, relatively soft, slightly woody and pulpy, but tense finish, which characterized the soil of Genévrières. Not ready to drink before another three years, potentially five.*

**2010.** *Pale yellow, green reflection. Lemony nose, discreet and concentrated. Slender and tense mouth, long and austere. Wait at least four years, remarkable with roasted Loctudy langoustines and a peak of "Neptune powder" of Olivier Roellinger. Bliss!*

**2008.** *Golden yellow color. Open, rich, honey nose. Wide and buttery mouth, very mature, beautiful structure in the end of the mouth, but relatively heavy. Demands a white meat of good breeding such as braised veal with porcini mushroom casserole.*

**2007.** *Pale yellow color, relatively fine and complex, white fruits and notes of honey, and then freshness. The palate has structure, refreshing, a good length.*

*Note that the greatest years are not always the best vintages. Sometimes, the lesser vintages, jealous, wake up with time and prove that the origins of a terroir can overcome climatic variations! The difference comes from the winemaker who gives birth to the wine and pours his soul into it.*

*And out of sheer indulgence, to conclude the tasting, Jean-Baptiste opened a bottle of:*

**2008 Meursault 1st Cru Les Charmes Dessus.** *Intense golden yellow and brilliant color. The nose is open, rich, fruity (exotic fruits), stewed notes, signs of maturity. Integrated and present wood. Round mouth, buttery, broad and generous. Slightly tense finish, supporting the whole. Nice length. A ready Meursault-Charmes. Perfect with a grilled lobster.*

# Domaine Roulot

*From Stage to Vineyards*

T THE ROOTS OF THE
DOMAIN'S FAME
we find the Roulot grandparents. The property's fame would
grow with Guy Roulot, Jean-Marc's father. Here is one of the
great names of the Côte de Beaune. A vocation for the theater
first attracted the man at the age of 20. Four years later, he joined the class
of the great Michel Bouquet at the Conservatoire. That was in 1980. Two
years had gone by when his father's illness brought him back to Meursault.
He had to take over the family's torch, but without renouncing his first
passion. And since 1989, all while having taken over management of the
family vineyards and having vinified his first vintage independently, he has
devoted himself to theater stages and film sets. He has learned too how to
conjugate other things, such as barrels. Through the vineyards, he became
the interpreter of different authors – the land and the sky – and various
characters: the Aligotés, Chardonnays and Pinots Noirs. For nearly thirty
years, he has given birth every year to wines from these terroirs. Each time
a creation of nature. Jean-Marc is the director and the author of each "theater
piece" of wine! He is also the successful performer and producer.

Meursault includes numerous domains rich in their diversity and styles,
beyond the particular hallmark of the Chardonnays made in this town.
Those of Jean-Marc are recognizable among all. What characterizes them
is their delicacy and finesse. These wines are more lingering than wide,
defined by a balance built on freshness, reaching sometimes a certain liveli-
ness. All these parameters require Jean-Marc's wines time to perform the
full range of their repertoire. Like many people in entertainment, Jean-Marc
is a discreet and reserved sort. He is very close to the style of his wines. Both
his professional and cellar choices appeared at the time of his father as original. The Meursaults were then more golden yellow, buttery, opulent or fat.
As with everything, standards of beauty evolve, and talents as well. Always
in search of greater precision, Jean-Marc redirected starting in 2000 towards
biodynamics.

With the arrival of Michèle, his sister, to manage the logistics and allocations to the happy beneficiaries of the family wines, the domain expanded
significantly. The latest acquisition in partnership with Dominique Lafon
of Clos de la Bouchère is the best example.

# MEMORIES

Thinking of Jean-Marc's wines leads me by patterns of action to associate him with wine lovers working in show business. Thus, among my fondest memories of sharing one of his bottles, I remember this meal in 2000, at the restaurant of Jean-Paul Arrabian, Chez Pierre, where the four of us, Philippe Legendre and our respective spouses, had dinner around a magnum of 1992 Meursault Les Tessons, Clos de Mon Plaisir. Here is a tip regarding bottle size: when four to six persons sit around a table with a single wine in mind, choose a magnum. Beyond the festive look of the bottle, the intrinsic quality of the wine is always optimized. Pleasure increases tenfold. This stems, among other things, from the fact that the neck of a magnum is substantially similar to that of a 75 cl bottle. The cork being of similar proportions, the influence of air managing to penetrate the fibers of cork is much more restrained, resulting in preserving better the wine from the ravages of time. As was the case for us.

Be that as it may, on that day, at a table nearby, Henri Salvador, one of our great men, who disappeared in 2008, an exceptional songwriter whose tunes rocked our childhoods, was lunching with some friends. What laughter, what joy, his face always smiling, like his eyes! Delighted to share our magnum, we had it served at his table, gratefully toasting to the happiness he had offered us throughout his career.

Speaking of show business, in 2013, at Le Cinq, during a luncheon for members of Club des Cent, the master of ceremonies turned out to be Pierre Arditi. Knowing of his coming to Le Cinq in the company of illustrious gourmets, Jean-Marc had arranged to deliver for Pierre magnums of 2006 Meursault Les Tillets. In honor of these wines and guests, we matched them, along with Eric Briffard, with a dish of roasted lobster from the Chausey Islands, with citrus, candied fennel and coral juice. The venerable and impressive members of this so prestigious centenary circle did not frown on this delight.

## BURGUNDY
## Domaine Roulot

# The Wines

The area covers 13.5 hectares of plots scattered across an impressive range of terroirs. The family produces some Auxey-Duresses and some Monthélies. But Jean-Marc's heart is in Meursault. The significant terroirs are cut sometimes to the size of gardens, which complicates the winemaking. Among the wines located in Meursault (mentioned in ouvrées, in the Burgundy way, with 1 ouvrée representing 4.28 acres or 1/24 hectare, a surface that the winemaker can prune in a day), these are the area's most famous that are not to be forgotten:
– The Perrières (0.26 hectares), located in the Perrières du Dessous and acquired by his father in 1976 for 50,000 francs for an ouvrée, with vines planted early in 1950
– Les Charmes (0.27 hectare), located in the Charmes du Dessous
– The Poruzots
– The Meix Chavaux (0.95 hectare)
– The Luchets (one of Jean-Marc's finest vineyards, with 23 ouvrées), located on the slope above the Meix. I still remember a 1993 magnum of Meursault Luchet that Jean-Marc had brought to the Paulée of Meursault in 2011. A wine of an incredible balance and complexity. Jean-Marc is very close to this wine. You only have to remember his name in the film *Les Saveurs*

*du Palais* – Jean-Marc Luchet – to be convinced. He plays the butler of the president portrayed by Jean d'Ormesson. In a short scene, the academician says to his cook, played by Catherine Frot – sort of Karen Blixen's *Babette* of modern times – some delicious lines from *Les Éloges de la cuisine française* by Edward Nignon.

Another of Jean-Marc's localities is emblematic of his wines:
– Les Tessons, lovingly nicknamed Clos de Mon Plaisir. This land of 0.84 hectare, planted between 1959 and 1961, remains a great signature style of the Roulot family. Although merely a locality and not even a *premier cru*, it is recognizable for its distinct magnitude in the mouth.

After years of experience, Jean-Marc focuses on greater purity in his wines. Like an actor who refines his performance on stage using an economy of means, which often leaves more memories than laughter. Sometimes, certain wines can reach a premier cru level or even higher, because of the choice of terroir coupled with the age of the vines from mass selection. Often, the age of the vines transcends the terroir, and this is the case for Les Tessons.

# Tasting of Meursault Les Tessons
# Clos de Mon Plaisir in 2013

**2012.** *Nose rich and concentrated. The mouth is spherical, full, complete. It is a Tessons, wider than long. Imposing. To be revisited in a few years. Incredibly concentrated.*

**2011.** *Here is a beautiful Tessons. It is fine, delicate and floral. A tad still discreet. But what a delicacy. The evoked floral aromas are revealed in the mouth, with more brightness. The wine is long and offers a stunning retro-olfaction. To keep in cellar for another five years.*

**2009.** *Golden color. Nose open, exotic. The palate is rich and complex, generous. It appears more solar, reflecting the vintage. Slightly woody notes reminiscent of light caramel. The finish is very tender. To be consumed now.*

**2007.** *A year deemed cool. Pale gold color, floral nose. In the mouth, the wine is tense, tight, structured. This is Jean-Marc's style: Austere wines in their youth, a slightly bitter finish emerges. Needs more time. At the moment, rather Jansenist.*

**2004.** *This vintage is the result of a wine which had time to mature. Roasted and fruity notes. The nose is exciting although a hair reduced. The mouth, on the other hand, is round and generous, expressive and tense with grilled whiffs being detectable in the nose. A slightly criticized vintage, initially for a white. For those who still own some in their cellar, it is today a treat endowed with a strong attraction. A wine calling for great pairings.*

2008
ursault-Perrières
Meursault Ier Cru Contrôlée
Domaine Roulot
CÔTE-D'OR, FRANCE - MIS EN BOUTEILLES À LA PROPRIÉTÉ
750 ml
SULPHITES - ENTHÄLT SULFITE - PRODUCE OF FRANCE

# Domaine Jean-François Coche-Dury

*Murisaltian Legend*

# I

T WAS AT THE BEGINNING OF THE 1990S

that I met Jean-François through Dominique Rézette. For several years I had wished to meet him, following the very first words I read about Domaine Coche-Dury in an article by Michel Bettane in the *Revue du Vin de France* in 1984. He was dazzled by the 1973 white Burgundies produced in the domain. I dreamed of them. There were several elements that when juxtaposed made the wine incomparable. And terribly attractive. More so here than elsewhere, man makes wine. He shapes it through vintages and through its maturity. Jean-François's Corton-Charlemagne is the jewel of a necklace that he crystallizes. All the while keeping the results that only chardonnay permits. In particular, the work with the lees, the pressing, the careful aging, and the bottling with a double spigot. A caring process that makes Jean-François's wines small master-pieces. The bottles, under these conditions, sell around the world like hot diamonds. It is possible to detect Jean-François's style in these Meursaults, though the typicality of the locality is respected. I have been serving these wines for twenty years, and, each time I do, I delight my customers. Especially with a sublime pairing that Chef Legendre and I developed a long time ago: a Bresse pullet with lobster served with Jean-François's Corton-Charlemagne.

Meeting Jean-François and Odile, his wife, is living a moment of peace, when time pulses an instant with a unique style. The Coche-Durys' logic relies on constancy, discipline, and the vineyard cycle. Although the wines are more sought after than access codes to the Pentagon and their prices reach stratospheric heights on the gray market, the life of the Coche-Dury family has not changed, and the beauty of their wines is not impacted. Odile continues to write delicious and tender poems. Jean-François continues to methodically number his labels, in order to bust those lacking scruples who prefer to increase the value of their allowances on parallel markets rather than serve or share them with friends. In short, it is an anti-star system. And this is also the reason why the wines remain faithful to the man and his own. Certainly, one perceives a different air with Raphaël, the emancipation of youth. But everything is credible. When one has the great fortune to taste a great bottle, one does not forget.

Jean-François is one of the few winemakers trading in white wines who has such appeal. Maybe also because of the prices that remain very consistent. The Coche-Durys maintain a substantial private client base related to the consumption of their wines, which do not fall into the star system. Indeed, the customer book of the Coche-Dury family is a true Chinese puzzle. A great importance is given to old and loyal customers. Most of them were already in Jean-François's father's books. Here, a new client represents bereavement, because such an entry means that one of the lucky recipients has departed for a world that is said to be better.

# THE BOTTLING PROCESS…

The bottling process in Coche-Dury is one of the highlights. "Must say," as Jacques Brel said, that the best cork makers and coopers are proud to count the Coche-Dury among their clients. Imagine: each cork used is checked by hand before it is pushed down the neck of a bottle, so that the mirror end coming into contact with the wine will be the end with no apparent veins, so as to optimize even more the preservation. This is because these cork veins that are sometimes noticeable in the thickness and visible on the mirror ends are paths through which the wine can break through, and, long term, this type of cork will more or less create "deviances" in the wine. Before this final stage, the wine will almost never have been dislodged from the barrel where it was stored. For here, there are no unwanted extractions, no filtration or assemblage before bottling. The pieces are bottled one after the other at the family's pace, and that's it. Principles are put forward by young winemakers sometimes claiming to belong to some ultra-reactionary chapel. Here, no one claims anything. They perpetuate the rituals transmitted by the elders. Current technologies allow the development of new filtration and clarification systems. So many developments that we must not reject, as they are critical to enable the production of certain wines in significant quantity. However, the wines that trigger the greatest emotions are those that have been the least tampered with. As everyone knows, the best wine is the one that has been aged in the cellar of the winemaker who brought it to life. A great wine comes from a vineyard worked by a gardener, and when nature is not rushed, it gives its best. These

# BURGUNDY
## Domaine Jean-François Coche-Dury

wines are the perfect example of the application of mastered craftsmanship techniques, based on empirical knowledge, with a hint of intuition. These wines are among the best white wines in the world.

# MEMORIES

We all have our favorite dinner tables, those landing pads to which we are attached like a desert is to an oasis. Among mine, there is the Surcouf, in Cancale, at the helm of which is my pal Jerome Pierpaoli. A grand dynasty of restaurant owners in Cancale. His father, Jean-Claude, was the director of the La Mère Poulard in Mont-Saint-Michel, during the heyday of the Michelin stars. So, on a beautiful summer day, Jean-François and Odile, taking advantage of a "truce" in the vineyards when nature was on good behavior, arrived in the region, at the port of Cancale. Searching for a place to have lunch, they stopped to check out the menu outside of a neat tavern whose storefront was in fresh colors. Through one of the windows, they spotted one of their bottles, empty, on a shelf in a cavity in the wall, next to famous names of the great hexagonal vineyards. Intrigued, Jean-François entered. A youth in shirtsleeves greeted him. It was not quite noon, and the room was empty. Bluntly, Jean-François pointed at the empty bottle, and with his accent as authentic as his wines said: "Good afternoon, sir, where did you get this bottle from?" Jérome had recognized him in a split second. "Mr. Coche-Dury, a local broker supplies me with them, but you know, it's at the George V and then at L'Ami Louis, where I discovered your wines." Without a word, Jean-François went back out and reassured his wife. "You can go in. It looks like a serious place." Lunch was lively, especially given that Jérome is loquacious. Since then, Jérome has been enjoying an annual allocation from the Coche-Durys. An extremely rare privilege.

Do not be surprised if this domain is absent from the Surcouf's wine list. The boss decides when and with whom he will open his precious bottles. As such, I must confess that Cédric Maupoint, Thierry, and myself, were able to feast on Jean-François's Meursaults with the famous grilled lobster in *beurre blanc*, staring into the vastness of the bay of Mont-Saint-Michel. The last time was in February 2015. We were coming back from Saint Malo, and Thierry was returning from a copious celebration of his 91-year-old grandfather in the Costarmorican land. After some dishes of Cancale and a bucket of 2004 Comtes de Champagne, we had the honor of sole meunière accompanied by a 2010 Meursault Village from Jean-François – meal so savory that Jerome's father came to drink a digestive at our table. No hesitation there: Calvados Reserve of Adrien Camut. A fascinating discussion followed because Jean-Claude knew Adrien's grandfather and is an old friend of the father of the current distillers, the Domain of Semainville.

## BURGUNDY
## Domaine Jean-François Coche-Dury

# Morning Tasting at the Domain, November 18, 2013

My friend André Bercoff and I were welcomed by Jean-François Coche-Dury early in the morning before the Paulée of Meursault. We always started by tasting red wines of the domain first. This time, we got to taste the very seductive 2010 Auxey-Duresses. Then, the Volnay in the same vintage. Closed and austere but with a precise fruit. Whatever the produced appellations, the wines aged remarkably. In fact, during the period when all the white wines oxidized – from late 1990 to early 2000 – the Coche-Dury remained intact. Then we addressed the reason for my visit, the heart of the tasting that brought us together: the place called Les Vireuils du Dessus, in Meursault (the name of the clos is not mentioned on the label).

**2010.** *This time Raphaël was making the wine, and he changed the wine press (a revolution in the domain, the entire Meursault was talking about it!). Pale gold color, little change. Green reflection a bit strict. Fine nose, open, lemony, floral, with average amplitude. Severe attack, a little firm, taut mouth, mineral. Very good length. Must wait at least three years. An unusual wine for the domain.*

**2009.** *Still pale color, with average intensity nose, though straight. In the mouth, it is in vintage style, although a little shorter, but balanced. Must wait.*

**2007.** *Delicate nose, refreshing, lemony. Ample and fine mouth. Very nice refreshing length. Amazing.*

**2006.** *Intense gold and brilliant color. The nose is seductive and generous. The attack on the palate is smooth and complete. Ready to drink. Magnificent amplitude.*

**1999.** *Here is a beautiful mature Vireuil. What a beautiful example of what Jean-François's wine can offer over time. All wide, long, chalky. Tasting of salt. A beautiful bottle. An example for the appellation.*

# Jean-François's Corton-Charlemagne

The terroir covers nearly 71 hectares. This grand cru evokes both respect and dignity. At the same time, I have to admit that on such a large surface, not all the wines come from "the best barrel." Between the top and bottom of the grand cru, the range of winemakers, there is a multitude of different wines. For the enthusiast that I am, to have the privilege of offering Jean-François's wines on the menu at Le Cinq is pure joy. "Among the very best" is for me the best answer to the potential of this great vintage.

2009 *(Tasted for the first time at the domain with Jean-François and Raphaël in January 2012). The nose is still closed, too young. Dense and powerful mouth. A timeless wine, which the family offers sparingly to customers!*

*I will always remember the first time I tasted the 2005. It was in 2012, at the domain. We had been tasting for a while, and the end drawing near. We had made the tour of 2011. Suddenly, Jean-François turned to his son and said: "Why not open a 2005?" Raphaël went to fetch the bottle, and we enjoyed the 2005 Corton-Charlemagne. Since at that time this vintage was still being stored in the cellars, Jean-François told us: "I think we'll put it into the allocations. It tastes ready now." Magical moment. Surreal.*

*I was tasting one of the greatest Chardonnays of my life! Which leads me to say today, "Whoever has not tasted the 2005 Corton-Charlemagne can only hope."*

2005. *Very great intensity. The Chardonnay expresses both the floral and mineral character at the same time. Exceptional density, incomparable width at once. Incredible persistence. With an extreme youth. For a pairing, I am thinking of a pie of blond duck livers of Bernard Pacaud. Exceptional. When someone tells you that no Chardonnay must follow a Montrachet, it is because she or he has not tasted one of the Corton-Charlemagnes of the Coche-Dury family.*

BURGUNDY
Domaine Jean-François Coche-Dury

# Domaine Jean-Marc Boillot

*A Great Friendship*

# I

## T IS IMPOSSIBLE TO TALK
### DE JEAN-MARC

It is impossible to talk about Jean-Marc without mentioning the man who introduced him to me for the first time, Dominique Rézette. He was to become a leading player in my professional life, a daily contact, a confidant. For me, he is the Serge Gainsbourg of the wine world. Beneath his unkempt appearance there hides a sharp mind, an accomplished scientist, an eminent pedagogue, an academic, an outstanding taster and a connoisseur of Burgundy's twists and turns, both those making up the terroirs, the clos (which he crisscrossed early on either running or riding his bike) and those inherent in the vicissitudes of the domains and families. He is also and above all one of the most famous mediators of the "Côte" between the large domains and the Paris gastronomic restaurants (and those beyond Paris as well) for over twenty years. Our meeting took place in 1993 in the Tony Garnier Hall in Lyon, during the presentation of the 1992 vintage in the Rhone valley (a vintage long forgotten… and for good reason). Paul Avril (head of the Papal Castel-Domain, an eponymous character who has done much at the INAO for regional wine appellations) had invited me there. Paul wanted me, as a Best Sommelier of France and working in the region, to taste a few wines for the press. Dominique Rézette was in the audience that day. After my presentation, he came up to me, and we quickly agreed to a meeting in Montrond-les-Bains. We soon struck up a friendship. Dominique insisted on introducing me to Jean-Marc in the following months. Since then, I have remained in touch with both of them.

Jean-Marc's adventure of working for himself in Pommard began well before these meetings. He settled there in 1985, after working on his family estate in Volnay, then with the trader Olivier Leflaive in Puligny-Montrachet. Today he manages 11 hectares of vines with his two children, Benjamin and Lydia. The plots are located across the towns of Beaune, Pommard, Volnay, Meursault, Puligny-Montrachet and Chassagne-Montrachet. The soils are calcareous clay and mostly on hillsides. On average 50 years old, the vines are grown distinctly towards the organic. For example, herbicides have not been used for over fifteen years. In the cellar, the number of new barrels does not exceed 25% per year. The maturing is generally long and smooth. The whites are stirred regularly.

## BURGUNDY
### Domaine Jean-Marc Boillot

A tireless worker, Jean-Marc has the soul of an entrepreneur. Discreet, quiet and serious, he is like his own faithful Jack Terrier who is not easily fooled. Behind this appearance, Jean-Marc hides a big heart. During my visits throughout the years, my palate has evolved. My vision of his wines, and of wine in general, has been refined. We have together, including Dominique, defended the concentration – like this 1995 Jarollières, as closed as a prison door, which, I hope, someday will open up. Ten years from now at least, it will have lost its fruit, and this is when things become interesting. Meanwhile, Jean-Marc has been able to gauge his style, making his wines more delicate with less tannin in the reds, and a more controlled maturing stage. A beautiful evolution. Having said that, more than once during dinners at Jean-Marc's, I blithely mistook one vintage for another regarding his whites for which I had not anticipated a good aging but which did, ultimately, preserve a remarkable freshness.

The friendship that binds us to Jean-Marc materialized with strong support right from the opening of the George V. It is thanks to him, and Dominique, when we can offer throughout the year in the Gallery the Puligny-Montrachet, the village of his domain. In fifteen years, I have never received a complaint from patrons who had chosen it from among all our wines by the glass both at the Bar or the Gallery. It is an undeniable asset for the staff to be able to serve a trustworthy wine. This is reflected in their approach, as well as in their comments. As I always say, the less sommeliers talk about wines, the more we must choose wines that speak for themselves.

# MEMORIES

The tastings of Jean-Marc's older vintages, such as the 1991 Volnay Les Pitures, bring me back to the time when he received us in the house of his grandfather, which he was to renovate tastefully some years later. We slept in an antique four-poster bed with twisted columns, in the grandfather's room. A sleeping situation that we shared with Thierry in conditions close to those of Bourvil and Louis de Funès in *La Grande Vadrouille*, because Thierry tends to breathe rather loudly when sleeping… What memories!

In the morning, Jean-Marc joined us for breakfast at the formica kitchen with chairs screeching on the multicolored tiles. We chatted about the tastings of the day ahead. Sometimes, we contemplated our abused spirits regarding the dinner the night before. All this with an open heart and, of course, smiling eyes, from Jean-Marc. These exchanges always took place at his home. The walls have remained the same. We stay on top of the famous room. We both breathe rather loudly, but since Thierry has become almost deaf with time, and I sleep like a rock, all is well. What has changed is that nowadays we eat on the ground floor with Jean-Marc and Veronique in their splendid kitchen-dining room. And each time, we taste bottles whose freshness is matched only by older vintages. Which explains why I make so many mistakes when he serves us blindly.

Outside the Pommardière – the name of the house – given the number of pairings made with fine wines from our man, one evening in January 2009, we had a sommelier dinner at Thierry. That evening, among many dishes, we savored a 2005 magnum of Bâtard Montrachet from Jean-Marc with a black-truffled risotto. An intense and powerful pairing. In 2010, for the same occasion, Jean-Marc sent me a 1990 magnum of Pommard First Cru Rugiens, for which we had reserved a Saint-Nectaire from Maillard's. Once again, a great time.

These bottles reflect the friendship that unites us. During these evenings, each of our sommeliers can actually taste these wines for themselves. It is no longer a question of looking for flaws as we tended to do during dining room service when we open the bottles. There, between us, the wines are appreciated purely for the sake of pleasure.

# BURGUNDY
## Domaine Jean-Marc Boillot

# The Wines

Initially, during my first visits, I was in favor
of wines designed with certain goals: deep color,
marked structure, dense wines, such as those
of the mid-1990s that many of us extolled.
I believed it. Like Jean-Marc, I had certainties.
"And now the days when I go around the earth,
where I pace about, I tell myself that all I know
is that you never know," (as Jean Gabin sung).
Otherwise, I focus less on the superpower
and more on easier wines with flexibility
indices mastered without too much extraction
research.

His style has evolved, and we can detect over
the last several harvests more delicacy in his
wines. The evolution of his whites is tighter,
and the reds, more tender. He was inspired by
his muse, Véronique. Pumping has been lessened.
The work of extraction inclines more towards

a research for blending. Many features that make
Jean-Marc's wines more delicate and refined.

His grandfather, Étienne Sauzet, planted the plot,
Champ Canet. Jean-Marc gives it his full
attention. At Jean-Marc's, cultural practices are
based on a very dense planting to induce
competition between the stocks and force
the vines to make deep roots in the soil –
the vineyards of the area have a minimum density
of 12,000 plants per hectare. This density
is enormous, even for Burgundy, where densities
of 10,000 plants are common. The wines
are plowed in a way as to limit the superficial
proliferation of roots and to oxygenate biological
life while preserving the beneficial fauna.
This results in the activation of natural defenses
by elicitors which must take place at the date
of harvest closest to its aromatic maturity.

# Vertical of Puligny-Montrachet 1ˢᵗ Cru
# Champ Canet, in February 2015 at the George V

*2012. Intense yellow straw color. Open nose, intense, young, fine, with exotic notes of pineapple. The oak is discreet and elegant. It has a concentrated and generous nose which does not show its full potential. Wide mouth, spherical, medium length. A light deep in mid-palate highlights a slight lack of nervousness. Nevertheless, the wine remains balanced. Drink now or within five years with enjoyment. It may evolve relatively quickly.*

*2011. Golden yellow color of medium intensity. The nose is discreet with candied lemon, vanilla, and hazelnut notes. The whole is still reserved. But already, what elegance. The mouth is full and tense with rectitude and depth. Nice length, discreet wood, with a fruity and spicy retro-olfaction. A beautiful first cru. It is balanced and holds its rank.*

*2010. Intense yellow and brilliant golden color. The nose is concentrated, discreet, fine with depth. Long mouth, concentrated, tightening in mid-mouth to the wood still present. The finish is very long, racy. A great wine still too young. I look forward to reviewing it again within the next three or four years.*

*2002. Intense yellow straw color. Sign of evolution. Open, rich, ripe, and fine nose. Very expressive. White fruit notes (pear, plum), slightly licorice. Lots of elegance, a dizzying smoothness in the nose. The mouth is full, rich, sweet, masking the acidity. Long lingering with fullness. A vintage full and dense. A great white wine atop its potential. Definitely a great gastronomic wine.*

# BURGUNDY
## Domaine Jean-Marc Boillot

170

# Vertical of Volnay 1ˢᵗ Cru Les Pitures, in 2013, at Jean-Marc Boillot's

**2011.** *Black color. Cherry nose, ample, fine and crisp. Sensual juicy attack, very good length, remarkable flexibility index. It can already be enjoyed now, which is a huge shift in the Pinot Noir winemaking process at Jean-Marc's.*

**2010.** *Maturation notes. Deep nose, tight, discreet. The full mouth is structured, square but without harshness. Very persistent finish. The archetype of a beautiful 2010 to keep.*

**2009.** *Open nose, kirsched. Notes of Mara des bois strawberry compote, exuberant. The wide mouth is extroverted, with an exotic touch, slightly spicy sweet finish. An almost sexy profile. Made to drink now while being careful of the room temperature which should be slightly lower than usual. The wine expresses an accomplished maturity.*

**2008.** *Nose straight, dense, open, floral, and fruity. The maturation is still dominant; the mouth has an average amplitude but remains tight and firm. It has a slightly austere style. Wait at least five years.*

**1991.** *An unparalleled success. At the beginning, it had the misfortune to be born in the shadow of the 1990. But today, the 1991 turns out to be cooler, lighter and so much more refined than its predecessor. A great attitude without being massive.*

# Domaine David Duband

*Passion Flower: The Reward*

# I

F I HAVE THE PRIVILEGE
TO RUB ELBOWS WITH DAVID,

it is once again thanks to Dominique Rézette, who very early identified this young talent. Located on the borders of Burgundy, in the land of Chevannes, in the Hautes Côtes, we are far from the customary route for wines. Tastings there have an aura of a holiday trip. The reason is simple: the Dubands settled in the area a long time ago. David's father was already vinifying there before his troublemaker son took his first steps in the vineyards. In the vault and in the cellars perpetual energy reigns, a vitality arising from David, which radiates onto his employees. All this exalts us. Each year, a story awaits us. The one of the domain first, which constantly grows with the contribution of new ouvrées (1 ouvrée is equivalent to 1/24 hectare) and of new appellations among the vineyards of the area.

All this was made possible thanks to the confidence and the means implemented by François Feuillet, a passionate man and a cornerstone of the area. Without him, David's beautiful adventure would not have come to light. The remarkable success of Mr. Feuillet in leisure transportation did not take him far from his native Burgundy to which he was deeply attached. With David, he found the ideal partner to carry out his project.

Today, the range of wines offered on the property is incredible: Chambertin, Latricières, Bonnes-mares, Combottes, Échezeaux, not to mention his remarkable 1$^{st}$ crus or the villages. All these wines make up a stunning Camaïeu, giving David the opportunity to vinify and manage very different terroirs. Each year, he reviews his methods and experiments and refines his wine philosophy. He dares and challenges present trends.

For some time, he has been experimenting with keeping whole grapes for maceration. This requires healthy sanitary conditions, harvesting in small crates, all these aspects and many more allowing for production of more complex and vivid wines. They need more time to mature. Colors are sometimes less intense. In short, everything the market and the current trends do not want! I deduce from this that he does not lack courage and does not hesitate to venture onto more chaotic roads. The results are encouraging. He is in constant motion and readjusts his approach based on trial and error. Our winemaker does not seek to create copies but to regularly realize authored wines, and too bad if he only produces best-sellers. He is part of the movement of young winemakers who have a deep respect for the Côte de Nuits, a major location.

Given this philosophy, he nevertheless strives to conquer the holy grail of what may be the best rendering of a terroir while minimizing the footprint of his parent. Besides, how many times have we discussed and expounded the relevance of a certain crop or winemaking choice. These are conversations I often have with winemakers because the subject fascinates me and it keeps me up with the current practices in viticulture and oenology.

# MEMORIES

During my wanderings in the vineyards, I always love to invite the members of my team along, the dining brigade such as the sommelier or kitchen staff. Sometimes, for certain journeys, I extend the invitation to customers who generally have become friends over the years. It is for me a way to allow them to discover and understand the intricacies of the passionate business of a sommelier. They are always happy to have access to domains previously unavailable to them. Certain properties such as the Carthusians in Isère are strict. When Elizabeth II presented herself at the doors of the abbey, they remained tightly closed. Birthrights or wealth do not open all the doors of the domains of Burgundy – or elsewhere either.

Since this is not the case at David's, I showed up in 2011 at Chevannes one morning around 9:30 am with a couple passionate about wine, who had travelled from Chicago. It was winter. The hills labored to free themselves of fog. As a great writer once said, "you could not see further than the tip of your nose… !" After tasting several vintages of the domain, roughly a dozen samples of the current vintage maturing, we got down to serious business. This appeared as a first – and then a second – 1999 magnum of Échezeaux from David. To accompany this grand cru, David's father had prepared terrines, black pudding from a pig killed a few days prior. Suffice to say that by 11 a.m., we were a happy bunch! Especially as our friend from Chicago who failed to spit during the first phase of the tasting… But what a mood!

# BURGUNDY
## Domaine David Duband

## The Wines

David built a new cellar because the property has grown considerably. He belongs to those winemakers who have chosen to be partners with the George V. So we meet with him every year. He is obviously a talented winemaker, who has the elegance of Pinot Noir, with a daring edge. Whereas at first his were marked by too much intensity, he was able to change his approach.

## Tasting at the Domain on November 19, 2013
with a vertical of Chambolle-Musigny Les Sentiers

**2007.** *Vinified with whole grapes. This is a 0.65-hectare plot. This choice leads David into a new style, where wines are of less intense color. This is why the color of this 2007 is frail, brilliant, with a bright ruby tinge. The nose is fine, open, fruity, spicy and flattering. The mouth attack is supple with that delicate touch keeping the acidity in the background. An affordable Sentier, with a beautiful density. To be enjoyed now.*

**2008.** *Dazzling color, medium density. Flattering nose, sexy. Black fruit. Tonic and tannic mouth. Woody touch. The finish is fruity, spicy, and long with a nice flavor. Please note: this still very firm wine is made out of 60% whole harvest.*

**2009.** *Brilliant color of average intensity for a 2009. Fruity nose, generous, warm and stewed. The whole harvest (here 100%) counterbalances the heat of that year by highlighting the final. So, overall, it is still very firm and demands at least another five years of aging. I was a bit skeptical initially regarding this vintage at David's. The wine snaps back in strength and complexity.*

**2010.** *Brilliant pale ruby color. Closed and fine nose. Full mouth, sappy, reveals nothing. The wine is austere at the moment. It will be ready within five years. A grand bottle.*

**2011.** *Sparkling ruby color. Nose open, wooded, beautiful density. Sensuous and full mouth. Structure far more flexible in the mouth than the 2010, without having the body. Already enjoyable.*

# Domaine Georges Noëllat

*Peaceful Pinot*

W HEN
DOMINIQUE RÉZETTE
told me about a young winemaker in Vosne-Romanée
whom he had just met, he piqued my curiosity. For, of all
the places where the chance of "discovering" a newcomer
is more than unlikely, Vosne-Romanée shines. Here, the crus and climates
are parcellized, fragmented. Alliances of families ensure a common wine
heritage. Vines venturing out of the domains are rare.

This domain is typical of Burgundy. To understand its name, you must go
back several generations. At the beginning, we find Georges Noëllat, the
founder of the domain. After his death, Augustine, his wife, took over the
management until 1986. In turn, her daughter, Marie-Thérèse, and her husband, Jacques Cheurlin, a winemaker in Champagne – the other homeland
of Pinot Noir – took care of the vines. Upon their separation, Marie-Thérèse
went back to Burgundy and managed the domain from 1991 to 2009. If the
domain has remained hardly known, it is because, for a long time, almost
all wines were sold in the Burgundian market.

In 2010, Maxime, Marie-Thérèse Cheurlin's grandson, decided to join his
grandmother in Vosne-Romanée. He spent his childhood and adolescence
between Champagne, where his parents operate the grandfather's domain,
and Burgundy, home of his grandmother. Being a winemaker's son, he
turned to vitiviniculture studies. Having a strong preference for Burgundy
wines, he trained at the wine school in Beaune.

Barely 20 years old, he produced his first vintage in 2010. He belongs
to the sixth generation of the family who has cultivated the 5.5-hectare
vineyards, of which 3.5 hectares are First Crus and two are Grand Crus
(Échezeaux and Grands-Échezeaux). The vines are now cultivated without
herbicides. The maturing is conducted exclusively in oak barrels ranging
from 30 to 100% of new wood. Maxime represents a new generation of
winemakers. He finds inspiration from people like Jean-Nicolas Méo,
Emmanuel Rouget and the DRC. He is certainly fortunate to own a
variety of exceptional terroirs, but he must still prove himself. For us sommeliers, this affords a rare insight to follow a young winemaker from his
first vintage and observe how his approach to the vineyards and vinification evolves.

# BURGUNDY
## Domaine Georges Noëllat

As with the first domain I was able to visit in Burgundy with Dominique, I discovered Maxime through him. I stopped counting how many hours I spent every day on the phone with "Domi" over twenty years. He is the most discreet broker in France, a man in the shadows, never in the spotlight. Thanks to him, although I am in Paris, I always have an ear and an eye on the coast. I live the daily life of the domains, the families' alliances, the stages of the grapes, via the handset. This is my Burgundy gazette. Every day, the two of us touch base. Though born in Paris, he is far from the stress of this gray Paris, "so beautiful, so sophisticated," as Pierre Soulages aptly says. So when he mentions to me a youth who looks promising, I waste no time in asking him to introduce me. Maxime is among the rising stars of Vosne. Every morning, he gets up with a view of his vineyards, the First Cru Chaumes, at the foot of the house. Here, I must mention an extraordinary detail. His grandmother's winter living room overlooks an area planted with an English strip of grass and several well-delineated squares on which to plant legumes, seasonal tomatoes and a fruit tree. The staging is charming, I confessed to Maxime, who, debonairly added, "It's true that it's very nice, though it is costing two ouvrées of Vosne-Romanée 1st Cru Les Chaumes!" Here is a young man endowed with wisdom, common sense and kindness. Our first visit took place in January 2012 with Thierry and Dominique. We tasted the 2011s, which were from the cask. The wines were promising. As much his Nuits-Saint-Georges as his Vosne-Romanée.

 EMORIES
Among the highlights of my half-yearly visits to the Côte-d'Or, I always lunch with Domi at Le Miotte. For the last twenty years, this inn has been the rallying place of journalists, sommeliers, restaurant owners and representatives of large Burgundian houses. This ancient seventeenth-century hunting lodge is located near the village of Ladoix-Serrigny, close to the railway track. This exceptional inn is managed by Lady Catherine, who officiates in the kitchen and the dining room. Here, you feel you are in Burgundy. The menu includes regional specialties: poached eggs, snails in garlic butter, beef bourguignon… and the decor is basic: the floor is made of large slabs of Corton, with massive

oak beams in the ceiling. There is a venerable Franche-Comté clock in a corner. On the mantelpiece, bottles bearing the labels of the most sought-after wines are worthy of a hunting landscape painting of an experienced amateur. On the walls, a rare collection of posters from the St. Vincent Festival recites the names of the wine villages of the Côte-d'Or. Domi's cat appears asleep on top of the oak chest covering the cast iron radiator. From the soft pillow of her chair, Tomate, Catherine's Yorkshire terrier, keeps vigil. Large windows overlook the park whose aspect recalls the freedom of an English garden. A brook meanders through the trees. The ambience is peaceful and slightly old-fashioned.

The true uniqueness of the place rests with the cellar. The wine list printed on the leaflets is rather sketchy and mostly focused on Burgundies. Up to that point, nothing extraordinary. What are, though, are the references displayed! Only famous and rare names of winegrowers from the Côte, virtually impossible to obtain, especially at these prices. Ah! We are far away from the "palace" prices. Beware, however; before being able to order one of these gems of the Burgundian climates, patrons must show their credentials to the watchman of the house: Dominique Rézette. There's a Houellebecq touch about him. For this former high-level gymnast and seasoned academic is a real connoisseur of Burgundy, the Yonne and the Saône-et-Loire. Woe to pedants and smooth-talkers who make the mistake of underestimating him. The verbal backlash is destructive.

This is where I tasted blindly for the first time a sample of Maxime Cheurlin! Dominique had poured me a glass without elaborating during lunch. Since we have become friends, he has insisted on offering us a remarkable magnum of 1979 Vosne-Romanée 1st cru Les Beaux Monts from his grandfather. A bottle that we savored in February 2013 during a George V sommeliers dinner, to which we have always invited a friend or two. The wine was delicious. Especially with David Bizet's roasted woodcocks.

I could not conceive of a stay in Burgundy without saying hello to Cathy. During this fine January month, Dominique regaled us with a 2009 Meursault Rougeot from Jean François Coche, paired with parsley ham, followed by a 2009 Gevrey-Chambertin 1st Cru Aux Combottes from Cyprien Arlaud. This domain is also part of Dominique's latest push to promote young winemakers of the Côte. We approached him through one of Arlaud's cousins,

# BURGUNDY
## Domaine Georges Noëllat

David Duband. In 2008, we went there, and the first vintage on the menu was the 2007. I must admit that this new venture did not really make an impact on me. The wines were quite angular, as if emaciated by the vinification. Meanwhile, the Arlaud brothers and sister went back to basics, listening to friends' and relatives' opinions, including Domi's. He pointed out during tough talks with Cyprien the right actions and vinification choices behind the rusticity sometimes felt in some of the vintages. He was not wrong to intervene, because too often the excessive interventionism taught in wine schools, during the phases of winemaking, leads to generic students whose sensitivity has been erased.

Cyprien's evolution has delighted me year after year. He is moving towards more refinement and delicacy in his wines. Especially since his palette contains prestigious terroirs: First Crus in Morey-Saint-Denis, Chambolle-Musigny and Gevrey-Chambertin and major sought-after Grand Crus: Clos-de-la-Roche, Clos-Saint-Denis, Bonnes-Mares and Charmes-Chambertin, not to mention beautiful well-located appellations.

Maxime and Cyprien are both the owners of great terroirs, which they have the drive to develop using their feelings and their taste sensibilities.

# The Wines

2013 Vosne-Romanée 1st Cru Petits Monts. *From the cask, roasted nose. At this stage, the maturing process is marked. The mouth is tense, tight structure. Nose reduced at this stage.*

2012 Vosne-Romanée 1st Cru Petits Monts. *Beautiful fruit, rich, fond mouth, wood traces not as present.*

2012 Vosne-Romanée 1st Cru Chaumes. *What fruit! Remarkable. Very rich and fond. More earthy.*

2012 Nuits-Saint-Georges 1st Cru Boudots. *What a fruit! Remarkable. Very rich and fond. More earthy.*

2012 Vosne-Romanée 1st Cru Beaux Monts. *Beautiful. No reduction, fine nose, long, small seeds, 80 years old vines. As Maxime says, "These are my old aces!"*

2011 Vosne-Romanée 1st Cru Petits Monts. *It is a stone wine as Dominique describes it. Strong fruit, much less woody than Maxime's 2011 Nuits-Saint-Georges 1st Cru Boudots tasted during lunch with Dominique. Mouth somewhat angular at this stage.*

2010 Vosne-Romanée 1st Cru Petits Monts. *This is Maxime's first vintage. Beautiful wine, rich, large, already pleasant. Clear fruit.*

2012 Échezeaux Grand Cru. *In cask. A lot of gas at this stage. The wood stands out, flattening the wine. Fine, long and rich seeds.*

2012 Grands-Échezeaux Grand Cru. *In cask. Orange peel in the finish. Tense and fine. Great acidity, nice frame, somewhat chewy.*

# Domaine Méo-Camuzet

## Men Come and Go, Vineyards Remain

# F

OR MÉO,
IT ALL BEGAN IN 1959,

when Jean Méo, father of Jean-Nicolas, inherited the property, legacy of a parent who was descended from Camuzet. It was for Jean, a native of Vosne-Romanée and a descendant through his mother from an old family of winemakers, the Lamarche family, another reason to go back to his roots. As a matter of fact, he had embraced a political career and joined de Gaulle's government. In this regard, I would like to share a true story that Jean Méo told us during his address for the domain's Jubilee in 2009 which I attended: "When I inherited the estate in 1959, I was working for de Gaulle. It was well known that he wouldn't accept gifts. But I got used to sending him, every Christmas, a case of Méo-Camuzet – not to the Élysée but to Colombey. They were never returned. His aides told me that he said in Colombey, 'Let's have a good time. Go down to the cellar and fetch a bottle of Méo-Camuzet. I'll take care of the menu myself,' and he added, 'I prefer Burgundy wines. They were the favorite wines of French kings: Charlemagne, Henri IV, Louis XIV and Napoleon.'"

Taking advantage of round trips between Paris and Vosne-Romanée, Jean Méo at first marketed his wines via merchants, in barrels, allowing him to continue his career in Paris with an eye on his Burgundian domain. The torch was passed to Jean-Nicolas – who trained alongside Henri Jayer – in early 1989. From then on, he managed and operated the domain.

As for my first exchanges with the family, I have to admit today that back then, I was very skeptical. Indeed, there were reasons. Was I not a young cub in the world of wine? How many parameters necessary for understanding them did I still not know? For example, I could not understand why Henri had moved away from these terroirs. The truth appeared to me much later, after talking about it to Jean-Nicolas. Henri Jayer had reached the age of a well-deserved retirement and, without a direct successor, the leases were not renewed. This misunderstanding on my part stemmed from my ignorance of the situation. This is a pitfall for many sommeliers, who sometimes lack sufficient knowledge and weave and interpret incomplete facts. The best solution to eliminate these miscalculations is to visit and talk to the winemakers. Still, my first memory of a Parantoux Cros is from January 1986. It was a 1979, tasted at the Écusson, in Beaune, run by the passionate-about-wine chef, Jean-Pierre Senelet. Sipping this wine, I understood what had been meant by the sensuousness of the great Burgundy reds.

Some time later, the Méo family appeared at La Poularde. Young, fiery, and unaware, I wanted to tear them apart, but, luckily, my friend Dominique Rézette – and I'm grateful – opened my eyes to Jean-Nicolas Méo's emerging talent. At the helm of terroirs handed down by a great name, he was able to continue the work, imbuing them with his style, not devoid of panache, elegance and a certain refinement. There is much perseverance, considerable conviction, a great focus on details, and a relentless rigor. Throughout this evolution, even today, his family, his father in particular, has continued to direct him towards his roots. Naturally, he had to confront family pressure. It is in this context that he can sometimes offer the best of himself and of his wines. Perhaps envious yesterday, Jean-Nicolas is now envied. If in the 1990s, he took over the vineyards of the "god" Henri Jayer, I remember that some, including myself, disparaged his first wines. The main reproach was often that his wines were too woody, too different from those of Henri. We were influenced by a style and an extraordinary character. Now, like his temperament, his wines are precise and very elegant. He made the choice regarding de-bunching of the grapes and then sought out the delicacy of extraction during fermentations. Power is not the prerogative of great wines. It is the intensity and finesse that accentuate them.

Jean-Nicolas always tests, doubts at times, and frequently questions himself. But for those who can wait for the wonderful vintages born from the terroirs and winery, pleasure comes. Today, his bottles are among the elite of great wines. In over twenty years of winemaking, he has managed to impose his mark. He occupies in the patchwork of the great names of the Côte de Nuits an appreciable position, rising up to the rank of a star among fans in Japan. He remains nonetheless humble. Jean-Nicolas has had the privilege of taking control of a first-class vineyard consisting of Richebourg, of Échezeaux of Vosne-Romanée 1st Cru Aux Brûlées, of Vosne-Romanée 1st Cru Les Chaumes, of Nuits-Saint-Georges 1st Cru Aux Murgers, without forgetting the famous 1st Vosne-Romanée Cros Parantoux. Among all these stellar names, the most famous among the Méo remains the Cros Parantoux. From a terroir that when first discovered was a fallow piece of land, though well exposed to the east however difficult to work, Henri Jayer was able to extract the quin-

# BURGUNDY
## Domaine Méo-Camuzet

tessence of Vosne-Romanée. The plot is sloped, with gravel, and a shallow soil. The situation is recent. In 1978, he produced his first vintage Cros Parantoux. His latest vintage was the 2001. Since the death of Henri in 2006, his nephew, Emmanuel Rouget, has had the task of sustaining the work of his uncle. He began with him in 1979 and was very present from 1985 on. Today, the Méos grow 30 acres of Cros Parantoux, to our delight.

But let's come back to winemaking. During many conversations with him, I mentioned that he might want to move towards a vinification with a whole grape harvest. He disapproved of this option. These differences characterize Burgundy. The paths that winemakers take during vinification give birth to very diverse wines, even if they are from similar plots. In Burgundy, the rule is absence of dogma and absolute individualism for each domain. You are in a regional area where the gates are sublime. It is rare that they are open to the sundry eyes of all comers!

 **M**EMORIES
Several years ago, in November 2009, I had the privilege of being invited to join an Aeropagus of fans of the domain, of international journalists and famous chefs – I was in fact seated next to a delightful couple, the Rostangs (oh, his truffle sandwich!) – for the Jubilee of the Méo-Camuzet Domain. For the evening, the family had taken over the grand hall of the château of Clos de Vougeot. We must remember that the founder of the domain, Étienne Camuzet, was the last private owner before selling the site to the Brotherhood of the Knights of the Taste-vin. The Domain had been in the hands of Jean Méo for fifty years, who inherited it in 1959 from Maria Noirot, the last descendant of the Camuzet family of this remarkable domain. That evening, between the songs and Burgundy benches and the typical regional dishes, we were fortunate to enjoy an impressive array from the domain. The meeting started with a tasting in one of the Gothic rooms of the Clos de Vougeot. Each table, in small committees, tasted the domain's wines dating back over the last twenty vintages. They succeeded each other at a steady pace:

– Nuits-Saint-Georges 1$^{st}$ Cru Aux Murgers: 2006, 1997, 1989

– Clos-de-Vougeot: 1999, 1996, 1995, 2005

– Corton-Clos-Rognet: 1991, 1990

– Vosne-Romanée 1ˢᵗ Cru Les Brûlées: 2002, 1994, 1990

– Échezeaux: 2007, 2002, 2000

– Vosne-Romanée Cros Parantoux: 2007, 2003, 2000, 1992

– Richebourg: 1993

Since we were in 2009, before going to dinner, we started with the wines of the "year" as a warm up:

– Vosne-Romanée 1ˢᵗ Cru Les Brûlées 2008

– Clos-de-Vougeot 2008

– Richebourg 2008

Then, over the four dishes that were served, sublime wines took turns. A "barker" announced them the way that important personalities at an embassy reception are announced:

Tarte tatin of duck *foie gras* and gingerbread
*2002 Burgundy white Hauts-Côtes-de-Nuits Clos Saint-Philibert*
*2003 Vosne-Romanée*

~

Lightly smoked sturgeon with a pumpkin cream and harenga caviar
*2002 Clos-de-Vougeot*

~

Charolais tournedos with a roasted bacon veil and juniper salt
*1999 Nuits-Saint-Georges 1ˢᵗ Cru Aux Murgers*
*1996 Richebourg*

~

Good cheeses from Burgundy
*1959 Corton*

~

A first cru chocolate Vougeotin
*Brut Rosé Crémant-de-Bourgogne*

# BURGUNDY
## Domaine Méo-Camuzet

To this day, I have not had again the opportunity to experience such a domain tasting. First of all, the family's generosity towards their guests that night has a lot to do with it, as is their ability to keep wines and vintages in large quantity over long periods. It must be said that it is a rare phenomenon in Burgundy, given the demand and the incredible fragmentation of the clos. So tasting these wines as they mature, comparing their evolution and discovering their surprises among vintages which we almost forgot is a real pleasure. Pinot Noir has multiple faces that only time and the terroirs can reveal.

# Tastings of Vosne-Romanée 1ˢᵗ Cru
## Les Brûlées in November 2013, at the domain.

For the most part, the first vines date back to the 1930s. As Jean-Nicolas said, "The grapes are the archetypes of small "millerand" grapes. They have all small seeds and a great concentration that can remain longer on the stems without damage." This cru is located at the foot of the Richebourg commune. The soil is rather shallow and the plow often "scrapes," getting caught on large stones or the bedrock itself.

**2003.** *Dark color, opaque, China ink-like. Kirsch nose, dense, compact. Sappy mouth, slightly sweet sensation. More ample. Spicy candied note. Fig slightly chocolatey. To be consumed within five years.*

**2001.** *Evolved color, open nose, floral, reminiscent of a cool vintage (hawthorn and pomegranate). Slender mouth, taut and shapely. Fresh wine, long and athletic. The tannins are fine and somewhat demanding. To be matched with a game bird, cooked in its juice right away.*

**1996.** *Here too, a cool vintage. Brilliant color, slightly evolved. Nose still closed and tight. An animal note reminiscent of leather. Note of stewed wild strawberry. Wide mouth, but tight in the finish. A little Calvinistic. The structure has presence and deserves pairing with a type of dish that is either simmered or grilled. It requires something succulent.*

**1988.** *A vintage from Henri Jayer's time, which he vinified himself. Tiled and stripped color. Tertiary nose. Accomplished mouth, ripe, fine, slightly tense. Complex with notes of cedar, leather and spices. Consider pairing with roasted thrushes with sweet raisins and spices.*

**1980.** *Tiled color. Open nose, fine. Tertiary. Recalling vieux garcon jam. Coffee and chocolate notes. Elegant palates, refined. The half-body finish remains present. The wine is different, a curiosity.*

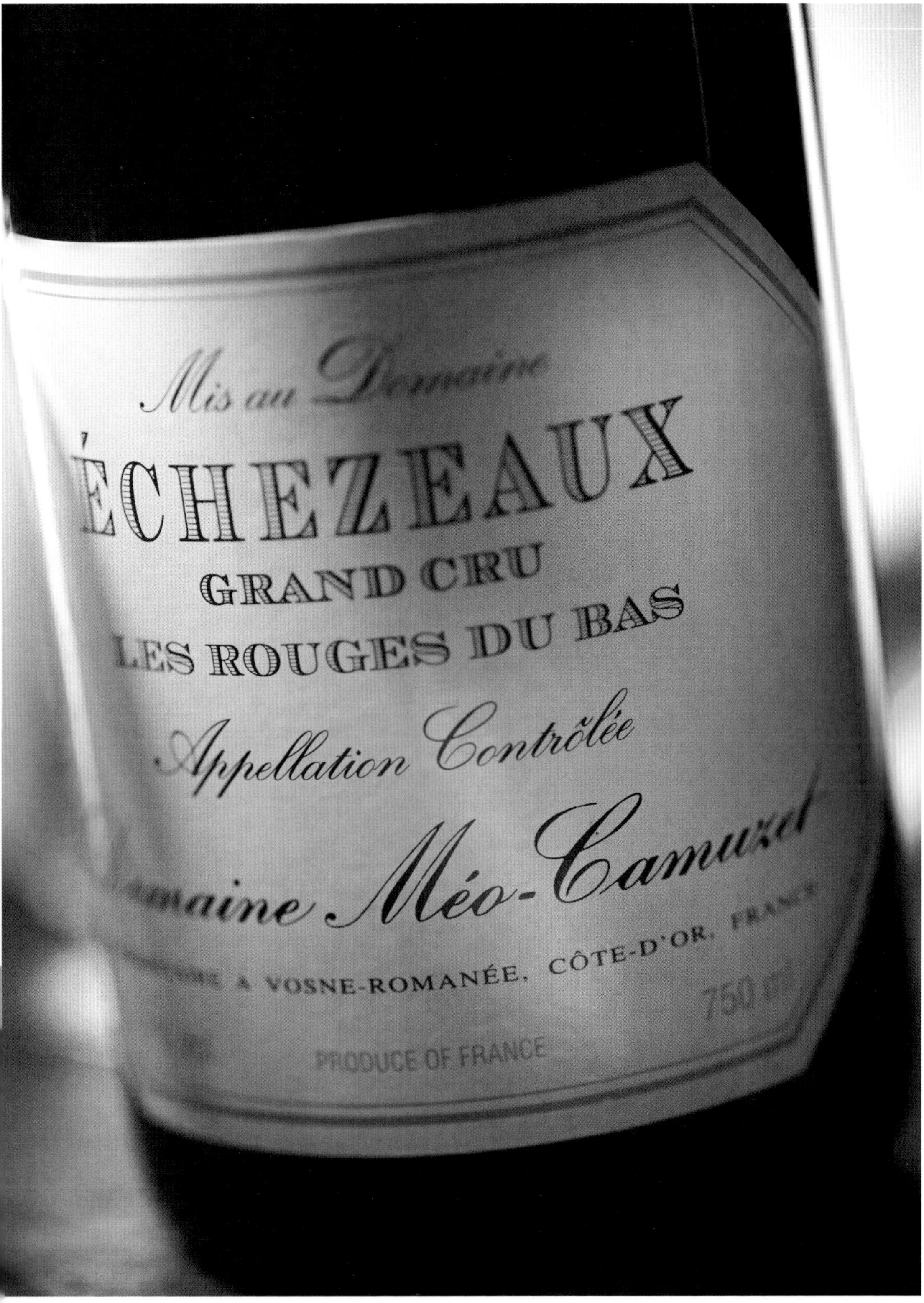
Mis au Domaine
ÉCHEZEAUX
GRAND CRU
LES ROUGES DU BAS
Appellation Contrôlée
Méo-Camuzet
A VOSNE-ROMANÉE, CÔTE-D'OR,
750 ml
PRODUCE OF FRANCE

# Domaine de la Romanée-Conti

## The Domain

**O ONE PASSES**
THROUGH VOSNE-ROMANÉE
without pausing at the foot of the Calvary erected in front of
the Romanée-Conti clos. This stop feels like a pilgrimage,
such as the one made by believers visiting St. Peter's Square
at the Vatican. Obviously, it is unlikely that the Holy Father receives them
for a hearing, but at least they have a sense of having drawn as near as possible. In some way, it is the same for the wines made in the Clos. They are
so rare that few tasters are asked to taste them. So, to be able to contemplate
the vines, to breathe in the land, enjoy the slope of this 1-acre plot, 80 ares
and 50 centiares, is a little like becoming its owner. And who knows, perhaps
later, once tasted, it would be possible to even better understand this much
sought-after wine. So, like all young sommeliers, when I started in early
1984, it was through books dedicated to wines (among them, those of Guy
Renvoisé) that I began to get closer to this domain and its Grands Crus. In
the restaurants where I came to work, I watched closely the recognizable
labels that sometimes emerged from the cellars, my eyes shining like those
of a prospector who has just spotted a gleaming nugget. Though I could not
claim to have tasted them, I had already positioned each cru on the map
engraved in my memory.

From 1987 when I arrived at La Poularde, I was able to access these treasures. My book learning was solid, and I only had to complement it with my
visual, olfactory, and gustatory memories. It was even more magical for, at
the time, our wine list included bottles such as the 1966 Montrachet, 1966
La-Tâche and 1971 Romanée-Saint-Vivant… Whenever I came back up
from the cellar carrying one, I had goosebumps.

To serve these fragile and delicate Pinots, we used a particular system, still
sometimes used at Le Cinq today. It involves a wine basket, attached to a
shaft, itself connected to a small screw, which a small crank allows to gently
tilt the basket without generating eddies and waves inside the bottle, and in
so doing to preserve the wine free from any cloudiness, which the light
sediments at the bottom of the bottle can generate. The wine remains limpid
and crystalline, without having to decant it, which weakens both the bouquet
and the mouth. During these services, I held my breath. The most delicate
step is the opening, because the cork does not necessarily let itself be extracted

easily. Some are glued to the neck; others crumble or break slyly in the last third of the extraction. Talk to François Audouze about it, a specialist in the opening of old wines. He is equipped like a surgeon of the Grand Army, ready to free the wine from the sealed cork, sometimes in place for half a century and more. The sole requirement is that no cork particle must obscure the clear wine. So, like the years, one must take time to complete the operation.

Speaking of which, I like very much Aubert de Villaine's philosophy regarding the aging in the cask and the life of wines in the bottle. As he puts it, "Wines sometimes revolt during their passage in bottle after having matured in a Burgundian cask (a 228-liter barrel). Suddenly they find themselves locked in a narrow glass bottle (75 cl), a glass prison. So they need time to get used to it. It's normal." We can then add that the cork is a form of hermetic door for which we have a key: the sommelier knife, which delivers the wine from its glass prison.

The supreme reward of our trades is that it is our duty to taste the wines we open. The little I knew then about old wines was shattered. These 1966 and 1971 wines (we were in the late 1980s) offered little color, but the flavors were sumptuous, complex, infinitely delicate. The tannins were still present. I was discovering the old Pinot Noir. I was entering the universe of wines designed for the nose. I was traveling between an English garden with old rose beds and a market with oriental spices. Dishes had to remain simple. The bottle deserved calmness and serenity.

The wines of Romanée-Conti were my first love. Since then I have never turned my back on the domain.

# BURGUNDY
## Domaine de la Romanée-Conti

# M EMORIES

My last recollection with the La-Tâche dates back to 2012. It took place in a discreet inn located in Champagne, in one of those former post houses described by Curnonsky, where – after a grueling day of a 150-champagne tasting marathon – we met with Serge Dubs, Olivier and David Poussier Biraud. To thank us, our host took us to this restaurant under the watchful eyes of Max, their butler.

He served us timeless bottles like this magnum of 1947 dry Veuve-Clicquot (which the cellar master, Dominique Demarvil, present at the meal and who brought it himself, certified). It was spicy grilled, with honey, toasted bread, marzipan, fresh Parmesan, discreet with fine bubbles. Coming from a small yield, the wine was very wide.

Our host, Jean-Marie Curien, offered us a bottle from his cellar and brought it up reverently. It had never been moved since the end of the war and came from a case of twelve bottles that his father purchased at the "domain" for some butter and fresh cream! Women made this 1942 La-Tâche. The silence at the table was palpable. An extraordinary silence, "We could hear a wine critic fly." This La-Tâche transported us with its complexity and finesse. The youth expressed by the wine got the attention of the Areopagus of tasters. The cork itself – the original – was still in top physical shape.

The 1942 originated from prephylloxeric Pinot Noir! The bright and clear color underlined the orange nuances, revealing a certain age. How to describe this nose, without forgetting the aromatic range, as rich as a Balzac's description?… Nothing was missing, as much the fruit as the spices. With no exaggeration. Each aeration delivered increasingly diverse aromatic experiences. The mouth, of a great roundness, surrendered with light touches the same impression as the nose. The whole experience was just dazzling.

So much so that we forgot the tasty dish. The game served was juicy and without pomp, simmered for quite a while and of a great tenderness, not to brutalize the structure of this wine. A gray partridge in bladder, cooked in its own juice, with a truffle-infused cardoon gratin.

These evocations invite a dream to dwell on. Here was a menu that I have rarely had the opportunity to serve during my career. I will not mention the sponsor, himself a lover of great wines, full of integrity, always preferring to share rather than speculate – an attribute that he waved off. He ignored these monetary considerations and always focused on the duality between two high-ranking lords and the dish used to distinguish them. The scene took place in 2004 in a private room at the George V. The walls were covered with wood paneling with warm tones. The fireplace adorned with lily flowers came from a chateau in the Loire Valley. The high ceiling seemed unattainable. A subdued light pierced the high-hanging windows. The table runner consisted of a richly woven fabric. The embellishing flowers expressly had been chosen to be odorless. A dozen friends were gathered around an oval table. The glasses were ready, and the chef was in place. After sharing in the adjoining living room a 1979 S champagne of Salon, the guests were invited to sit at the table with the famous statement: "*Monsieur* is served." We must imagine these gastronomes such as those described by Marcel Rouff in his masterpiece, *The Life and Passion of Dodin Bouffant, Gourmet*.

# BURGUNDY
## Domaine de la Romanée-Conti

Once everyone was seated, here is what was served during the next three hours:

Sarlat soup with Périgord black truffles
*1955 Pavillon Blanc of Château Margaux*
*1945 Pavillon Blanc of Château Margaux 1945*

~

Red mullet fillet, with a liver verjuice sauce and smoked eggplant
*1959 Château La Mission Haut-Brion – 1961 Château Haut Brion*

~

Racan country pigeon and its roast from Abatilles
*1918 Château Haut Brion – Magnum of 1928 Château Léoville Poyferré*

~

Venison fillet with Jerusalem artichokes
*1929 Romanée-Conti*

~

Cheese from the Cistercian Abbey
*1947 Bonnes Mares Monassier*
*1942 Richebourg Domaine de la Romanée-Conti*

~

Quince and honey millefeuille, with caramel cream chibouste
*1894 Château Coutet – 1937 Château d'Yquem*

~

Mocha coffee from Ethiopia and chocolate candies from Jacques Genin
*1858 Fine Champagne*

And to continue at the table, in the English fashion, with endless discourse and tasting of cigars from Havana (still allowed at the table at that time…), we opened with a pair of pliers a 1900 Wiese & Krohn Porto…

All wines for lunch came from the personal cellar of the hosting power. Not a single wine had a flaw. All had a complement, except the 1929 Romanée-Conti! Not only because no other wine in this vintage could compete with it, but also because it remains an absolute rarity.

# The Wines

January 2014. We had just arrived from Paris with Thierry on the 9:00 a.m. train to Dijon. Once the sedan was rented, we took the road for the great vintages. What better opening could we expect before entering the domain! One after the next, before our eyes, we passed villages with evocative names: Marsannay-la-Côte, Fixin, Gevrey Chambertin, Morey-Saint-Denis, Chambolle-Musigny and Vougeot.

Everywhere around, bundles of vine twigs were strewn on the hillsides. These rough cuts, used for cooking, warmed up the winemakers in the vineyards (it was 0° C on the thermometer). At the appropriate time, we stood at the gate. We found Aubert for a tasting of the 2012 vintage in cask with Bernard Noblet. The tasting was by the book.

**Échezeaux.** *Comes with a beautiful fruit, elegant, charming at this stage. It is more open.*

**Grands-Échezeaux.** *Spicier, fine, rich. The wine is ready to be bottled. The yields were low: 22 hectoliters per hectare.*

**Romanée-Saint-Vivant.** *More powerful, more pronounced bitterness.*

**Richebourg.** *More sappy, square, with a vegetable dash.*

**La-Tâche.** *Nothing is missing. With a slightly salty side in the finish. A lot of elegance, with some restraint. The last replanting in this terroir dates to 2008. Two plots are currently fallow and replanting is ongoing. The estate owns 6 hectares of La-Tâche.*

**La Conti.** *Very tight, still closed, with finesse, and dense. Airy, carnal, a star of the opera, the nave of a cathedral. And what a length. Subtle finish, delicate, refined.*

*Then we headed towards the second cellar for the vertical of La-Tâche. We chatted while walking quietly through the quiet, empty streets of Vosne-Romanée, wrapped up in our coats. A light mist wrapped up the houses. The smoke from the twig fires burning in nearby vineyards reached us slightly. While listening to Aubert, I automatically inserted my nose in the glass where a drop of 2012 Romanée-Conti remained; a tart cherry aroma with an incredible sharpness oozed out of it. A rare and ephemeral moment. What bliss!*

## BURGUNDY
### Domaine de la Romanée-Conti

# La Tâche

To describe the place called La Tâche is to understand the intimate relationship between man and the land. La Tâche is a good example of labor performed by the winegrowers on this ungrateful land, with a limestone outcrop. A parcel of 5.03 hectares, this terroir represents rectitude and attitude with subtlety. Often more rigorous than the Conti. After several years in the bottle, drinking the La-Tâche is like taking a journey between the East and West. This terroir and this variety deliver a spicy bouquet and fruity notes between sandalwood and cedar, and morello and roses. Nonetheless, it remains powerful and intense. From the road that leads from Beaune to Dijon, one can see the hill of Vosne capped with a strip of white earth. But at the foot of this land, you come to understand its power and scope. La-Tâche is for me, with the Romanée-Conti and Musigny, what Mother Nature, helped by centuries of monks' patient work, has given birth to of the very best.

2012. *From the cask. Dangerously seductive nose. The fruit recalls the small morello. The wine has a great frankness. Slightly spicy. The wide and suave mouth offers at this time the most beautiful balance since the beginning of the tasting. Everything is intense, complex, and sappy. Already a great wine.*

2011. *Small-yield vintage. Deep garnet color. Clear. Powerful nose, a little warm. Rigorous enough. The aging is perceptible. A closed nose. Not happy to have been opened so fast obviously. It must find its place in the bottle. The full mouth, tight at the attack, gives a serious impression, a little compact. To be revisited.*

2010. *Deep garnet color. Nose fine and open, delicate, very intense, a lot of reserve. Woody, fruity, and spicy notes. The experience is incredibly elegant. The mouth is lavish. Tight and spherical. With an incredible energy. Great wine.*

2009. *Made completely with whole-grape harvest (the grapes are dropped into tanks with their stalk), dark and opaque color. Rich fleshy nose, spicy, fine but still confused. Dense and floral mouth recalling faded roses. Of a great power, with a slightly solar retro-olfaction. Wine is very full and slightly extrovert. At this stage, I prefer the 2010.*

2008. *Intense and brilliant ruby color. Open and fine nose, slightly tart. Incredibly elegant, red berries, floral violet iris. The whole is extremely attractive. A wine for noses. The palate is classic. That is to say, with width, with some restraint in a cool sophistication. It is balanced and refined. The retro-olfaction reminds one of spicy red fruits and ginger notes. The tannins are melted. The experience is extremely*

elegant. Let's not forget that the harvest happens later in the domain and that the wines are not as square as the 1988 could remind us. Late harvests and longer sunshine exposure have the effect of burning some acidity and give more seductive and rounder wines.

**2006.** *Ruby color. Medium intensity. The nose is surprisingly already open for a vintage whose reputation is rather austere. However, the maturing dominates. Light cocoa and vanilla notes, blond caramel too. Slightly flattering, masking the fruit. The mouth is full and soft. The mid-palate gives the impression of a half-bodied, with a good length. It is a docile and flattering La-Tâche. Ready to be enjoyed.*

**1998.** *For the record, this wine was bottled piece by piece. Intense ruby color. Slightly cloudy. Reduced and severe nose, with evolved notes, which after the aeration, becomes earthy. Virginia tobacco notes. The average width mouth gives a slightly rigid impression, with quite a harsh finish. This La-Tâche needs more time. To be revisited.*

**1988.** *After a long gestation period, this cold and austere vintage is poised to reveal itself to the enthusiasts. The ruby color with orange reflections is very clear. The complex nose is spicy, fresh, where the spices mingle, humus and dry floral, a tad of gentian leather. fireplace smoke. As well as notes of fruit in eau-de-vie. This is nose wine. After a few minutes, cocoa notes. Black truffle. The mouth remains, however, tonic and svelte. A little sharp in the finish. To appreciate this 1988, long-cooked meats with strong flavor are needed.*

**1961.** *The surprise of the day. Served blind since it looked so young. The color is moderately intense ruby orange. Some topaz reflections. A classic for the domain, which is not known for black wines. The nose has an impressive finesse and complexity, reminiscent of notes of leather, sandalwood, cedar, fruits in eau-de-vie, kirsch cherries, and withered roses. Spice and cocoa. It has a bouquet with a fragile and ultimate balance. For a 50-year-old wine, an incredible intensity distinguishes its generous mouth. It does not have much flesh left but is remarkably light and diaphanous. It was the first time that I tasted this vintage. The balance of the mouth is the reflection of the nose. And the eyes. All converge to describe this wine as a heavenly one. I am thinking of pairing it with a venison fillet with a Périgueux sauce and tuberous chervils with fresh black truffles.*

ROM
CO

ANEE E

TI

# Château Thivin

*The Claude of Mount Brouilly*

W HEN
I ARRIVED AT LA POULARDE,
I started by visiting the nearest vineyards, those of the Loire department: Côtes du Forez, Côtes Roannaises, the local wines of Urfé, Condrieu and Château Grillet. Quickly, I turned my attention towards the Beaujolais – a wine that dominated the hills of the Lyonnais region through Arbresle and Villefranche-sur-Saône. It is through these roads that I began to understand the role of the granite foothills of this vineyard. The ten Beaujolais crus are home to a great diversity of subsoils: some volcanic schists, and in other parts sandy granite. Together they form a mosaic that has built up over successive erosions.

Of these terroirs, I only knew at the beginning the production of the "sea" of vines, spreading at the foot of the Beaujolais crus. There, it was not necessarily a question of terroir but rather, in the words of an immortal expert, of "cash-terroir." The craze for the production of new Beaujolais hardly concerned me at La Poularde, and today, at the Georges V, we consume twenty-four clos each year, which we purchase via the illustrious Tim Johnson from the *Juvéniles*, in Paris, the Domaine de Vissoux, whose 2014 vintage was particularly delicious. In fact, the first appellation that attracted me was Morgon. I enjoyed my exchanges with Marcel Lapierre. At the time, he was experimenting with several paths. He was "the" disciple of Jules Chauvet, a prominent trader and maker of Beaujolais. Chemist in his spare time, he worked on yeast, malolactic fermentation and carbonic maceration. Pedagogue, gifted with a great sense of conviction, he is something of the father of the natural wine movement. Hence, we could enjoy at his home the same wine in three different forms: unfiltered and non-sulfite, unfiltered slightly sulfite, and filtered and sulfite. My choice tended to lean towards the second choice. Especially given that, one year, we had issues with the first choice during transportation. The wine began to labor again in the bottle.

While still enjoying the wines of the Lapierre family, we extended our escapades in this genuinely charming region. The landscape is dotted with hills where the vineyards are cultivated in cups. Important people from Lyon or families rooted for generations in the region maintain lovingly the numerous castles visible along the roads in the distance. These appellations offer a wide range of styles of rich wines. One can create a cellar with bottles full of surprises. For enthusiasts, the Beaujolais is a gold mine.

Among the nuggets ostensibly standing out from the hills: Mount Brouilly. On the flanks, surrounded by greenery and vines, almost hidden from view, is the Thivin Château. It is recognizable for its two towers and glazed-tile roofs, worthy of the Brothers Grimm's tale *Hansel and Gretel*. Since the late nineteenth century, the Geoffray family has owned the castle. Zaccharie, a distant ancestor of Claude Geoffray, bought it at an auction in 1877. Back then, the property was only 2 hectares. It stretches now over 25 hectares of vineyards. Here the subsoil is composed of volcanic rocks, with diorite and porphyry mixed with clay. As for this stately property, it takes its name from the individual who bought it from the Marquis de Vichy in the wake of the Revolution. This member of Parliament was called Thivind.

Among the major celebrities and customers who were faithful to Thivin well before us was the great Colette. The passion of the author of *Gigi* for Beaujolais wines is not a secret. Claude Geoffray once told me something Colette said during a visit to the castle in 1947, at the time of the harvest: "The covered courtyard resounded with voices, wheels, heavy-shod foot-steps, because forty pickers of the domain were going for lunch, guarded by their alert and vinous smells. I would have liked to trail them."

The Geoffrays have always been at the forefront of their terroir. Claude II, the grand-son of Zaccharie, was one of the major architects of the creation of the appellation. Today, Claude IV – because for the Geoffrays, like the Müllers in Sarre, the eldest still bears the name of the grandfather – is the only winemaker of his region to serve as a member of the illustrious Academy of Wine of France, chaired by Jean-Robert Pitte, member of the Institute.

His son, Claude Edouard, joined the domain in 2007. He runs the domain as a wise winemaker, concerned about its environment, in order to pass it on to one of his three children: Tobias-Claude, Nicolas-Claude and Florina Lavinia Claude. The succession seems assured!

BURGUNDY
Château Thivin

# M EMORIES

Among the generous, rebellious wines to share with friends, without frills, the Beaujolais crus occupy a prominent place. If vineyards become increasingly out of reach for enthusiasts because of their often prohibitive prices, it is not the case here. The pleasure of uncorking a bottle of Beaujolais remains unchanged.

The day of our visit to Thivin castle, we did not think we had time to stay for lunch. We had to leave quickly to catch a train to Mâcon. But Évelyne, Claude's wife, saw to it that things would turn out otherwise. After all, it had taken me more than fifteen years to come back. Shame on me! So, after the tasting and a great tour of the castle's adjoining vineyards with Claude, we were surprised to find the dining room table set up for a good spread. The ambience of this room is very warm. Rather small, it is used for the family. In this still cool month, a roaring fire crackled. The old wooden floors, the cat purring on the windowsill, the paintings, the old wood moldings, played their parts to make the place inviting.

No sooner were we seated then Ms. Geoffray handed me a salad of warm green Puy lentils. A delight that I had not enjoyed for a long time, as was the dish which followed: a *sabodet* and a pistachio poached *saucisson* flanked by English-style Charlotte potatoes, with chopped parsley and butter. These Lyonnaise charcuterie specialties are refined and tasty, perfectly suited for a beautiful and intense fruity Gamay.

The dish was all the more appreciated given that breakfast on the train had been summary and poor quality (let's rehabilitate dining cars!). Besides, tasting sessions always awaken the appetite. Which means that we still had room for the cheeses when they arrived: a Fourme of Montbrison in memory of the plains of Forez, a goat brick from the Lyonnaise hills and a great Saint-Marcellin as at M. Paul's. For the last two cheeses, we went back to the 2013 white Beaujolais, a private production of the Geoffray family.

And while having a cup of coffee, we indulged in a delicious fine baked apple tart. Simple dishes shared in this friendly, family setting, paralleling the Geoffray family and their wines.

## The Wines

At the origin of the Beaujolais hegemony is the nobility of the black Gamay with white juice. This variety was widespread throughout the medieval Burgundy, until 1395 and Philippe II of Burgundy, known as Philippe the Bold (1342-1404), who, through his birth and marriage was granted additional titles: Count of Flanders and Artois, Count Palatine of Burgundy (Franche-Comté), Count of Nevers, Rethel, Étampes, Gien, Charolais, Lord of Salins and Malines. A prestigious page in the history of Burgundy began with him.

The Valois dynasty of Burgundy, which he founded, reigned during more than a century. But at the end the fourteenth century, he ordered the uprooting of the Côte de Nuits in Mâcon of all the vines of Gamay, a grape variety labelled as a "vile and treacherous plant." Therefore, the Beaujolais vineyards were expressly reserved for him. Some claim that his goal was intended to end the competition of Gamay wines in Burgundy. They also took into account the qualitative differences in production of the two grape varieties and considered the Pinot Noir more "noble."

## Vertical of Côte-de-Brouilly tasted at the château in March 2014

Thierry and Marc Le Gallic, one of our young sommeliers, were present. The latter has the advantage – like all our young people – of having a driving license. As I often say,

"we can often change clerks but not the license!" mainly because the police is not too soft with sommeliers (among others).

**2012. Vintage Sept Vignes.** *A vintage that we currently serve at the George V. Vegetal nose, lighter mouth, a soft wine, lower acidity, inviting. Lots of raspberry.*

**2011. Vintage Sept Vignes.** *More precision, sharpness, fine, noble. The winemaking process has become more precise, racy. Alert and long. Without warmth, lots of flavor, a dish in sauce is needed, such as an eel stew or a sautéed hunter rabbit.*

**2010. Vintage Sept Vignes.** *Less dense color, finer nose and mouth, violet nose, refined. Mouth with a nice tension, some freshness and light bitterness. Skimmed at 30% vol. Do not serve too cold. With a red meat, medium rare, a steak or a flank.*

**2009. Vintage Sept Vignes.** *It seems impulsive, clear color, intense, with density, without the cooked side of the 2003. Average degrees in this vintage: 13 to 14% of vol. Quite chewy and large. Noble, powerful, without cooked fruits. A food wine, for juicy braised meat.*

BURGUNDY
Château Thivin

**2001. Vintage Sept Vignes.** *Less massive vintage than was the 2000. A time of crisis in the Beaujolais, morello nose, tart red fruit. A full mouth, a very fine wine, rich, lovely refreshing acidity, a success (without a scrape).*

**1999. Vintage Sept Vignes.** *This is a wine that we serve even today at the George V, originating from a blend of parcels in the domain. Intense color, nose more alcoholic, kirsch, stronger mouth. Massive.*

**1995.** *Coffee nose, licorice, more angular mouth, a reduced peak, sharp and tense mouth.*

**1993.** *Old Pinot Noir nose, mouth tight, a little long, but still of interest.*

**1991.** *Tiled color (whole grapes), smoky nose, mineral, mushrooms, rich mouth, still with energy, held back by acids. Sapid finish. This was the first vintage ordered for Montrond-les-Bains. With this wine, a good plate of porcini would be adequate.*

BURGUNDY
Château Thivin

# Cuvée Zaccharie

This is the name of the grandfather who created the domain in the late nineteenth century. The wine is fermented in barrels of 228 liters, from 1 to 10 years of age. There is only 8% of new wood in total so as not to give too much wood. The aging time runs from 10 to 12 months. It is a wine created in part to meet the demand of the Lyon market that wants denser and more powerful wines.

2012. *At this stage, the maturation process still shows up a little. Vegetal nose, delicious.*

2011. *Very nice wine, the wood remains pronounced, but has some tension, some voluptuousness, more digestible, has retained character.*

2009. *The density is such that the wine seems "off region" to the extent that it is dense, heavy, powerful, candied cherry burlat, 14.8% vol. Satiating. Sweet spices, saturation of almost bitter cocoa. Marked cask, vanilla.*

2007. *Much more pleasant, especially after 2005. Tannic structure, more digestible too. Traces of wood less marked.*

2005. *Deep color, misleading, austere vintage, tight, dense, sappy. Still very serious, chewy.*

2003. *Harvested as early as mid-August. Massive density in the mouth, concentrated grapes, dried but no phenolic maturity (around 15% vol. in certain vintages). Wood nose. Dark chocolate finish, bitter (12.5% vol.).*

2001. *Slightly cloudy color, no filtration. Black pepper nose, coated, easier to drink. Very chewy, dense.*

*To the question "Can a Beaujolais get old?" this tasting proves, if required, that the Gamay with white juice can pass the test of time with class. To achieve this, healthy grapes – as with all wines – are needed. In the Beaujolais, the harvests cannot be but manual. Besides, for plots on hillsides and those where the Gamay is grown in cups, man is indispensable. Since the winery is on a hillside, the different stages of winemaking are achieved with gravity, without using conveyor pumps. Then, it is customary to minimize interventions during macerations and fermentations. Only some crushing and pumping to promote the extraction of tannins and the color, and finally a gentle pressing. The fermentations end quietly in casks (sometimes centuries old) and the wine is refined for six to eight months. Then it begins a long life in the bottle.*

P 216 CHÂTEAU HAUT-BAILLY

P 222 CHÂTEAUX HAUT-BRION & LA MISSION HAUT-BRION

P 229 CHÂTEAU RAUZAN SÉGLA

P 234 CHÂTEAU PALMER

P 240 CHÂTEAU MARGAUX

P 246 CHÂTEAU LÉOVILLE BARTON

P 252 CHÂTEAU BATAILLEY

P 259 CHÂTEAU LYNCH-BAGES

P 264 CHÂTEAU MOUTON ROTHSCHILD

P 270 CHÂTEAU LAFITE ROTHSCHILD

P 276 CHÂTEAU LATOUR

P 282 CHÂTEAU CALON SÉGUR

P 286 CHÂTEAU SOUTARD

P 294 CHÂTEAU FIGEAC

P 303 CHÂTEAU AUSONE

P 311 CHÂTEAU CHEVAL BLANC

P 320 PÉTRUS

P 328 CHÂTEAU LAFLEUR

P 334 CHÂTEAU DE FARGUES

P 341 CHÂTEAU D'YQUEM

# Wines of

~

# Bordeaux

# Château Haut-Bailly

*From Sanders to Wilmers*

# S

INCE 1998
## THE WILMERS FAMILY

has owned the domain since 1998, and it is managed by Véronique Sanders, granddaughter of Jean Sanders, the former owner. With this, the Haut-Bailly philosophy has persisted: continuity is a prerequisite. Véronique undertakes all that is possible in order to extract the best from her terroir, while entrusting its outcome to Gérard Vialard, the Cellar Master. Véronique has the owners' full confidence.

The Haut-Bailly terroir remains quite unique. In fact, the faluns (limestone outcrops) have the capacity, during colder years, to enable vines to produce deep and generous wines. At the heart of the estate is a parcel of 4 hectares of vines that is very special to Véronique - this rare ampelographic heritage (from the heart of the Haut-Bailly varietal conservatory where the grape varieties are drawn) contributes to the Growth's stylistic preservation. Here, you will find Merlot, Malbec, Carmenère, Petit Verdot and both Cabernets.

The second important point here is, of course, that the size of the vineyard has never varied: 28 hectares. This case remains exceptional in being the only châteaux within the appellation that had been classified without a cadastral restriction as far as plot development is concerned.

The dependability of Haut-Bailly is remarkable. The wines are always distinguished by an unparalleled pulp and a singularly Burgundian elegance.

# M

## EMORIES

In my initial journey to Bordeaux, I quickly encountered Château Haut-Bailly. Jean Dessalle is one of the best brokers I have ever known. It was in February 1989, at the château with Gilles Étéocle (then chef and owner of La Poularde) and Veronique's grandfather. That day, he had us open a 1959 Magnum accompanied by a mature Mimolette cheese; then, as we were well on our way, a 1955 Magnum! I simultaneously remember the man's generosity, the refinement of a great wine in its fullness – magnum size – but also a divine agreement, for here the bite of the Mimolette, its palatability and aromas, provided all the necessary materials for the expression of these matured vintages, without hurting them or removing the slightest characteristic.

In the wake of this tasting, we went to dinner at Jean Ramet's, one Michelin star at the time, the best of Bordeaux. I still remember the menu:

–Spanish elvers with a 1986 Château Saransot-Dupré. First time I ate elvers. I loved the soft, fine texture of the elvers, the delicacy of the preparation. Followed by…

– Pan-seared veal chop with a 1976 magnum Haut-Bailly. Very good vintage. Established on faluns, Haut-Bailly is protected from the heat, and its terroir conserves the wines' chill quality. This is why the 1976 Haut-Bailly is one of the few to have lasted…

M. Dessale drove on the way back. He was more than 70 years old at the time. In Montrond, we ordered up 300 bottles of each vintage of Haut-Bailly. It was Pierre Troisgros who had informed Étéocle of this great broker.

## BORDEAUX
### Château Haut-Bailly

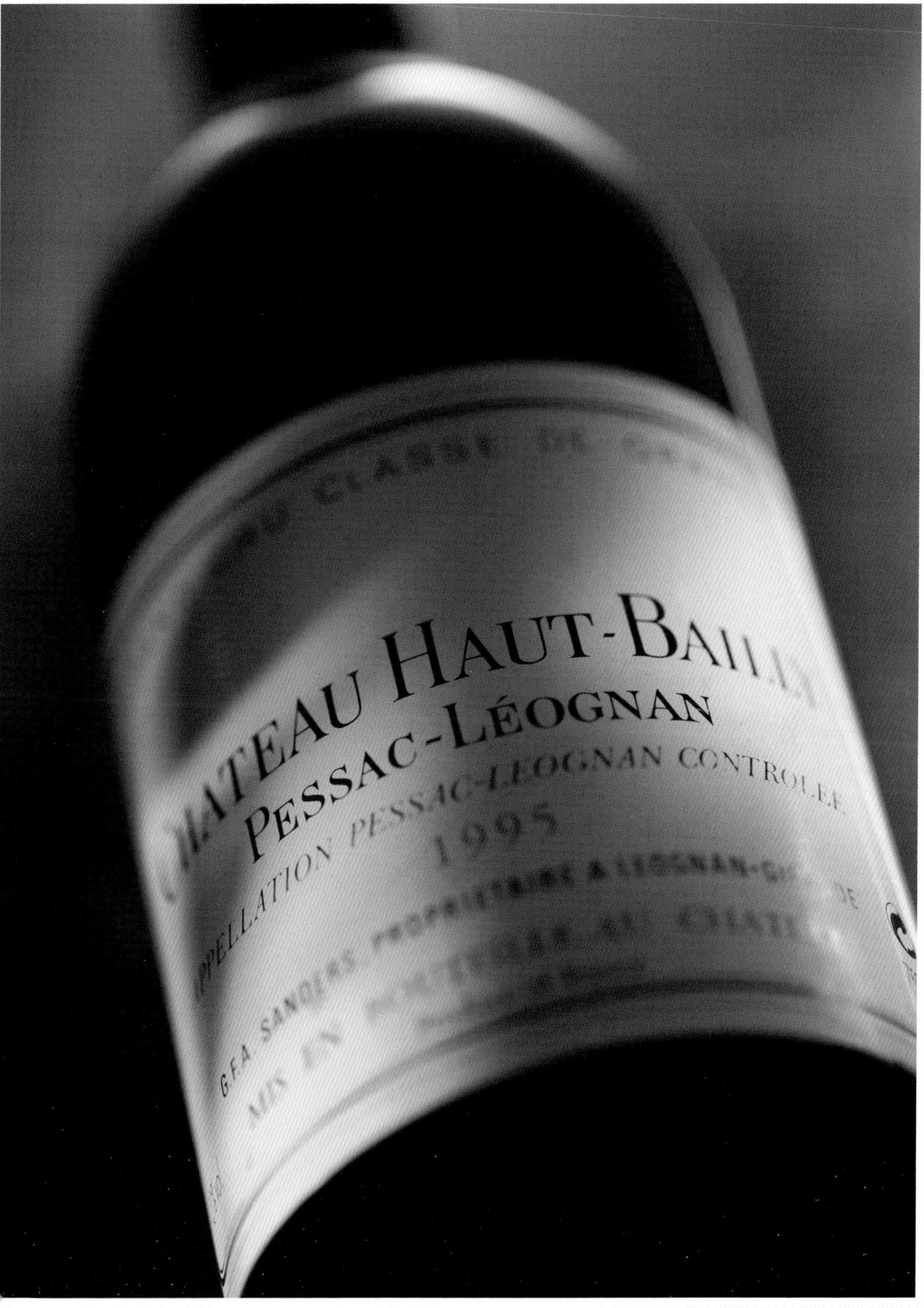
PESSAC-LÉOGNAN
1995

## The Wines

The creation of great wine is the result of outstanding work carried out in the vineyard in which parcels are defined over the course of the wine harvest, or, to be more precise, the intra-plot.

Here, there is no desire to change the image of the château or modernize its label or participate in the race of some passing fad. None of that. It is for these reasons that it remains one of the great châteaux, opened regularly at our Le Cinq tables.

## 2013 Wine tasting at the Château

2010. *Compact, deep nose, a touch of reduction. Wide mouth, quickly overtaken by extreme density. The best wine of the tasting. One of the greatest Haut-Bailly wines I have enjoyed.*

2009. *Warm and powerful nose, pulpy, recalling plum, hint of kirsched burlat cherry. Dense mouth, very fleshy. Long lingering mouth finish. The whole is very consistent and generous.*

2008. *Straight, fresh nose, fruity, remarkable, beautiful. Slender, structured mouth, delicate and ripe tannins, remarkable length. Needs more time.*

2007. *Fruity nose, resembling Cabernet, the mouth is quite soft, a bit fluid as Cabernets are weak.*

2006. *Fresh, fruity nose, discreet, structured, sappy mouth, slightly salty, refreshing. The whole is complete. Needs more time.*

2005. *Closed, compact and truffled nose. Deep attack on the mouth, great structure, complete, needs at least 10 years, the whole is very balanced.*

2004. *Closed, dense nose, full and rich mouth, very nice balance from a successful, drastic selection.*

2003. *Exotic nose but not too ripe, surprising, large attack, slightly sweet with tannins that are not too aggressive, ready to drink.*

2002. *Charming nose, supple attack on the mouth, a little fluid, easy, slight touch of dry tannins in the finish, ready to drink.*

2001. *Touch of reduction during aeration, after a few minutes, delicate, fine, very fruity, good aromatic expression, supple and elegant mouth, surprising for a 2001, a revelation in this vintage.*

2000. *Solar, mentholated nose, macerated fruit, profound. Dense, rich, round mouth, hint of licorice at the finish, very long. A great wine.*

1999. *Fine nose, fruity, amiable, supple and tender attack, ready to drink.*

1998. *Ripe nose, kirsched, sappy. Graphite notes. In the mouth, it's revealed as smooth, slightly fluid attack, tannins present, harmonious.*

# Châteaux Haut-Brion & La Mission Haut-Brion

*The Prince and the Delmas*

# L ES CHÂTEAUX
## LA MISSION HAUT-BRION

and Haut-Brion châteaux are part of the Clarence Dillon Domain, alongside Château Quintus (formerly Château Tertre Daugay) and Dragon de Quintus. Historically, the Dillon family acquired Château La Mission Haut-Brion in 1983 from the Woltner heirs. The family had already owned the Chateau Haut-Brion since 1935. The purchase was made at the time by Clarence Dillon, a New York financier. Today, it is his great-grandson, Prince Robert of Luxembourg, who manages the Clarence Dillon properties.

Recalling the year of the Haut-Brion purchase, a memory springs to my mind. It is of the lunch given in 2005 to honor the fiftieth anniversary of Fernand Point's death. I was permitted to speak before an assembly of the fifty most famous chefs of France about a 1933 Haut-Brion. I was amazed by its intensity, this bouquet of cypress, turpentine, black macerated fruits, graphite. And with it, on the palate, an incredible thickness. There was genius in this wine.

Haut-Brion and Mission share an unusual history. It is also a history shared by the Delmas family: the grandfather of Jean-Philippe Delmas (Georges) was manager of Haut-Brion from 1923 to 1961, then his father (Jean-Bernard) until 2003. Jean-Philippe Delmas started at Haut-Brion in 1994. He is now the director of the Dillon family châteaux.

To describe Haut-Brion is to dig through the memory of Bordeaux. It also requires understanding the modern idea of wine. Haut-Brion evokes the idea of Urban Vineam. In any Gallo-Roman city, it was inconceivable not to have surrounding vineyards. Haut-Brion obviously quickly distinguished itself in terms of: quality, proximity to the port and a reputation in England. It made perfect sense that in the famous 1855 classification, it was present among the crus of Médoc.

BORDEAUX
Châteaux Haut-Brion & La Mission Haut-Brion

# The Wines

In early spring, at the invitation of Jean-Philippe Delma, it was a pleasant surprise to find myself at Haut-Brion with the Head of Cultivation, the Cellar Master, Sylvain Boivert (Council Director of 1855 crus classé) and Thierry.

## Tasting of March 11, 2014

**2010. Château La Mission Haut-Brion.** *This vintage makes up only 47% of the great wine sold under this label. Opaque garnet color, very dense. Closed nose, generous dense and deep. Fruity and tight attack. Relatively smooth. Very long finish with bold and fine tannins.*

**2010. Château Haut-Brion.** *This harvest yielded only 42% of the great wine in the Haut-Brion vineyard. Dense, opaque garnet color. The nose is complete, delicate and sensual. Note of spicy black fruit compote, woody, delicate. Silky and spherical mouth. Very high density, extremely long and sappy. Very good potential. A great 2010.*

**2009. Château La Mission Haut-Brion.** *Color as deep as the 2010. The nose is rich, dense, tight. Very young. The mouth is splendid in the attack, spherical, tight, very long and the finish exhilarating. A very good, relatively creamy 2009. A great Mission.*

**2009. Chateau Haut Brion.** *Opaque garnet color. Dense nose, delicate, complete and tight. Closed but is very deep and quite young. The mouth, ample, is rich and caught by a fine, tight tannic structure. Impressive. Very tight, long tannins. The power seems a bit generous in retro-olfaction.*

**2008. Château La Mission Haut-Brion.** *Bright garnet color. Open nose, fresh and delicate. Fruity, slightly tart. Note of crushed black currants. Very flattering and oceanic. The medium-bodied mouth possesses present and tense tannins. A classic and austere style unlike preceding vintages.*

**2008. Château Haut-Brion.** *Garnet color. Medium density, bright. The nose is open, flattering, rather woody. However, very fruity and fresh. Square and austere mouth of medium body, dense and sappy.*

**2007. Château La Mission Haut-Brion.** *Bright garnet color. Open, expressive nose, woody, pleasant, relatively fruity. In the mouth, soft and caressing attack, quite complete. However, the finish is of medium length.*

**2007. Château Haut-Brion.** *Garnet color of medium intensity. The nose is open and flattering. The finish, rather fruity. The oak is discreet. The mouth is soft and slender, with a discreet structure and a tender finish of rich and smooth tannins.*

**2006. Château La Mission Haut-Brion.** *Dense garnet color. Rich, powerful, concentrated nose, woody, licorice. Rather delicate. The mouth is compact, a bit extreme on the mid-palate, revealing slightly square tannins. At this stage, lacks charm. A bit heavy.*

**2006. Château Haut-Brion.** *Deep garnet color, brilliant. Closed nose, dense and concentrated, lacks charm for the moment. Wide and square mouth. It needs time. Reopen within 5 years.*

**2005. Château La Mission Haut-Brion.** *Opaque garnet color. Closed nose, nothing reduced. Concentrated, black fruity, spicy. The mouth is full, broad, structured. Beautiful tension. Long and serious. Delicate tannins. The whole is harmonious. A Mission built to withstand time.*

**2005. Château Haut-Brion.** *Opaque, garnet color. Open nose, dense and profound. Very pulpy. Notes of black fruits, frank, very elegant. Powerful mouth, spherical, highly refined tannins. An immense wine by its density combined with great finesse.*

**2004. Château La Mission Haut-Brion.** *Garnet color with medium density. The nose is open, delicate, fruity. The mouth is soft and fluid, somewhat easy, disappointing even. The tannins are a bit dry and supported at this stage by a dominant woodiness. Leave it quietly in the cellar and revisit in two to three years.*

**2004. Château Haut-Brion.** *Intense ruby color, slight sign of evolution. Open and accessible nose, fruity notes, spicy and animalistic. Somewhat surprising. After a soft attack, the mid-palate is revealed to be a bit thin. The finish is tannic, slightly dry at this stage. Revisit in time.*

**2003. Château La Mission Haut-Brion.** *Dense and opaque garnet color. An open, confit nose, exclusively spicy. The mouth is full, soft, with a supple mid-palate buffered by dry tannins in the finish that are not yet integrated.*

2003. Château Haut-Brion. *Dense, opaque ruby color. The nose is open, exotic and stewed, woody, solar, accessible, even exuberant. In the mouth, during the attack, a slight impression of sweetness and low acidity. On the other hand, slightly square tannic finish, losing its original charm. A great and massive wine.*

2001. Château La Mission Haut-Brion. *Ruby color, sign of evolution. Open nose, slightly vegetal, fruity. Fresh, quite simple nose. Mouth of medium body. Soft, the finish is nice and caressing. Ready at the time of tasting.*

2001. Château Haut-Brion. *Brilliant and striking ruby color. The nose is open, expressive, generous. Animalistic and fruity notes, spicy, pencil lead, smoky note. A dense nose. The mouth is smooth, expressive. Finish of delicate and easy tannins. A good length. Perfect today.*

2000. Château La Mission Haut-Brion. *Deep ruby color. Sappy and slightly open nose. Fruity and spicy. Already pleasant. A lot of potential. In the mouth, the polished structure of the tannins and depth give an impression of fullness in the finish. We are on the plateau of maturity. A remarkable wine, it will certainly keep long.*

2000. Château Haut-Brion. *Opaque ruby color. Open nose, dense and fruity, complex. The mouth is smooth, long and pulpy. Great fullness in the finish. A full and charming wine. Great potential.*

# Lunch on March 11, 2014, in Haut-Brion

Strips of monkfish with tartar sauce
*2009 Château La Mission Haut-Brion Blanc*
*2009 Château Haut-Brion Blanc*

Landes chicken on a spit, Vichy carrots, fingerlings gratin
*1998 Château La Mission Haut-Brion*
*1998 Château Haut-Brion*

Extra mature Mimolette cheese, Ossau-Iraty
*2005 Château La Tour Haut-Brion*

Chocolate cake, English cream
*Mocha coffee, Tesseron Cognac No 29*

## BORDEAUX
## Châteaux Haut-Brion & La Mission Haut-Brion

# Château Rauzan Ségla

*Renaissance Perfume*

# T

HE MARGAUX TERROIR
WAS BORN IN 1661,
with Pierre des Mesure de Rauzan. He bought this vineyard
from the Gassies family and gave it his name. It remained in
the same family until 1866. A share created a second property
in 1766, and it took the name of the last descendant of the family, Baroness
Ségla. Rausan Ségla became Rauzan Ségla during its last change of ownership in 1994. On that date, the Wertheimer family, owners of Chanel,
acquired the estate. They appointed John Kolasa, formerly from Château
Latour, as Head of the Château. He launched huge projects at full speed.
Everything was done to ensure that Rauzan Ségla found a place among the
Second-Crus Classé of 1855. The park and the château were renovated with
the intention of preserving the maximum number of historical elements that
the residence evokes. Benefitting from this approach, work also ensued  in
the vineyard buildings. In addition to the wineries, the fermenting room was
redesigned and completely rebuilt. It was then the vineyard's turn to be
renovated. Drains were installed to absorb an overflow of water in certain
parcel areas. In 1998, John grafted 3 hectares of Cabernet Sauvignon Merlot.
Grafting consists of changing the grape variety while retaining the existing
rootstocks. It diversifies the plantings, losing only a year and not six or seven
as is the case with grubbing-up. A rest period for the land must then be
considered before replanting, then another four years before harvesting the
grape that can integrated into a vintage. Added to these improvements were
arrangements for the 2004 harvest receptions, with more efficient sorting
tables, especially since the harvests are carried out through parcellary methods. This, in turn, helped to refine the blending of vintages and, lastly, the
breeding in the wine cellar.

# M

EMORIES
Here, I have no memory of a great dinner or lunch on the
grass. Nothing. I recall above all, with a touch of nostalgia,
the before and after of our tastings at Rauzan Ségla. Yet this
memory dates back only to the beginning of spring 2014. In
fact, in order to taste the primeur wine (wine futures) of Rauzan and other
surrounding châteaux, John Kolasa had invited us, with my faithful aide-

## BORDEAUX
### Château Rauzan Ségla

de-camp, Thierry, to stay at the château. So, we stayed there several nights. The site could not be quieter and further away from the road, seldom busy in any event. Beyond the cozy comfort of the rooms, our breakfasts and late evening returns stood out most in my memories.

Every evening, we would dine in a château to which we had come to taste the primeur wines. Our friend Sylvain Boivert would drive us back to Rauzan later. From the entrance gate to the heavy service door, we crossed a courtyard of crunching gravel, raked by invisible steps. We then reached the dimly lit large salon. On a small table near the cigar case, the housekeeper, before leaving, had placed two cut crystal glasses and a bottle of 1976 Bas-Armagnac from my friend Pierre Laberdolive. Of course, we barely had more than a drop (already thinking of the next day's tasting), but the consideration was charming, and I must admit that these moments of relaxation, during which we could review the day with Thierry, are rare among our countless trips together. I remember a time when he would always bring a flange of aged JM Rhum, which we would share in the evenings after dinner, unraveling the day and the wines tasted. In this salon floated a slightly outdated atmosphere, yet it was refined and classy. Works of art referring to the equestrian arts dear to the owners were tastefully scattered in the living rooms. Confidence in us was absolute, as during these hours we were left to ourselves in the château. I loved the hushed, quiet atmosphere. These annual transhumances that I (gladly) imposed on myself in Bordeaux have allowed me, over the years, to penetrate the heart of the Médoc art of living – a clarity of vision which helps me better understand the wines. With this sense in our core, John would join us during our breakfasts, dressed at times like a gentleman farmer. Dedicated to this purpose , a table was set in a dining room in front of our bay windows – one which looked towards the morning sun. The antique porcelain tableware seemed, like the silver, to have a soul. Do we have as much at the George V?

These moments allowed Thierry and me to escape before the very rhythmic first tastings of the day. At night, we would have a drink before getting back to our rooms – rooms found at the end of a long corridor with creaking floors smelling of wax and polish. Even the Persian rug seemed to glide. Life here is a dream.

# Tasting at the Château in March 2014

The blend is generally around 60% Cabernet Sauvignon and 40% Merlot.

**2011. Rauzan Ségla.** *Black color. Full nose. The mouth is sappy but austere. The wine is complete. Tight finish. A sappy vintage to be opened in at least 5 years.*

**2009.** *Rich and deep, very extroverted nose. Condensed fruit, explosive bouquet. Spherical and generous mouth. Rich tannins, lingering finish.*

**2005.** *Deep, luminous ruby color. Open nose, fruity, spicy, recalling mild tobacco. Elegance. The mouth is smooth and supple. The pulp is apparent. The tannins are rich and delicate for a sappy year. Wide and generous mouth with a full and tight mid-palate. Long finish. Very nice aging bottle.*

**2004.** *Deep garnet color. Rich and pulpy nose. Rich and square mouth, demonstrative. A full, sappy wine.*

**2001.** *Garnet color. Open nose, elegant, fruity, mentholated. The fruit stays fresh. The medium-body mouth is soft and elegant. The 2001 is balanced, long, delicious. Very balanced, successful.*

**1998.** *Color with signs of evolution. Open nose, spicy mild tobacco, fruity confit. Soft mouth with a massive structure, elegance.*

# Château Palmer

*A Diamond in the Shadows*

# V

ERY EARLY ON,
I WAS FASCINATED

by Palmer, its history, its wine, perhaps because of its rarity at the time when I started in the business in the 1980s. The first time I came across a Palmer was when Serge Dubs, head sommelier at L'Auberge de l'Ill, mentioned it in an article appearing in *L'Écho des somme-liers*; this was a few months after his winning the title of Best Sommelier of France. We were at the beginning of the 1980-1990 decade. For him, Palmer was the greatest of the Bordeaux. For me, a young cub in the world of wine, it was a word even more important than what he marvelously spoke of – a dream I wanted to attain.

Palmer was a name inherited in 1814 from a General Palmer, a Wellington Staff Officer, who bought the estate from Mme. de Gasq, the former name of the property. He passed it on to the Péreire family in 1853. It was the Péreire family who established the current château in its Second Empire style and which no one ever inhabited. In 1938, it again changed hands, and this time, it would be the last time. These hands belonged to the Sichel, Mälher Besse and Bouteiller families, who still preside over Palmer's fate.

For several years now I have had the opportunity to meet with Thomas Duroux, Palmer's Chief Operating Officer. A distinguished man, a polyglot. Thomas is the man behind the Palmer – his renovation making the premises function on a large international scale. This has earned him collective rec-ognition from the owners. He leads the work by putting his heart into it for future generations.

# M

EMORIES

I remember a pairing that took place during the literary eve-ning that we organized every month at the George V, con-necting an author and his latest book with a great estate. That night, we paired a sublime 1990 Imperial Palmer with a foie gras escalopes fried in Margaux, Timut pepper and chard braised in wine.

The most vivid memory, however, is of two magnums of 1998 Château Palmer shared at the restaurant Le Pharamond in the mid-2000s with the brigade of maitres d'hotel, one night after service. This restaurant is one of the few to have survived the demolition of the Halles quarter. The fact that the decor is classified certainly contributed to its preservation. At the time, the place was run by a friend Sylvain Lebardier, former sommelier of Louis Gadby, head of the Ami Louis. Accompanying these large bottles, Sylvain had prepared for us Charolais beef ribs with mushroom cassolettes and large English-cut fries. Following this dish, our friend still served us on a tableside the Centennial specialty of the place: tripe, Caen-style. The best I have eaten in Paris. As always at Le Pharamond, we were treated to the most delicious of desserts: hot butter madeleines, with crispy edges, accompanied by a creamy caramel ice cream. And a lovely yellow VEP Chartreuse!

This was the only night of the year where I could find myself with the maitres d'hotel and the directors of Le Cinq. That night, surrounding me were Patrice Jeanne, Christophe Kelsch, Eric Koszyczarz, Jeremy Évrard, Olivier Legros, Frank Clinchamp, Frank Painchaud and Ghislain Chabaille.

BORDEAUX
Château Palmer

# The Wines

Let's talk about this amazing Margaux wine. Here, the proportion of Merlot is rather unusual for the Margaux appellation. At Palmer, the Merlot percentage is generally around 45 to 55%, shared with the Cabernet Sauvignon, the few remaining percentages being reserved for the Petit Verdot. That being said, this choice in the varietal creates this pulpy, sensual side, characteristic of Palmer. It retains pulp and texture for a long time. Merlots have a depth, an unparalleled structure on the left bank. At La Poularde, I had many 1970-1980 Palmers, but I was stuck on these from 1959 and 1961, which remained for me special vintages, where the fruit is matched only by the depth of the finish of an indeterminable length.

Of course, those we serve in the dining room of Le Cinq are more precise than the 1970-1980 years (apart from the excellent 1983). The 1995 and 1998 now work wonderfully with a braised lamb shoulder in a well-reduced jus.
Recent vintages produced by the Thomas Duroux team are remarkable. Then, there is this touch of Petit Verdot so maligned and dismissed, like a convict in Cayenne, from major projects and great works. And yet! The latter has resurfaced for some time under the guise of a distant uncle, a kind of messiah.
Reflecting its label, Palmer lives often in the shadow of other names of its appellation, yet such a diamond, it flickers when a ray of light shines upon it.

## Vintages of Château Palmer Tasted in 2013

**2010.** *One of the very good bottles of the vintage. The nose is deep and dense. The climate again made this year a little warm, but this time the mouth at the finish has a large structure. Needs to wait at least ten years. Grand and sophisticated!*

**2009.** *Palmer is powerful here, opulent, full, maybe a little warm? Finally, yes, a 2009! That said, everything is here, so we'll have fun when the time comes to open it.*

**2008.** *A creamy, dense wine, produced from low yields, balanced. And in this vintage,* *it was and remains a very good price/quality ratio.*

**2007.** *We return to a more flexible Palmer like most of 2007. The extractions were milder during vinification, so as to mitigate the most unique aspects of this delicate vintage. The fruit here is slightly tart. The finish 'crisp'.*

**2006.** *A Palmer more tense than long. Corseted at this stage. The fruit is seductive, with slightly marked graphite notes. The mouth, savory, is fresh. Less demonstrative than in 2005.*

**2005.** *Deep, full, a success with a kirsched nose, a little 'Burgundy'. A great Palmer, too young today, very long, perfect balance.*

**2004.** *A Palmer for a great table today. This is what I often call a 'half-body'. Namely, a gourmet wine but without the charisma of a great vintage. A fun wine. Here, fruity, elegant, unpretentious, medium length, agreeable*

**2003.** *At the first approach, we perceive all at once licorice, white truffle, menthol, an exotic touch. The whole taste is*

*elegant. To drink now and within five years.*

**2002.** *Good management of rapid concentration. The whole is coherent but without the harmony of the 2001.*

**2001.** *With 44% Merlot, a lot of elegance. Less pulpy than the 2000, but mentholated, fresh. Such style! The mouth is caressing. Delicious at the moment.*

**2000.** *A complete wine, full mouth, needs to wait and must be decanted.*

# Château Margaux

*The Margaux Club of Five*

T O ME THIS APPELLATION
OF 1,400 HECTARES
whispers elegance and refinement. And it is not because we named our eldest daughter Margot! Incidentally, these characteristics have been recognized since 1855, when the château was honored to represent the appellation in the famous Club of Five, which were the first Crus Classé (there were only four at the time).

This terroir, located south of the Médoc, is one of the best examples of 100% (or nearly) Cabernet Sauvignon. I was able to set foot for the first time on the property at the time of the global competition. It was thanks to Paul Pontalier, who started in Margaux in 1983 and became its general manager, a position he retained until his death in March 2016, at 59. Paul Pontallier, the general manager, agreed to play along with the TV crew to have me (of course, with the permission of Mme. Corinne Mentzelopoulos, the owner of the estate). When the special delegation team drew up the program for this show, on such a compelling topic – the competition for the 1998 World's Best Sommelier – I naturally thought of Margaux, as I had contacted Paul to visit his property in Chile that he managed with Bruno Prats, owner of Cos d'Estournel at the time. So, the appointment was made. We went to the château, where I could not help but be impressed in front of this neoclassical building. I was still a young sommelier. Later, thanks to Jacques Dupont and Sylvain Boivert, I would be involved in the primeurs tastings each year.

M EMORIES
The pace of the tastings with Jacques Dupont is always intense. But the time spent at the table is always exceptional. In this context, we had in 2010 the rare privilege of lunching in Margaux with Corinne and Paul. Here, as at Le Cinq, our adage always works: 'Great House, no hesitation!' It's the least you can say when you are greeted with a glass of 1998 Krug Clos du Mesnil. There were four of us surrounding our hosts. In the Empire style of this abode, particularly in this salon of beige and honey tones, this great champagne was proof of its distinction. With lobster and eggplant and mushroom duxelles, we savored a 1995 Pavillon Blanc. The Blanc is produced from 90% Semillon and 10% Sauvignon.

I always prefer it in a cool year, cold even. In fact, although located beside the Château Bel Air Marquis d'Aligre on the limestone plateau, it is often very rich. This 1995 is no exception and reveals a golden yellow color. The classic nose of pollen and wax blends with notes of citrus. This Pavillon is wider than it is long. Afterwards, two Château Margaux accompanied the rack of lamb and vegetable stew: a 1996 and a 1982 in magnums. The 1996 vintage was just beginning to speak. Black fruit and truffles dominated its bouquet. But the structure remained imposing, contrasting with the 1982's perfect coolness and length. I have often been wary of this bottled vintage, with frequent disillusionment due to premature evolution.

BORDEAUX
Château Margaux

# The Wines

The property offers four labels:
— The Grand Vin is resolutely the quintessence (30% of production).
— The second, the Pavillon Rouge, is always a lovely maturity to experience. A lot of grace in this wine, especially in 2000.
— The Pavillon Blanc (90% Sauvignon Blanc and 10% Semillon). I have often complained of the Médoc white wines that have no appeal other than their rarity. Well, the Pavillon Blanc is a case apart. Let's just say that its richness is sinful.
— And, since the 2009 vintage, the Margaux of Château Margaux.

## Tasting at the Château Margaux in 2014

**2010. Château Margaux.** *Opaque garnet color. Closed nose, fruity, uninspiring at this stage. Long and smooth mouth, without great length. Great finesse. The whole is remarkable. The most classic and of an incredible breed.*

**2009.** *Same depth of color as the 2010. The nose conveys some very seductive oriental fragrances. A nose of great body, a lot of depth supported by this unwavering, creamy sensation of ripe fruit. Such brilliance! The mouth does not disappoint. The volume is incredible, the tannin concentration is impressive. Such length! Certainly the château's greatest vintage in twenty years.*

**2008.** *Bright garnet color. The nose is closed, fresh, mentholated, with hints of sour fruit of discreet undergrowth. Elegance. The mouth confirms this impression with a sharp attack that evolves by undergoing a beautiful tension. The finish of the mouth is long and slender. A sharp and Jansenist Margaux.*

**2007.** *Deep ruby color. Fruity, mentholated nose, slightly woody, open and delicate. Soft mouth without dips. Average length but elegant. Delicate and subtle tannins. Example of a great wine in a climatically difficult year. The sorting was lucrative, no flaw. This is not a mythical wine but it offers a real consistency of touch with a proportion of very light Merlot. An amiable wine, voluptuous and sensual.*

**2006.** *Bright ruby color. The nose is closed and delicate. It evokes blackberry, cherry and sandalwood. The whole is cool, sharp and dense. Without extravagance. The mouth is full but slender and long. In terms of flavor, the barrel still dominates. This vintage reminds me of the 1986, but more modern and with less Merlot. It needs more time.*

2005. *The nose remains a classic. The fruit is expressed in its fullness without being obstructed by the woodiness. The mouth coats the palate, remains dense and finishes in a peacock tail. A complete wine. Reminiscent of the 2009 and 2010. However, it has an extra freshness and this perfect balance with incredible length.*

2004. *Bright ruby color. Open nose, slightly softer fruitiness than its less flattering successors. The Merlot gives it a juiciness I don't care for. However, the taste profile conveys somewhat severe tannins, long but a little square. In conclusion, a wine to drink now or within three years.*

2003. *In this case, the terroir concept carries some weight, for in a year as solar as 2003, I have not really felt the stewed fruit. On the contrary, the color remains opaque and ruby. The nose is fruity, with notes of spiced jelly. The mouth is sensual in the attack and then tightens in the finish, creating a welcome relief. It is a success for 2003. It can be enjoyed now.*

Regarding the aromas, it should be noted:

– *The fruits that characterize most Margaux are undoubtedly the black cherry and sweet almond, evolving towards cedar and pencil lead – graphite.*
– *These aromas were present in the greatest wines of the estate that I remember having tasted. I think with emotion of a magnum of 1900 Château Margaux and, later, a 1959. Both vintages were still fresh and complex. A touch of camphorated cedar mixed with macerated red fruits, tannins of a superb delicacy and that signature graphite.*

# Château Léoville Barton

*Family Home*

# T

HE SAINT-JULIEN
APPELLATION

covers about 910 hectares and includes few domains, of which only eleven are Grand Crus Classé. First. Léoville Barton – 45 hectares – is one of five Second Crus Classé, while Langoa Barton – nearly 20 hectares – is a Third Cru Classé. These châteaux have been owned by the Barton family, since 1821 for Langoa and 1826 for Léoville, the latter property being issued from the great Léoville estate which belonged to Alexandre de Gascq and included, at the time, the three current Léoville estates: Barton, Las Cases and Poyferré.

Since 1983, Anthony Barton has been at the helm of the châteaux, with his daughter, Lilian Barton-Sartorius, at his side. Situated somewhat north of the St. Julien appellation, the vineyards of the châteaux, rather fragmented and intermingled with their neighbors, are close to the Gironde estuary. They lie on rather hard gravel covering a base of clay.

It should also be noted that the Bartons are among the last owners of Médoc Crus classé to reside there throughout the year, a further proof (if any was needed) of their commitment to this vineyard. Mme. Eva Barton, her husband Anthony and their daughter Lilian, who also manages Langoa Barton, live in the château.

For me, Léoville Barton ranks among the temple guardians of Saint-Julien and, more broadly, of Médoc. Château vintages such as the 2000 and 2005 are the peaks of the appellation, the perfect reflection of this terroir.

One detail: among the topics which no one will remember from all the tastings in my company over the years, there is one – incongruous, to say the least– which, I am sure, will stick. My *spit*, as the English say. In a word, the jet of tasted wine that is spat after extracting the quintessence in the mouth. Quite a few people stain themselves during this perilous exercise. In my case, the jet is clean and bright, projected like a sword blow. Woe to whoever is too close to the spittoon when I get started… They know who they are, and I offer all my apologies for these 'projections'… But every time, he or she leaves with a beautiful 'stain' from a big name!

During one lunch – which I will discuss later – we entered the château from the garden side at the end of our tasting in the cellar. As we walked along the border of these magnificent flowerbeds, we inquired about the number of gardeners needed to maintain these masterpieces. Anthony Barton thought for a moment, contemplating the park, and said, 'There are three… and a half'. To our dazed and interrogative looks, he added, with his wonderful humor but in a more serious tone, 'Actually, we have four gardeners, but the fourth is so inconspicuous that we count him as half'. This was, again, a testament to his warmth.

# MEMORIES

In April 2011, we had the privilege of being invited to eat with M. and Mme. Barton at their château. From the aperitif in the salon, the tone was set by the 1990 Laurent-Perrier Grand Siècle (exceptional, and a rarity of such that I barely remember it!). Having expressed my happiness at tasting this sublime wine with our hostess, at her signal, a second bottle immediately appeared, prolonging further this fleeting moment of bliss.

At the table, the wines were served blind. We were surprised by their freshness. In a word, not one of us could distinguish the good vintage!

The dishes, presented French-style (the guests serve themselves using cutlery service), were welcome, forming beautiful pairings. What a site! As a restaurateur, I had never seen so much refinement on a table. Near the cutlery, each one of us had for our enjoyment a tiny crystal boat set in silver containing salt flowers and a delicate pepper mill of the same metal, equally discreet. Everything there was so that everyone would be as happy as possible.

BORDEAUX
Château Léoville Barton

# March 2014 Tasting

In the presence of Mme. Barton-Sartorius, the daughter, and on a second occasion, of M. Sartorius and their daughter (Anthony Barton's granddaughter).

**2012.** *Château Mauvesin Barton. A recently acquired property. It covers almost 40 hectares in the Moulis appellation in Médoc. The wine tasted is endowed with charm, gourmet and maturing.*

**2005.** *Château Langoa-Barton. Great success. Nose in a secondary register. Spice, macerated fruit. Sappy mouth. Tannins still tight in the finish. The nose seems more evolved than the mouth.*

*Regarding the blending, in Léoville Barton, it is generally 72% Cabernet Sauvignon, 20% Merlot and 8% Cabernet Franc. The vinification involves a great deal of classicism, with a wooden fermenting room and, above all, a will to not produce wine extracts. The great wine is aged 50% in new wood and 50% in 1-year-old wood.*

**2012. Château Léoville Barton.** *Silky, refined, delicate and lacy wine. At this stage, a slight sample of wood. Voluptuous, beautiful seed, superb.*

**2010.** *Powerful and delicate, a great success. Still the refined style of Barton. Delicate, spicy, beautiful seed of very delicate tannins. Serious and sophisticated. No alcoholic impression.*

**2009.** *September 23rd harvest. During vinification, extractions were well proportioned. The seeds of the tannins are very delicate. Not overripe, lacy. No drought, greater rainfall, finesse, delicacy. Great Barton success. Very deep.*

**2008.** *Here we find a classic vintage, fruity, slightly tart, with a touch of firm oak. To be preserved for the time being (at least four years). Great elegance.*

**2007.** *No vegetal aspect here. Slight note of cooked spinach, all the same. Beautiful fruit. Mouth: very good acidity. Some chewiness, not too much wood, a certain thickness, some material. To be served immediately.*

**2006.** *A more classic vintage in its definition, in the spirit of the 1996 and 1988. Fresh, spicy, tight, needs more time. It will develop upon maturity the complex bouquet of cedar and blackberry jelly. Still austere today.*

**2005.** *Léoville is actually rounder, fuller, chewy and present. A great, sappy wine, pulpy, and still very tight. A lot of freshness is felt. At this stage of evolution, don't let its sensations be filtered. 'It's starting to be amiable'. Tender attack, intense nose, tannins of a tight seed, dense.*

**2004.** *Here is a Barton vintage that we serve at Le Cinq, particularly during business lunches. The tannins are without great power. The woodiness is slightly blended. Nonetheless, there is a nice, long finish. After the 2003 Vintage that had dried up the plant, the 2004 was a great yield. Here, the nose appears more evolved than the mouth. Good density. The wine still has tension and present tannins.*

**2003.** *This is the year of density, of rich and ripe juices. But, here again, thanks to the choice of judicious early harvests, the result is remarkable. Even though many observers agree – myself included – that 2003 was marked by the overmaturation of grapes, Barton has an additional finesse. To drink now by decanting 1 hour before.*

**2002.** *Here again, we are in the presence of a vintage for which Anthony has chosen a low extraction during pressings, ensuring*
*Barton gets a fine and delicate style. To drink now.*

**2001.** *Not very intense color. Nose of marked truffle. A deep, sappy wine. The flexibility index is high and, what's more, the wine is complete. Delicious, to drink now. A stunning bottle.*

**2000.** *A great model of elegance thanks to a freshness preserved through early harvests. The wine is all the more digestible, and the tension of the tannins is dazzling. It will take it a good fifteen years to reach supreme happiness.*

**1999.** *Château Léoville Barton. Open nose, fruity, expressive. Mouth with beautiful material. Spicy and macerated fruit. At this stage, I would pair it with braised meat, with succulence. A Bordelaise beef cheek.*

**1996.** *A wine with a lot of tension, chewiness, freshness, savoriness.*

# Château Batailley

*President Castéja*

**B**ATAILLEY IS
ONE OF THE PEARLS
of the wine necklace composed of Crus of which Philippe
Castéja has charge; even more, he feels a duty to impart this
knowledge to the next generation. Noble principle. Rare today.
Beyond the walls of this Batailley domain in Pauillac, he also represents the
Council of 1855 Crus Classé, a sort of plenipotentiary ambassador of these
vineyards that also form part of our country's prestige.

Philippe Castéja is the head of this beautiful property of 58 hectares, where
the clay is more discreet but where the wines acquire shading through the
years, a sublime balance, therefore not losing any aging potential. The wines
of Batailley remain classics in plantings, with a significant proportion of
Cabernet (67%). More precisely, they are parcellary vinifications – each laid
within small tanks, an elaborate process that better helps in understanding
the full potential of this terroir. The winery has gained elegance, while still
retaining its well-structured system.

**M**EMORIES
Among the great table moments which I preserve as my
fondest memories are the lunches in Batailley. Here, within
the rich decor of a familial past upon which each generation
made their mark upon without erasing the contributions of
the former, we are exposed to more than a century of a great Bordeaux
family's life. It is in these places that we still encounter a rare and otherwise
endangered noble class: the domestic servant.

To better visualize the faithful maitre d'hotel of the place, think piously
of the memorable performance of Robert Dalban (Jean) in *Les Tontons
flingueurs*, by Georges Lautner, and there you have it. Better than anyone,
he knows what it is needed at the precise moment it is needed, foreseeing
each stage of lunch so that the sequence of dishes and wines unfolds perfectly. Believe me, few of our restaurants and dining rooms could boast such
service.

Though not devoid of comfort, the salons and the dining room are of
intimate proportions, favoring hushed discussions befitting the tasting of

great wines  the very same that the civilized householder chose with discretion after consulting the family's Head Chef. A protocol throughout.

It is certainly at this table that I tasted the best Lamprey à la Bordelaise. Especially alongside a 1949 Batailley, an anthology that surprised us with its freshness. We also had a 1949, 1959 and 1961, all outstanding. Intense colors. The 1959 evoked cedar, black currant jelly.

### Lunch on April 7, 2009, at the Château

Asparagus with Mousseline Sauce

~

Beef Filet with Périgueux Sauce

~

Small Seasonal Vegetables

~

Cheese Platter

~

Chantilly Strawberries

~

*Champagne Pol Roger Brut*
*2005 Château Lynch-Moussas*
*1995, 1989, 1962, 1955 Château Batailley*
*1997 Château d'Yquem*

BORDEAUX
Château Batailley

# March 2014 Château Batailley Tasting

The synthesis of Batailley terroirs is based on slightly calcareous limestone soils with deep gravel.

**2013.** *(Sample from barrel). 95% Cabernet Sauvignon and 5% Merlot. Deep color. Preservation of fruit in nose. A wine saved from the waters. This is the first 2013 that I tasted this year in Bordeaux.*

**2012.** *80% Cabernet Sauvignon, 18% Merlot, 1% Cabernet Franc, 1% Petit Verdot. Intense color, medium depth. Nose of red fruits. The mouth is wide and gourmet, surrounds a downy structure. A relatively sexy and pleasing wine.*

**2011.** *85% Cabernet Sauvignon, 11% Merlot with Cabernet Franc and Petit Verdot. For this vintage, 38 hectoliters per hectare. Opaque garnet color, modern nose. Smooth, charming mouth. Woody, delicate, slight sweetness supported by its maturation. A serious and strong wine. To wait.*

**2010.** *78% Cabernet Sauvignon, 19% Merlot, 2% Cabernet Franc, 1% Petit Verdot. A vintage where the summer was very dry. Deep garnet color. Powerful nose, intense, a clear vintage, black fruit, solar sensation. High-density mouth, square but developed structure. Very good length. A long-keeping wine.*

**2009.** *74% Cabernet Sauvignon; 22% Merlot. Almost black color, deep. Rich and powerful nose. Concentrated, ripe, spicy notes, long and still closed. The mouth is full and sappy. Large. Not frosted. Wait another ten years.*

**2008.** *Deep garnet color. Opaque and intense. Expressive nose, fresh, slightly mentholated and fruity. Recalls fresh red fruit. Still a bit monolithic. Requires aging. Will evolve into graphite and cedar. In the mouth, a classic flavor profile is expressed, ample and fresh, with a charming fruit. Good length, at a level fitting its classification. Beautiful Fifth Growth. A classic vintage, fresh, elegant, structured. The woodiness is present and delicate. The selection work is felt.*

**2007.** *This was a complicated vintage requiring a lot of work in terms of extractions. The nose is floral, fruity, open. The mouth remains supple and smooth. Slightly fluid. A vintage to drink with pleasure.*

BORDEAUX
Château Batailley

2006. *70% Cabernet Sauvignon,*
*28% Merlot. Year benefitted from*
*the new fermenting room. Bright*
*garnet color. Profound, open and*
*delicate nose. Spicy, the woodiness*
*is integrated and delicate. Mouth*
*has average body. Boosted, however,*
*by a tonic acidity. Ripe and delicate*
*tannins. A serious wine, to be*
*decanted.*

2005. *73% Cabernet Sauvignon,*
*23% Merlot. Black garnet color,*
*dense. Full nose, delicate, firm,*
*fruity dominance, spicy, touch*
*of camphor. Full mouth, sappy.*
*Tannins present, delicate. Very nice*
*work on the extractions. A complete*
*and balanced wine. It deserves*
*a great maturing. This is a great*
*year for Batailley. A grand bottle,*
*sublime. Complicated vintage.*
*Demands extraction work.*
*A dense, powerful, perfect wine.*
*It has everything and more. A very*
*great, sublime bottle.*

2004. *69% Cabernet Sauvignon,*
*26% Merlot. Slightly degraded garnet*
*color. Open nose, nice intensity, sharp and*
*delicate. Heavy fruit. Discreet woodiness.*
*Relatively soft mouth. A flattering, clear*
*wine. Ready to be served.*

2003. *72% Cabernet Sauvignon,*
*24% Merlot and 2% Petit Verdot,*
*Cabernet Franc. First vintage of the*
*current cellar master who arrived ten*
*days before the beginning of the harvest.*
*Ruby color. Note of evolution. Open,*
*fruity nose, exotic, mentholated camphor.*
*Pleasant. Smooth and sensual mouth.*
*Relatively discreet acidity. Beautiful*
*preservation of the vintage despite a*
*severe climatic context that could have*
*quickly overripened.*

2002. *Last vintage from Philippe Castéja's*
*father (still residing in Batailley). Garnet*
*color, signs of evolution. Open, fruity*
*nose, delicate, pleasing. Soft mouth,*
*consensual. A juicy wine of medium*
*length. To be immediately consumed.*

# The following notes were taken during lunches

between 2011 and 2014 at the Château Batailley.

**1962.** *Still intense color. Ruby hue. Healthy, sumptuous bouquet, cigar box. The mouth is fruitier, velvety texture. Long and harmonious. Elegant vintage with good acidity that is rarely seen at tables today, as it was overshadowed early on by the success of 1961.*

**1961.** *Ruby color with orange reflections. Beautiful brilliance. Open nose, dense, tertiary, complex and delicate. Spicy and woody dominance (cedar, shoe polish, black truffle). A lot of charisma. The mouth is full, dense and elegant. Smoothed out and velvety tannins, velvety patina. Retro of fruit compote, leather. Mentholated. A great wine at perfect maturity, to be served with delicacy.*

**1959.** *Evolving, browning color. The nose is marked by notes of fruit in brandy, spicy, leather. The mouth still offers a certain charm, slightly velvety, delicate. It fades discreetly.*

**1955.** *Clear, evolved ruby hue. Nose of macerated black fruit, cedar, mild tobacco, slightly camphorated. The mouth is fleshy, with a beautiful spine. Fine length. It's a vintage rarely spoken of today, highly regarded for many years.*

**1949.** *This is the third post-war vintage together with the 1945 and 1947. Ruby, browning color, evolved. Open nose, tertiary, noble woodiness, truffled, spicy. The mouth is wide, soft, balanced. Great allure for its age.*

# Château Lynch-Bages

*Masterpiece of Cazes*

# I

N THE MID-
1980s,
I discovered the wines of the property thanks to Steven Spurrier and the tastings organized in Berryer City. This was the era of Blu Fox and the magazine *L'Amateur de Bordeaux*. It was through a client-friend that I was able to approach the domain. This occurred during one of my trips to Brazil, where I was traveling as part of a George V presentation with the marketing management related to operations with potential hotel customers – first, during the time of Didier Le Calvez, then alongside Christopher W. Norton. It was during one of these trips that I met Sergio Mendes. Today, the celebrity has been a friend of the Cazes for thirty years. A great photo in the Lynch-Bages tasting room attests to this. Throughout the 1980s, Sergio was at the piano in the vineyards during the harvests, surrounded by the Cazes family and a team of pickers, incredulous and delighted.

Among the Médoc properties that shine, not by their classification, but by their wines, and above all by the men who run them, there is Lynch-Bages. Lynch-Bages, in addition to strong wines and great aging potential, has very loyal customers. Its location is outstanding: in the heart of Pauillac, on the Blages plateau overlooking Pontet-Canet. The blend is almost solely composed of Cabernet Sauvignon on this clay-gravel. It provides wonders. So, of course, this 1855 Classification Premium was first a handicap. Yet this Fifth Cru is now considered as a Second. Jean-Michel's father did not compromise on quality. Now his son has taken the reins. He has found his place in no time. One of my clients and friends had asked me to organize a visit to Bordeaux, and I planned a dinner at Cordeillan Bages, at the time when Thierry Marx still managed the kitchens. This trip remains memorable because I was able to introduce my friend Tor Peterson to Jean-Michel.

BORDEAUX
Château Lynch-Bages

# M EMORIES

How could I forget this lunch in 2004 – so complicated to organize – which brought together such dynamic protagonists? It is thanks to Roxane Debuisson, the only woman in Paris who has helped me with unfailing generosity. She took care of so many things. The magnum of 1990 Dom Ruinart Blanc de Blancs was already chilling under the arches of the Place des Vosges, at the entrance to the Ambroisie. In addition, Mme. Pacaud and Bernard, the lucky chef, were also present with the three of us: Didier Le Calvez, Philippe Legendre and myself. An incredible restaurant that had still survived amidst four years of tension in the George V.

My friend Pierre Le Moulec came to me to take over, pointing out that there remained a magnum of 1990 Lynch-Bages. I knew the bottle well, and I needed the aid of Bacchus for such a complex lunch. I admit it fulfilled its duty with Bernard Pacaud's truffle salad and lobster stew. We finished with a chocolate tart of incredible creaminess, served, as usual, with an aged malt. Whiskey and chocolate: a love match. Before letting Bernard leave to play Pétanque on the Place des Vosges with his friends. I'll remember this scene all my life. I touched the hand of major actors in the art of entertaining and cooking *à la française*; I cannot but thank Roxane who knew so early on how to help me with Philippe's recommendations, accommodating me for four months in her garret room and waking me every morning to the sound of the Republican Guard's trumpet, whose quarters were in front of the building.

# Tasting in Lynch-Bages in March 2014

**2009.** *Lynch-Bages. Intense garnet color, opaque. Delicate nose, full, spicy, ripe and generous. Dense and sweet in the attack. Present and delicate tannins. Opulent and solar finish. Great aging potential. Remarkable.*

**2006.** *Bright garnet color. Open nose, mineral, green reflection. On the nose, notes of pencil lead, black fruits, truffled. Very complete. The mouth is tight, full and sappy. Long. The slightly crisp acidity brings out the square tannins. It is the first vintage of Nicolas, cellar master, and Jean-Charles Cazes.*

**2001.** *Ruby color, touch of evolution, browning, good brilliance. Open nose, complex, tertiary, notes of leather, truffle, macerated fruits, cedar and cigar box. Sensual mouth, smooth, creamy, round and spherical mid-palate. Nice length. A vintage where the reflectivity in the vineyard was important. A Lynch-Bages of medium depth to serve with a braised meat or a stew of game birds.*

**2000.** *Darker, opaque color. Severe nose, delicate, pulpy and generous. Marked black fruits. Full and fleshy mouth, buttery and long tannins, complete, massive even. Very long finish. A great Lynch-Bages to reopen within 5 years.*

*As Daniel, the former cellar master, said: 'It's not a big fake!' A wine that I envision very well with a large ribbed steak on vine shoots and a Cabernet sauce.*

**1996.** *Evolved color. Open color, delicate, truffled, tertiary, with notes of mocha and licorice. The woodiness is delicate and complex. The mouth is full and sappy, very elegant, nice finish. An elegant and consensual Lynch-Bages.*

**1995.** *Deep ruby color. Some signs of evolution. Closed nose, delicate, concentrated. Notes of red fruit, licorice. Mentholated notes. On the reserve. Smooth mouth with aromatic freshness on the mid-palate, recalling camphor and blackcurrant leaf. Long finish highlighted by austere, slightly square tannins. Jean-Charles tells me of a high water stress in August. At this stage, the vintage appears somewhat on the inside, or folded in on itself.*

**1990.** *Intense ruby color, evolved. Open nose, full, complex, with notes of wild blackberry, truffled. Sensual. Great richness and deep nose. Full and rich mouth. Delicate and rich tannins. Very long. Mineral retro and dry floral. Still a great success. Especially since I don't feel* any presence of 'bret'. Behind this contraction hides what can in wines be the unpleasant animal odors of leather, stables, sweat or horse urine. The organism responsible for this is often a yeast of the Brettanomyces type.

**1989.** *Evolved, ruby color. Open nose, delicate and generous. Recalling spicy fruit and truffles. Notes of cocoa, camphor. The mouth is very smooth on the attack, moving towards a concentrated mid-palate, dense, without softness. The tannins have calmed and bring snap and great length. Great wine. Retro-olfaction recalling woody boletus. This 1989 must wait until ready. It seems to me a monument upon which the veil is still in place. It awaits inauguration.*

**1986.** *Intense ruby color, open nose, delicate, complex, tertiary. Licorice, graphite, black currant compote, eucalyptus, dried mint. Powerful. We sense a great Cabernet Sauvignon in line with those of his father in the 1970s! Wide mouth, smooth, very complete. Great wine.*

**1985.** *Evolved, ruby color. Delicate nose with fruity notes, dried plant. The Cabernet Sauvignon is characterized by its slightly vegetal, pharmacopoeial aspect. The nose seems tired for this bottle. The mouth with a soft attack is released mid-palate. A little flat in the finish.*

**1982.** *Intense ruby color, black even! Open nose, rich, delicate and complex, tertiary, with original notes recalling tar and licorice, black fruit compote, spices, mild tobacco. The mouth is full, generous and still tight. The wine is dense. Such youth at 34 years! The mouth's finish with a touch of tannins recalls taffeta. A great wine, still young. Exceptional.*

# Château Mouton Rothschild

*Living collection*

I T WAS IN THE COMPANY OF THE ASSOCIATION OF SOMMELIERS of France and under the guidance of Hervé Valverde, a Bordeaux native and renowned sommelier, that I first discovered the Château Mouton Rothschild in 1985. We visited several châteaux, including that of the two Blondin brothers in charge of winemaking at Mouton Rothschild, where Raoul Blondin greeted us. During these first forays to Mouton, I was fascinated by the longneck carafes of Baccarat crystal that were encircled with red waiter's cloth to prevent drops of wine from spilling on the tablecloths. The vintages presented were 1978 and 1979. I was introduced, upon his arrival, to Baron Philippe de Rothschild, a nobleman who devoted body and soul to Mouton. He has been the source of his family property's rebirth – a property which Nathaniel de Rothschild acquired back in 1853. This first visit to Mouton Rothschild encouraged me to seek and purchase some of the domain's vintages (starting from 1988) for La Poularde in Montrond which I could immediately serve. Through a broker close to the Château, I was able to see wines by the glass from 1971, 1975, 1978, 1979 and 1982 quickly appear on the menu. I recently tasted 1961 and 1962. They revealed the intense efforts of the Baron to become a classified First Cru, which occurred in 1973 thanks to Jacques Chirac, then the Minister of Agriculture. The terroir deserved it.

Several years after the classification change, the partnership with Robert Mondavi that created Opus One in California, the commercial policy of Mouton Cadet, and the export to the United States of the ex-second wine, great vintages were still being produced. The 1986, for example, was graded at 100% for its rigor by Robert Mondavi. Alongside it, the 1988, 1989 and 1990 are success stories. However, it seems to me that there could have been more concentration and precision. After the death of Baron Philippe in 1987, Philippine, his only daughter, devoted herself to the family estate. After Patrick Léon (from the great Maison Georges Duboeuf), Philippe Dhalluin, then Head of Château Ducru-Branaire in Saint-Julien, shifted mentalities and methods and restored it to First Level.

The property extends over 80 hectares on the Pouyalet plateau, wedged between Lafite and Pontet-Canet. The vineyard is planted with more than 80% Cabernet Sauvignon. So much so that in 2012 this vine accounted for

90% of the Grand Vin (top wine). The rest is planted with Merlot and Petit Verdot. Since 1993, the second wine, Petit Mouton, had carried a Jean Carlu-style label from 1924. A second wine was needed. The selection of lesser-grade parcels went towards Baron Nathaniel, a trading wine. There is substance to shape this second wine. Worthy of the Pauillac First Growth.

It is impossible to ignore the cultural and artistic character of the property, housing a remarkable wine museum built by Baron Philippe and Pauline Fairfax Potter, his second and much adored American wife. Of a sentimental disposition, she was a poet and translator of Shakespeare, Marlowe, Christopher Foy and *La nuit a sa clarté*, a romantic drama played by Madeleine Renaud at the Odéon in the 1970s. Julien de Beaumarchais, the youngest son of Philippine, displayed the allure of a young Prince of Vines, in encyclopedic culture. He was the source of a beautiful book on Mouton Rothschild published by the National Printing-House, a virtual masterpiece of Bordeaux wine history.

In the early twentieth century, Phillipe Dhalluin made considerable efforts; he managed to have Philippine approve a percentage for the Grand Vin that was increasingly low – the key to a great Bordeaux wine. Serious work on minerality, precision and length were performed. Since 1988, a true identity has been found in Mouton.

## MEMORIES
**A dinner in Mouton, April 6, 2009**

Nage of the Sea
Roasted Beef Tenderloin
Anna Potatoes
Mushrooms Forestier
Apple Pie

~

*2005 Aile d'argent*
*1999 Château d'Armailhac*
*1996 Le Petit Mouton de Mouton Rothschild in magnum*
*1947 Mouton Rothschild*
*1898 Château Coutet*
*Vieille Prune from the domain of Le Cassis de la Baronne...*

# BORDEAUX
## Château Mouton Rothschild

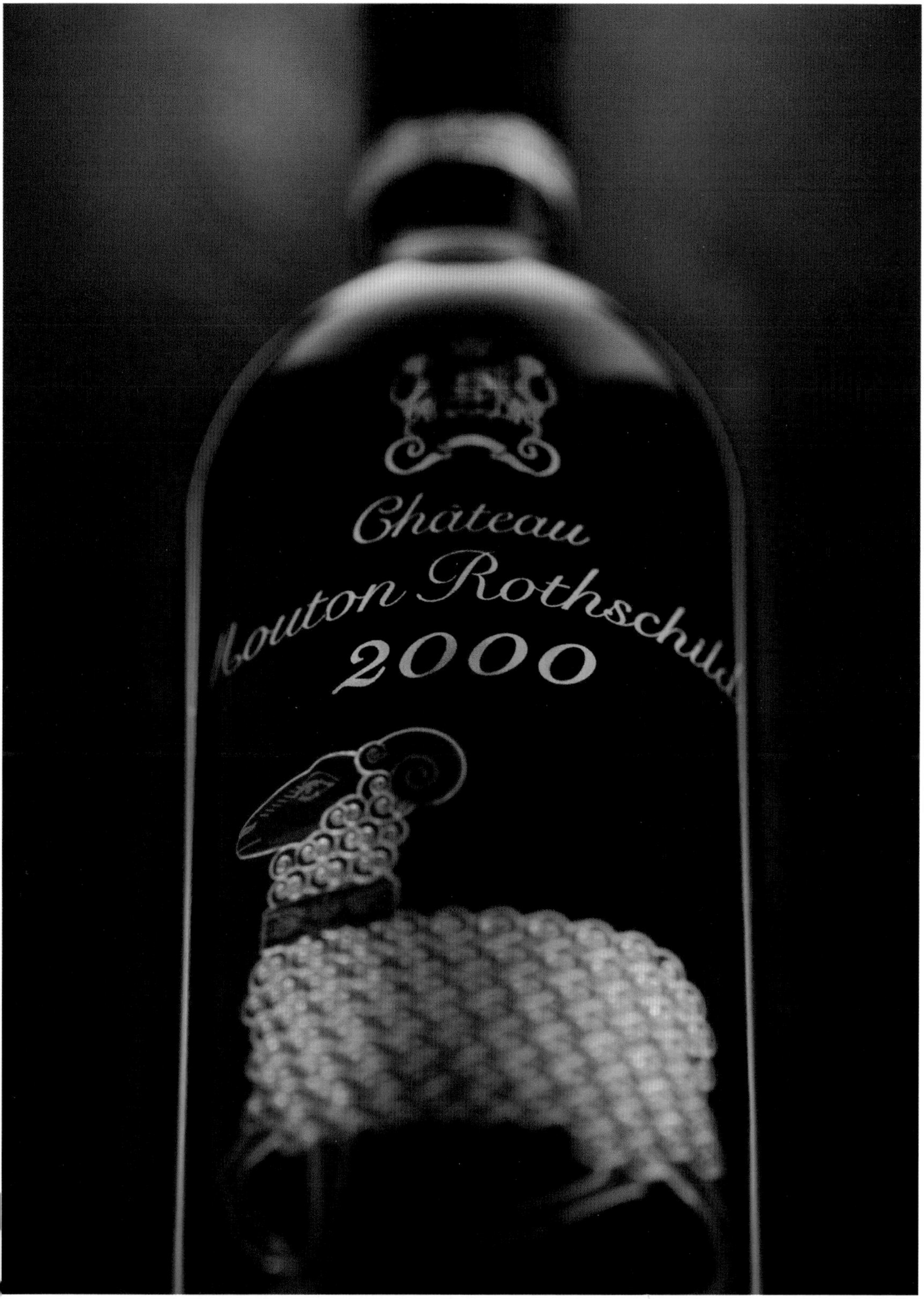
Château
2000

# 2014 Tasting at George V

**2012.** Château Mouton Rothschild.
*Almost black color. A delicate nose,*
*complex, still closed at the time*
*of tasting. Full and fleshy attack.*
*The tannins are ripe, dense and firm.*
*A very successful vintage, sappy,*
*fleshy, a little square.*

**2011.** *Intense color. Nose of red fruits, spicy.*
*Mouth with unctuous attack. Excellent*
*balance, great length. A classic Mouton,*
*which constitutes a great success in this*
*delicate vintage.*

**2010.** *Deep and intense color. Spicy nose*
*develops notes of black fruit. Complex*
*attack in the mouth, powerful tannins.*
*A relatively rigorous wine at the*
*moment. In several years, it will*
*be magnificent.*

**2009.** *Deep color, very young, rich,*
*in its teens, too seductive, complete,*
*to be tasted again.*

**2008.** *Smooth and long. Remarkable year.*
*Fresh, very nice Cabernet. Finish of*
*roasted coffee, mocha chocolate. One*
*of the finest 2008 of the appellation.*

**2007.** *In the finish, the tannins have light*
*vegetal notes. Freshness. To be opened now.*

**2006.** *Delicate nose. Mineral mouth.*
*Not at all vegetal. I prefer it to the 2005.*
*Body, tension, without brutality. A fresh*
*mouth and a very fine tannin grain.*
*Note of undergrowth in the mouth.*
*Great Mouton.*

**2005.** *It still lacks expressivity, austere.*
*A monster. Dense, precise, rigorous*
*selection, parcel. The vines suffered*
*water stress that is felt in the tannins.*

**2004.** *Fewer new barrels, choice of Philippe*
*Dhalluin. Light, successful, stretched*
*like the 2001.*

**2003.** *Evolved. Dry tannins. More balanced*
*than the 2002. A wine with lots of body,*
*mocha, vanilla.*

**2002.** *Generous, small yield, successful.*

**2001.** *Tasted with Philippe Dhalluin,*
*even the intermediate years are*
*successful, more tender than the 2000.*
*Woody notes, vanilla.*

# Vintages tasted in recent years

**1986.** Château Mouton Rothschild.
*More severe, French-style, Cabernet,
serious, more intellectual. The bouquet
– acidity and tannins – perfect. Very
complex. Aromas of mocha, truffle,
cigar box. Delicious.*

**1982.** *Total opulence, euphoria, everything
overflowing, spherical, no troughs,
voluptuous, chewy, will shed in time,
served at Mouton in 2007 in an
Imperial.*

**1971.** *Great achievement, best of
the vintage with 1971 Pétrus, density,
elegance, maturity. I remember in 1985
at La Poularde in Montrond, we offered
it on the menu for 90 euros!*

**1970.** *Generous, volume, aromas
of the typical Mouton cedar.*

**1962.** *Offered by Philippe de Rothschild
to French academics when he was
a candidate to join the illustrious
company under the Dome. He was
not elected. The 1962 was tasted blind
in May 2012 at the Château Margaux.
One of the most successful of the vintage.*

**1961.** *Black color, stewed fruits, woody
notes of Cabernet, huge, full-bodied,
mineral, pencil lead (graphite),
still in its adolescence…*

**1959.** *A masterpiece, the finest wine
of the place, with eucalyptus aromas,
menthol, such freshness!*

# Château Lafite Rothschild

*The Value of Time*

# O

N THIS STRETCH
OF FLAT LAND
in Médoc, a mound, a hillock, becomes a summit. The coast of
Lafite possesses a hilly appearance. In this town of Pauillac, in a
place called the Pouyalet, the description of a "gravelly mound"
fits perfectly. This is the heart of the Lafite vineyards. We are entering the land
of one of the most famous surnames in the world: Rothschild. Bought by Baron
James de Rothschild thirteen years after the 1855 Classification, this unique terroir
also has the qualities of a great one. As the saying goes, "it always comes out on
top." The property is vast (almost 107 hectares, including a historical parcel on
Saint-Estèphe). Here, the Cabernet Sauvignon takes precedence.

# M

EMORIES
April 2012. Like any year, Jacques Dupont, Sylvain Boivert,
Thierry Hamon and myself arrived at the château to taste the
2011 primeur. A special moment: Charles Chevallier, who has
officiated at Lafite since time immemorial, greeted us. From the
outset, Charles told me that the Baron wanted to be there at lunch to welcome
us. What a joy for me (this was the first time that I would have the opportunity
to converse with him).

After the traditional and always satisfying tasting led by Charles, we entered
the château. We were introduced in the red salon and announced. Eric de Rothschild came toward us. Here, we need a freeze frame to describe this room. The
living room was lined with crimson red damask. Niches in the corners housed
life-sized statues of grey gypsum. Sofas, armchairs and other loveseats were
upholstered in the same fabric. Nothing had been changed in this décor designed
by Betty, Baron James's wife, the first Rothschild to own Lafite.

The family champagne was served. The Baron, meanwhile, stuck to his Fine
with water created by our fellow countrymen of the Far East during the Second
Empire and a perfect reminder of the beautifully preserved Napoleon III salons
of the château. To accompany the "blanc de blancs," we feasted on white estuary
shrimp, scented with a touch of wild anise that blended with the champagne
beautifully. Not long after, the doors to the dining room were opened, and we
sat down at the table. As is customary in great Bordeaux houses, the dishes are

served French-style. They consisted of eggs Florentine accompanied by a white wine from Domaine d'Aussières, a 2010 Pays d'Oc wine, 100% Chardonnay, a Languedoc domain acquired by the family in 1999. Shortly following was a 1989 Lafite, matured by the years, containing notes of "copper cap," a touch mineral, particularly long, prodigious, giving tone to the smooth and gourmet Crécy sweetbread, simply accompanied by a quick coffee. Saint-Honoré worthy of the capital's best pastry chefs is found in the 1997 Château Rieussec, a smooth and sophisticated companion.

What most moved me was the timelessness of Eric de Rothschild. Although the Celestial Empire worships his wines, the values of which have soared like never before, Baron Eric remains unfazed. Here, he is the guardian of a heritage to be passed on to his descendants, having undertaken everything to improve the result. He evolves into another "course" of time. He is, above all, a considerate host, funny, who knows to move beyond the present, indispensable parameters to continue sharing his great bottles, from which he derives the enjoyment of his guests. For me, it was a wonderful lunch.

What most moved me was the timelessness of Eric de Rothschild. Although the Celestial Empire worships his wines, the values of which have soared like never before, Baron Eric remains unfazed. Here, he is the guardian of a heritage to be passed on to his descendants, having undertaken everything to improve the result. He evolves into another "course" of time. He is, above all, a considerate host, funny, who knows to move beyond the present, indispensable parameters to continue sharing his great bottles, from which he derives the enjoyment of his guests. For me, it was a wonderful lunch.

To this lunch, I would like to add a dinner at Lafite. It was March 2014, after the tasting described above. Baron Eric was absent but had conferred to Charles Chevallier and his wife the task of organizing the dinner. We all met with Sylvain Boivert, Gerard Sibourg-Baudry, Thierry, Charles Chevallier and his wife, as well as a great-aunt of Charles (she seemed straight out of an Agatha Christie novel, a *Death on the Nile* heroine, who lived elsewhere, I learned, between Marseille and Constantinople). The dining room of Lafite had an unusual feature: the Electricity Fairy was not among the guests. A soft light emanated solely from the candles, torches mounted in the chandelier, sconces in the walls, and candelabras on the table. Here is the domain of M. Didier, a maitre d'hotel worthy of the Charles Carson character in the *Downton Abbey* series. He always

## BORDEAUX
## Château Lafite Rothschild

ensures that, whatever the dishes planned for dinner, I'm not embarrassed to take them from the serving dish or cut them.

We began with a muslin of fava beans, mushroom blood sausage and veal, and a 2008 Château Duhart-Milon. Then, a filet of sea bass, celeriac and black truffles, mirroring Cabernet. With a 1998 Château Lafite Rothschild. A dashing wine, graphite, fine. Good acidity that melts from the beginning. Nose of tobacco, cigar box. Very nice harmony with the truffle sea bass. Three cheeses followed: an Alpine Beaufort, a Stilton Cream and an aged Mimolette. For this service, Charles planned a 1978 Château Lafite Rothschild. The nose gave off aromas of cedar, precious woods and macerated fruits. Woody, delicate. Nice balance, very noble length, yet endowed with freshness. The mouth offered a nice creaminess, delicate upstroke. No asperity, melted, impression of fullness. A bite of chocolate and caramel was then served, accompanied by a 1976 Château Rieussec of great complexity with notes of honey, spices and light caramel – a liqueur very well assimilated through the years. A great, great Sauternes.

The doors reopened, and we retired to the salon. For its size, the "Rothschild green" salon is conducive to conversation. The walls are covered with the same dark green damask as the one upholstering the armchairs. The lamps harmoniously arranged on consoles, or standing mounted, provide a soft light that doesn't impede the flame in the fireplace from glowing. While coffee and teas were served, we tasted a drop of aged Armagnac, letting the wisps of Havanas escape. The wines of Lafite are like the domain of Baron Eric. They are unsoiled from the trends and ravages of time. They retain an aura of mystery that no other cru possesses.

## The Wines

The domain markets two labels, the great wine and the second, les Carruades de Lafite – actually from a duly cadastrated terroir, which annually produces this wine, indissociable from the château. Overall, there has been some revival in the area since the 1980s, with a remarkable 1986 that turned out to be both rare and tense; a refined and exhilarating 1988, and a 1989 and 1990 whose respective opulence and charm comes with a more severe tannic touch in the latter. Then the 1995 and 1996, still closed. Too early to judge at this stage, but how sappy!

Lafite is the breed and the discipline. In recent years, the wine has returned to the supreme level of this outstanding 1959 shared in May 2012. Although this vintage was solar, the wine remained fresh and elegant since this terroir has the ability to retain freshness in the wine even when the year is hot. The body, the flexibility in an intermediate year is always amazing. Up next are the vintages for their time: 2000, 2009 and 2010, which will pass through three or four decades without flinching.

## Tasting in Lafite, March 2014

With Charles Chevallier, Director and Winemaker of the family wines, including Pauillac, Gérard Sibourg-Baudry, Manager of Caves Legrand, in Paris, and Thierry.

**2011. Carruades de Lafite.** *55% Cabernet Sauvignon and 39% Merlot. Deep color, clear. Nose still closed. Fresh mouth, fine tannin grain in the finish.*

**2011. Château Duhart-Milon.** *Lots of work done on this property in recent years. The sorting in the vineyard and on the table, plus the optical sorting upon arrival of the harvest in the fermenting room, when the vintage requires it. Beautiful tannin seeds. More sensual, amazing vintage.*

**2011. Château Lafite Rothschild.** *Very great! Racy, an incredible charm. Unexpected at this stage. Very fine tannin grain. Still ripe, all the same. Pretty serious vintage. Quite crunchy. Note that the great Lafite wine is around 90% Cabernet Sauvignon. Very rare. The remaining few percent reverts to Merlot and a small portion of Cabernet Franc.*

**2009. Carruades de Lafite.** *A great wine! Density, power, bitterness in the mouth still very present. Spices, macerated fruit, large, ripe. For Carruades, only 10 to 15% of new wood is used, so no trace of new barrel is perceived in the blending. A very good stage.*

## BORDEAUX
### Château Lafite Rothschild

2009. Château Duhart-Milon.
*Dry plant, structured mouth, straight, tight, slightly bitter, dense, 50% new wood in this vintage. Mocha notes. Less strange, all the same!*

2009. Château Lafite Rothschild.
*Black, deep density, yet very expressive nose, transition between primary and secondary nose. Fine seed lining the chaffs. Long, delicate. Some sap. Very sensual. Coated, will cut through time.*

2001. Château Lafite Rothschild (in magnum). *Tasted in April 2014, during a meal at the George V. Color showing signs of evolution. The nose is fine, open, of medium intensity, dominated by macerated fruit and red berries, still flattering. Elegant. Precise. Mouth of a still present acidity, but not too refreshing. Medium-bodied. Fine tannins and finish.*

# Château Latour

L'Enclos

# T

## HE TOWER THAT
## LONG AGO LENT ITS NAME

to the domain no longer exists. It was gradually demolished from the many conflicts that punctuated the Gironde when the English coveted it. The one that now stands as the emblem of the château is happier, since it is an ancient dovecote of the thirteenth century. A tower, therefore, but of peace.

The domain, like others mentioned on these pages, such as Calon Ségur, Lafite and Mouton, was created by the Ségur family and remained in the hands of their descendants until 1963. It successively passed through the portfolios of two British business groups. After this last English "occupation" of the terroir of the former Guyenne, a great Breton name, François Pinault and his family helped Latour regain its French status in 1993. Soon after, I was in contact with Frédéric Engerer, with whom we would regularly exchange ideas so as to better understand Latour, as well as the group's expansion projects: the Domaine d'Eugénie in Burgundy (formerly Domaine Engel), the Château Grillet, the Condrieu micro-growth and, more recently, the Domaine Araujo, in Napa Valley. To these properties, a significant share-holding needs to be added with the Château Siaurac (Lalande de Pomerol), the Château Vray Croix de Gay (Pomerol) and the Prieuré (Saint-Emilion, cru classé). Latour remains the heart of this passion for wine in Frédéric. He will support, invest and showcase the great wine throughout the world. As Roger Dion clearly explained, without sizable financial support, there can be no large-scale, sustained development in the realization of a great wine.

Since the arrival of the Pinault family and the appointment of Frédéric Engerer to manage the domain, Latour has seen considerable growth in defining purity. The parcellary work was completely necessary. As a sommelier, I always want to know which plot, in the assembly, is the most important for the realization of a great wine. During parcellary tastings in Latour with Frédéric Engerer, I discovered that the heart of the great wine of Latour included 47 hectares of L'Enclos. I keep, on my desk, a chunk of blue clay from a core sampling 10 meters in depth. This segmenting in L'Enclos de Latour remains the most beautiful testimony of knowledge of this terroir, consisting of clayed gravel, gravelly sands, and finally, the blue clay mentioned above. It is this clay that helps the plant, during summer months, to locate the deep water resources needed to grow, without too much stress. When we taste a wine of Latour in its early youth, still being aged, it takes several minutes for the palate to detect all the components that submerge it. This is the Cabernet Sauvignon in all its power and rigor, since Latour is from 80 to 85% Cabernet Sauvignon, even 90% in recent years. This concentration is so natural in Latour that the tasting room has something monastic about it. We are on the drawing board. The wine and the terroir, visible by the berries, are the only elements that stand out.

Defining the data identifying a great terroir takes time. When possible, as was my case over the years, to expand one's scope of knowledge by constantly tasting these wines, one can then go back in time to those sought-after vintages, such as the 1982. For example, I remember a lunch at Le Cinq when I had to confront the 1987 Château Pichon Longueville Comtesse de Lalande and the 1982 Château Latour. They were both served in an Imperial (bottle with a capacity of 6 liters). It was a meal game; all the dishes were "feather" or "fur." At the time, Enrico Bernardo had just won the title of World's Best Sommelier. We each defended a cru. Having a penchant at that moment for Pichon, I had chosen it for my defense. Enrico, the Latour. Glasses in hand, despite my argument worthy of a litigator, I was beaten by the dazzling 1982 Latour. It was at the top and still is.

# MEMORIES

Tuesday, June 21, 2005, I had the honor of being invited along with a distinguished Areopagus of tasters, all representatives of great restaurants and importers from all over France and the world. There were about thirty guests gathered. The lunch menu was very nice. It consisted of a soup of Tarbais beans with summer truffle, followed by line-caught sea bass, wild mushrooms, among which included Bordeaux mushrooms, chanterelles, and a rack of Pauillac lamb, garden vegetables and a 7-hour juice. All topped with a refreshing iced nougat. However, the purpose of our meeting was more about the wines served. To warm us up, a 1976 Champagne Salon; then, over the course of the lunch, a 1949 Château Latour (which I uncovered blind) and a 1945 Château Latour (which my tablemate, a prominent taster and

wine journalist, Michel Bettane, uncovered). Then a 1919 Château Latour. It emanated a scent of the wine cellar, with kirsched red fruits. Light in the mouth while retaining a certain complexity. And a 1911 Château Latour: really red-tiled color, with leather nose, from Havana. Marked acidity. Light mouth, pretty short. It passes through the mouth like a zephyr.

# April 2014 Tasting at the Château

**2010. Les Forts de Latour.** *Black color, opaque. Dense nose, with hints of black fruits, creamy with an impression of thickness, velvety structure. The mouth is rich, concentrated, sensual. Tannins of extreme elegance. A great Forts in the image of Latour success in this vintage.*

**2006. Les Forts de Latour.** *Garnet color of medium intensity. The nose is open, loose and flattering. Notes of red fruits, resinous wood, with a measured complexity. Mouth tight throughout.*

**2011. Latour.** *Black color at this stage. Closed nose, fine, tight, a little woody. Mouth a little tense, concentrated, without greenness. Is closer to the 2008, but a little smoother and thicker. Remarkable tannins with a texture that is mineralized. A somewhat tense vintage. The 2011 was somewhat shunned by the market.*

**2010 Latour.** *Black color, opaque and dense. Concentrated nose, full, delicate, of an incredible depth. Notes of very refined wood. Spectacular mouth, full, sappy, tannins are elegant and precise. Great finish. It gives me the impression of a 1961 – modern – and is, in my opinion, the most successful since 1982.*

**2009 Latour.** *Bright, opaque color. Nose of incredible density. Creamy, fruity, notes of wild blueberry compote, fine, violet and licorice. Amazing. The mouth is extremely tasty. Quickly becomes lean in mid-palate. Fine and buttery tannins. Great length, spicy finish, fruity, licorice. A terroir. To be enjoyed in ten years.*

**2008 Latour.** *First year where a significant part of the Latour vineyards was managed through organic farming. Opaque color, intense garnet; delicate nose, dense, closed. The mouth is sappy, classic, notes of graphite. In the words of Alain Passard who was familiar with it: "a root wine." Like entering the plant. The Cabernets are fresh. Very nice length, an elegant wine, a little austere. A Latour longer than it is wide. Wait at least five years before opening.*

**2007 Latour.** *Bright color, intense garnet. Closed nose, rich, notes of black fruit. A fine and straight nose. The mouth is smooth, beautiful. Texture with volume. This 2007 vintage is still elegant and successful.*

**2005 Latour.** *Dark color, opaque garnet. Concentrated nose, unfathomable, fine. Nothing else can pass through it. Impression of great maturity. Wide mouth, plump, firm. Delicate and square tannins. Very long, sophisticated. A very balanced wine. The most serious since 1975 but more modern and so precise. Must absolutely be preserved in the cellar and not rediscovered for another five years...*

**2004 Latour.** *Intense garnet color. The nose is closed. Notes of black fruits, black currant, delicate, discreet. The attack in the mouth is firm, monolithic. Finish of medium length. The mouth remains fresh without vegetal sensation (through a strict selection at harvest).*

**2003 Latour.** *Garnet color. Slight sign of evolution. Open nose, wooded, a charming little thing, spicy, fruity, slightly stewed. Touch of mocha. Sensual mouth, rich, dense, sweet sensation. The tannins are present, quite rich. The finish is a little fluid. The whole remains balanced, roasted retro-olfaction. A gourmet wine to drink now.*

**2002 Latour.** *Garnet color of good intensity. Open nose, roasted, fruity, quite sensual and approachable. The fruit is ripe and fleshy. Soft mouth, medium-bodied, fairly fluid in the finish. Remains quenching and svelte. Noticeable acidity without harshness. Very pleasant, to open now.*

# Château Calon Ségur

*From Denise to Vincent*

# B

EING FROM BRITTANY,
I SEE THE VINEYARD
of Saint-Estèphe as a Finistère of vines. Calon Ségur is also the
northernmost of the 1855 crus classé. Its history is inseparable
from that of the Médoc. The Marquis de Ségur (1697-1755),
nicknamed the "Prince of vines," who already had in his possession the
Lafite and Latour domains, acquired this cru during his marriage. He loved
to recall: "I make wine in Lafite and Latour, but my heart is in Calon." The
origin of the cru's name is similar to *calones*, the flat-bottomed boats that
lined the Gironde estuary.

The current director of the estate, Vincent Millet, was a key advisor to the
late Mme Capbern-Gasqueton. Seamlessly, Vincent was able to change
course and reassure her. The cru has come a long way. In 2000, the vineyard
was almost declassified because of the weakness of the vineyard's planting
density. At the time, around 5700 vines were planted and, shortly after the
arrival of Vincent Millet, it expanded to 7200. Today it is around 10,000. The
Calon Ségur replanting cycles are scheduled to finish in ... 2025! At that time,
all will be in production, and the great wine is expected for 2036! The terroir
of Calon consists of seams of clay, sandy gravel and other clay areas. The
53 hectares of the Calon Ségur vineyards have been redesigned to develop
the qualities. The cru was recently taken over by a large French banking
group. The death of Mme Gasqueton and the estate expenses left no other
choice for her daughter. Her family was the owner of Calon Ségur from 1894
to 2012.

Vincent was our second contact in Calon. It was through my association
with Jacques Dupont that I was able to join the primeur tastings and first
heard the energetic words of Denise Gasqueton. She led the debates and
almost seemed to dictate Jacques's comments. He didn't mind – I sensed that
Mme Gasqueton sincerely esteemed the great journalist. Over the years,
Vincent was able to take part in this meeting, and, in recent years, he got to
lead the discussions. Vincent knew to be patient – it was through his work
in the vineyards and cellars that he gained Mme Gasqueton's trust. Today,
this Grand Vin represents 40% and the second, Marquis de Calon, 45%. The
remaining batches fall within a third wine, La Chapelle de Calon.

# March 2014 Tasting

With Sylvain Boivert and Thierry. Vincent Millet and the Cellar Master also attended.

The varieties of the cru consist of 53% Cabernet Sauvignon, 38% Merlot, 7% Cabernet Franc and 2% Petit Verdot.

**2011. Calon Ségur.** *Dark garnet color. Precise nose. Ample and sophisticated mouth, elegant end of the mouth rather than concentrated. This is a precise wine and a great success for Vincent.*

**2010.** *Vintage hailed in Saint-Estèphe. This can be understood. The wine is complete, but the finish is still marked by tannins.*

**2009.** *Dark garnet color, opaque. Dense and complete nose, spicy, woody. Rich mouth, sappy and long. Very young, a great Calon.*

**2007.** *Slightly stripped garnet color. Open nose, flattering and fruity, of a medium density. Supple and loose mouth.*

**2006.** *Vintage marking the arrival of Vincent Millet. An elegant wine without being sharp.*

**1995.** *Tonic mouth, beautiful substance, enough fluid. At the time, the concentration did not develop a high density in the mouth.*

BORDEAUX
Château Calon Ségur

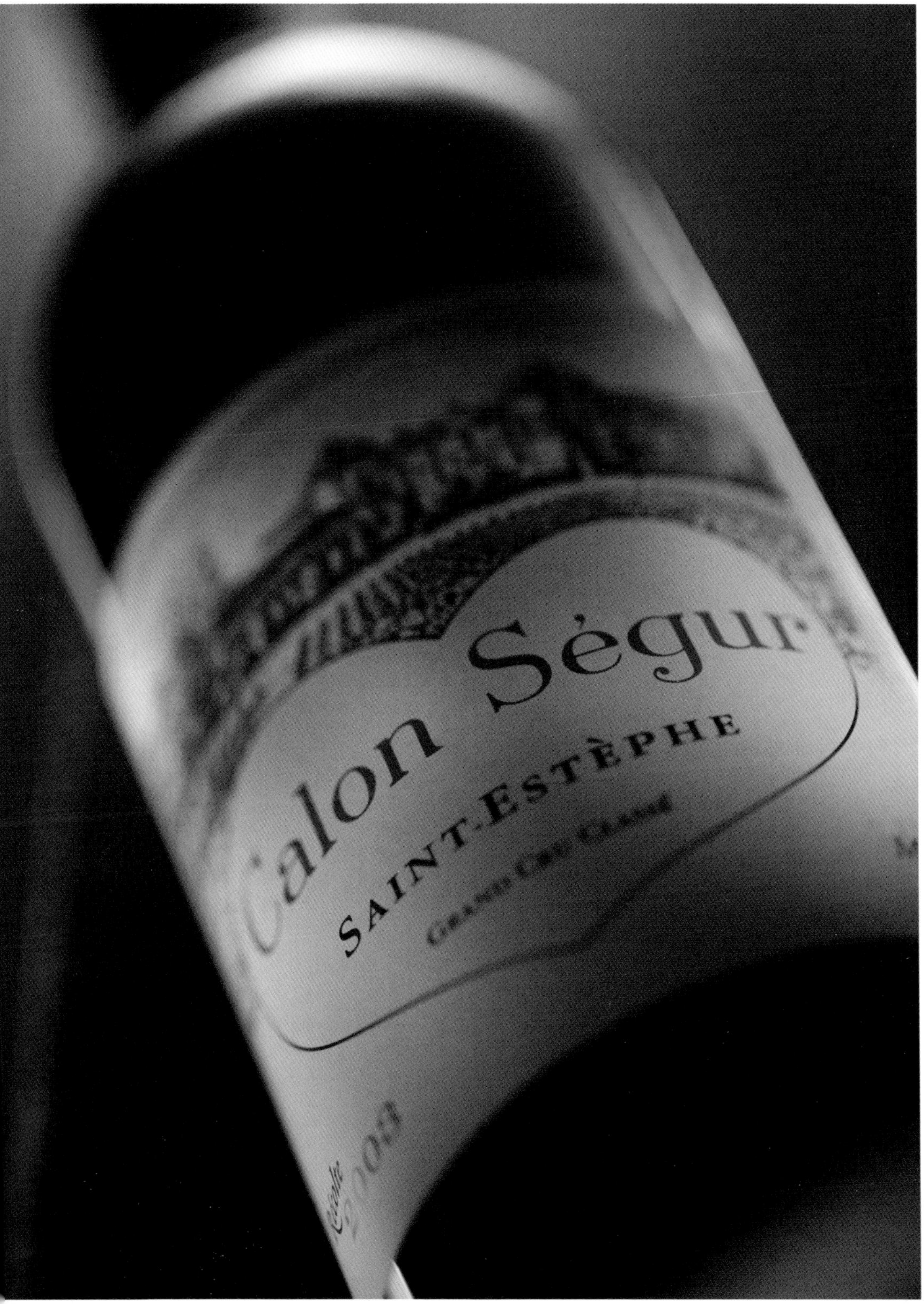
Calon Ségur
SAINT-ESTÈPHE
GRAND CRU CLASSÉ

# Château Soutard

*What I came to know*

# I

AM FACING
AN UNUSUAL CASE.
In fact, the property that we are now about to wander still exists, maintained and developed with great interest by the current owners. The domain was not dismembered; the storerooms, the cellars, the house itself benefitted from substantial, exemplary work. Nevertheless, the period that I describe to you lies in the past. Ultimately, however, as many as the bottles from that era will survive, that past is still alive somewhere.

The period is 1987. The final contest for Best Young Sommelier of France was in full swing. I won. First national title. During the cocktail party following the award ceremonies, in a Vinexpo room, Christian Péchoutre (who was the best man at my wedding) pointed out a blue-collar character somewhat out of step with the participants. Then, Christian said, "Eric, may I present to you the owner of Château Soutard, Comte François des Ligneris!" François managed the domain with his parents and sisters. Later, it turned out that my main broker of Bordeaux Grands Crus, Marcel Dessalle, had, in his name, a supply of Soutard. With him, I found myself one evening at Ramet, a famous Bordeaux restaurant, in the company of the Comte and Comtesse des Ligneris. Over the course of the dinner, well-watered with wine, those whom I now call François and Isabelle invited me and my wife for the harvest. We accepted with pleasure, and it was with Margot, our first daughter, then 1-year-old, that we landed at the château. All three of us slept in the cellar, with sounds in the background of singing fermentation in the tanks. (For amateurs, I recommend *Sound of Wine*, a CD released in 1996 by the tireless Willi Opitz, star of Austrian winemaking, prepared in Burgenland, a true melody of happiness!). If memory serves, the 1990 vintage was solar. A providential year, with superb maturities and concentrations.

We stayed a week for the harvest, living in the rhythm of the château. Sometimes, François's father would invite us to the château to taste the succulent desserts he would find in Libourne. We would have lunch in the vineyards. Dinners took place near the washing station with the pickers. At the time, François used a large family of gypsies. All the siblings obeyed at the patriarch's point of a finger and glance. He was the only one who received instructions from the Head of Cultivation. During the evening vigils, the women would dance around a fire, and the men would play songs reminiscent of Django Reinhardt on the guitar. What an atmosphere! What a great life!

Soutard is an eighteenth-century Asterie limestone château, surrounded by 22 hectares of vineyards, including 16 on clay-limestone soils. For us, entering a home like that for the first time was a dream world. During this first visit, I could perceive the whole character of François, from his honest address to the politically correct antipodes. A born pedagogue, he allowed me to better understand the workings of the National Institute of Appellations of Origin (INAO), appellation committees, the famous Appellation of Controlled Origin (AOC) (now Protected Appellation of Origin, AOP) approval committees, contest juries… A world in which many parameters are considered beyond the merits of competing wines.

François was often at war with the Saint-Émilion appellation union, of which he is no longer was a member, and the exasperating winemaking dogmas to which everyone had to conform. As such, Soutard was, at the time, extremely affordable for a Saint-Émilion cru classé. In maturation, he was unfailing regarding the harmful effects of wood that was overly heated, not hesitating to saw staves that were "too hot" to better understand the cause. The breeding was consistent year in and year out, at 33% new barrels, 33% barrels of one wine and 33% barrels of two wines. No one had ever spoken to me about wine in this way, and always with kindness, no mood swings. Aristocratic soul – let's not forget that the des Ligneris had resided in Paris from 1560 in a hotel built by the architect Pierre Lescot (also known for his achievements in the Louvre where a wing still bears his name), now better known as the Musée Carnavalet and where the family coat of arms is still visible – François had an altruistic side; he was a "defender of the widow and the orphan" you could say, and this drive sometimes turned him into an outsider. His outspokenness at every turn of a phrase or chosen quotation displayed a fine intelligence tinged with friendliness, and coupled with extreme sensitivity. A poet wisely wielding metaphors. An unrepentant orator capable of holding an audience spellbound for hours. I remember one of his witticisms during primeur wine tastings, held each year in early April: "These are wines for eaters, I prefer wines for drinkers."

BORDEAUX
Château Soutard

**EMORIES**

It is a special memory that I retain among the moments of great camaraderie lived with friends. It was the last evening in the adjoining washing room in the château in 1999, on the occasion of a Mad Wine Waiters of the World (MWW) sale, created a few years prior with some sommelier friends, among them Gérard Basset, Olivier Poussier, Bernd Kreis, Eric Boschman and Eric Duret. Big names! Here, the gala dress was most uncommon: evening dress or tuxedo, white socks and black diving flippers. Such class! We met with about twenty bon vivants seated in the washing room, ready for a hearty and necessary meal. In addition to the bottles prepared by François, everyone needed to bring bottles worthy of the guests and their number, hence the influx of magnums. Among the special guests was Edmond Vatan, accompanied by his daughter, Anne. They wondered what was happening all around them. What an atmosphere! The wines were tasted in a predetermined order, according to their characters, and then the dishes and supper were served. That night, I found myself paddling in the washing room before sinking in 60 centimeters of water. My tux never recovered.

Another time, another place, with Soutard as the headliner. We were at Le Cinq. Between 2000 and 2005, every Sunday night or almost, we would serve one of our most wonderful hosts at this restaurant. A man of Lebanese origin who made his fortune in Brazil and who had for some time been free from any existential obligation. Every Sunday, he would dine at Le Cinq with six to ten friends. The ritual was immutable. Throughout the week, his butler would call Legendre, the chef, referring to him as "Monsieur." Together, they would establish the menu to be served. Always the great classics: all the soufflés made an appearance – gruyere soufflés, lobster soufflés, soufflés with black truffles – but also lobsters à la parisienne, vols-au-vent (for six to eight people!), crusty game pâtés… The dishes ranged from whole turbots with champagne, to half-mourning chicken in bladder, milk-fed veal chops, hares à la royale served entirely on a silver torpedo… all dishes carved and served at tableside. The wines, on the other hand, never changed: a well-chilled magnum of Moët & Chandon Brut Impérial and… 1990 or 1995 Château Soutard in a carafe (bottles never visible). We would present the guests with bottles upon request.

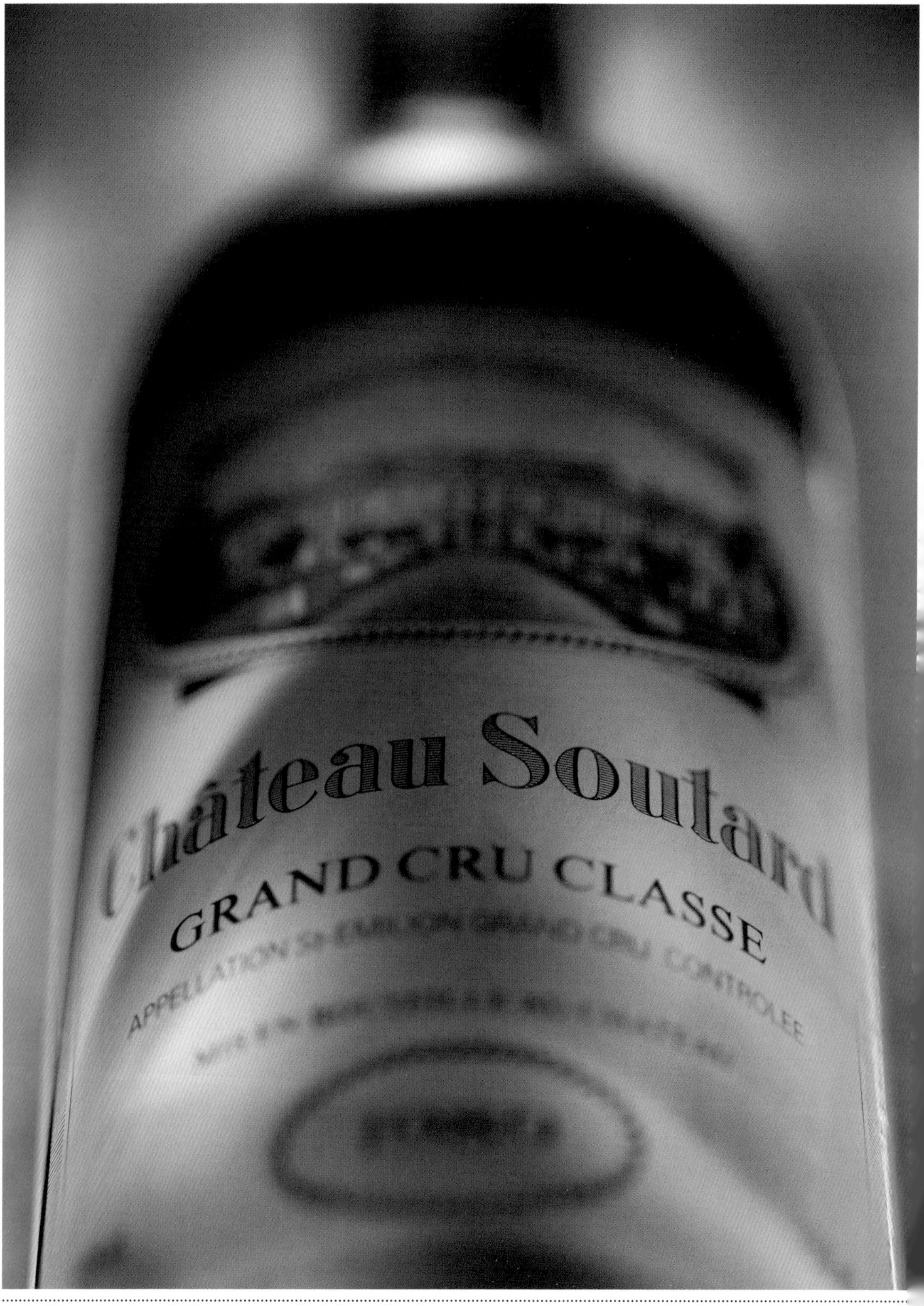
Château Soutard
GRAND CRU CLASSE

He had "adopted" Soutard and always praised it to his guests. The vintage always lent itself well to sharing and to the complex preparations of the chef. We adapted the year to the dishes and vice versa. The chauffeur of M. and Mme A. would transport them (from their residence on Rue de la Trémoille, 200 meters away) to the George V at 8:00, so that they were in the Salon de l'Horloge to greet their guests.

M. A. was always generously perfumed with Hermès cologne. Always very well dressed, with brightly colored puffy cravat, large dark tortoiseshell glasses. Sparse and perfectly slicked hair, he was short and mostly cylindrical. He spoke to each of his guests in their language, with an inimitable accent. Madame was very slender and more severe in nature, always in an understated Chanel suit, wearing two rows of pearls and matching earrings. I remember Madame's menu, very different from her husband's, as she only consumed wine accompanied with her meal: unsweetened peppermint iced tea, and for her entrée, smoked Norwegian salmon with chestnut honey and Melba toast.

After payment, we would draw up a table for him and his coffee, out of sight from his friends. He would have his coffee and a glass of cool water and would discuss with the maitre d'hotel (at the time, the lively Michel Carrez) the dishes served and convey his opinion to the chef.

Upon the death of his wife, he informed us that he would not be continuing these receptions, no longer having the appetite. Some time later, he joined her, most unfortunately. Yet, he will never truly leave Le Cinq as we had lived in contact with him for many delightful hours. He was a great gourmet, a host of refined taste, a remarkable man of the world.

Since selling Soutard in 2006, François has been tucked away at L'Envers du Décor, where I have seen him several times. The steamroller inherent in any succession defeated two hundred years of des Ligneris presence in Soutard. But the ideals of François remain.

A book of his family has closed on the history of this domain. Another volume has been opened with the current owner. This is the case with many properties.

# The Wines

In Soutard, the clay-limestone plateau was cadastrated during the eighteenth century. The parcels already defined indicated the suitable grape varieties: here no excessive concentration, no touch of woodiness. Above all, elegance, finesse. François insisted on it.

He segmented the parcels enormously during vinification, always raising the Merlot (30% of the vineyard) separately from the Cabernet Franc (70%). My visits provided me with so much in terms of wine comprehension. None of my questions were off-limits. François wanted, through his wines, to convey messages. There was especially the desire to be original without seeking to belong to such or such school, with the will for continuing in a world already endangered at the time of his debut alongside his father in 1978.

This spirit of patrimonial legacy, I discovered in the wines of the château, such as this 1964 vintage, vinified by his father, enjoyed by candlelight in the cellars of the château.

It was also uncovered blind by Eric Bordelet who would become, years later, the great pomologist that we know. This wine revealed to all the finesse and power of this great terroir. François is among those who have always supported me in my efforts in sommelier competitions. I still remember this long tasting in March 1998 in his wine bar: L'Envers du Décor. Pierre Lurton and Stéphane Derenoncourt had coached me well.

I had tasted a hundred and ten wines blind; everything had been organized by François! To complicate the exercise, I was being filmed by the *Envoyé Spécial* team for a story covering me, offering a window into sommellerie on a national level.

From this time period, I still retain memorable moments. Like these raids in Saint-Émilion after the morning snack, to order at the counter of the bistro a very thick Lillet Blanc in tapered glasses with an orange peel, listening to the latest gossip of this city dedicated to wine, known today throughout the world.

# Tastings

2005. *This is the last one that François vinified. The wine contrasts with a number of those from 2005. Here the tannins are fine, complex, full of elegance. Very good length.*

2004. *What emerges in this delicate vintage is the Soutard ability to maintain great elegance. The signature of a terroir.*

2000. *Tasted at the time, then at Le Cinq, where it remained on the menu a long time. It was, and for those who still have it, is one of the great successes on the plateau. A complete vintage, like François.*

1995. *The black fruit expressed in the nose is candied today, the mouth dense yet balanced, fulfilled.*

1990. *An ever-present vintage at the George V. Time has passed, and it is now at the peak of its career. The nose is expressive, with notes of chocolate, spices. The mouth is powerful. A winter wine.*

# Château Figeac

*The Manoncourt Panache*

# THE ORIGIN OF THIS PROPERTY

dates back to Roman times and is named after its first owner, a man named Figeacus. Its history over the centuries proved to be tumultuous. Two families particularly stand out in the life of the domain. From the mid-seventeenth century to the early nineteenth century, the Carles family developed, improved and raised the quality of the Figeac wines until a slow decline driven by a succession of unfortunate heirs separated the domain, over the decades, into smallholdings. One of them became famous under the Cheval Blanc name. When the Comtesse de Carles-Trajet separated from the domain in 1838, of the 200 hectares, including Figeac at the peak of its glory, only 130 hectares remained. Multiple owners who then succeeded at a steady pace accelerated the dismemberment of the domain. This splintering helped create properties such as Château La Tour Figeac, Château Mayne-Figeac or even Petit Château-Figeac (the latter cru was restored in 2002 by Manoncourt, thus reinstating the old domain).

In 1886, the decline that then passed through Figeac led the Féret family (publishers based in Bordeaux since 1812), in the fifth edition of its guide *Bordeaux et ses vins* to strip Figeac of its premier cru ranking in the Graves of Saint Emilion. For the record, this famous guide, published for the first time in 1850, published its nineteenth edition in 2014!

In 1892, when the Manoncourt ancestors bought the domain, it only had, including the garden, 54 hectares. The great-grandson of M. de Chèvremont (whose coat of arms still appears on the label), Thierry Manoncourt, was leading the domain when, in 1954, upon the creation of the crus de Saint-Emilion, he saw Figeac become classified as a premier cru classé. However, it was blandly placed in the panegyric of great names of the appellation.

Today the estate has 40 hectares of vineyards, 30 of which make up its major terroir, composed of Günziennes Graves. The same as those found in… Cheval Blanc. This terroir is perfectly suited for Cabernet Franc and Cabernet Sauvignon, which make up between them 70% of the vine population, completed by 30% Merlot. From 1947, the year of his first harvest, to his death in 2010, Thierry Manoncourt was, for more than half a century, the progenitor of Figeac's qualitative renewal. He was simultaneously benevolent and determined in everything, with great elegance. He also embodied the archetype of a great lord. And what panache! He was an unequalled communicator, breathing a wind of rebirth into the domain, whose potential, proffered by the terroir, he was certain of. It was through his knowledge and convictions that he was able to maintain his course, preserving Figeac from the affronts of trends. He was indifferent to the enthusiasm of a more conventional, international style in which many big names engaged, consequently retreating. By not adhering to the trend of overpowering wines, Figeac is sometimes depicted as thin, puny. We simply have to give it time. Thierry Manoncourt could have adopted the famous tirade of Edmond Rostand's "No thank you" in *Cyrano de Bergerac*. And I wager that in the evening of his life, he enveloped himself in the last words of the unloved herald:

CYRANO: […] Ah, I recognize you, you old enemies of mine!
Deceit…?
*He strikes his sword in the air.*
There, there! – Ha! Ha! Compromises,
Prejudices, Cowardices! …
*He strikes.*
That I make a treaty?
Never, never! – Ah! There you are, Stupidity!
– I know that you'll lay me low in the end;
No matter; I fight on! I fight! I fight again!
*He makes passes in the air and stops, breathless.*
Yes, you take all from me: the laurel and the rose!
Take them! Despite you there is something though
I keep, that tonight, as I go to meet my God,
will brush the blue threshold beneath my feet,
something I bear, in spite of you all, that's
free of hurt, or stain,
*He springs forward, his sword raised.*
And that's…
*The sword falls from his hand; he staggers,
and falls back into the arms of Le Bret and Ragueneau.*

BORDEAUX
Château Figeac

ROXANE, *se bending and kissing his forehead:* That's?
CYRANO: My panache.

(Edmond Rostand, Cyrano de Bergerac, act V, scene 4)

The refinement of thought in Thierry Manoncourt was a melodious echo up to the service of his wines. I realized it at a party in Figeac when I was with Nicolas Charrière, our first sommelier. The bottles succeeded each other in a sustained rhythm. They were served in incredible Baccarats, dating from the nineteenth century, whose distinctiveness was such that they discreetly housed, in a hole at the bottom of the carafe, a music box! The freshness of Figeac emerged across vintages such as the 1995: deep, intense and sophisticated. Or the 1983: very successful in Figeac. It could cross swords with the famous 1983 Château Margaux.

In Figeac, vinification gimmicks are not in favor. The style is classic, and its aging capacity remarkable. At present, I think that Figeac has the freedom to return to the forefront; this Sleeping Beauty has been renewed with vigor. The breath of Thierry Manoncourt has not been extinguished. The current director of the estate, Frédéric Faye, watches over Figeac. He first entered in 2002 as Head of Cultivation and then became Technical Director. He now leads the domain in its wine-making and wine-growing operations, management and marketing. He infuses all his energy into the cru's future, one that is imbued with the philosophy of Thierry Manoncourt. Let's welcome and look forward to the next time these wines are opened.

EMORIES

With certain friends, we see each other once every quarter, either at one of our homes or at a friendly restaurant. In June 2013, we gathered in a place that attracts me because it contains everything we could need: Le Laurent. This legendary, hidden institution in the gardens of the Champs Élysées, close to the Marigny Theater, is run by Philippe Bourguignon. He is the General Manager, the Sommelier, the soul. He provided us with an upstairs lounge with a terrace. The weather being lenient, the table had been set there. My six companions, including Thierry and myself, met there at the height of the foliage of the surrounding trees. The view extended to the Dome of the Grand Palais. The evening was fresh, the faces were happy – everything went smoothly.

M. Coquillette's magnum of 2000 Saint-Chamant Champagne gathered us around Robert, my friend Laurent's stepfather, a member of the happy team. Robert told wonderful stories. He had seen the heyday of Chambord, the gourmet restaurant of the *France* ocean liner, and continued his career at Lasserre. Here he served as first maitre d'hotel until his retirement. At Lasserre, he met members of high society during the reign of René Lasserre, one of the three greatest restaurateurs in Paris (along with Claude Terrail and Jean-Claude Vrinat). Philippe had prepared his famous spider crab entrée with its juice in jelly, fennel cream, served with a magnum of 2006 Les Clos de Raveneau Chablis Grand Cru. The wine began to open with notes of honey hawthorn, yellow fruits and fresh hazelnuts. The mouth, long and elegant, balancing perfectly with the crab flesh, reminded me of the delicacy of moussettes served from April to May. For the dishes that followed, I provided a double magnum of 2004 Château Figeac. Prime example of a serious bottle. We were eight bon vivants – it was just what we needed. The chef, Pégouret, then prepared for us red Genevan mullets with crushed livers. A dish that was not without relief. Then came a wonderful, milk-fed veal shank slowly cooked in its juice and French-style peas, accompanied by pommes soufflées aériennes. The wine was presented in a vintage somewhat discredited by amateurs. It proved to be perfect in every way. Its success supported a good management of yields associated with a high proportion of Cabernet Sauvignon and Cabernet Franc grape varieties. In a word, my comrades were enraptured. So much so that by the end of the evening, we had decided the date of our next reunion. Well underway, I proposed a site that was the antithesis of the usual location of our feasts.

In September of the same year, we found ourselves in Granville, heading towards the Chausey Islands! The crossing was invigorating. Within an hour at sea, we disembarked in Chausey. A few hours after our arrival, a myriad of small islands appeared and seemed to emerge from the waves, retreating backwards like courtiers waving their white plumes. It was one of the highest tides of the year. We took up quarters in the island's Vauban Fort bunkers, where we met up with some fishermen friends, including Eric Collet,

BORDEAUX
Château Figeac

provider of the George V sommelier group dinners. There were twelve of us: six from Paris and six fishermen.

As usual, the luggage was heavy with… bottles! Everyone came armed. One was responsible for the contingency aperitif. In the invigorating context of seafarers, the licorice drinks are often put to use – and this case was no exception. It was delicious, with just poached shrimp and prawns with a wild fennel branch. Here we call this appetizer "Chausey peanuts." For the entrée of raw clams, whelks in court bouillon and large periwinkles, we had the support of two 2010 L d'Or magnums of Muscadet Cuvée from Pierre Luneau-Papin. The delicate sautéed scallops with Bordier Yuzu butter were treated to a magnum of 1999 Salon I had brought. The Parisian friends opened their eyes wide, and the fishermen found the bottle "really good."

The following dish had to be as distinguished as the bottle: a Jeroboam of 2001 Château Figeac. Luckily there were carafes in the lazaretto of the fort, allowing us to decant it. As for the glassware, I came armed with four cartons of glasses just in case… Seeing me wipe them down, one of the fishermen pointed out that they were already clean. I placed one glass freshly from the carton and another one freshly cleaned under his nose. It made him smile. Amused, he promised to remember.

For me, there was no question of tasting this Hussar-style Figeac. After a necessary resting period, I served it delicately. Its color was very bright and deep. The earthy nose, truffled; the mouth, harmonious, intense, broad. In these rustic and Spartan surroundings, power emanated.

## BORDEAUX
### Château Figeac

Then came companies of covered lobsters fresh from the water, mere steps away, which were sliced and grilled alive on the flames of an immense brazier in the fort's courtyard. I put jars of a delectable bordelaise sauce created by David Bizet, one of the chefs of the George V, to cool in a makeshift water bath. One of the men had brought Touquet Ratte potato baskets which we sautéed in butter and generously smeared with truffle butter. I had the good idea of bringing some with me before leaving home. Everyone described the wine with their words, their impressions. The pairing was a first for the fishermen, little accustomed to Bordeaux with lobster. Here the encounter between the iodine, the thick lobster flesh, the sauce mirroring the Cabernet, deep and raised, the potatoes exhaling a rustic butter truffle scent, formed a link as inseparable from the Figeac as the size of the container was wonderfully preserved. It took two or three services for the Sea Cardinals to appreciate the Jeroboam. One of the fishermen, called Cricket, even found it "very lively"!

Already, the Breton songs resonated between the thick stone walls. The sour rice pudding in my care, enriched with vanilla beans that a friend had brought from Tahiti, provided strong support for the 1950 Montebello Rhum. The cane brandy from remote islands reached its peak with a case of Monterey *Hoyo des Dieux* cigars.

Late at night, we reached our sleeping bags. Crammed into the bunk beds of the fort's inconvenient bunkers, we rested rather poorly.

But what happiness, at dawn, alone on the shore, to witness the sunrise in a glowing red blaze rising over the still sleeping waters, the color of emeralds.

# Tasting of Château Figeac in situ, in 2013

**2010.** *One of the great successes of Saint-Emilion. Remarkable for its intensity, frankness and without too much alcohol. Rare for the vintage, due in part to the use of Cabernet Sauvignon.*

**2009.** *Full-bodied, powerful, squared, slightly hidden, and will come together within ten years.*

**2005.** *It already ranks among the grand Figeacs; alone, it has long substantiated its classification.*

**2001.** *The troublemaker, maligned, yet so moving in its scope and sensuality; combines sweet spice and macerated fruits with an elegance of huge tannins.*

**1995.** *Another monument of righteousness. More Médoc than Saint-Émilion.*

**1990.** *Medium today. Marked animalistic notes in the opening. But sensuality covers this aspect, a wine. Very large, deep complex, where the structure is melted and loose. No hardness, which is a great quality for this year. The truffled notes blend with spices and black fruits. A great success.*

**1985.** *Deep ruby color, slightly tiled reflection. Good intensity. The nose is complex and flourished. The macerated fruits mingle with hints of undergrowth. Soft mouth with the wide classic trough of the 1985. However, the finish is beautiful and elegant.*

## BORDEAUX
### Château Figeac

# Château Ausone

*First Visit*

THE VAUTHIERS FORM
AN INTEGRAL PART
of my memories of wine. This dates back to July 1984, the first
time Marie and I came to Saint-Émilion, and I began the visit
with… the mayor's office. In fact, I was provided with a letter
of recommendation sent by a friend of my father's from Louvigné-du-Désert,
where I'm from. The idea was to otherwise find work in the region, or at
least visit some domains. However, the mayor was none other than the father
of Alain Vauthier. The job hunt seemed elusive – he kept me until his son
picked us up to visit Ausone. For the first time in my life I was going to visit
a wine estate. I didn't understand much about wine. Yet from the very beginning, I was fascinated by vineyards, the terraces, the stone cellars, the ancient
quarries, the chapel, the history of this château. These were revelatory
moments. The day after the visit, more than ever, I knew my career would
be in wine! Since then, Bacchus has accompanied me every day. We came
with Marie, without knowing too much, entering the world of the great
age-old terroirs of Saint-Emilion. And not just any one!

At the time, the property was undivided between the Vauthiers and their
aunt, Mme Dubois-Chalon, and the relationships between them were rather
tempestuous. After years of legal battles and family conflicts, the vineyard
and the château regained calm and serenity through its rebirth, in the hands
of Alain Vauthier and his sister, Catherine. Since 2005, his daughter Pauline,
licensed oenologist, has been at his side. This succession is the final act of a
special Ausone rarity in the world of wine. Since its inception, only three
families have succeeded as the head of the property:

– The Lescours family, from the thirteenth to the sixteenth century,

– Jacques de Lescure and his heirs, in the seventeenth century,

– The Chatonnet-Cantenats of the late seventeenth century to the late
nineteenth century.

Since then, the Dubois-Challon-Vauthiers, from the same line as the previous one, have kept the property within the family.

Ausone was named after a fourth-century poet, Decimus Magnus Auso-
nius, who lived in Bordeaux and Saint-Emilion. The site where the domain
was built is in a locality called Roc Blancan (White Rock). From the sixteenth
century, it was the subject – like all the Saint-Émilion area – of a great page

# BORDEAUX
## Château Ausone

in the history of the Gironde: underground mining of Asterie limestone. This stone takes its name from the presence of Asteria fossils, a sister organism to the starfish, which are found here. On the site of Ausone, the vast galleries that meander endlessly, snaking under the château, the chapel and the vineyards, reflect the importance of these excavations over the centuries.

Open-cast quarries, like the galleries in Saint-Émilion, abound in the village. The extraction of stones by galleries and not digging in the open was chosen because of the high added value generated by land surfaces. Destroying a source of income, such as wine, by digging in vineyards, was out of the question. In Gironde, it was established that the total surface area excavated exceeded 2,000 hectares! All the great buildings of the Gironde, from the eighteenth century to the early twentieth, were reared with these limestones. This trade was heavily relied on by the region's economy from the thirteenth to the nineteenth century, until competing, at certain times, with the revenue generated by vineyards.

The galleries of Ausone also include the wine cellar. It covers an area of 1,800 square meters under the château. On the same level as the cellar, another underground quarry spans 3,800 square meters with galleries 4 to 6 meters in height. Then, on a lower level, a third quarry is the most extensive of Ausone: 8,000 square meters. Its galleries are supported by a forest of pillars (153 in all). In total, 13,800 square meters of open quarries. Added to this incredible amplitude are three kilometers of galleries whose entrances were blocked in the nineteenth century to facilitate the cultivation of mushrooms. In fact, the lower galleries, the largest, were for another, similar use. Until 1985, they were used for the production of cultivated agarics, i.e. button mushrooms. It can be estimated that the entirety would be as vast as what the George V covers, with its nine floors above ground and three floors underground (the cellar is 15 meters below the hotel), an area of 38,000 square meters. This is why Alain Vauthier always said, "A small portion of the quarries is used for wine aging in barrels."

Today, the domain is oriented towards the light with its 7 hectares of vines (45% Merlot and 55% Cabernet Franc) in terraces and on the limestone bedrock, in the form of a headland. A site all at once sober and monumental. It is one of four châteaux to benefit from the status of premier grand cru classé A, confirmed at the last review of the classification in 2012 (Saint-

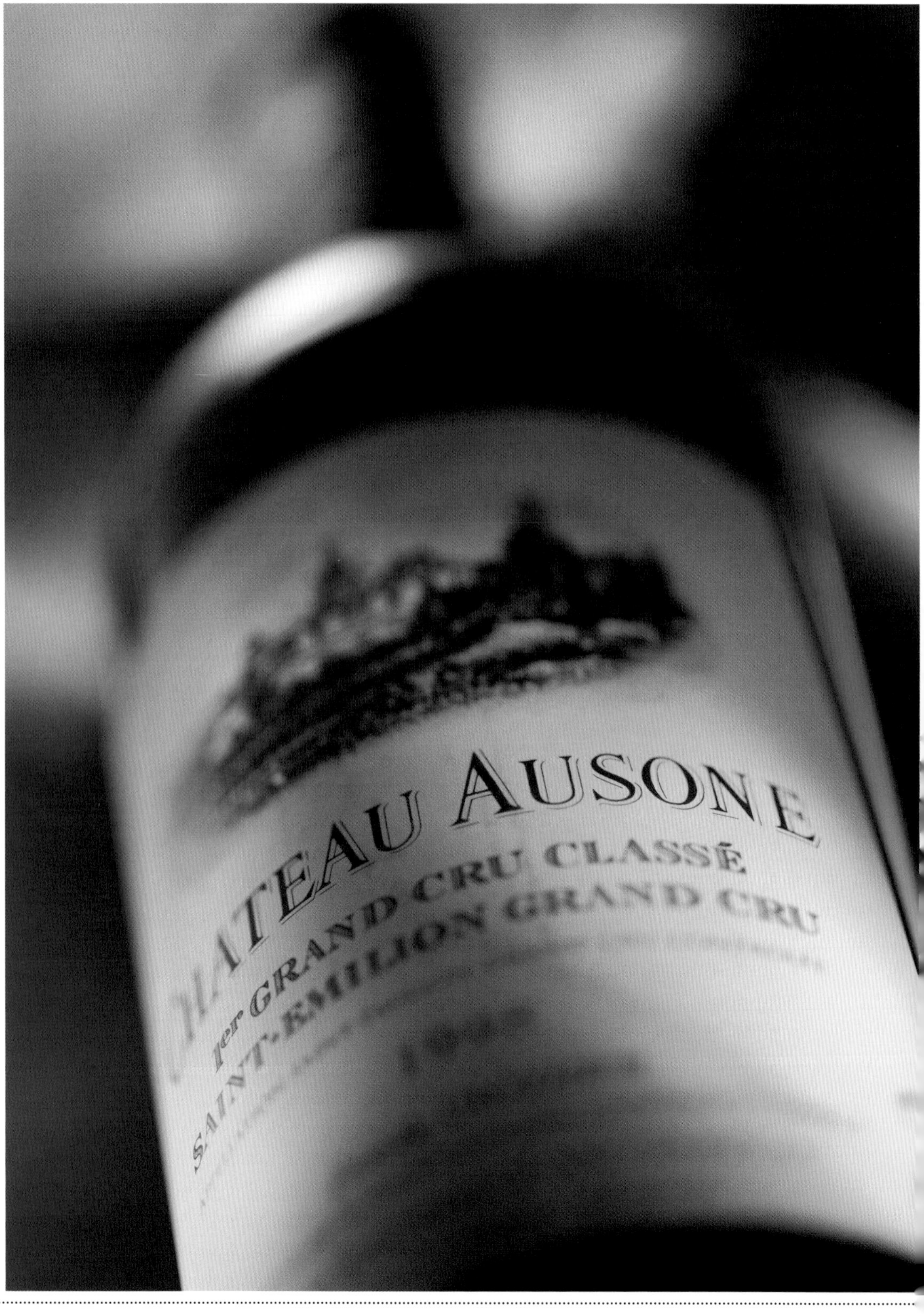
ATEAU AUSONE
1er GRAND CRU CLASSÉ
SAINT-EMILION GRAND CRU

Émilion is the only appellation of the Bordeaux region to review its ranking every ten years). The three other châteaux are Château Cheval Blanc, Château Angélus and Château Pavie.

The Vauthier terroir is easier to understand than elsewhere. In some places, landslides and rock explosions have exposed the clay and limestone terroir in its layer. When you enter the cellar, looking up towards the roof, there are the Cabernets and Merlots rootlets winding through. In front of you, the wines in barrels, born of the same vines, continue maturing.

Those were my first steps in a wine cellar.

# The Wines

I have had many opportunities since 1984 to survey the vineyards of Ausone, to taste its fruits and wines alongside Alain. Admittedly, over the last fifteen years, Ausone has become a world reference, so much so that every year, one of the most anticipated releases of Bordeaux primeurs is from this cru.

Even though it was long forgotten by rating tabloids, today it leads the industry. The only downside to this success is its scarcity among gourmet restaurants in France. Its current coastline does not facilitate access, like other great châteaux of Bordeaux elsewhere.

## Tasting carried out in 2013, at the château

**2009.** *I close with this vintage, harvested ten days earlier than the 2008 and entering history like the 2000. But I will – I hope – be patient if I want to enjoy it like the magnum of 1900 Ausone served in 2005 at the George V, which had not lost its sensuality! At this age, it's rare! A wine where the spices, candied fruits and notes of dried flowers express the long and slow work of time on a masterpiece of nature. This 2009 wine could well be of that caliber.*

**2008.** *Sublime wine that we like to refer to as classic. Harvest between 15 and 20 October. A taut style, precise. Will need decanting before serving. Will be a gastronomic wine within five years.*

**2007.** *This is the vintage for Pauline since taking over the Grand Vin and her second, Chapelle d'Ausone. It is half-body, soft, with an almost feminine sensuality. A vintage needing to breathe a bit after two great years of aging. It will be ready to be served within three years.*

**2006.** *Very successful, this time with more apparent tension, but what tannins! A textbook for beginner tasters as they are both large and delicate. Pure elegance.*

**2005.** *With this vintage, we enter another category. This is a big year in the sense that the Cabernets and Merlots were sublime, without problems associated with drought or concern of any kind. The work in the cellar was therefore not too exciting. A wine that is sappy, velvety, intense and dense. A wine to keep for a long time…*

2004. *The efforts are paying off and this wine is reaping the benefits. Although this vintage is somewhat ungrateful, it remains sensual, fine and fruity at all points. Long in the mouth without displaying power. Very nice juiciness. Remarkable. Distinguished terroir. A delicious wine within five to eight years.*

2003. *Vintage was very scorching, as you know. The right decisions throughout the plant cycle. A great terroir that helped to avoid or mitigate the water stress as well as a high percentage of Cabernet Franc saved the vintage. It's not an extroverted wine – by no means stewed. A touch of mint camphor, black fruit, a marked density, still needs to settle down.*

2002. *Complicated vintage, as the Merlot foundered. The Cabernets fared better and allowed for a soft, fruity wine of medium density, balanced, to enjoy now. Among the many pairings, I would consider fresh hazelnuts with Sologne venison loin, chanterelle ravioli and a cocoa sauce poivrade.*

2001. *A great expression of a vintage where the intensity has given way to more elegance, without too much structure, letting the floral side be expressed. A half-body Ausone but balanced. Very nice bottle within five years.*

**2000 Château Ausone.** *A blend of 55% Cabernet Franc and 45% Merlot. The creamy Merlot is refreshing, balanced by the very pure tension of Cabernet. A high density, a remarkable length. It can be opened but it will reach its full potential within 10 years. At least! Just because… Ausone demands it now. An almost clinical absence of aromatic deviation and a taste frame as tight as a corset. This is a great, rigorous wine. This vintage tasted admirably at a 2008 tasting, during a lunch with Jean-Luc Thunevin, the originator of the famous Saint-Émilion micro-cuvées, which he developed in his home… the former Saint-Émilion garage. Also present were his wife and Alain Vauthier. Alain's 2008 faced off with the 1989 Château Monbrison, a beautiful cru (eminent member of the l'Union des Grands Crus de Bordeaux), a 1995 Pingus. The latter is one of the great wines of Ribera del Duero (birthplace of the famous Vega Sicilia Unico). For the record, in 1990, this appellation had 9,000 hectares. It now covers 22,000 hectares. It is the flagship cuvée of Dominio de Pingus. A property created in 1995 in a… Quintanilla de Onésimo garage by Peter Sisseck. The man has become one of the most famous winemakers in Spain, despite his Danish origins. By creating this wine, 100% Tinto Fino cuvée (synonymous with Tempranillo), he created a myth: Pingus. That was its nickname in Denmark. Facing this matador, Ausone admirably played the game.*

# Château Cheval Blanc

*An Iron Fist in a Velvet Glove*

# T
HE DOMAIN
WAS BORN IN 1832.
Previously, it was attached to the immense property then called
Château Figeac. From its ten-hectare beginning, after several
nearby acquisitions, the cru reached its final size of 37 hectares
of vineyards (for a total of 41 hectares, including the garden) in 1871.
Originally known as Vin de Figeac, the owner baptized his cru in the name
of the Cheval Blanc locality that bore the former Château Figeac's small-
holding. Legend has it that Henry IV, coming back from Navarre, made a
stop at the inn. In recognition, the innkeeper renamed his post house
Auberge du Cheval Blanc. Consequently, in 1853, the Château Cheval Blanc
name appeared on the labels. The cru quickly gained great recognition – it
won a bronze medal in 1862 in London, a gold medal in 1878 in Paris, then
Antwerp in 1885 and Brussels in 1910. The Cheval Blanc label still honors
this legacy with its two nineteenth-century medals framing the vintage.

The Fourcaud Laussacs remained in charge of this grand cru for a hundred
and sixty years, always through direct transmission to each generation. However, the wine would be nothing without those who gave birth to it. At
Cheval Blanc, an iconic character managed the cru from 1943 to 1987:
Gaston Vaissière. He would witness his work honored in 1955 by the classification of Cheval Blanc as a Saint-Emilion premier grand cru classé A.
Throughout his career, he was at the helm of famous vintages. He officiated
at a time when modern oenology, research and technical advances were still
in their infancy.

Nevertheless, despite cellar conditions which today would make a freshly
minted oenologist shiver, vintages of legendary proportions have come to
life: the 1947, 1948, 1949, 1950, 1961, 1964, 1966 and 1982. In those years, the
terroir, its exceptional climate and the gaze of Men were already deeply
"rooted." A perfect example of technical developments and familial resources
invested over the years to nurture and expand this cru of clay-gravel terroir.
The grape varieties are generally composed of 55% Cabernet Franc, known
as "Bouchet," and 45% Merlot. I had the good fortune of meeting
M. Vaissière once during my first visit to Cheval Blanc. It was in 1985, with
Jean Frambourg (charismatic president of the Sommeliers of France), my

## BORDEAUX
### Château Cheval Blanc

good friend and wine poet Christian Stévanin and an Areopagus of somme-liers from all over France.

In 1998, because of the inability to properly manage the domain with so many successors, the cru was yielded to Bernard Arnault and Baron Albert Frère. They, in turn, entrusted the direction of their cru classé to Pierre Lurton, who arrived at Cheval Blanc at the age of 34, in 1990. The man comes from a great and ancient family of Bordeaux landowners. (The Lurton family owns twenty-five domains in the Bordeaux region, equalling about 1600 hectares.) His career has been dazzling. At 23, he left the university benches to manage the Clos Fourtet, Saint-Emilion premier grand cru classé, which had belonged to the Lurton family for many years. It was his uncle, André Lurton, who entrusted him to lead this great cru, of which Merlot is king. It was at this age that Pierre Lurton made his first cuvée, alongside Émile Peynaud, "the father of modern oenology." Later, as if to confirm a sublime destiny, he was chosen among fifty candidates to lead the Château Cheval Blanc. As Pierre recounts, "In an interview, the Fourcaud Laussac heirs informed me that the Lurton name was perhaps not ideal due to my family's influence and suggested that I take my mother's name instead. It complicated things when I responded that my mother was a Lafite!"

Beyond his obvious qualities, reflected as it were in his singular ability to lead two premiers crus classés, Cheval Blanc and Yquem, Pierre possesses an uncommon sense of humor. His sense of timing is formidable and his comebacks, feared. Not content with directing *two* legendary crus, he also owns a domain in Entre-Deux-Mers: the Château Marjosse. At the moment, we serve two of his 2011 and 2012 white wines for receptions at the George V salons. He defines his situation well, "I'm in heaven every day, and I come back down in the evenings at Entre-Deux-Mers. There's this sweet vertigo in between. Then there's the Château Marjosse – that's what makes me respectable!"

To this, I can add a touch of derision, like the night in 2012 when he joined us at the Bistrot du Sommelier, a famous Bordeaux restaurant run by Hervé Valverde, a great local figure of sommellerie and proven bon vivant. This is the home base of Jacques Dupont and his staff during his annual campaigns of primeurs tastings. Pierre Lurton walked in, carrying a shopping bag fit for a housewife, and handed it to us: "I brought you some products of the region." His Bordeaux specialties consisted of a 2007 Yquem, a 1990 Cheval Blanc and a 1988 Yquem!

The following year with Nicolas Charrière, our first sommelier, and Gérard Sibourg Baudry (owner of the Caves Legrand), we went to the château to discover the new wine storehouse designed by architect Christian de Portzamparc. It took five years of work to achieve this wonder, both architecturally and technically. Pierre Lurton and the architect opted for vinification in concrete vats. They were curved, optimizing, like a tasting glass, the oxygenation of musts. They were segmented into fifty-two units and their dimensions studied according to the size of the parcels in the vineyard. The storage cellar was below, like a crypt, with a completely different atmosphere, lined with perforated brick walls to facilitate natural ventilation and to allow, by gravity, the wine to flow. A place with clean lines. Simple, soft. Yet the imposing building, adjacent to the château, seemed poised on a cloud.

# MEMORIES

My first memories of Cheval Blanc were not wine tastings but close encounters with the wine. In 1979, when I was a cook apprentice at Roc Land, a restaurant in my provincial Bretagne, on Sunday afternoons I would see the maitre d'hôtel recover, with great care, a bottle from the cellar, always the same one, for the same customer. It was the 1947 Cheval Blanc. At the time, this wine cost 900 francs! A fortune for me, who earned 100 francs a month as an apprentice. Not long after, I learned the value and rarity of this wine (and why this customer came from Rennes specifically for it!): because the 1947 Cheval Blanc is an icon of Bordeaux and one of the legendary vintages of Cheval Blanc. For proof, just read the beautiful pages devoted to it in *Au Cheval Blanc: Une Histoire de Millésimes* by Claude Fourcaud-Laussac (Mollat Publishing, 1998).

Several decades separate the young apprentice from the seasoned sommelier today. In 1979, I never dreamt that thirty years later, in September 2009, I would be flying over Cheval Blanc. Yet that was what was happening at the request of a client, a personal friend of Christopher Norton, a great wine lover and patron of Le Cinq. The man ranks among America's television stars. Idolized, always in a hurry, he had long wanted to visit Cheval Blanc. Having a free day, he asked me the impossible: a visit and lunch at the château and then to be back in Paris for a big gala he was invited to! Between the airport transfers and very congested traffic… the George V concierge was conclusive. He saw only one way to pull off this magic trick: not only by air, but in a helicopter! For me, this was a first. Throughout the flight, I was able to describe to Ryan the different terroirs over which we were flying low enough to recognize and describe. A wonderful way to introduce the vineyards, great domains and major sites of our wonderful country. He devoured the landscapes with his eyes.

After three hours of flight, we landed in the garden of the Château Cheval Blanc. The moment was even more exceptional as it was in September of 2009. With a fantastic climate, Cheval Blanc was then on the eve of producing perhaps its greatest vintage since 1990.

We were greeted by Pierre Lurton, after a tour of the wineries and a tasting of the 2008 vintage in the barrels. This vintage, still developing, was marked by major qualitative advances in the vineyards. Cheval Blanc would initiate the futuristic work of the cellars a few years later. Projects that require a great deal of energy combined with team management capabilities. As I said sometimes to Pierre, "I am here in the image of Cheval Blanc: an iron hand in a velvet glove."

We went inside. To begin, Pierre had a 2007 Y d'Yquem served, full-bodied and powerful. It accompanied us at the table with a light and refreshing entrée. We awaited the announced dish, saddle of lamb prepared by Chef Philippe Etchebest. The two chosen wines were exceptional. Without further ado, we tasted a 1908 Château Cheval Blanc, which was a revelation to me as the wine was still holding very well. It was still there. The color, very deteriorated, tiled, did not foreshadow the aromatic complexity of the nose. The mouth, in lace, was maintained by a lively acidity that must have been vivid in its youth. A slender and delicate mouth. Refined. We then tackled a magnum of 1966 Cheval Blanc. This was a pivotal year for Cheval Blanc as it marked the baptism of a new fermenting room. Cement vats replaced the former wood, ageless and inconvenient. It was a very big year, long underestimated, which has nimbly overcome the decades. Wines such as this

# BORDEAUX
## Château Cheval Blanc

one, in magnum, are still impressive. This proved to be the case. Michael Broadbent (creator of the Wine Department at Christie's in 1966), who tasted it on multiple occasions, preferred it to the famous 1947 and defined it as the "epitome of elegance." In 1987, it again gave him a quarter of a century without problems. He was right.

The dessert selected, a soltana salad and cookie with almonds and saffron cream, complemented the 1988 Château d'Yquem very well and still reminds me of the first ones served in Montrond.

We still had time to take a few steps outside with a cup of mocha. The afternoon was beautiful. Already, however, the pilot came to tell us that we could no longer delay departure. We were lifted above the vineyard and took flight, like a dream on a summer's day.

# Some of the wines from a château tasting, in 2013, with Nicolas Charrière

**2009. Cheval Blanc.** *Intense, concentrated and, at the same time, very delicate.*

**2008.** *Year when the work in the vineyards played a greater role in order to further refine the qualitative aspect and maturities. Very classic vintage, fresh, tight, tannins present without harshness. Good concentration. Less fluid than the preceding.*

**2000.** *A great Cheval, still closed today. The Cabernet Franc was outstanding and achieved a rare balance with the maturity of the Merlot. To enjoy, decant an hour beforehand. This is the birth year of the family's youngest. After Petit Cheval (second wine of Cheval Blanc), a generic Saint-Emilion is created.*

*N.B.: Don't forget to maintain carafes, while decanting, at the right temperature, i.e. between 15 and 17°C.*

## BORDEAUX
## Château Cheval Blanc

# Tasting at a wonderful dinner at the château, in 2005

Pierre invited my wife and I – and a great man, who did so much for me during a "pivotal" time in my professional life, Raymond Garcia, an extraordinary character, a man of heart.

**1990. Cheval Blanc.** *Modern, slightly more sophisticated version of Cheval Blanc, great length, a little wiser than its elders. To drink with relish.*

**1982.** *It's as if everyone knew a great vintage would result, which is amazing since we talk of low yields as an irrepressible gauge of quality. In 1982, the yields were particularly high in the Bordeaux region. And yet! Thirty years later, these wines are still exciting, and we praise their qualities. Here, this means a total fullness, notes of macerated red fruits, black spices, Lebanese cedar (like the venerable one at the domain).*

**1966.** *One of the greatest tasted. Intense and deep. The black fruit is mixed with camphor and woody, resinous notes. It is less impressive than the 1947 but much more balanced.*

**1947.** *Considered the greatest vintage of the century. The then director found it superior even to the 1929. However, after World War II, the technical means were not great. Everything was lacking, starting with the barrels. But the harvests were super, the grapes of great quality, the fermentations took place without incident and despite the virtual absence of new barrels, the wines lived through a wonderful breeding. During my tasting, it was still impressive, extroverted, solar, pulpy, generous. Almost sweet, remarkable length, not a wrinkle, a great wine.*

# Pétrus

*The Lord of Pomerol*

# P

ÉTRUS!
AN ILLUSTRIOUS NAME,
evoking for some the first bishop of Rome, for most, an ancient name, while still for others, a great sommelier: Antoine Pétrus, head sommelier/director who succeeded Gérald Louis-Canfailla, the so-called "Monsieur Louis," at the Lasserre restaurant in Paris. Mostly, it is a name globally recognized to be that of the Pomerol wine. Pétrus is humble. Here, the title of château or domain is not highlighted or even claimed. Along with this unique fact, at this level of excellence, there has never been a second label created. The undesirable Merlot batches invariably take the path of trading.

The vineyard takes root on a clay ridge, a geological "caviar" over an area of 11.5 hectares, at the heart of a sea of vines. It is a macroterroir that has always sparked passions and inspired lusts. Here, the ambrosia of the gods was born. From the beginning of this cru, there was a family: the Arnauds. Throughout the nineteenth century, they watched over this terroir and gave it its name. In 1930, an innkeeper from Libourne, Mme Loubat, was interested in wine and began to purchase shares from the Arnauds. At the time, the economic crisis was in full swing, and the vineyards saw their values plummet. After the war, she became the sole owner of Pétrus. In the 1950s, she teamed up with an up-and-coming merchant, Jean-Pierre Moueix. In 1961, when Mme Loubat passed away, there was no doubt that St. Peter would open the pearly gates to welcome her. The nephew and niece of "Aunt Lou" bickered over the inheritance, the nephew selling his shares to Jean-Pierre Moueix. It was passed on, in 1972, to his son Jean-François, who acquired it from the last heiress, Lily Lacoste-Loubat, whose remaining shares allowed him to become the sole owner of Pétrus. Everyone gave, every day, the best of themselves to maintain and constantly refine the work of their predecessors on this unrivaled terroir.

It lies on the 45th parallel, not far from the Dordogne; further west, the Gulf Stream awaits the influence of the ocean, a boon for the entire region. This clay-limestone terroir, this hilltop of montmorillonite clay, these Merlots and the experience of two hundred years allied with Correzian commercial instincts formed Pétrus. Pétrus, as well as other timeless vineyards, are national treasures in line with *The Mona Lisa* or Versailles. Who would dream of seeing these wonders altered? It is not a matter of luxury, but one of art. This is not only the result of expertise, as it is also nature which dictates its conditions year after year. Man is only an interpreter.

My relationship with Pétrus began in 1987 when I joined La Poularde. The stepfather of Gilles Étéocle (the owner chef), Joannès Randoing, had accumulated in the cellars of his inn a solid collection of Pétrus through M. Boyer, the manager of the Wine Company from 1970-1980. At the time, Mr. Randoing acquired thirty-six to forty-eight bottles per vintage, without batting an eye. La Poularde had a clientele that perfectly adhered to this great wine. The pleasures of the palate occupied an important place in the landscape of the Forez plain, as in the neighboring departments. Organizing a dinner at La Poularde was of a selective nature, the equivalent today in Paris of an evening at the Comédie-Française or the Palais Garnier. At the time, between 1987 and 1999, the prices that we followed were far from our reality in 2015. For example, in 1999, the 1983 vintage in Montrond was priced at 1,800 francs on the menu, and recently, we served it at Le Cinq for 2,300 euros. I dare not make the conversion. It also sold out – it was the most affordable. Great vintages like the 1982, 1978 and 1975 were frequently opened, but also some rare pearls in the intervening years: 1981, 1979, 1976… And the crates were well stocked.

In the kitchen, Bernard Barret, owner/chef at La Poularde, prepared, among other wonders, flaky turnovers with truffles and foie gras d'anthologie. We had, during the season, one loyal customer who, every Sunday, would come with his wife from Clermont-Ferrand for the turnovers and a bottle of Pétrus… provided that the price of the bottle did not exceed 1,000 francs. What a joy it was to serve and open older vintages with such regularity for these gourmets (of a certain age) who traveled over 100 kilometers to indulge themselves. An era that seems so far away…

At the source of these vintages, there was one man: Jean-Claude Berrouet. Arriving in 1964, he began with, as his son revealed to me, "only a table, a chair and a mustimeter for the whole laboratory." He vinified and oversaw forty-three Pétrus vintages. Since 2007, Olivier, his son, has been running the property. He works closely with Jean Moueix, himself the son of Jean-François. I dare say, they both act and think under the watchful eye of their fathers.

BORDEAUX
Pétrus

In the last fifteen years, Pétrus has gained even more presence than before, with greater accuracy and density. Perhaps without equaling the post-war vintages that are essential in the pantheon of the great wines of Bordeaux, which we still taste today. Yet the cellars of the Bordeaux region sixty years ago were less well-equipped than they are today. Like *enfants terribles*, musts must have been difficult to manage, and wines to raise. However, the remarkable 1989 is a monument and the 1990, one of the most successful of Bordeaux in this vintage.

# MEMORIES

The list of memories that binds me to Pétrus is long, especially since I joined the George V. It would be easy for me to fill pages describing incredible visits with famous guests, facilitated by heads of state, as the international market and the rating achieved by our wines have significantly slowed their consumption and sharing among amateurs. They are still tasted by amateurs but often under distant latitudes.

It is through the arrival of these guests at the George V that I have maintained and even developed the rhythm of my tastings. Bearing witness to the fact, within the depths of the cellars lays an impressive collection of bottles sampled at Le Cinq by the most passionate of our Pétrus fans. My special relationship with the domain allowed me, on numerous occasions, to visit Pétrus with friends, upon which they would suddenly revert to a child-like state at finally being allowed to discover and touch the cherished object. It must be mentioned here how wonderful it is to be received at Pétrus by Jean-François Moueix or the Berrouets. Their proximity and simplicity are the antithesis of the luxurious image conveyed by this great wine. For when you love this wine, treading the terroir that witnesses its birth, feeling the earth, meeting its creators, these things are the ultimate recognition. Tasting it at its birthplace makes sense, as it always does in the world of wine. These are wonderful moments that blur the material existential contingencies. You live in a dream. It was in this state of being that on an evening of February 2013, in a great location just steps from the house, reserved for the occasion, I organized, with the whole team's partic-

BORDEAUX
Pétrus

324

ipation, a memorable dinner for the Le Cinq sommeliers. We had invited three friends: Laurent Plantevin, one of the finest gourmets of France; Philippe Bourguignon, a prominent businessman and friend of Laurent, and Pierre Arditi, whose palate matched his panache. Our faithful David Bizet, chef of Le Cinq, had agreed to take over the kitchen, having just left the George V.

Maggie Henriquez, the fairy godmother of Krug, privy to this rare evening, had delivered a Jeroboam of 1996 Krug Vintage. A wine of incredible density, great tension. The format in Jeroboam gave it a great youth. The mouth was almost tannic; the wine lively, frisky. To escort it, we had a few baskets of wild Granville oysters and clams in breadcrumbs with lime gratin. Pierre brought a bottle from his cellar: a 1999 Haut-Brion Blanc in magnum. The color was yellow gold, the nose with a beautiful evolution, notes of plants, propolis, wax and vanilla infusion. In the mouth, it was wide and dense, of a great maturity. David, meanwhile, was in charge – aided by two assistant sommeliers – of scallops prepared in brown butter, Granny Smith juliennes and celeriac, which succeeded roasted Chausey lobsters, coconut sauce and combawa…

For the birds of Bretagne that a friend brought for us, served with their roasts, I went all out: 1989 Château Lafleur. A great one. The color is still very dense, black. Fine, complex, truffled, licorice, black fruit compote. Very full-bodied mouth, supported by a present tannic structure but with a fine and buttery seed. Still very young.

One of our former sommeliers, whose Périgord family had truffles at their disposal, sent us something for everyone. David prepared them in green cabbage, étoufféed in a cast iron skillet. For this fragrant and refined dish, I had acquired from a wine merchant friend a 1959 Pétrus. My idea was to share this wine with all our young people, under the best conditions. We were entering another world. The color had not one deep wrinkle. Very concentrated nose. It took a good hour decanting it before beginning to understand it. At this stage of maturity, candied fruit, spices, camphor notes, earthy humus. Delicate fragrances, continuing to amplify. Mouth of great concentration. Spherical, buttery tannins, fine, extremely long. The overall impression was that of a great, balanced wine. Coming from a very hot year, exhilarating. A lot of sensuality. Even Pierre, who had yet lived some incredible moments with wine, could not believe this harmony and these moments shared between us, in the middle of the night!

A whole truffle, with cabbage, was served to everyone. Our young apprentice, Ludovic, then leaned towards Thierry, sitting on his left, to ask how he was supposed to cut... and eat... the black diamond.

These moments are a reward for me, every year. It is my pleasure to share these wines with my sommelier team annually. It was a dream when I was their age. In memory of a La Poularde specialty in Montrond-les-Bains, Thierry had left a Fourme d'Ambert in a stone jar to soak for a week, marinating in a ten-year-old port. For this purplish-rimed cheese, fat and soft, we went for a magnum of 1979 Vosne-Romanée premier cru, which Cheurlin Maxime from the Domaine Noëllat had offered me. A smooth and delicate wine, spicy, with kirsched notes. It was certain that, out of Pétrus, the gauntlet had been thrown.

Then, as always, the unmoveable dessert arrived, carried by two servers: the La Luna Rhum Baba, abundantly topped with a vanilla whipped cream and aged Bally rhum raisins. For this masterful baba and the grand finale, I had prepared a rarity. From a wooden box, I took out a bottle wrapped in a paillon: an 1885 Saint-James Rhum. Topaz color, black, high viscosity. Thickness. Stunning, lively nose. Yet, subdued with bouquets of vanilla, rhum raisins, caramelized pineapple and sandalwood. A stunning nose, plunging us into the exotic. In the mouth, the attack, slightly sharp, lines the entire palate with a long length. The minutes do not exhaust the length in the mouth. Notes of leather, licorice stick, Zan.

Around 6 o'clock in the morning, rhum and fatigue overcame me. However, I will never forget sharing this brandy and 1959 Pétrus! That night, Nicolas, Mikaël, Gabriele, Florent, Victor, Edmond and Ludovic, and our friends, infused their memories with masterpieces.

BORDEAUX
Pétrus

# Tasting in Pétrus, 2013

The first vintage in Pétrus that we tasted was one from the creation of a new label to help prevent forgeries – in fact, there was a trial run with the 1999. Starting from this vintage, there would be tiny, almost undetectable holographic chips placed in two different locations.

**2009 and 2010.** *These are monuments with not enough distance at this time. Today, I preferred the 2010. These are vintages to be served at my kids' weddings (a small gathering).*

**2008.** *It's a warm year, meaning that the alcoholic aspect of the wine needs to be digested so as to be expressed.*

**2007.** *It was at least rainy, but above all the first vintage for Olivier Berrouet. But, as they say, "rainy wedding, happy marriage!" I wish him as much happiness as the head of this property that his dad had throughout his life as Cellar Master. The happiness of giving birth every year to something unique, something that surpasses itself. As for the vintage, I would call it serious, a thinking wine.*

**2006.** *A serious vintage, structured, tannic, to be forgotten still for five years.*

**2005.** *Once again, smart extraction has offered Pétrus body and remarkable balance. A long-keeping wine for over fifteen years.*

**2004.** *The most oceanic in recent years. The structure in the mouth is long, but the wine is more of a Savile Row three-piece suit than an Arnys velvet. An already appreciable wine.*

**2003.** *Reveals the exceptional nature of the terroir due to its water-retaining clay. In short, a successful 2003, not too drying, structured.*

**2001.** *A success for this more difficult vintage, with notes of dried roses and softness in its tannins. Pétrus generally does not allow immediate approach. It has fire, but it will need ten to fifteen years of maturation.*

**2000.** *It is a delight, harmonious and smooth. Of great length.*

# Château Lafleur

*Buried Treasure*

# T HIS SECRET PROPERTY,

covering only 4.58 hectares, reflects the adequacy of an unusual family structure for a historic cru of this order. This is not really a château, but rather a beautiful stone gardener's cottage, with sky-colored shutters, overlooking the... vineyard... peeking through the threshold.

This "Garden of Pomerol" was created in 1872 by the great-great-grand-father of the current owner, M. Henri Greloud. Jacques and Sylvie Guinaudeau, now masters of the site, exude harmony and kindness while passion and tenacity radiate from Baptiste, their son.

One of the most striking points of this great terroir is the absence of any fragmentation or modifications of any kind to this vineyard since its inception. The Robin ladies, aunts of M. Guinaudeau, maintained the integrity of this coveted land for almost fifty years. This family continuity has helped to preserve the old vines in mass selection even after the frost of 1956. The Robin ladies respected the terroir, safeguarding the spirit of their father. Here, we understand the "value" of time as well as that of the cru. Neither's role can be diminished. This jewel, Lafleur, is a carefully polished diamond, where each facet reflects a piece of the place's soul and perhaps also those who have shaped it throughout the twentieth century.

In Paris, the famous restaurateurs of Tan Dinh, rue de Verneuil, in the seventh arrondissement, the Vifian brothers – Robert in particular – had spoken to me about it for many years. Yet it was only after twenty years of experience that I really got to know this cru. My ignorance was due to the fact that this wine is mainly sold abroad. It was, furthermore, in California, in 2012, that I was able to taste it and to include this property at the top of my strongest emotional responses.

It is a siliceous, clay-limestone terroir, limonaire. The Cabernet Franc and Merlot complement each other equally and wonderfully to give us a pulpy nectar, fine, extremely long and singular.

# M

EMORIES

The discovery of Lafleur is attached, in my memory, to a particular dinner. It took place in October 2013, at the initiative of a collector friend and prominent taster, Maurice Marciano. While visiting the cellars, he perceived my interest in discovering his collection of Château Lafleur across the great vintages of the twentieth century. Over the course of my stay with him, he had prepared a huge surprise for me.

This great moment was held in the dining room of The Restaurant at Meadowood, three Michelin stars, in California, with Chef Christopher Kostow. A few wine-loving friends were invited. There were six of us around the table, which was generously filled with glasses. Nearest to the chef, our host had brought a few bottles from the cellar. We began with a 2002 Dom Pérignon Rosé. His favorite champagne. It was served with crackers and cheese, caviar and garden herbs. Then the first wine appeared: 1983 Château Lafleur. We had begun! The 1983 vintage was medium. No decanting. Open nose, notes of macerated and candied fruit, very ripe. Mouth of a great silkiness, fine and delicate, none of the slightly drying, harsh side often found in the 1983. A vintage to be savoured smoothly. To accompany it, the chef offered us a Wagyu beef entrée cooked back-and-forth on a teppanyaki plate, simply seasoned with sauteed shiitake mushrooms in aromatic herbs.

Then came a 1989 Lafleur. Thinking about this wine, I recollect recently having a conversation with Jean-Claude Berrouet, Pétrus winemaker for nearly half a century. I indicated to him my feelings regarding Pétrus and Lafleur in this vintage. For me, I found that the 1989 Lafleur exceeded the Pétrus. He said, "You're right!" For him, there was an additional maturity in the tannins that benefitted Lafleur, while Pétrus, less so. Still very young during the tasting. Such potential!

We prolonged this tasting with a broth of black truffle and cannelloni with calf sweetbread. The 1982 Lafleur was next to arrive. This is "the" 1982 which my memory places at the firmament of my personal rankings. Unparalleled in this year of 2013. After fifteen minutes spent arguing amongst us about this incomparable wine, the kitchen served us young crispy cockerels with candied turnips, white soy and black truffles.

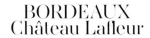

BORDEAUX
Château Lafleur

Then came an avalanche: 1975 Lafleur, intense, deep, truffled, sappy, served together with a 1979 Lafleur, which, although appearing "amiable," proved upon opening to be of an unusual density. Juxtaposed in the wake was a 1970 Lafleur; for my part, I find that most of the 1970 Bordeaux are on a slippery slope at the moment, yet it amazed us with a flesh and lack of thinness on the mid-palate. I must say that the vines well withstood the frost of 1956, as we still had old vines here. An outstanding 1970, not thin or metallic. We could turn to the crusted steak with morels and foie gras butter. With a 1950 Lafleur, obscure vintage that had its heyday in England (and France) as it was among the post-war greats (with 1945, 1947 and 1949); a success in Pomerol with Pétrus, tasted several times in a magnum bottle and still very sappy, concentrated, fruity and floral. Less truffled than Pétrus, but an exceptional texture. Here, there was a beautiful Stilton teamed with port cherries and pecans to close the feast.

No dessert for lunch. I just asked to keep the glasses and switch from one to another for a few more minutes. Although we had been received at one of the finest restaurants in the region, the work of the chef came in second place that day. I was completely absorbed by the vintages that succeeded one another, recording every detail that I perceived. I only remember the dishes because I scribbled them in the evening when resuming my notes of the lunch. This tasting remains the most memorable that I have had the privilege of experiencing. This is a great wine that made me wait a long time. I think Lafleur, just like the taster, should be approached only after it has reached sufficient maturity. We must be worthy of it. It's a wine that I compare to the Opera. It is an absolute art, an absolute wine. However, to understand it, to perceive all its refinement, you must master a number of parameters in the acquisition of knowledge, the art of drinking and also the art of living well.

# Tasting of Château Lafleur at the domain, in 2014

**2009.** *A Lafleur with elegance, line of lace. Rare for this vintage!*

**2007.** *The nose, with a present fruitiness, suggests a wine that will quickly "arrive." The mouth again offers woody notes that must blend.*

**2006.** *This vintage evokes more so the left bank than its own – the reason being the percentage of Cabernet in the blending blows away the classic characteristics. In a word, maintained class, a very good length. An outstanding wine. Very floral.*

**2005.** *It remains one of the great Pomerols in this vintage and competes with its neighbor (Pétrus) without blushing. In fifteen years it will unveil – for those who can wait – a balance, a finish, an incredible finesse.*

**2003.** *Completely sharp with a spicy and kirsched side reminiscent of the Pinots of Côte de Nuits; the mouth is sensual, gourmet, a delight.*

**1982.** *"The" 1982 which my memory places at the firmament of my personal rankings. And unmatched in the year 2013, still a "youthfulness" to rival its coreligionists… from any bank!*

BORDEAUX
Château Lafleur

# Château de Fargues

*Golden Key of de Lur Saluces*

# F

OR MANY YEARS,
I ONLY ASSOCIATED

Lur Saluces with Yquem. Yet, another very old domain binds the family of Comte Alexandre de Lur Saluces, last of the line to oversee Yquem, to a neighboring vineyard five kilometers from the former. Fargues is a fortress pierced with arrow-loops that Comte Alexandre began to energetically rebuild, with the expertise and knowledge of the Sauternes motivating him to complete this masterful resurrection, surrounded by 15 hectares of Sémillon and Sauvignon vines.

From the outside of the court, the fortified château of 1306 was stripped of the ivy that covered its majestic ruins, witness to a troubled time when wars lasted a hundred years. Guillaume de Fargues, nephew of a cardinal, was the first resident builder of this proud fortress, from which invaders could be observed and one's own defended. During uprisings and conflicts, farmers of the region of Langon would take refuge in Fargues, a lordship of multiple services. In 1472, Pierre de Lur, husband of Isabeau de Monferrand, settled in Fargues. The family remained there until 1687 when a fire destroyed the château. The fire sparked physical and moral neglect: the Lur family abandoned the premises. The château was purchased by an older branch of the family, then focused on Yquem. The strength of this ruin's walls is prodigious. Each generation of de Lur Saluces participated in renovations, consolidation work and its upholding within the Sauternes landscape.

Upon returning from WWI, Alexandre's uncle (the Vice President of the National Institute for Appellations of Origin), Bertrand de Lur Saluces,) replanted a portion of the plateau in white grape varieties while abandoning the production of local red wine. From this headland, we find the château Malagar, owned by the Mauriac family. Lower down, the Garonne and Ciron flow – an important waterway for all of Sauternes. "The Sauternes is a mystery," says Alexandre de Lur Saluces, present on this terroir for forty years. The first Fargues was the 1943 vintage, bottled in 1947. After the historic Yquem adventure, which he managed for four decades, Alexandre withdrew to Fargues where he sought to faithfully refurbish these ruins: a long-term task that does not frighten the Comte. The majestic beauty of Fargues helps him confront the risks and constraints of such an undertaking.

BORDEAUX
Château de Fargues

It is a patronage. Fargues produces 1,000 bottles per hectare! So little. A calling. In 2014, he bought 8 hectares of vines in the Fargues vicinity, bringing the operational surface area of the vineyard to 15 hectares today, or about 20,000 bottles annually. Within ten years, Fargues will be a new configuration, of 30 hectares. We are far from the 103 hectares of Yquem's vineyards.

The wine-growing capacity of Fargues is reduced compared to Yquem. This factor plays a major role in aromatic diversity. However, by constant attention to detail, work in the vineyard, sorting of the best *Botrytis* during harvests, these mornings and afternoons of uncertainty about the time change, Comte Alexandre maintains - more profoundly with each passing year - the depth of the Fargues terroirs. The desire to produce a great sweet wine reverberates. Here, producing a dry white wine is out of the question.

For the moment, the recent renaissance of the cru's vineyard does not allow us to revert in time like the other great names of the Sauternes, such as the Médeville family – ancient Sauternes – and their remarkable Château Gilette Crème de Tête that could cross the decades of time. Lacking the bottles born under former generations, in Fargues, the alliance of two such illustrious names as de Lur Saluces and d'Orléans is in itself a measure of continuity and a testament to the will of these families to pass on the fruits of their labors and leave their signature on an age-old tradition. It takes pugnacity to maintain these viticultural selections in our current world. Alexandre de Lur Saluces and Eudes d'Orléans work tirelessly – like all great Sauternes and Barsac landowners – to promote their great sweet wines. However, the fickle business environment reflects the serious commercial difficulties encountered in this region. The entire appellation suffers from a lack of visibility. The wines of Sauternes, although loved and adored, are not consumed. They lie, like gold bars, in the cellars of individuals who are reluctant or who no longer dare open them. It's terrible.

At our level, we are major influencers for Sauternes. We only have to simply replace these wines with a service per glass. This is easy as the purchase price of these incomparable wines is extremely low. Herein lie the major problems of this region. Sale prices are not in correlation with production costs. In fact, in the Bordeaux brokerage world, the Sauternes prices are aligned with those of reds. However, a sparsely quoted red vintage leads brokers to lower the price of Sauternes, regardless of their quality or the production costs incurred.

Moreover, as Alexandre de Lur Saluces stated, the media, very happy to be promoted to influencers through their ratings, just relay, with neither reflection nor agricultural or economic competence, demagogic speeches. In a word: "Indulge in the pleasure of a Maserati for the price of a Twingo." When we refer to the current Sauternes rates, we observe that they have gradually dropped to those of fifteen years ago. In this, the properties producing only Sauternes are condemned to debase their production or even convert to the production of dry white wine. It would be like forcing the Médoc to produce rosé! Alexandre said bluntly, "The prices charged by the commercial environment condemn the Sauternes crus classés to sell at a loss. The interests of the châteaux, the brokerage community and professionals must remain complementary and convergent but not at prices that have no future!"

EMORIES

Often my tastings "uncork" memorable, sometimes legendary meals. One reason for this is that the best part of the day to taste is in the morning between 9 and 11 o'clock. This is why, over the last thirty years in cellars and vaults, opportunities to engage in table discussions have never been lacking. But often, there is an unprecedented event, a rare, unexpected moment that enriches and imprints the memory. This day in September 2014, for example, includes a number of gems that shine in my memory. The weather, dry, was tinged with uncertainty after a rainy summer. The trend focused on passerillage on vines and not on the development of *Botrytis cinerea*. Yet, a few weeks and some sparse rain showers later, the famous fungus grew, spread and illuminated faces and hearts. Meanwhile, Baron Nicolas de Rabaudy and I were in a Fargues tower room, boarded up, soberly yet tastefully redecorated. For the first time in centuries, lunch would be served there. Alongside the Comte Alexandre de Lur Saluces were his son Philippe and the director of Fargues, His Royal Highness Prince Eudes d'Orléans, Duke of Angoulême. For this unusual occasion, our hosts had provided a 2002 Taittinger Comtes de Champagne.

Only one possible entrée in Fargues: white asparagus and scallops in Maltaise sauce. Because, for the All-Bordeaux, there is only white asparagus from Fargues! This restricted production of highly sought, white asparagus is an ancient family tradition. We tasted it with a 2007 Fargues. Harmony of reason and pleasure.

The chef then served us carved medallions in a Bazadaise fillet with Rossini. Here, Comte Alexandre chose a Saint-Émilion cru classé, the 1998 Château Corbin Michotte. There was no need, in creating this dish, to leave the de Lur Saluces

estate, as the domain also makes Bazadaises, a local, unclaimed race that the family re-introduced on the domain and for which Aquitaine chefs eagerly seek out prime cuts. After an improvised blade of Roquefort Le Vieux Berger, escorted by a 2004 Fargues, a fluffy and airy soufflé of saffron and almond blancmange was warmly served to us. There, it was a 1998 Fargues, which undertook through its own aromas to prolong those of the soufflé.

Fargues is not only a Sauternes. It represents a larger whole, preserved by the ravages of time, despite conflicts and shares. A rare example of a patrimonial preservation of this magnitude.

# Tasting at the Château with Nicolas de Rabaudy, September 2014

**2009. Château de Fargues.** *Intense straw yellow color, with large, green reflection. Open nose, fine, develops exotic and floral notes, verbena and lime. The nose reveals elegance and class. Beautiful length in a full-bodied mouth; the liquor is well integrated and the woodiness isn't too dominant. Balanced finish with bitter notes of grapefruit. To wait ten years.*

**2008.** *Light gold color. Open nose, rich, notes of caramel, vanilla, woodiness. Dried mango and pineapple. A seductive and concentrated nose. Rich, slightly heavy mouth, broad and bold. Powerful and long. A finish of medlar jam and currants. A generous Fargues.*

**2005.** *Intense yellow gold color. Fine nose, precise, fairly delicate, floral, still closed. Wide mouth, medium-bodied, but without the intensity of the 2004. Roasted finish, notes of pastry and squash. Balanced. A pretty easy Fargues, however.*

**2004.** *Intense golden yellow color. Fine nose, rich, sophisticated, complete, honey, with the notes of saffron characteristic to great years. Rich, pulpy mouth with relief. Nice acidity giving it structure. The mid-palate is squared and still tight. Great Fargues with an incomparable base, a real success.*

**2001.** *At this stage, the golden, intense color reveals all the intensity of an incomparable vintage. The full and rich nose lacks expressiveness, however. Some citrus notes, like mandarin, reveal all the freshness and elegance of this vintage. Ample and rich mouth, but lively and tonic. The quality of botrytis will reveal a great wine within ten years.*

**1999.** *Golden yellow color. Note of evolution. Open nose, fine, more elegant than powerful, aromatic notes of candied grapefruit, mango, pastry. Medium-bodied, remains smooth but is characterized by a relatively soft finish. A consensual Fargues.*

*In conclusion, this recollection from Alexandre, "John Sanders, from Haut-Bailly, always said to me about Fargues: 'It's a wine without too much but with everything you need, like the flower beds of Le Nôtre.'"*

# Château d'Yquem

*Imperishable Perfection*

T HERE
ARE TIMES
that we forget. There are times forever engraved. Yquem is of
the latter. It was 1985. I had just joined the Association of Sommeliers of Bretagne, whose annual conference was held that
year in Bordeaux. I was there with our delegation, led by Christian Stévanin,
charismatic and iconic character of French sommellerie throughout the 1980s,
1990s and 2000s. No title, no job, but with passion and determination, I found
myself at the château where a meeting between the sommeliers and the maître d'hôtel, Comte Alexandre de Lur Saluces, was taking place. He served,
for one hundred and twenty guests, among many vintages, the famous 1937.
On that day, it was Jean-Luc Feutry, recently having claimed the 1982 title of
Best Sommelier and Restaurateur in France, who had the pleasure of describing it. I'm sure I would have been incapable of doing so! A wine of topaz
color, dense. The nose is, from the opening, as plural as the opening of the
skies upon contact. Candied citrus, saffron and chestnut honey all at once.
The liqueur is of an indeterminable length and imposes itself unconditionally
over all mankind. It is the ambrosia of the gods. How could I still remember
it? Maybe because it was given to me to taste several times since… In any case,
this wine is among those that inspired me to enter the world of wine.

Here we are at the heart of over 100 hectares, a property with global
influence unmatched in the world of sweet wines. Its etymological origin is
closer to the Aquitaine surname of Eyquem, of Germanic origin: *aig-helm*,
*aig* meaning "to have" and *helm*, "helmet". The most famous bearer of this
surname is still none other than Michel de Montaigne (1533-1592). From
1785, when Françoise-Joséphine Sauvage d'Yquem married Louis-Amédée,
Comte de Lur Saluces, colonel of the regiment of Penthièvre-Dragons, until
1999, with Comte Alexandre de Lur Saluces, the family has developed, and
continued to create the myth: Yquem. As of 1999, the LVMH group became
the majority shareholder of Château d'Yquem. Initially, Alexandre de Lur
Saluces continued in his position, which he held until 2003.

Since May 2004, Pierre Lurton has worked on the creation and development of this nectar. With Pierre, I accomplished a long-term partnership
that allowed us to serve Yquem at Le Cinq by the gl ass, with greater regularity, opening between two to four bottles a week. This great wine must

### BORDEAUX
#### Château d'Yquem

be cultivated by sommeliers and chefs. For it is, above all, a wine of harmony and gastronomy, once it attains several years of aging. We have to discuss it with our customers, present it to our cooks and pastry chefs (for making desserts and low-sugar sweets). In a word, we must create the event – simply including it on the wine list without bringing it to life would be a shame. Beyond the gaze, it must be debuted, tasted. It has so much to teach us. And this, from the beginning of a meal. In fact, the following harmony may seem unexpected to you. In April 2012, during a rogue dinner organized by Jacques (Dupont), Pierre (Lurton) was able to join us *in extremis*. When he appeared, he said bluntly: "I brought you some products of the region." In this case, a 2007 Yquem, a 1988 and a 1989 Cheval Blanc. It was during the aperitif that we opened the 2007, with a few thin slices of Médoc grenier, a famous Bordeaux delicatessen specialty, and toast. It was remarkable.

EMORIES
The world today seems ever farther away from the one attached to Yquem. Here, time takes on its full meaning; hedonism is unfeigned value. How many wines have the ability to gleefully bypass the course of fifty years of aging? Also, I would like to pay tribute here to Pierre Lurton and the de Lur Saluces who always managed to preserve the identity of the only Sauternes premier cru of the 1855 classification. When we taste an Yquem, we interpret it. Why, after tasting, can we not, like the actors from the time of *Au Théâtre Ce Soir*, honor those who are behind the wine's creation?

Here, we applaud the Director, M. Pierre Lurton; the Vineyard Steward, M. Francis Mayeur and Cellar Manager, Mme Sandrine Garbay. Let's not forget the respective teams of each, who safeguard the property remarkably. We must also not forget that this "text" would not have the nose or the soul without the past work of great writers such as M. Latrille, who retired in 1996 (the Monsieur Noblet d'Yquem) and was at the helm of forty-four Yquem vintages! Let's applaud them.

# The Wines

The vine population corresponds to 80% Sémillon and 20% Sauvignon pruned into cots. The terroir consists mainly of a clay sub-layer, but it should be noted that all the vineyards of the domain cover the entire geological range of Sauternes. The drainage dating from the nineteenth century is systematic and has been revamped throughout the history of the domain.

Here, the production is minimal. The official decree authorizes yields of 25 hectoliters per hectare. At Yquem, yields are instead between 7 and 8 hectoliters per hectare, or slightly more than 1,000 bottles. Compared to the almost 10,000 bottles per hectare in Champagne, the scarcity of production makes sense.

Before beginning the tasting, I must mention one absence. A wine created in 1959 by Alexandre's uncle, the Marquis Bertrand. This is of course the famous Y d'Yquem. Since then, how many "solaces" have been created with Bordeaux labels?

It's a dry white wine from the château. It is produced from rum (or slightly candied) raisins, which we sometimes call the "tails" of the harvest, referring to the Master Blenders that cut the "tails" of distillate upon judging the result of the distillation unworthy. As recalled by the eminent Michel Bettane, "In the nineteenth century, the château produced dry and semi-dry white wines." For the *Botrytis cinerea*, without which the greatest vintages could not have been born, does not show itself every year. In this, the numerous vineyards, the creations of the Appellation d'origine Contrôlée (AOC) and their inherent power have, in a way, "depleted" the diversity of wine products.

# Tasting in Yquem, 2013

**2009. Château d'Yquem.** *I remember the harvest arriving at the wine press. That day, according to the grimoire, which annually collects the harvest data, the Cellar Master so much surpassed the quantity of grapes entered that it was comparable to the harvest of 1893, as evidenced by the château archives. It was the second sorting, with a rare balance: 155 grams of residual and 13.5% vol. It gave forth a pure wine, solid, incredible, with notes of frangipani, the fruit mixing with notes of flower honey, with a long length. To be kept for thirty years and beyond!*

**2008.** *Cooler vintage than 2009, less liqueur in the mouth. An elegant vintage, gifted with a beautiful sense of tension.*

**2007.** *The harvests dragged on as there were seven sortings in the vineyards. This gave the wine an incredible complexity. A complete vintage, very full. A success.*

2006. *A year with a small harvest in terms of quantity. The month of August was cold. The result is a classic year, still with 130 grams of residual sugar.*

2005. *Rarely are sweet wine vintages of Bordeaux attuned to the great reds. 2005 is an exception to the rule! The 2005 Yquem is a legendary vintage, complete and rich, but without excess. Notes of sweet almonds, pistil, saffron, honey. To keep… for a long time!*

2001. *First vintage without the de Lur Saluces name on the label. This vintage has a liqueur of 155 grams. A supercharged harvest. It was the largest since 1967 and 1937. We have often served it at Le Cinq with a brioche perdue of apricot and peach and saffron ice cream.*

1988. *A thought for this year of amazing finesse, with the 1986 and 1983. Vintages I have served since my time at La Poularde and which continue to be on the menu of Le Cinq today. Proof that great sweet wine vintages accompany a sommelier's career beyond the places he practices. There is one downside: I am aging quicker than Yquem's wine!*

1945 *Tasted at the George V in 2010). In the words of Michael Broadbent, "The miraculous post-war vintage."*

*The color is in itself a palette of gold from its core to the edges of the disc. Perfect bottle, incredible nose of quinces, medlar spices, buckwheat honey, date, infinite perfumes. The mouth carries the mind through time. Simply gliding.*

1937 *(Tasted at the George V in 2011). Among the greatest vintages of the century. It is one of the legendary vintages of Yquem along with the 1929 or 1921. The color is mahogany with amber reflections. A nose close to perfection. Bitter orange jam, honey, rich and intense. Wide mouth, a rare balance. We serve it by itself during dinner, ordered by the inviting host.*

1929 *(September 2014). Mahogany color with reflections of Maduro Havana. Open nose, touch of oxidation, chestnut honey, caramel figs, loquats. Sensual mouth, full-bodied and caressing attack. Finesse, coats the palate, infinite length without heaviness. Orange zest, a caramelized lightness. The balance of this great wine, yet it's a wine that deserves to be alone with you. At this level of balance, a dish should be avoided. It is a meditation wine. It succeeded in a fantastic tasting including the 1947 Cheval Blanc, 1947 Lafleur, 1967 Barbaresco San Lorenzo, 1929 Romanée-Conti, 1945 Lafite, 1937, 1952 and the 1961 Pétrus.*

P 350 DOMAINE ANDRÉ PERRET

P 357 CHÂTEAU GRILLET

P 366 DOMAINE JEAN-LOUIS CHAVE

P 376 DOMAINE JEAN-PAUL JAMET

P 389 DOMAINE SAINT-PRÉFERT

P 395 LE VIEUX DONJON

P 402 CHÂTEAU RAYAS

P 410 DOMAINE BONNEAU

# Wines of the
~
# Rhone Valley

# Domaine André Perret

*Gentle and good-hearted*

# H

ERE IS AN APPELLATION
THAT SITS AT THE INTERSECTION
of three departments of France: Ardèche, Loire and Rhône. This location, unique to say the least, is the home of Condrieu. Sitting on the granite arenas of Mont Pilat, these hillsides face southeast, on the right bank of the river, where one can contemplate the beautiful flora of the Isère across the Rhone. The closest appellation to the north is none other than the mythical appellation Côte-Rôtie, recognized the world over for its distinguished Syrahs. Isolated at the heart of the Condrieu vineyards is where you'll find one of the smallest *appellations d'origine contrôlée* (AOC) in France: Château-Grillet. But let's not dive into these two appellations just yet – we'll come back to them. The appellation covers 250 hectares, 140 of which are vineyards. To put that in perspective, many of the great domains in Bordeaux have about 100 hectares of vines. From a geological standpoint, Condrieu is made up of decomposed ancient granite, which has been planted with viognier vines. This varietal, native to Dalmatia, is said to have been chosen by the Greeks and then imported, like other varietals, by the Roman Legions.

The domain d'André is located in Verlieu, which straddles two villages, Chavannay and Vérin, 50 kilometers south of Lyon. This is the farthest north that viognier grapes can fully ripen, allowing the potential for producing wines that are subtle, delicate, elegant and particularly aromatic. It is the greatest vineyard in the Loire region, which is also home to Grillet, as well as two less famous wines for which I happen to have a sentimental fondness. In the northernmost part: the hillsides of Roanne are home to several passionate young winemakers alongside the region's historic domain, the Sérol family, partners of the Troisgros family. Closer to me, the Côtes du Forez, with its vineyards that back up against Auvergne, passionately defended by Jack Logel and his wife Odile Verdier. It is the story of an Alsatian carpenter who landed on this volcanic terroir intended for Gamay. I can still see the label of his treasured vintage, Côtes-du-Forez La Volcanique. Our man couldn't resist planting a few acres of his native Pinot Gris in a granitic parcel – a nod to his roots. What an endearing and warm character, much like André Perret.

Over almost thirty years, André built a domain that covers nearly 13 hectares. There, he produced two great appellations: Condrieu and Saint-Joseph.

Initially, his father's domain was mostly focused on arboriculture, as were many families in the region, for that matter. It was the apricot that reigned supreme. His mother crafted marvelous jams from the family orchards, which we devoured before heading down into his grandmother's cellar. Little by little, and with great perseverance, André planted vines in place of the orchards. He began digging and planting his dream in 1986. I arrived at La Poularde in 1987. Much like him, I had everything to prove, although I had already earned some recognition for my work. This is why when I mention my friend André, I am transported back in time to Montrond-les-Bains. Still a young sommelier, I had just met a young winemaker. At the time, the quantities provided were very small, and I remember that Patrick Gerbaud (back then the sommelier for Pierre Gagnaire in Saint-Étienne) and I were always at each other's throats over who would get the bigger lot. I should clarify that in the late eighties, other than Marcel Guigal and, of course, Georges Vernay, the appellation wasn't very well represented on wine menus. As I was intent on building a cellar representing all regions, I built a relationship with André. I visited more and more often, so much so that I ended up asking him if he could give me a few clusters of Viognier grapes. We dried them in the lofts of La Poularde and served the seeds as a condiment to accompany a *foie gras au torchon* prepared by chef Bernard Barret. I was proud to serve this great wine – it sat in the Cenacle of my favorite wines, and very few guests could order some.

Since then, André and his wife have managed to establish themselves amongst the great names of this micro-appellation. André has his own style, as much in his Saint-Joseph Syrahs as, and especially, in his Viogniers, of which the Chéry, with its elegant richness, is the standard bearer. At this time, I would compare it to two other expressions of this grape variety: the Vernon by Christine Vernay for its density and depth, and the revival of Grillet, with its unparalleled finesse.

Remembering this micro-vineyard brings back a memory from my time at La Poularde. In the mid-nineties, chef Étéocle struck up a relationship with a winemaker, Alain Paret, from the village of Saint-Pierre-de-Bœuf in the Loire. Their idea: revive an historic escheat terroir in the commune of Malleval, on the terraced granite hillsides at the foot of the Château de Volan. It became the vintage Lys de Volan. To complete their assembly of *bon vivants*,

# RHONE VALLEY
## Domaine André Perret

they partnered with a friend and powerful gourmet: Gérard Depardieu. This period was one of my first forays into the art of single-varietal wines. I soon communicated to the chef my doubts as to the finesse that could be brought out of this terroir. For me, the wine lacked tension, as the sunshine on the hills often led to overripe grapes. But he quickly made it clear that this was "his" wine and that he fully intended to add it to the wine list at La Poularde and to introduce it to his friends. This was when I first understood an ongoing struggle faced by many sommeliers: how to serve and highlight their employer's wines, irrespective of their own opinions about the products in question! In my case, it was not easy, as I was much younger and more impetuous than I am now, and certainly less diplomatic. And so, I generally avoided discussing the subject with the chef. However, this gave me the chance to meet Gérard, with whom I would later have many festive encounters. As for the Lys de Volan vintage, Chef Étéocle ended up abandoning his shares. The vintage still exists today, though without its original protagonists. Gérard collaborated with the Condrieu terroir until 2011 along with a heavyweight of similar stature: Marcel Guigal! Somewhat of a battle of the Titans.

MEMORIES
Quite a while ago – this was in the early nineties – I had just finished a lovely tasting with André and Thierry when hunger suddenly struck. It was 11:30 a.m., and a snack was an absolute necessity. We caught Dédé unprepared! I winked at Thierry, who opened the trunk of his sedan and brought out a wicker basket covered with a lovely Vichy linen kitchen towel. From it, he pulled out an impressive *jamón ibérico*, a plentiful round loaf of sourdough bread with a crispy and fragrant crust, and the appropriate knives. Dominique and André in turns completed the picture with some *rigotte de Condrieu* goat cheese.

I must briefly digress at this point and explain that, back then, we ate much more hastily during our visits to the vineyards than we do nowadays. Since we scheduled visits to at least six domains per day, we had to optimize our lunch break. So sometimes we brought something to snack on during the drive or by a vineyard between two visits. This was often the case because, with the exception of our first visit, we were always behind schedule for the rest of the day (I confess that we haven't made much progress on that front). The fact remains that the *jamón* proved to be delicious paired with a spirited Saint-Joseph by André, and we went back to the Condrieu to accompany the *rigottes* with dried apricots before having our coffee.

Afterwards, I have frequently dined with André and his wife at very fine tables. I think back fondly on the wonderful moments we shared at Patrick Henriroux's La Pyramide in Vienne, where the table, the kitchen and the cellar, are magnificent. And yet this snapshot, if you will, of a cheeky and greedy moment, remains to this day our most treasured memory.

## RHONE VALLEY
### Domaine André Perret

# The Wines

The two major terroirs are Clos Chanson
and Chéry. Over time, André's wines have
acquired richness and structure from
his old vines.

## The following is a tasting from Spring of 2013
with Nicolas de Rabaudy and Thierry

**2012. Saint-Joseph white** *(tasting
on barrel). Quite a respectable and
delicate wine. I made a mistake in not
thinking to order some for George V.*

**2012. Condrieu** *(tasting on barrel).
This is André's generic vintage. It is a
Condrieu, light and clean, perfect served
by the glass and immediately enjoyable.*

**2011. Condrieu.** *Great success, pleasant,
more approachable than the 2012.*

**Clos Chanson.** *This comes from an
enclosed, terraced parcel that André
began renting in 1986. Today, it is
one of his greatest successes.*

**2012 Clos Chanson** *(tasting on barrel).
Pale color, floral and understated,
very elegant. The mouth feel is chiseled,
with citrus, yuzu and floral notes.
Remarkable. A formidable success.*

**2011. Clos Chanson.** *This Chanson
is simultaneously balanced and long.*

# The famous vintage Chéry

This is a terroir with granitic soils rich in mica and schist, facing south-southeast. Here, the average age of the vines is 60 years old. According to a charming local legend, when the Roman emperor Probus ordered half of the vineyards in Gaul to be ripped out, he spared this hillside because, the legend states, this particular slope was already producing exceptionally good wine. "Chéry" is one of the Condrieu parcels characterized by "chaillets," which are low walls built from dry stones extracted from the parcel over the generations by the winemakers, forming tiers up the slope of the vineyard's steep hillside. At regular intervals, channels that run perpendicular to the hillside serve as drains during springtime rains, simultaneously providing a better distribution of water to all of the vines. In this poor soil, the roots and radicles of the vine stocks have to penetrate through up to 3 meters of granite to get their nutrients. The vines are pruned in a single guyot and held up with stakes – often three per vine. When strolling along these foggy hillsides on a chilly winter morning, I am reminded of the rifles of the Imperial Guard interlaced in a cross pattern before entering into battle for the Rhone…

2012. Chéry *(tasting on barrel).*
*Intense, golden color. Rich open nose, luxuriant. Notes of apricot and vanilla. Nice attack, wide, nice length, without being heavy. In this vintage, the Côteau de Chéry was particularly well exposed to the sun, which gives it a great strength.*

2011. Chéry. *The wine from this vintage is more bracing. Notes of violet mingle with apricot. The mouth feel is an absolute success, especially as it remains very fresh.*

RHONE VALLEY
Domaine André Perret

# Château Grillet

*The Amphitheater of Viognier*

T HIS TINY VINEYARD COVERING JUST 3.8 HECTARES, located in the Loire, has quite an ancient reputation. I offer as an example the events Michael Broadbent told me about his work dedicated to ancient vintages: "In 1892, the Neyret-Gachet family, which has owned Grillet since 1820, received from James Christie, Lord Steward of King George IV, an order for two cases of 72 bottles of Grillet for St. James Palace." Later on, in the beginning of the 20th century, the prince of gourmets, the infamous Curnonsky, ranked it as one of the five great white wines of France. This royal flush of great names was made up of prestigious vineyards: Clos de la Coulée de Serrant, Château-Grillet, Montrachet, Château-Chalon and Yquem. In listing these celebrities of our vineyards, I cannot help but think sadly of the first on the list. The Coulée de Serrant is going through what we often call a "dumb phase," a period during which the wine is less open to tasting but which later wakes up as if being pulled from a long slumber. This time shall come.

Let's get back to Vérin, to this jewelry box of wines. It could not have escaped my palate, especially since I worked for many years at the doors of this domain when I was in Montrond-les-Bains. It was then that I endeavored to understand this terroir, which is great in that it allows the grape varietal to express itself, all the while letting the soil and the microclimate shine through with elegance and finesse. In Grillet, the terroir manages to temper the ardor of the Viognier grape and gives it an uncommon complexity. The credit is due to the new team, managed by Frédéric Engerer and the domain's winemaker Alessandro, who will keep on glorifying this enduring winemaking rarity. Speaking of which, we must not forget the former owner, Isabelle Baratin, who, for better or worse, always did her best to protect this jewel. Grillet has always aroused envy and stirred the passions of the great names of the Rhône.

One is free to continue speaking highly of these precipitous and well-sheltered granite terraces that look out over the Rhône, whose heart of the vineyard produces the most fascinating variety of grape: Viognier. Soon the château, a structure dating back to the middle of the 18th century, will come back to life after having been left rather uninhabited. The 80-centimeter-thick walls need to be restored. The cellars have already awoken after a deep, hollow sleep. This is evidenced by the latest 2012, with an energy that

## RHONE VALLEY
### Château Grillet

has once again struck the sweet spot. The nose is of sublime violet. The intense mouth feel is candid and delicate. It epitomizes everything that aesthetic canons shall henceforth require.

To reach this point, Frédéric Engerer and his team were forced, with the owner's approval, to make a major decision. It was to preserve the heart of what Grillet meant for them when they bought the site. The selection process during the tastings was strict: 30% less than the previous vintage – about 3,800 bottles of 2011. The 2012 didn't fare any better, with just… 3,000 necks for the entire world!

And so the decision was made to create a second label. The wines from the domain that did not quite meet the Château Grillet standards were given the only possible appellation: Côtes-du-Rhône white. This vintage features the parcels from the bottom of the hill, in addition to others located to the west of the château. Let us not forget that such a financial effort is rare, if not unheard of! And there are still damaged vines to be regrown, soil and leaves to be revived. The work here is firing on all cylinders! There is so much to do.

It has sometimes seemed to me like there weren't many of us who supported Isabelle Baratin in her efforts to preserve the reputation of this mythical domain. So I was stunned when, over lunch at Le Cinq, François Pinault asked for my opinion about the terroir. I quickly learned that he had become the controlling shareholder. This was a pleasant surprise, as we all know how hard-working the entire team is and the considerable means that have been granted to Château Latour since he took the helm of the vineyard, alongside Frédéric Engerer.

Waking the sleeping beauty required a healthy dose of determination. They did what they promised to do, and the results were not long in coming. The 2011, the first vintage, shows more clarity than in the past. The 2012 combines this quality with controlled strength. To accomplish this, they first had to refurbish the barrels and the wine press, not to mention undertake a complete cellar renovation that preserved the soul emanating from these three hundred-year-old walls. Like Edmond Sailland (Curnonsky), I have always been confident about this unique terroir. It is quite simple: just being there is the only evidence you need. All of the conditions are present to create great wines. Go there – a visit will tell you more than any words could say.

# MEMORIES

If Château-Grillet had a favorite place, it would be La Pyramide in Vienne. For good reason – Mado Point and Louis Tomasi (who long ruled its cellars) have been important clients of the domain since the beginning. The Michelin-starred chef Patrick Henriroux, while at the helm of this house and its fabled past, enabled the establishment to stand the test of time and maintain its place amongst the great gastronomic destinations in France and the world. Bravo!

Some years ago now, in 2005, on the fiftieth anniversary of the passing of Fernand Point, all of his legendary former students came together around a table: M. Paul, Pierre Troisgros, Louis Outhier, Michel Guérard and Alain Ducasse. How could I forget to mention Régis Marcon, Michel Bras... the crème de la crème of French chefs, reunited within the walls of La Pyramide, in which his memory lives on. As I had worked for a long time in the region, I had the honor of attending as one of the sommeliers. That day, we were served a 1990 Château-Grillet. A full-bodied, powerful and generous wine, whose full expression includes notes of sweet almond mingle with a rustic quality, and minerality. Remembering this wine makes me think back to a wonderful dish from Joannès Randoing, an illustrious chef and owner of La Poularde in Montrond-les-Bains: his shrimp gratin in a copper casserole. What a memory! However, in the context of this lunch, and taking into account the other wines served alongside it, I would have preferred the 2011 Grillet with, for example, a dish of Verneuil white asparagus blanketed in a creamy blood orange mousseline sauce... but, hey, now I am just nitpicking.

The other moment that stayed with me from this lunch, during which I gave a speech, was when the 1961 Château-Haut-Brion was served. It touched me. Tertiary bouquet, dark berries, intense, full-bodied, concentrated and long. What a marvelous wine we enjoyed!

It's almost as if global warming and the urbanization around Haut-Brion enhanced the balance of this *Grand Vin*, making it surprisingly generous. But from a complicated point of view, it remains the model for its genre, with a balance between Merlot and Cabernet Sauvignon, all in the low notes. This gives the Haut-Brion a sensual quality, a creamy texture, and an unparalleled charm. No brutal tannins.

## RHONE VALLEY
### Château Grillet

# The Wines

In June of 2013, the 2010 vintage was representing Château-Grillet on the market. This was the vintage that carried the torch between two chapters of this noble terroir's history. It is delicate and tense, but personally, I find that it is missing some charm and fullness. Previously, I defended it out of respect for the terroir, for what it represented for the pioneers of appellations, the commitment of those who brought it before the baptismal fonts of the AOC and contributed to the renown of an entire winemaking region that goes well beyond the borders of the Rhône-Alpes. Now, it is with conviction and passion that I support this phoenix that waited for its moment and has once again taken to the skies.

**2011. Château-Grillet.** *As I pointed out, what characterizes the Grillet is the influence of its unique terroir that gives a certain distinction and nobility to Viognier. It strengthens the heart of the terroir. The production of this Grand Vin has been cut in half. For agronomical reasons, the plants also had to be revitalized. This 2011 Grillet with a golden yellow color is luminous and radiant. The open nose is intense. It has gained depth and maturity. The fruity notes are carried by delicate floral notes that call to mind lime blossom, violet and dill. It is full-bodied and smooth in the mouth, lightly woody but not excessively so. The richness, more pronounced than usual, gives it a clean and lively finish. If it had just a hint more energy, it would be singing to the heavens. But honestly, what a turnaround!*

**2012. Pontcin.** *This vintage was subject to rigorous cuts before blending. This resulted in the creation of a vintage, under the appellation Côtes-du-Rhône, called Pontcin. If the Grand Vin is going to be available in small quantities, this micro-vintage will be just as rare, with only 780 bottles produced. The wine is clean, precise, already open, but doesn't possess quite the same sparkle and elegance that we have come to expect from Grillet.*

**2012. Château-Grillet.** *Along the same lines as the 2011, in even smaller quantities. But what I highlighted in the finish didn't appear in the 2012. The nose is more succulent and rich, with mango tones and a hint of menthol, but remains understated. The nose is often trimmed with a slightly mineral freshness. Anise and lemon. Has an airy quality for such a rich wine. The mouth gives an extra measure with its endless length. The whole is still dense but very harmonious. To understand the 2012 Château-Grillet, you must taste the 2012 Pontcin, which sets the tone for density, with a very charming character, of course.*

**2013. Pontcin.** *This vintage is more lively and fresh than the previous vintage. More sensuality. A lovely wine.*

**2013. Château-Grillet.** *This vintage will be one of those rarities that connoisseurs will fight over, and for good reason: less than a thousand bottles were produced. The open nose is delicate and relatively accessible. 2013 will go down as a defensive year, which left its mark on the wines. All of a sudden, Viognier has become more violent again. The rigorous selection process meant it kept the upright, distinguished qualities, but without the sparkle seen in the 2012.*

# Domaine Jean-Louis Chave

*It all began in... 1481*

BOUT
50 KILOMETERS
south of the Côte-Rôtie vineyards, between Vienne and
Valence, on the left bank of the Rhône, terraced along the
south-southeast-facing hillsides, is where the vineyards of
Hermitage are located. This is a miniscule appellation covering less than
140 hectares, or just a little less than the area of the two *Premiers Crus Classés*
of Pauillac. The quality of the wines grown on this hill has been recognized
since the 17th century. You only need to read Boileau's verses about a fake
Hermitage served in a well-known café in Paris, the Pomme du Pain, run
by a certain Crenet, not far from the Pont Notre-Dame, to be convinced:

> "Such a compound a lackey pour'd into my glass!
> *Lignage* and *auvernat* together, I am sure,
> Such as Crenet exposes for *hermitage* pure.
> It's colour was red, and its taste sweet and flat,
> And oh, what a villanous tang after that!"
> "Le repas ridicule," *Satire III*, 1663

Later, in the mid-18th century, Hermitage wines were used by certain
châteaux of Bordeaux to enhance their wines during difficult years. It was
then said the wines were "hermitaged." Incidentally, Château Palmer
brought it back into fashion recently with a vintage called: Historical
XIX[th] Century Wine. A nod to the history of this *"vin de France."*

But instead of that episode, I prefer to remember that in 1862, *"vin de
Mauves"* is mentioned in Victor Hugo's seminal work *Les Misérables*. It is the
drink that the Bishop of Digne serves to Jean Valjean. Mauves is located
across the river, on the Ardèche side, across from Hermitage. The village is
crossed by local route 86, running parallel to the symbolic national route 7
on the other bank of the Rhône, which Charles Trenet sung about so well.
In the middle of the village, by a rusty sign whose colors and letters have
faded over time, unchanged for generations, is the only external publicity
that marks the enclosed façade of the house of the Chave family. Since the
end of the 15th century – more precisely, since 1481, as indicated on the neck
label of their bottles – the Chave family has been making wine in Mauves.

That makes twenty-two generations of Chaves who have helped make Hermitage an unrivaled masterpiece over the centuries.

Today, the domain covers almost 15 hectares, 13.9 of which are in Hermitage. Add to that the terroirs of Jean-Louis's treasured Saint-Joseph red: 9.3 hectares are planted with Syrah in the vineyards of les Bessards, l'Hermite, le Péléat, le Méal, le Beaume, les Diognières and les Vercandières, and 4.6 hectares are planted with Roussanne and Marsanne in the vineyards of les Roucoules, le Péléat, l'Hermite and la Maison Blanche. The appellation is located at a unique convergence of geological and climatic factors, a granitic peak formed by glacial deposits over the millennia that led to a heterogeneous terrain. Thus there is no *one* Hermitage, but rather Hermitages. Understanding this notion is essential for anyone who wants to understand Gérard and Jean-Louis Chave (the latter returned to the domain in 1992 after venturing out to discover the world and, more specifically, California).

Over the years, over many tastings, I've had the chance to walk the dizzying slopes of this rocky peak alongside them. For me, Hermitage is in the enchanting names of the parcels: les Greffieux, le Méal and les Rocoules. The Chave family draws on these terroirs for their energy, their passion and very reason for existence. A terrestrial, almost mystical power, emanates from this mountain.

As the Chave family says, "these wines from grape varietals originally planted by the Allobroges have been grown in this region for more than two thousand years in harmony with these choice terroirs at the edge of the continental and Mediterranean world." The history of the Hermitage varietals is rich and diverse. On this subject, Jean-Louis has been fighting a constant battle against clones that are implanted in the vineyards in an extremely controlled manner. These "individuals," all perfectly identical, are so strong that often even a great terroir is unable to transcend the varietal. This leads to varietal-type wines without any expression. A disaster. And to help choose the clones, like for many other winemaking parameters, quite a few winemakers seek the services of consultants. Yet, as Jean-Louis says, "there are consultants everywhere, as if you could simply call up a consulting firm to create something with a soul." Therefore the entire domain is produced from companion-planted vines with an average age that hovers around a substantial 50 years old, with some parcels that are more than 80 years old.

## RHONE VALLEY
## Domaine Jean-Louis Chave

# M

EMORIES

If I were to describe Gérard in one word, it would be "hedonist," for the number of wines he has brought forth into the world over the years shows his desire to see Hermitage in all of its complexity and intensity, so that he might eventually share it at the table with friends. They say loud and clear, "In schools of enology, we should be incorporating the history of the vineyard, instead of solely focusing on technique. As for chefs, how many know their culinary history? A chef who isn't interested in wine is not a great chef. One cannot dissociate wine and food. We sit at the table to enjoy them together."

Over the last thirty years, I cannot tell you how many wonderful moments I have spent at the Chave family table with Gérard, Jean-Louis and his mother. So when I dig back in my memory, what comes to mind are classic dishes and impeccable pairings. I should say right away that Gérard is what we call a *cordon-bleu*, a refined gourmet with a discerning palate, close to nature, to the waters, to the forests, ready to cross an ocean to taste a rare delight or to better understand a product. I remember one of these meals, a lunch during the summer of 2011. The weather was sunny. After a meandering tasting in the depths of the cellars, we came back up (two of our young sommeliers accompanied me, as always) to have an aperitif under the shade of the plane tree in the courtyard. Madame Chave had prepared *caillettes ardéchoises* (ground bloody organ meats wrapped in caul fat) according to her secret recipe. We savored them, warm, sliced fresh on toasted country bread, with a 2008 Hermitage white. At that time, it was still quite restrained in the nose as well as in the mouth, but it delivered tension coupled with a very fleshy quality. At the table in their dining room, which was cool, familial and, in a word, intimate, the first course was a sea bass that weighed more than three kilos, line-caught off the tip of Brittany and received just that morning, cooked in the oven in a salt crust. The tag that came with the fish, which Gérard brought from the kitchen for me, showed that it had been swimming in the turbulent waters between the Île de Sein and the Pointe du Raz just a few hours before. The master of the house promptly removed the shell and lifted off the fillets, which were served with a cloudy *beurre blanc*. Speaking of which, as Jean-Louis likes to remind me, at this latitude, it is Ardèche "*au beurre*," since the 45th parallel passes at the very southern border of the kingdom of butter. Once you have crossed this line, the olive tree reigns supreme. Ardèche becomes "*à l'huile*," heralding a different cuisine, different wines, and different varietals. That is where a 1995 Hermitage white took up the baton. The wine had already been open for a while, served at a temperature that allowed it to express all of its aromatic richness and complexity in the mouth.

The *plat de résistance* consisted of two sturdy roasted Bresse chickens, perfectly browned, accompanied simply by the well-seasoned drippings and colorful heirloom carrots. The 2008 Hermitage red was prominently featured. This dish – family cooking at its best – allows for a wide variety of pairings. Depending on how seasoned the drippings are, denser wines may be served, which was the case here.

The cheese course consisted of creamy Saint-Marcellins and a large slice of blue cheese from Vercors-Sassenage. Gérard and Jean-Louis honored us by pairing it with a 1998 Cathelin. A heavenly moment. I must admit that we all poured ourselves a bit of the 1995 Hermitage white to accompany the Saint-Marcellin. We reserved for the blue cheese the privilege of being served alongside the vintage Cathelin which, by the way, did not require the cheese, as this little bottle possesses a near infinite repertoire.

And to finish this fantastic feast, the cook placed a very delicate earthenware fruit bowl in the middle of the table, overflowing with sun-drenched, juicy Bergeron apricots, a rare and refined fruit. There was, of course, only one possible choice: the family's legendary Straw Wine from the year in progress: 1996. The other vintage produced during that decade, the 1997, was being aged. It was absolute perfection. In that amber yellow nectar, with a rare sophistication made up of charm, intensity and length, mingle aromas of apricot, honey and preserved candied fruit. What a dream! Gérard revived this wine in the 1970s. It is made mostly with Marsanne grapes, dried on beds of natural rye straw in a secret loft (I've never been allowed to visit) and barrel-aged for six to seven years.

When coffee was served, accompanied by a sponge cake – soft, light and still warm – I glanced at the watch on my wrist and was unsurprised to discover that we would not make the train back to Paris at the scheduled time. We are well accustomed to this, which is why I always end my trek through the northern Rhône with a visit to the Chave family, so that we can enjoy the exceptional hospitality without worrying about time. The return trip to Paris can wait…

# RHONE VALLEY
## Domaine Jean-Louis Chave

## The Wines

Tasting in the cellar with Jean-Louis, Thierry
and my dear friend Jean-Claude Chatard in July 2014

# Hermitage white

**2012.** *Jean-Louis presents us with three possibilities for different blends, differing by only a few percentage points in each lot.*

**2011.** *Notes of grapefruit and propolis, dense and powerful with nice bitter notes. Clean, precise.*

*At this moment, noteworthy arrival of my friend of thirty years, Jean-Claude Chatard. He was arriving from Saint-Étienne, where he is an associate professor at the Université Jean-Monnet. Jean-Claude is one of the preeminent French experts in applied medicine for elite athletes. And a lover of wine and good food!*

**2008.** *Intense golden color. Shimmering. Rich, open, creamy nose. Minty notes mingle with buttery ones. Beeswax, verbena. The full-bodied, smooth mouth feel retains a hint of wood and licorice. Notes of honey and infused herbs appear in the finish. Long and powerful.*

**2007.** *Now here is the Hermitage white in all its splendor. Golden color, nose of sweet almonds and honey, Comice pear, propolis. The mouth feel is buttery and unctuous. A fantastic wine to accompany food.*

**2003.** *Intense golden color. Nose of pastry, frangipani and marzipan. Notes of breadbox. Spherical at the back of the mouth. An opulent wine. Progresses to notes of sweet spices.*

**1985.** *Otherworldly! Smoky nose. We're between mineral flavors and the complexity that develops over time. It is not due to oxidation, but thanks to a wealth of smells and tastes. Refined. Finishes with aged rum, dried mint. Timeless. This wine resembles certain old Rieslings, with less acidity.*

*Before tasting the Hermitage reds, we wandered towards the barrels of Saint-Joseph. Since he returned to the domain, Jean-Louis has been working with his characteristic passion and energy to revive certain forgotten vineyards in the appellation that were abandoned after the phylloxera disaster.*

**2012. Saint-Joseph red.** *This wine hasn't yet been blended and is already remarkable. Precise, clean, distinguished. More subtle than powerful, gourmet. This vintage contains 100% grapes grown in the domain.*

2013. *Tasted six barrels in the new cellar, its walls and rib-vaulted ceilings built with stones from Montpellier. It's incredible. The Chave family has been there for almost five hundred years, yet they continue to dig deeper and make it more beautiful for the wines and future generations. After the first barrels, we tasted a special wine planted in granitic clay, from the vineyard of Dardouille, which is very special to Jean-Louis.*

# Hermitage red

2013 *(Tasting on barrel) We were able to taste the essential expressions of the different terroirs that make up Hermitage:*
*– L'Hermite (above the Bessards): powerful, long, dense*
*– La Beaume (terroir located near Rocoule): lots of finesse*
*– Le Méal (located above the Greffieux), the heart of the vintage: dense, with very fine-grained tannins, more vivacious*
*– Bessards: Transcendent style. Especially big. Brings density and length to the blend*

*This tasting allowed us to fully grasp the definition of Hermitage. The blending of different terroirs. The wines that we tasted are some of the finest wines from the hill.*

2012 *(Tasting on barrel) This vintage is blended. We are tasting it after it was recently decanted. Very nice balance, delicate, less powerful than the 2013.*

2012 *(Another barrel) This is another unblended terroir: l'Hermite. The wine is remarkably reminiscent of Pinot Noir. What I mean by that is that both the nose and the mouth show a great deal of finesse and delicacy. The wine is less sunny, but still sappy. Exceptional.*

2011. *Still austere in the nose and mouth. It needs more time to find its bearings in its glass prison before it can begin expressing itself. It is of the same caliber as Jean-Louis and Gerard's 2001, tasted last night.*

2003. *This vintage was drastic in terms of yield, which was cut by two thirds. Nose of very ripe dark berries. Seems very sunny, even though we tasted it in the cellar at a fairly low temperature. But still, what a delight. Jean-Louis served it blind, and I admit that it was the particularly rich nose that led me to this vintage. Given the sunny circumstances of this grape harvest, it is a great success.*

Ermitage Cathelin *(four possible ways of spelling it exist: with or without H, preceded by L' or not). At the home of the Chave family, there is an extremely rare vintage that wine lovers the world*

*over hunt like the Holy Grail:
the Cathelin! This vintage was named
in homage to the work of painter
Bernard Cathelin (1919-2004),
a friend of Gérard Chave, who created
the painting we see on the label.
This vintage is produced from several
terroirs, dominated by the Bessards
and the Méal. Only a chosen few have
had the pleasure of "reading a few
pages" of this wine, as it is produced
in miniscule quantities (2,500 bottles
on average), and only when the vintage
allows. Therefore, we only have 1990,
1991, 1995, 1998, 2000, 2003 and 2009
vintages. This is the deepest and densest
blend of Syrah and Hermitage that
I have ever had the opportunity to taste.*

*You will always remember your first time
tasting certain wines, and this is one
of them. It was in 1995 at La Pyramide
in Vienne, celebrating the creation of
the Syrah glass by the Riedel family.
Surrounding Georg and Maximilian
Riedel were Alain Graillot, René
Rostaing, Marcel Guigal, Gérard Chave,
Jean-Claude Ruet, Patrick Henriroux
and myself. Before us were placed two
distinct glasses. One was called Syrah,
machine-made, and the other, blown
by hand, was named Hermitage. The
first glass was slender with a very large
bowl, and the other, with its narrower
rim and diameter, was perfectly suited
to Hermitage. These glasses were
developed into four series, each including
four major expressions of the region:
1990 Crozes-Hermitage La Guiraude*

*from Alain, 1990 Côte-Rôtie
La Landonne from René, 1990
Côte-Rôtie La Mouline from Marcel
and… the 1990 Cathelin from Gérard!
As I often say, "the game had punch!"
(or in the French expression that I love,
it was throwing logs into the boiler
of a steam train that has gotten
white-hot).*

*During the comparative tasting, Gérard
Chave confessed to me that he wasn't
sure of the relevance of creating
micro-vintages, because in making the
necessary choices, there was a risk
of "undressing" the mother vintage.
However, at the end of the discussion,
he presented us with the first Cathelin
in a series, which we will discuss
at length.*

# Three Cathelins tasted throughout 2014 at Le Cinq

1998 *(tasted at Le Cinq in January 2015).*
*Deep garnet color, signs that it has*
*become more opaque. Nose is delicate,*
*open, complex, distinguished. Notes*
*of preserved dark berries and spices.*
*Not extravagant. Full-bodied and sappy*
*mouth. Very long on the mid-palate,*
*with an ethereal finish.*
*Very delicate and distinguished.*
*An elegant Cathelin, more refined than*
*powerful. We brought this bottle up*
*for a dear friend who wanted for his son*
*to taste a great expression of the red of*
*his choosing that evening (following*
*a 1983 Alfred Gratien champagne,*
*then a 2008 Premier Cru Perrières*
*Meursault from Jean-Marc Roulot).*
*Considering the rarity of the bottle,*
*he hesitated for a moment and then*
*shared his choice. His father had spoken*
*to him about it, as had we, so the bottle*
*was brought up.*
*And our friend, seeing that Philippe*
*Foreau was at a nearby table, asked*
*me to serve him a glass if he would like*
*one. To which I obliged. As Philippe*
*said, after taking the time to taste it*
*and argue its merits, "You see, Eric,*
*this wine needs feathers, not fur, but*
*lovely feathers like a long-billed curlew."*
*And I must admit that he was right.*
*It was the first time he had tasted*

*the Cathelin. When I learned this,*
*I couldn't help but think how gifted*
*sommeliers are when it comes to*
*approaching and discovering the greatest*
*expressions of the rarest and most*
*sought-after domains. Even better,*
*we have the pleasure of meeting*
*the winemaking elite, when they*
*often don't even get the chance*
*to visit each other.*

1995. *Very intense ruby color. Still so*
*young. The mouth feel is firm but*
*full-bodied. Truffled. The finish*
*is impressive.*

1991. *Here is a wine that is remarkably*
*precise, while proving even more delicate*
*than the 1990.*

1990. *The firstborn of this vintage.*
*It has the light garnet color that*
*certain Pinot Noirs have when mature.*
*The nose is delicate, complex,*
*shows incredible finesse. Notes of violet*
*and wild blackberry. The mouth feel*
*is perfectly balanced. Simultaneously*
*fragile, juicy, and very intense.*

## RHONE VALLEY
## Domaine Jean-Louis Chave

# Domaine Jean-Paul Jamet

*Syrah Speaks to Him*

# T

HE DOMAIN
IS LOCATED

in the heights above Ampuis, in a small place called Le Vallin. The view there is spectacular, and when the weather is clear, you can see Mont Blanc – if you know what you are looking for. It's on the "plateau," as people call it here. It was the perfect place for the Jamets and their father Joseph to build the cellar of their dreams. This is how the project became a reality and is now fully operational. That being said, most of the family's parcels are located on the hillsides, consisting primarily of schist; here, there are two major entities.

On the one hand there is the southern part of the appellation, often called "Côte Blonde" because the soil here has a blonde tinge and is made up of a rocky mountain spur facing directly south, south of Ampuis. The Côte Blonde is attached to the Massif Central and has a granitic subsoil, covered in a layer of sand. Wines growing in this terroir tend to be more charming, more precocious, fragile and subtle in their aromatic expression.

On the other hand, there is the northern part of the appellation, facing the southeast which has more graphite schist and clay, heavier soils that contain iron, making the soil look darker. This is called the Côte Brune. Here, the Syrahs are often deeper and require more supervision due to their impetuous, extraverted temperament. But Jean-Paul Jamet breaks with convention: he is as retiring as they come! And he mostly produces Côte Brune. Understand this: his Côte-Rôties have been admitted amongst the best of the appellation, but don't ask him to get up on stage and talk about them in front of an audience – heavens, no! To hear him, you have to go to him, into the dark depths of his cellar. He is like a painter, begrudgingly presenting his works at the opening exhibition. With him, you've got to listen to him chat about his demi-muid barrels, comparing them. Because here, it is out of the question for the aging process to even slightly dull the full expression of the Syrah or of his native terroir. So, for each lot we compare barrels: one that was racked (a process that aerates the wine) versus one that was not, as was the case in 2011 – one of the keys to the success of his wines from that vintage. He left the wine alone without roughing it up. The result is sublime.

Jean-Paul's wines bring to mind a work by Rembrandt that hangs at the Louvre, *Philosopher in Meditation* (1632). There are similarities between them – a depth in the color of the Syrah that is like the mood of the canvas, the mystery of a wine that doesn't always give itself over easily at first, that requires you to contemplate the bottle. Here, for example, in the artist's canvas, the spiral staircase, with its stairs that seem to disappear into the darkness that seizes you, reminding me of the aromas of a dark and deep Syrah. There is also the duality of Côte-Rôtie, between the Côte Blonde and the Côte Brune, represented in the painting by the swaths of brown on one side and the soft golden light filtering through the open windows. It would be natural when contemplating the venerable philosopher to think right away of a subdued vintage, like the 1991 Jamet that has reached a maturity that allows it to be tasted with exquisite enjoyment in a place similar to this painting. Wine is also a kind of work of art. Sacha Guitry, favorite dramatic writer of Thierry Hamon, explained the idea well, "A painting one has at home is an extra window to sit in front of." And so long as you savor the wine in its prime as one does here, the voyage is even more real because the analytical mind mingles with the other senses.

Like any visit to an enthusiast in his lair, there is one rule here: make sure that it is the last visit of the day, and that dinner isn't scheduled too early, because once in the cellar, Jean-Paul takes off, and we must simply buckle our seatbelts. One must follow him, pipette in hand, from one demi-muid to the next, revealing details along the way about the soil, the maturity, the choice of one barrel over another, having already held one or more wines. And each time, we discover different ranges, densities and tonalities, like a complex variety of tessituras that come together into a harmonious ensemble. Over the hours spent in the cellar – because we can easily spend long periods down there – Jean-Paul's Syrahs speak for themselves.

annual visits to the Jamets started in the earlier nineties. I remember that in Montrond-les-Bains, the first Jamet family vintage we had on the menu was the 1988, which still had father Joseph Jamet's name on the label. I went to visit every year, which was quite easy since geographically we were not far apart. After fantastic years in 1990 and 1991, 1992 and 1993 proved to be difficult in terms of quality. At that time, certain clients were objecting to maintaining the quantities that they were allotted during the two fantastic years before. But at La Poularde, we did just the opposite. Because in addition to the two-Michelin-starred restaurant, the Étéocle family had just created a more casual branch, le Domaine de Cordes, located in Firminy, not far from Saint-Étienne. Just as a side note, this turns out to be the native village of Gérard Basset, recipient of the award for the World's Best Sommelier in 2010. The fact remained that we were in need of wines that could be consumed quickly, "on the fruit," as we say. And, in 1995, the 1992 and 1993 vintages served that function perfectly.

This support and confidence in Jean-Paul solidified our relationship for the long term. I will always follow this ethical code with winemakers. We owe it to ourselves, particularly when we are presiding over great houses, to keep our promises to domains, no matter what the cellaring prospects are for a particular vintage. If the winemaker works his vines and wines with heart, he will always be able to preserve the best aspects of a given year. Jean-Paul and his wife Corinne demonstrated the continuity in our relationship and our thirty years of friendship when we opened George V. Thanks to their support, we were able to include 1990, 1991 and 1995 Côte-Rôties on our wine list beginning in the first few months of 2000. This gave us a solid base and helped form the bedrock of our cellar. To this day, he still brings us a few bottles from time to time that have reached maturity and never fails to delight our guests at Le Cinq. What a joy!

# MEMORIES

Like sommeliers, gourmets are defenders and propagators of winemakers' wines. Two such gourmets are a couple of clients I had in Montrond who quickly became dear friends. They have devoted, and continue to devote, a sizeable portion of their income to the pleasures of the table. For him and his wife, anything that enters their home must have a story. This couple of passionate veterinarians has frequently invited Marie and me to attend unbelievable feasts. During these dinners, several of the dishes were remarkable accomplishments. I remember one dinner in particular, in the winter of 1996.

The Bonnets live in a little village in the Haute-Loire, Saugues, which has maybe 1,800 inhabitants in all. Though it is little known today, this hamlet had its glory days in the mid-18th century, when it was a part of the Pays de Gévaudan (now in the department of Lozère), the land where the infamous

Beast of Gévaudan was hunted! That day, we had some trouble on the snowy road, which hadn't been well plowed. During that season, it was quite the adventure to get there from Montrond. But I'm not complaining, because a couple of friends had also set out on the road from Laguiole. So we arrived at the same time as Sergio Calderon and his wife. Sergio, the "Argentine from Aubrac," has been the incomparable restaurant manager and head sommelier for the Bras family for almost twenty-five years.

We had barely walked through the door before some of us were tasked with setting the table while others were sent to help Sylvie and her cook who were in over their heads. There were six of us around the large table in their dining room. Their four sons were dining at the high oak table in the kitchen. They then went into the living room in front of the TV screen tuned into the world.

We stood by the imposing granite fireplace to enjoy the aperitif, a boletus mushroom tartelette – a specialty of Michel Bras – since Marc is crazy about mushrooms. It was served with a 1985 champagne from Egly Ouriet in Ambonnay. When we moved to the table, Marc brought us *langoustines royales* from Guilvinec, with lots of garlic, the way he likes them, served with a 1992 Silex Pouilly-Fumé from Didier Dagueneau.

That's when things started getting serious. The grilled lobsters from Brittany, accompanied by a *beurre blanc* and boletus mushrooms sautéed in crustacean butter were fantastic. Impressive bottles appeared in rapid succession: a 1992 Meursault Premier Cru from Dominique Lafon, then a duel: a 1990 Bâtard-Montrachet from Étienne Sauzet versus a 1990 Bâtard-Montrachet from Jean-Noël Gagnard. At the time, Marc was a fervent supporter of Jean-Noël, and as for me, I swore by Sauzet's wines. These tastings were incredible because these were difficult wines to access, and my budget at the time meant that I wasn't able to add any to my personal cellar. Our friends were not only enthusiasts but also incredibly generous. For that matter, for them, the wines were only worthwhile when shared.

Next, the cook appeared singlehandedly carrying an earthenware dish with two superb hens poached *en demi-deuil* ("in half-mourning"), which Sergio promptly carved. It was a succulent and elegant dish, moist, and perfumed by the black truffles slipped under the skin. Our gracious host brought three sets of glasses during the carving and announced: 1990 Clos

# RHONE VALLEY
## Domaine Jean-Paul Jamet

Saint-Denis grand cru from Philippe Charlopin, 1991 Bonnes Mares grand cru from Dominique Laurent (the year when he was "discovered" by Robert Parker) and a 1989 Vosne-Romanée premier cru Cros Parantoux from Henri Jayer. The debates carried on nonstop and were riveting. Almost an hour went by in this manner.

Once the table was cleared, out came a Saint-Nectaire from chez Maillard and a piece of Comté from chez Bernard Antony, which I tried for the first time that evening. Almost twenty years later, both of them are still included in the cheeses served daily at the George V. The next debate was led by the peasant emperor of the Rhône Valley, represented by his three graces: Turque, Mouline and Landonne, from the 1985 vintage (the first vintage from La Turque, which were young vines at the time), up against a new domain that I had brought: a 1991 Côte-Rôtie from Jean-Paul Jamet! Here, the pairings were not the focus, though the Saint-Nectaire did pair perfectly with a big red wine. Instead, the discussion focused on the respective qualities of the three vintages of Côte-Rôtie from Marcel Guigal, and how they compared with Jean-Paul, the young secessionist. Before he and his brother decided to work solely in bottling, their father used to deliver his grapes every year to… Guigal. That evening, Jean-Paul's wine already possessed a style that set him apart. A precision, a chiseled quality, a new chromatic range.

Mercifully, dessert was often put off until the next morning… but not the digestif! Marc, a lover and collector of Chartreuse, brought us still a yellow Tarragone from the 1950s! Our wives retired to our rooms, and the three of us sat around the fireplace in endless discussion, building a new world… of wine.

Then, late into the night, we in turn decided to go upstairs. At that time, there was one crucial thing to remember: the two essential bottles of water. Wine may intoxicate you, but the alcohol it contains also dehydrates you, especially after a marathon of this scale. Despite the glacial atmosphere of the season and the old granite abode with its vast rooms that were impossible to heat, I didn't run the risk of getting cold during the night.

When I think back to the wines that we shared, I realize that in 2015 it would be impossible to bring them back together without spending an exorbitant amount of money, even if you remove the 1989 Cros Parantoux from

the Henri Jayer years, which today is often considered to be the most expensive wine in the world. That also means that these wines have become luxury goods, inaccessible to many enthusiasts. My friends from the Haute-Loire have since updated their cellar book, but they remain relentless supporters of quality products, discerning tastes and respect for the seasons. And so they, perhaps even more than myself, deserve to be knighted by the Legion of Honor for having always been such champions of agriculture.

Recalling the 1991 Côte-Rôtie from Jean-Paul reminds me of a fine supper that remains one of the most prestigious meals that I have shared with the sommelier team. It was in January of 2005. This time, it was set at the Parisian apartment of Enrico Bernardo – his last supper with the sommeliers before spreading his wings to embark on his own great projects. To accompany the pre-dinner morsels, we made quick work of a bottle of 1995 Dom Pérignon rosé, and then a thousand and one grams of Sévruga caviar from the Caspian Sea, which dissolved on contact with a magnum of 1990 Dom Pérignon rosé. A sensuous and marvelous pairing. Enrico, the former cook who had not lost his touch, whipped up a Carnaroli risotto with Alba white truffles that was tender and fragrant, paired with a bottle of 1982 Château-Margaux in its prime.

What could our boys possibly hope for after these extraordinary dishes… as it so happens, in came a jackrabbit stew cooked up by David Bizet – the brains behind the kitchen at Le Cinq – who is very close to the team. This is when Jean-Paul's Côte-Rôties took the stage: a 2001 Côte-Brune, a 1999 Côte-Brune and, particularly, a 1991 Côte-Brune! This was the first time I had tasted it since I first sampled his "village" vintage from this vintage

# RHONE VALLEY
## Domaine Jean-Paul Jamet

almost ten years prior. The wine had gained a fabulous complexity. An intense and flavorful moment. I don't think I am misspeaking when I say that the entire team still remembers it. Since then, everyone has advanced wonderfully: Fabio Masi, head sommelier and director of Il Lago at the Four Seasons Hotel les Bergues Geneva; Cédric Bilien, wine importer in Hong Kong; Cédric Maupoint, head sommelier at L'Abeille in the Shangri-La Hotel in Paris; Sébastien Allano, head sommelier at Caprice in the Four Seasons Hong Kong; Jérémy Evrard, associate restaurant manager at a restaurant in Hong Kong; Claudio Boreggio, wine merchant near Vevey, in Switzerland; and Oriane Chambon, an apprentice at the time, and now head sommelier at the Château de L'Yeuse, near Cognac. That evening was also rare in that Thierry and I were accompanied by our other halves, Marie and Nicolas.

For this exceptional supper, we insisted that everyone contribute something to the feast, according to his position. Enrico, Thierry and I were in charge of the "extras." And even if it is true that dinners like the ones in Sauges are no longer possible, I will always continue to share such great expressions of winemaking terroirs with our young people. These evenings always lead to moments of togetherness and brotherhood that bring so much to my life.

# The Wines

Here, the wines have a style that is personal, recognizable, chic. That is quite miraculous. Jean-Paul's Côte-Rôties are recognizable by their deep colors, the notes of black olives, a touch of smoke. They are full-bodied in the mouth, dense in certain vintages, with notes of camphor or menthol that can appear in cooler years.

Though it may be definitively true that wine is "made" on the vine, the talent displayed in the cellar is very real. Jean-Paul is a strong example. He is a precise winemaker as well as a peerless maturer. For aging wine, Jean-Paul always chooses demi-muid barrels, and his domain can make from eight to ten wines. He is there to track and perfect the vintages that are made by individual parcel. He understands what each wine needs so that it can reach its fullest possible expression without being overwhelmed by its container! Even during barrel tastings, the wines are never too severe. Which is ever more remarkable considering that here, the Syrah grapes are almost never de-stemmed. The domain only has two vintages: the blended Côte-Rôtie and a special vintage, the Côte-Brune, which requires all of the necessary attentions and also... patience. These wines do not give themselves over until they have been cellared for five to fifteen years, depending on the vintage. A rare vintage and very sought-after by enthusiasts. But the heart of the cellar lies with the generic label – a Côte-Rôtie produced according to the traditions of the appellation. It is the fullest, most colorful image of a vintage, and Jean-Paul's signature.

## Tasting with Thierry and Nicolas de Rabaudy in July 2013

2012 *(Tasted on barrel). We tasted several demi-muids, some of which contained very full-flavored vintages, others that were more fruit-focused. He doesn't customarily de-stem. This vintage required as little intervention as possible, without overly dynamic maceration or excessive woodiness. This led to a touch of reduction in the barrel, which is normal at this stage. The mouth feel is of average structure, but the finish is elegant.*

2012 Côte-brune *(tasted on barrel). The Brune has more tannins, with a more sustained structure. It is the terroir that gives the most power.*

2011 *(tasted on barrel). At this stage, the 2011s have finished aging. There has been no racking since they were put into barrels. And not an ounce of reduction on the nose. Above all, such freshness, balance, juiciness. Simultaneously fresh and dense. This is true for all of the 2011 vintages.*

DOMAINE JAMET
Côte-Rôtie
Côte-Rôtie contrôlée
CÔTE-BRUNE
2006

2011 *(another barrel). This latest Syrah is insanely charming. The nose is well preserved. The mouth feel is sublime. I had a hard time placing it with the other 2011s – Jean-Paul confided in me that it was a vintage grown in the terroir of Landonne. Yet the domain doesn't have a label for this wine! One day, perhaps… a great success along the lines of the 2001.*

2011 Côte-brune *(tasted on barrel). Strong graphite, long, complex, distinguished grain, fabulous. Austere at this stage. Not de-stemmed.*

2010. *Tight, closed at this stage. But no reduction, on the contrary, very nice fruit. Opaque garnet color, closed nose, notes of dark berry, wild blackberry, a hint of violet. Feels delicate, subtle. Full-bodied and structured in the mid-palate, which is still austere. Showy finish without harshness. A great 2010.*

2009. *The fruit is very ripe. We are not used to this type of wine from Jean-Paul. It's also the fruit from a particularly sunny vintage. This is why we were able to serve this vintage beginning in 2013,* and particularly by the glass at Cinq, paired with chef Éric Briffard's dishes during the hunting season. It was a wonderful success.

2004 Côte-brune. *Tension delivered by the tannins, still very tight. Superb, should wait.*

1998. *Color has changed, notes of black olives verging on camphor, graphite. The tannins are melted, buttery, superb. We needed a nice jackrabbit à la royale to accompany this. Right now in the cellar!*

*Upon concluding this tasting, the takeaways are:*
*– The 2012s have a sustained structure, and at this stage, several of the wines were sharp, to say the least.*
*– The 2011s displayed a very fleshy quality, very sensual with a touch of creaminess.*
*– The 2010s will make us very happy… in ten to fifteen years!*
*Here we have an excellent cellaring year. The wine is sumptuous, still quite restrained; it doesn't allow itself to be easily approached but is so very alluring.*

# RHONE VALLEY
## Domaine Jean-Paul Jamet

# Domaine Saint-Préfert

*A Four-Hand Melody*

# I

T WAS MY FRIEND
HENRI BONNEAU
who spoke to me about this domain, confiding that Monsieur Serre
had co-planted certain ancient varietals in the middle of the
Grenache vines in Saint-Préfert, giving a distinctive complexity to
the wines grown in the domain. Meanwhile, we met Isabel in 2007. I remember because my father was there, and that was the year of the antediluvian
rains. It was a chance to meet someone from outside the inner circle of
Châteauneuf-du-Pape. Isabel disclosed Châteauneuf-related information
that no other winemaker had ever shared with me before. She had the
advantage of coming from a world that was certainly connected to winemaking, but not through family connections. Most of her professional career
was spent playing the role that Romy Schneider in the film *The Lady Banker*
made famous, helping fund winemakers in the Gard. Before beginning her
search for a domain, she studied viticulture for two years at the viticultural
high schools of Carpentras and Orange. From that point forward, she found
herself on the other side of the counter, but she was determined and had the
support of an incredible man – her husband.

In 2002, after a long period of negotiations, Madame Serre (a widow with
no children, the daughter-in-law of Fernand Serre, an apothecary and the
creator of the domain) agreed to sell her the buildings as well as the
13.2 hectares of vines remaining from the original property (which covered
80 hectares in the 1930s). Isabel rolled up her sleeves and harvested her first
grapes in 2002 and made her first wine in 2003. The success of a domain is
directly correlated to the determination of its directors. Isabel is a go-getter.
Very early on, when Daniel Combin, exclusive distributor of Henri's wines
and patron of the Bonneau family, introduced me to her, I sensed a great
skill for listening to advice and adjusting accordingly. Of course, it takes
years for a new arrival in Châteauneuf-du-Pape to be accepted. But the same
could be said of all of the high-profile French vineyards. Isabel was able to
strike the right balance between kindness, ambition and vision.

The domain covers the southern slope of the village of Châteauneuf-du-
Pape, a terroir of pebbles and gravel, known for being very sunny, well
drained and warm. From the beginning, Isabel created three vintages of
Châteauneuf-du-Pape red:

# RHONE VALLEY
## Domaine Saint-Préfert

– The classic Village vintage, which could be a Burgundy, made from 90% Grenache from 70-year-old-vines, plus 5% Cinsault and 5% Mourvèdre.

– The Auguste Favier Réserve: 85% Grenache and 15% Cinsault from vines ranging from 40 to 100 years old.

– The Charles Giraud Collection: 90% Grenache, 5% Mourvèdre and 5% Syrah. These vines are between 60 and 100 years old.

Then in 2004, she created the Domaine Isabel Ferrando when she acquired 2 additional hectares in her own name, in sandier terroirs.

In 2009, Isabel bought 1.7 hectares of sandy land in the *lieu-dit* Cristia. The three famous terroirs of the appellation – the sands of Colombis, the red clay of Les Roues, and the marl and sand of Château Rayas and Cristia – were blended together to create the Colombis vintage, made 100% from Grenache noir. Isabel has a great talent for making wines without weighing them down. Her style is evolving towards wines that are stripped down, more taut. Year after year, she raises the bar. This is one of the domains of the appellation to keep an eye on. It is full of promise, a real rising star.

# MEMORIES

After a morning spent tasting at Henri Bonneau's in December of 2013, we got together for a lovely lunch at the home of Isabel and Germain. The location of their charming house is splendid. Its large bay windows open out onto a view that is like the paintings of the great masters coming to life. Your eye gets lost amongst the rows of vines, the houses of the village of Châteauneuf-du-Pape visible in the distance, towered over by the castle ruins. This image, as we enjoyed an aperitif in the living room, the fire crackling in the hearth, shall forever be associated with Isabel and Germain.

In that month of December, the bare vines with the vine shoots still trained to the wire looked like a staff of music, and the dark vine stocks like the regularly spaced notes of the symphony for which each winemaker holds the key signature! It was in this setting that Isabel fulfilled her dream, a four-hand duet played with the powerful and wondrous love that unites her and Germain.

The lunch that followed was delicious on all counts, thanks first and foremost to the caliber of the guests. Lucien and Marie-José were there from Vieux Donjon, as well as Lionel Michelin and his wife. Lionel is a passionate collector and enjoyer of old wines. He was valiant enough to take over the famous cellar of Jean-Baptiste Besse on Rue de la Montagne-Sainte-Geneviève in Paris. He has been dispensing sound advice since 2004 in this sanctuary now renamed De Vinis Illustribus. Together with our hosts and their daughter Guillemette, we made quite the merry crew.

Their faithful housekeeper served us a light and fragrant salad of frisée lettuce and black truffles to start, accompanied by a 2003 Saint-Préfert white (90% Clairette and 10% a blend of Grenache blanc and Bourboulenc) that had retained an incredible freshness. Its color showed a certain maturity, but the nose and mouth were equally remarkable.

Next came chickens of noble bearing, plump and round like only our small farms can produce. After being faithfully spit-roasted for an hour and a half, they had reached the *summum* of flavor, to use an expression worthy of Édouard Nignon. They were accompanied by fingerling potatoes sautéed in goose fat with pink Lautrec garlic. Alongside them, we had the pleasure of tasting a 2007 vintage Colombis and two vintages from Charles Giraud: a 2005 and a 2003.

As an interlude, Lionel offered us a wine to taste blind. The color showed quite a bit of bricking and wasn't very deep, the nose recalled kirsched red berries and hints of spices. The mouth feel had held up remarkably well, still chewy. An old vintage, to be sure. After enough hemming and hawing to resemble a tasting by Mimi, Fifi & Glouglou, the heroes of the comic book by Michel Tournier, we admitted defeat. Each of us had gone in an opposite direction, and we suspected that the answer would not be simple. Nevertheless, both Thierry and I were absolutely certain that it was like no wine we had tasted before. And for good reason: Lionel unveiled the bottle, revealing a wine from Algeria. A Royal Kebir by Frédéric Lung dated… 1942! Lionel explained that this family of Alsatian origin had established itself in Algeria and was, until the 1940s, the largest wine merchant in Alger.

What a voyage, and what a lesson! Because, after all, the wine was still quite coherent and lent itself well to tasting. Our friend's passionate explanation confirmed the philosophy developed by Talleyrand that wine

# RHONE VALLEY
## Domaine Saint-Préfert

explanation confirmed the philosophy developed by Talleyrand that wine lovers echo to this day: "To love wine is to talk about it."

What a trip back through time for Isabel, who was born in Provence between Ventoux and the Dentelles de Montmirail, and whose father's family comes from Algeria. She spoke to us of the perfumes of her childhood: notes of cinnamon, saffron and the spices of the Orient. The cuisine of fried delights, of honey and dates, mingled with her mother's heritage, purely Provençale, bursting with olives.

As we pontificated, we enjoyed *briques* of goat cheese from a farmer in Lozère, firm on the outside and creamy within (here, our hands instinctively reached for the 2003 Saint-Préfert white). A light and befitting dessert of fresh fruits was served. Then came delicate fried pastry *oreillettes*, prepared by their housekeeper – an authority on the subject – perfumed with orange blossom water and dusted with vanilla sugar, airy and flaky as can be. When coffee was served, the pairing was irresistible and devilishly indulgent.

It is terribly hard to pull oneself away from such a congregation, especially since the volley of conversation is never-ending in such circumstances. This separation wasn't too sorrowful though, as we were due to meet later that evening at the Palace of the Popes in Avignon, where Lionel and I were to be initiated into the brotherhood of *Échansons des Papes* (the cupbearers of Châteauneuf-du-Pape) alongside such famed figures as Michel Troisgros and Jean Alesi.

For the time being, we set out on the road – more than half an hour late – to the Clos Mont-Olivet, where the Sabon family was expecting us.

# Châteauneuf du Pape red

Tasting at the domain in December of 2013

**2012. Colombis.** *Deep ruby color. Nose is closed, still austere at this stage. Just a few fruity and floral notes of black currant and violet come through. The mouth is supple and smooth. The tannins are subtle. Great attention to detail and a realistic approach to the vintage once again. Bravo.*

**2011.** *Nose is firm, dense. A bit austere, but refined. Feels like it has real potential. It has matured in a balanced manner. The mouth feel is sensuous, and the tannins are perfect. Great structure. A refined and long wine.*

**2010.** *Intense ruby color. Nose is dense, closed, fruity and refined. Subtle notes of wood and vanilla. A great deal of potential. Here we finally see the results of Isabel's work. An aromatic purity of high intensity. A real pleasure. The full-bodied mouth is a testament to this vintage's real potential and to Isabel's maturity.*

**2009.** *Color has turned to garnet. Nose is open. Notes of stewed fruits. A little simpler than the 2007. Smooth mouth feel, a little thinner. Subtle tannins. A little shorter in the mouth. The 2009 at this stage is less sophisticated than the previous vintage but falls flat due to a lack of fullness.*

**2007.** *Intense garnet color. Slight development. Open and complex nose of spice, wood and fruit – fairly elegant. Notes of candied blackberry and vanilla enrich an aromatic expression that is subtler than that of the 2006 vintage. The full and juicy mouth feel confirms the nose. The tannins are present and fairly long. This elegant wine is rich and sleek. You can feel a nice progression in the winemaker's touch.*

**2006.** *Color has turned to garnet, gleaming. The nose is open, rich, generous. Notes of candied stewed fruits. The mouth is wide, a little drying. Retronasal aromas of licorice and stewed fruits. Feels like it has potential. At this stage, it seems the winemaker is looking for the right touch. Isabel is on the right path.*

## RHONE VALLEY
## Domaine Saint-Préfert

# Le Vieux Donjon

*The Plural of Singulars*

LONG THIS WINE'S COURSE,
I HAVE DISCOVERED
tributaries full of talent, rivers of kindness and sharing, streams
with fine and fragile beds, hidden in the meanders of a few
valleys, each with its own nature, its own deep and noble soul,
as only the earth could bring to life.

It is a discreet property, of unassuming size, still underrepresented on
Parisian tables at the time of our first encounter. It all began in the early
2000s – I was an active member of an international tasting circle created and
led by François Mauss: the *Grand Jury Européen*. During several of these
blind tasting sessions, I discovered this domain from Châteauneuf which
was previously unbeknownst to me and stood out as one of the best wines.
I should specify that we were tasting the likes of their 1978 and 1990 – both
incredible! I could not speak highly enough of their forthrightness and
finesse. Following one of these tastings, I called Madame Michel and made
an appointment to meet her and her husband Lucien, the winemaker of Le
Vieux Donjon. As it turned out, the domain already figured prominently in
a well-known guide, that of the powerful Robert Parker. The latter had
fallen for this appellation and gleefully reintroduced it to the American
market.

In terms of the quality of the wines produced by the domain, this appraisal
was not insignificant. Marie Jo and Lucien's vines are predominantly located
on the Pialon, the highest point of the vineyards, located in the northern part
of Châteauneuf-du-Pape. The signature style of the Pialon results from a
combination of clay-rich soils and high elevation. This gives rise to wines
that are more tense and less candied, endowing them with power.
In Châteauneuf-du-Pape, it is customary to identify the various vineyards
surrounding the village according to their geographical location using cardinal directions.

These terroirs, combined with Lucien's traditional winemaking, without
new barrels, make a Le Vieux Donjon red worthy of cellaring. The style
here makes wines that are rather rigid when young. The spiced notes only
develop after ten or so years. Here, as is often the case, the wine resembles
the winemaker: Lucien Michel speaks infrequently but wisely, and his argu-
ments are far-reaching.

We have often conversed about the virtues and the vintages of Châteauneuf. Nowadays, it is with their daughter Claire and their son that we discuss these subjects. They run the domain. Lucien and his wife are taking a step back, while still keeping an eye on the vines and sharing their expertise acquired over years in the cellars. Their presence is therefore advantageous and appreciated by their children. Lucien is not the type to boast. He is a recluse, passionate about his Lozère region and his Purdey rifles with their delicately engraved platinum. As for Marie Jo, she is a passionate champion for her terroir, maintaining the values passed down to her by her father, who fought for the wines of Châteauneuf to be recognized, including through the *Échansonnerie de Châteauneuf*, of which I have happily been a member since the Winter of 2013. During the initiation, I met wine lovers and saw old friends, such as Marie Pierre and Michel Troisgros (chef of the renowned La Maison Troisgros in Roanne), with whom I spent a delightful evening at the Palace of the Popes in Avignon.

The Michel family's philosophy is uncommon in this appellation. Here, instead of producing multiple vintages, there is a single label with two expressions: white and red. We are far from vintages made by individual parcel, with low yields, matured in carefully selected containers of rare and esoteric woods. These choices beget wines worthy of agricultural shows, where the beasts presented have rippling muscles so seemingly devoid of marbling that one wonders if they were created solely for the photo opportunity. These "prize specimens" are produced by certain winemakers who covet the points – oh, the precious points! – awarded by a few gurus whose choices guide the wine market. Is it the wine most loved by its creator? This is generally not the question. It's so very tedious! For when this style develops and spreads to appellations and to entire regions, it can lead domains to try and outdo one another to produce more of certain "made to measure" vintages. But you'll see none of that from the Michel family. For Lucien, ramping up production is out of the question. Besides, as the label states, it's "Le" Vieux Donjon! The only multiples here are the years in which wine is made. And in any case, isn't client loyalty over the years the most important score? Thereby protecting oneself from the inflationary effects of this quest for points and the pernicious setbacks of these egocentric pipe dreams.

RHONE VALLEY
Le Vieux Donjon

# MEMORIES

At the George V, we quickly exhausted the few 1978 and 1990 bottles that Michel was able to provide us for the wine list. But thanks to these wines, we were able to preserve the most recent vintages for some time. Now, we are able to offer Le Vieux Donjon by the glass during the season when chef Briffard makes savory *pithivier* pies filled with grouse, mallard, gray partridge, foie gras and braised winter vegetables – held captive between two rolled-out pieces of puff pastry and glazed with chestnut honey. A true delight!

This flight of game birds reminds me of my first visit to Le Vieux Donjon, during which Lucien offered to prepare thrush kebabs over the dining room fireplace. This meal has since become a ritual that we religiously repeat every year in December.

When we arrive, a hearty fire is crackling in the imposing living room fireplace. There, the *amuse-bouche* is served: toasts generously buttered with black truffle butter concocted by Marie Jo – the best that I know of. With this fare, the best pairing is a Châteauneuf-du-Pape white that has been cellared for a few years.

After this delectable hors-d'oeuvre, we move to the dining room, where the guests are seated around the large oval table, immaculately set. The first course – delicious and unchanging – is a creamy and fragrant dish of scrambled eggs. The intensely yellow yolks of the farm eggs mingle with a *brunoise* of fresh truffle. There, a young and lively red is a good fit, provided it has a fairly youthful structure. Pairing wine with eggs is always complicated.

Then comes the much anticipated dish: the little birds, nestled against one another on skewers, bundled up in their jackets of lard, served on toasts with foie gras… that we enjoy with wines from Isabel Ferrando, at the table alongside us, and with vintages of Le Vieux Donjon that have reached maturity (a 1990 or, as was the case last year, a sumptuous 1995). What a joy!

This is followed by a wide fan of cheeses, then candied fruits from Saint-Rémy-de-Provence, *calissons* from Aix, blanched almonds and Marie Jo's exceptional quince jelly. These treats, combined with the pleasant company, always delay our departure. We do eventually leave but with the absolute certainty that we will return the following year to see these wonderful hosts again.

# Tasting in their new barrel cellar in December of 2013

In the presence of the children who are now at the helm of the domain.

**2013. Le Vieux Donjon white.** *Produced with a blend of 50% Clairette and 50% Rousanne. The pale golden color is already open, fruity, reminiscent of peaches. The mouth feel is broad and generous, long. This wine should be aged for two to three years. Perfect to accompany linguine with truffles.*

**2012. White.** *Pale golden color, dense. Subtle nose, rich, refined, fruity, reminiscent of pêche-de-vigne, tender apricot, still young. Slightly closed. The mouth feel is wide, concentrated, powerful, long, with a strong tension that supports such a big wine (14.5% ABV!). A wine that is balanced, nevertheless, with a hint of salinity on the finish. Cellar it for a few years if you can.*

**2012. Red.** *Blend of 75% Grenache, 10% Syrah, 10% Mourvèdre, 5% Cinsault. The winter of 2012 will forever be remembered for the temperatures that dipped to 5°F in a region that is unaccustomed to such wintry weather. The cold temperatures combined with humidity, which devastated many of the old vines. The 2012 Le Vieux Donjon has a dense color, with an already expressive nose of dark berries and chocolate. The mouth is broad. Both the acidity and the tannins are subtle. As a whole, it is indulgent and succulent, accessible. I think it will develop slowly.*

**2011. Red.** *This vintage is more severe. The nose is still closed. The mouth remains slightly angular, and the tannins are more present, giving us a sappy Vieux Donjon. Five to ten years to reach its full potential.*

**2010. Red.** *The color is black and deep. The nose is very concentrated, mentholated. The mouth remains fresh, despite the wine's considerable fullness. The finish is long and dense. This is a classic style that should wait at least six years. Grand vin.*

**2009. Red.** *The color is dense, opaque. The nose, powerful and sunny, leads to aromas of red berry compote and sweet spices. The mouth feel is spherical, warm, powerful and very long. The finish remains sappy. It will likely mature in the same fashion as the 1989.*

**2007 Red.** *This is the charmer of the last decade, a great success from the terroir of La Crau. It is Robert Parker's chosen vintage from the domain, with his famous 100 points! In my opinion, it is just the teensiest bit too sunny, if not a little tiresome. My preference tends toward wines with more gustatory resonance. This vintage seems far too sweet, too filling. My tastes align with what is called the old world, versus what was called new. The latter often dominates the conversation nowadays. But in the end, it doesn't matter to me, so long as everyone finds a wine to his liking.*

## RHONE VALLEY
### Le Vieux Donjon

# Château Rayas

*The Raynauds: a Dynasty*

# T

**HIS SHORT,**
IBERIAN-SOUNDING
name conjures up the mysterious race of the Raynauds, proud
and stern, like the late Jacques Raynaud and the legendary
commander Raynaud before him, who were able to protect
Rayas throughout the century. Today, Emmanuel Raynaud carries the torch
passed down to him by his uncle, defending the castle as his forebears once
did. Though it has no high ramparts or even fences to prevent entry, crossing
its threshold is so intimidating that the site seems like an impregnable, secret
fortress. Here, traditions are respected, as is the work carried out by previous
generations to better preserve this inimitable little island of Châteauneuf.

Simply finding the château the first time requires patience. There are, of
course, no extravagant signs here, no ten- by ten-foot billboards. Instead
there is a barely navigable path that you head down, uncertain as to whether
you are even headed the right way. Then you arrive at a fence surrounding
a respectable structure. On the fence is a message that reads: "Not here"!
(This charming sign was taken down several years ago now.) And indeed,
just a little further down the road, you finally see the only existing sign, as
far as I know, which speaks volumes… You already get the feeling that the
moment you are about to experience is something that must be earned, and
that is, in a word, a good sign.

The Rayas terroir is "concealed" to say the least, as just finding it borders
on the miraculous. It makes more sense when your foot touches the ground
as you step out of a sedan in the rain. A city slicker's brogues will not get
sullied by a swampy splash; no, here there are no puddles or mud, for the
soil is rich with marl. This means that it is sandy on the surface, which allows
it to filter and absorb the rainwater into the ground without getting water-
logged.

Next, the vineyard: it is divided into three hilltops from the East to the
West. It is precisely these soils that give the wines from this domain that
elegance and finesse. The freshness of the wines is maintained by the unique
freshness of the terroir, owing to the woods that surround the parcels
throughout the property. At Rayas, there are as many hectares of woods as
there are of vineyard. Some would likely have cut down most of these trees
and razed the thickets and underbrush to the ground to make room for more

RHONE VALLEY
Château Rayas

404

vines. But they would have inevitably lost the originality of this place. This rare context – a balance between the vineyard and the surrounding forest – is something I found, on a different scale, at Vega Sicilia in Ribera del Duero. We will come back to that.

One does not often speak of the East and the West in Châteauneuf-du-Pape. Emmanuel, however, refers to them often, as the terroirs of the Raynaud family have clearly marked orientations. In the 2012, a fairly drinkable year, the noses are elegant and aromatic. The vines located in the East are spicier. The parcels in the West make bigger wines, more under-stated, even mentholated, with notes of sage. There, once again, Emmanuel – who, let's not forget, has been making the Rayas reds since the 1990 vintage – was able to express the full potential of this vintage. Here, there are no tricks, no oaking or extraction techniques, but rather a winemaker who has taken a perfect inventory of the vines. One of the star grape vari-etals of the domain is Cinsault, which is enjoyed here like nowhere else.

I should also mention the Grenache noir, as it must be discussed in order to truly understand Rayas. Châteauneuf-du-Pape is the northernmost appellation where this varietal can be grown in Europe, and therefore the world. Growing at its northern ripening limit intensifies its qualities, making it more refined and complex. The Rayas vineyards are also the coldest part of the appellation, which adds to the complexity that defines these wines.

Emmanuel Raynaud resembles his late uncle, and can come across as reserved and not particularly forthcoming. His words are few but always relevant. Like his wines, he takes his time in all endeavors, a believer in the saying, "Time won't remember the things we do without it." Once you've gained his confidence, he opens up, and his simple and pertinent explana-tions allow you to further understand his wines, like an expert interpreting a canvas to help you perceive the subtlest nuances in the tone, down to the tiniest brushstroke. In 2013, he was offering – quite sparingly – his 2001 and 2004 vintages to his delighted clients. He will always be against any speculation or snobbery about his wines. This domain protects its individ-ual clients, who have always been its dominant clientele, distilling the bot-tles according to the needs of the many, as opposed to the means of the few. Very symbolic!

MEMORIES

Amongst the many rarities that have been produced at Rayas, I remember the 1955 demi-sec Rayas white (with the incredible title on the label: *Premier Grand Cru Réserve*!) that we had at Montrond-les-Bains in the early nineties, which we served to accompany a plump spring chicken with Albuféra sauce. It was a moment of sheer delight! The aromas of the wine were reminiscent of *calissons* from Aix, orange marmalade, beeswax and wild fennel. Impressive. It was at that time that Thierry and I made our first visit to the domain, back in 1996 when Jacques Raynaud was still alive.

Unfortunately, as is too often the case during our treks, we had arrived more than twenty minutes late. Sometimes, that's fatal. Lesson learned: we waited for a few moments outside before Jacques' sister came to let us in. While outside, we saw the Master of the House's inscrutable face appear in a window on the second floor without making a gesture or saying a word. As soon as we crossed the threshold, we wanted to wipe our feet on what we thought from a distance was the doormat. This was the wrong move – as we approached it, we saw it shift! It was the family dog, an improbable-looking creature.

Madame Raynaud was wearing fatigues (as was her brother, by the way), certainly from an army surplus store, a large county cap on her head. She shot us an icy stare, making it clear that we were not to move. "Jacques is coming," she told us.

At that moment, a house painter in coveralls emerged from a door at the back of the small entryway and entered the room, a Gauloise cigarette hanging from his lips, a can of white paint in one hand. He stopped to look around the room, evaluating the handiwork, then sighed and continued to the next room. In the hopes of filling the silence, I ventured, "Are you remodeling?" – "Well, yes, we're whitewashing the walls. You know, you have to resign yourself to doing it once in your life." Jacques Raynaud came down and invited us to taste a white wine in mismatched, stemless glasses that had become opaque from what I imagine to be long and frequent use.

The wine, which had likely been decanted several days earlier, showed a few faults and a touch of uncontrolled oxidation. In truth, this first wine was a developing bath (like the chemical baths that reveal the latent image of a photograph) designed to reveal any potential hypocrisy of the taster. One

RHONE VALLEY
Château Rayas

glowing comment and the tasting would have been over! But we responded diplomatically, without overdoing it, hinting at our thoughts about the "state of the white," which seemed to be rather weary! We passed the test, and went down into the cellar to taste the reds in casks and barrels. After a few steps on the beaten earth floor in the dimly-lit place – incidentally, without meaning to, I stepped on a lightbulb that had dropped from the overhead light like a ripe fruit – we tasted wines that were impressive in the clarity of both the nose and mouth. What a pleasure! And what a lesson! When we emerged, our understanding of Châteauneuf-du-Pape had been deepened. The wines from the property that we have tasted since then revealed themselves much more intensely.

We didn't have to travel far to find nice pairings. In the center of the village, we had reserved a table at La Mère Germaine. Our table was set in the back dining room, with a lovely arbor framing the wide bay windows that opened out onto the vineyard below. Here are my evocative notes, taken in the early 2000s: "First course of thin slices of raw scallops plated in a checkerboard pattern with slivers of black truffle and dressed with a drizzle of olive oil, a squeeze of lemon and a sprinkle of freshly-ground Szechwan peppercorn. A superb dish that gave the 1989 Rayas white free rein to express its full potential: appealing yellow color, a nose of candied lemon, wax, dried plants. Wide mouth with a nice fullness, notes of minerals, seashells, which mingles with the silky scallops and communes with the flavors of the truffles. Then we had the pleasure of enjoying a rare delight from the recipes of Édouard Nignon: the jewel of gourmet stews (it is a stew made with a doe – a female hare – cooked in Châteauneuf-du-Pape, brimming with shallots, crushed garlic, thyme, bay leaf, a pinch of cinnamon, a blend of *épices fines* and a hint of ginger, to which mushroom caps and lardons are added). To do the honors, we called on a 1985 Rayas red. That year was one of the greatest successes of the decade, thanks to a fantastic summer and rain at just the right moments. The color and the nose were at once Burgundian and Piedmontese. The mouth married silkiness with a pleasing strength. Marvelous, in its prime."

These words validate the notes that we took during our tastings. It is a real joy to delve into them once again. My memory rekindles them, and my nose relives their perfumes.

# Rayas white

It is produced from old vines of Clairette
and Grenache blanche and is very distinctive.
No "cold fermentation," giving it bouquets
that become more mineral over time,
developing accents of saffron and flint.
In the Summer of 2013, we were tasting
the château's 2000 whites, which are
remarkable accomplishments in terms of finesse
and have reached maturity, working wonders
alongside sautéed milk-fed veal chops.

**2003 Rayas white** *(tasted in January*
*of 2015 at Le Cinq). Intense yellow gold*
*color, gleaming. Rich nose of honey, sweet*
*almond and ripe pear. The nose expresses*
*a nice maturity. A few notes of bread*
*crumb, dry floral. The mouth feel is full,*
*tense on the finish from the Clairette.*
*Notes of chalk, licorice and dry yeast.*
*A powerful, broad wine. Needs to wait*
*a little longer.*

# Rayas red

When you taste with Emmanuel,
his county cap screwed firmly onto his head,
the astonishing mystery and beauty of Rayas
comes alive. The latest vintages in the anthology
are the 2009 and 2010. They will be offered…
when ready.

# Tasting in December of 2013

*When Emmanuel invites you to taste,*
*you mustn't expect to taste the vintage*
*in progress… because it is inherently not*
*ready. What a respectable point of view!*
*We began with the 2012 white. And boy,*
*are those 2012s astounding. The Clairettes*
*possess a remarkable richness. The fruit*
*is very nice and clean; opening them will*
*bring such pleasure! For the 2012 red*
*varietals, the Grenaches, Cinsault and Syrah*
*from Château Fonsalette are very successful.*

*I couldn't possibly hide my admiration*
*for the Rayas terroir. Here, convention*
*is turned on its head – the reds are pale*
*colored, far from the archetype of the*
*appellation, but no less intense. Next,*
*the wines are offered when Emmanuel*
*determines that they have reached maturity,*
*and then only in dribs and drabs. Finally,*
*the wines mature in antique casks*

*and prehistoric demi-muid barrels. If my*
*memory serves me correctly, they have been*
*there since his uncle's tenure.*

*These factors combined result in wines*
*that are dazzling, complex, refined and*
*delicate. They are what we call "Grand*
*Vins," for which one shouldn't attempt*
*to find a rational explanation and certainly*
*not an oenological one, coldly deduced*
*in a laboratory. It works well the way it is.*
*For example, though they are usually*
*intended for rosé wines, here the Cinsault*
*grapes are intense and deep, very spicy.*
*Peppery, with notes of bay leaf.*
*Though frequently vegetal in this climate,*
*here, the Syrah is very delicate.*
*As for the Grenache, when it is translated*
*by this terroir, it becomes supple*
*and delicate, with a very pale color*
*but such a mouth!*

# Domaine Bonneau

*The Wonderful World of Henri*

# F

IRST AND FOREMOST,
IT MUST BE SAID
that Henri – he died in March 2016 at 78 years old – was a man of
integrity. With him, there was no detours, no pretentiousness or
subterfuge. He assessed you with one look… and that said it all.

It was in July of 1998 that I met him for the first time, by way of my friend
Christophe Tassan from Avignon (an eminent sommelier I met during sommelier competitions, who was long the head of Les Domaines, one of the
best restaurants at the foot of the Palace of the Popes). To enter the Bonneau
home is not an opportunity granted to just anyone. Fortune, titles and hon-
orifics have no sway here; they fall on deaf ears. Incidentally, for a long time,
the label next to the doorbell, where one would normally find the name of
the resident, read "No guests!" Do not say you were not warned… (all the
better if this clever stratagem helped fend off all sorts of nuisances and other
unsavory characters).

In the world of winemakers' wines, very few can be opened blind and
reliably be recognized for its "progenitor." Henri's was one of them. At Le
Cinq, the policy is to only open his wines for guests who will be capable of
understanding them, because to serve them is first and foremost to talk about
them. This is true of all the *Grand Vins*. Our man's wines are created in his
image: uncompromising, of a singular temperament, expressing a journey,
a past life that cannot be imitated. Welcome to the home of one of the last
lords of Châteauneuf-du-Pape!

If you were expecting Henri's vines to be a lesson in viticulture and vine
training, all perfect cordons and tidy terrain, then move along. Here, all of
the man's originality is visible in his vines. The philosophy is to "release the
hounds," like the hunt masters would say during hunts of unrivaled panache.
Like Henri. Here, the star varietal is Grenache noir, which is grown in the
terroir of La Crau to produce the Cuvée de Célestins. There is also another
label: the Cuvée Marie Beurrier, grown in different areas of Châteauneuf in
the southern part of the appellation.

Our man liked what is natural and free. A free thinker down to his soul,
which was abundant. It is important to remember that though his vineyard
has many critics who sit in the alcoves of Châteauneuf snickering about the

aforementioned vines, there is not a single winemaker who does not dream of treading its soil and its grapes.

Of the many important moments in the life of any self-respecting sommelier, entering Henri Bonneau's cellar is one that is both highly anticipated and nerve-wracking. Because, after all, if there is one "singular" place in terms of cellars, this is it!

The house is situated in the heights of the village, on a narrow road across from the church. The door is understated and discreet, revealing nothing of the place that it encloses. Over the decades, both people and harvests have entered through this door. The miniscule basket press – like at Yquem – is located just steps from the dining room, as are the vats the hold the nectar of the vine. The various steps of vinification take place right below the living space, in the warren of cellars. Wine is at the center of the house, intertwined and indivisible from the walls and those who live within them. It occupies so much of it that it might as well be the master of the house! To cross the threshold was an acknowledgement from Henri: he accepted you. For one of his dinner guests, it was akin to being knighted by a great lord – a high priest of wine – which is what sommeliers are, in a way: at the service of the wine and the winemaker. Upon entering, I understood that here reigns a sort of oenological counter-culture, an ascetic, archaic vision of the world of wine. The labyrinthine Bonneau cellars are unique. The beaten earth floors are slightly sticky here and there, and further in, a grate covers a deep hole. The atmosphere is like none other. The vaulted ceilings are of the same hue as the floor and the antediluvian barrels.

Nothing disturbs the atmosphere of these cellars where some of the most sought-after wines of Châteauneuf-du-Pape mature patiently, peacefully. One of the maxims is that wine should only be bottled when it is ready.

And sometimes that takes four years, if not more!

Even the pipettes used to pull samples of the wine from the casks are of the same unidentifiable but consistent hue. As is often the case with winemakers, the chalk markings on the barrels prove indecipherable to everyone else. Lacking the genius of Champollion, I abandoned my search for their translations. After all, why bother when Henri was there, in tune with his wines, sublimating them when needed, keeping in mind the pleasure of he who shall one day enjoy them.

RHONE VALLEY
Domaine Bonneau

# M EMORIES

Of all the moments I have shared at the home of the Bonneaus, I remember one dinner a few years ago in particular. It began with seasoned tripe *caillettes* wrapped in caul fat from Chez Bouquette, washed down with a 1999 Marie Beurrier, followed by a 1998. Next came woodcocks roasted on skewers over the hearth, accompanied by toasted bread that had soaked up all that flavor, which Henri paired with one of his father's famous 1955 vintages, with kirsched notes reminiscent of the great pinots of the Côte de Nuits. There was also an exceptional 1989. Tasting one of Henri's wines is like tasting a part of him – his quick wit, his humor, his generosity, a rare sensibility. It is a wine that has heart. And his cellar is like an Ali Baba's cave that one is always happy to get dragged into.

In order to understand his maturing process, one must first put aside all prior knowledge and… trust him. Not a single bottle brought forth from his cellar has failed to move me when opened. I have enjoyed exceptional moments dining at his home, certainly some of my most treasured memories, imbued with good humor, human warmth, a simple and sincere friendship. I remember a terrine of wild boar that one of his hunting companions had brought for him several days prior, that he opened especially for us. With a few hearty slices of country bread and a 1998 Marie Beurrier, we were ready to set the world to rights.

During one of these visits, we had brought a couple pounds of boletus mushrooms with us which Thierry pan-fried in the kitchen with a veal stock reduction… Believe me, this is a base that always pairs well with mature red wines.

Another fantastic pairing was one evening in 2001, when we savored the 1990 Special Vintage – close to 17.5% ABV – with a Provençal beef stew prepared by Stéphane Tassant. What a delight! I opened it again to accompany a jackrabbit stew that my wife cooked up. If I had tasted it blind, the strong notes of spice and fruit compote without any overripe qualities might have initially led me to assume that it had been pulled straight from the barrel.

This larger than life epicure will never lose his sharp mind and joyful spirit, or the sparkle in his deep blue eyes. Thanks to his generosity and friendship, I have had the chance to taste an astounding number of old vintages, often bearing a coating of dust from a bygone era. One cannot truly understand his wines without knowing him. He embodies this paradox: "War is the darkest act of destruction that Man has created, but each great wine that is shared is one of his best creations."

And contrary to the rigor of the military, with Henri, wine is synonymous with freedom! It is a universal message.

Thank you, Henri.

RHONE VALLEY
Domaine Bonneau

# 1999 Cuvée des Célestins

This wine is grown on the famous plateau of La Crau. It is a terrace dating from the Villafranchian age, covered in the famous *galets roulés*, the smooth pebbles typical of the appellation. The terroir of La Crau – coveted, idolized – is the real treasure of the Popes.

The canonical vines with very low yield produce extremely concentrated grapes that will later stand up to six or seven years spent maturing in the cellar. This is when Henri, along with his son Marcel, and Daniel Combin's support, got into the game. Over many years, the wine will become more refined, more complex, in barrels so old that certain staves have been caulked with putty to prevent them from leaking.

As they mature, Marcel and Daniel will rack off and evaluate them several times. This method, which would take the wind out of most wines, is what creates the incomparable hallmark of his Cuvée des Célestins. The wines remain creamy, silky and big, indulgent and intense. During vinification, no de-stemming and no new barrels! And no filtering before barreling. The wine is subjected to a training regimen like that of a legionnaire preparing for a mission in the Sahel desert. Speaking of those desert expanses, I will not expand on the percentage of alcohol in Bonneau's wines, which can reach record heights. Looking past this simplistic parameter, the wines are often very coherent as a whole. Take, for example, the 1988 (tasted in 1998) still in barrel, which was astonishing. Deep, tight, dense, rigorous, with a discernible freshness despite blithely reaching 14.5% ABV.

# A few vintages tasted on the barrel, late 2013

*The morning of December 7, 2013, when I rang Henri's doorbell accompanied by Thierry, I had a knot in my throat as I do each time I visit. Jacqueline came to let us in, and Henri was waiting for us at the end of the hall, a happy look on his face, as well as ours! We went into the dining room where the wood-burning stove was purring, as was the cat, coincidentally.*

*We then went down into the cellar, Henri leading the way, leaning on his cane, which he uses with much protestation. When entering this den of wine, I hearken back to so many memories, all of them happy, epicurean, full of moments of sharing and a respect for time. After reminiscing about Alger and Constantine, Henri plunged his pipette into the antiquated barrels – the real strongbox of the house – and we began a vertical barrel tasting of the Cuvée des Célestins:*

**2012.** *The nose is smooth, full, sensual. The mouth is broad and long. It could strengthen quickly. Let's not forget the Célestins spend an average of six years in the barrel before bottling.*

**2011.** *Nose has marked notes of sour cherry and spiced fig. The mouth is structured and a touch austere at this stage of development.*

**2010.** *For Henri, this year falls a bit short of the 2009. Henri's wines need to stock up on sunshine before their slow maturation in barrels. Yet the 2010 didn't take advantage of it. Nevertheless, it is a great Châteauneuf. The mouth feel is firm, dense, distinguished and tense. This one will be a great bottle!*

**2009.** *A very good year for Henri. The Célestins is deep, dark, thick and firm. The influence of the maturation is of course imperceptible. The length is incredible. The same density as the 1989s. This is a wine that requires 10 years of cellaring… once it is bottled.*

**2007.** *2007. One of the batches of Célestins currently still in the barrel. It is the home turf of the vintage: the heart of the La Crau terroir. Only very old vines are represented. It is a delight of dark berries on the nose. Without the over-ripeness of the 2007s. An example of balance at more than 15% ABV.*

## RHONE VALLEY
### Domaine Bonneau

# Others wines tasted after bottling, sometime in 2013

**1999. Célestins.** *Creamy, fruity,*
*a smidge easier than the 1998. Still warm*
*and powerful during an awkward phase.*

**1989.** *One of Henri's greatest successes.*
*Deep, sensual, very structured.*
*As frequently occurs, it was decided that*
*the 1990 vintage was better, but the 1989*
*just needed more time. To put it simply,*
*it is one of the greatest Châteauneufs that*
*I have ever had the chance to taste.*

*Of course, ill-tempered critics will tell me*
*that deviances are a dime a dozen*
*with Henri, and that the wines have*
*a very high alcohol content. To them*
*I say that drinking Bonneau is not*
*mandatory… even if they have often*
*been convinced to taste some!*
*What is important to understand is*
*his outlook on life and wine, characteristic*
*of Marcel Pagnol's provençal soul,*
*interwoven with a touch of Tartarin*
*of Tarascon. The fact remains that for me,*
*Henri, with his rare human values,*
*is one of the common threads*
*of the appellation.*

# ALSACE
# JURA
# SOUTH-WEST

P 421

P 432

P 438

# Other Vineyards of

~

# France

# Domaine André Kientzler

*Pure as Crystal*

# T

HE FAMILY. THEIR VINEYARD,
WE ARE HERE IN RIBEAUVILLÉ,
where this family has lived for generations. It is the end of
summer. The cellar seems like it was set down in the middle
of the vines at the foot of the hillsides, near the entrance to
the village which is a little further off. To speak of André Kientzler is above
all to highlight this winemaker's humility and kindness – a kindness which
he has been able to instill in his sons.

For a long time, many Alsatian domains were obsessed with reaching
maximum maturity, often leading to the presence of residual sugar, and in
doing so, developing a simplistic image of the vineyards. Other winegrowers,
like André and his sons, chose to stay on course making tense, lively, crystalline wines.

Here, respect for the terroir is shown through efforts to make wines that
are dynamic, tense and svelte (these are nuances that aptly characterize the
Kientzler's). Without much ado, André was able to make a place for himself
with enthusiasts and sommeliers, as was the case at Le Cinq, where his wines
have always been positively received. The family land registry contains four
*grands crus*. The one that garners the most attention is the Geisberg. To think
that the grandfather built his house in the middle of this vineyard! Today,
no one would allow it. The domain is situated at the entrance to the village.
From the large bay windows of the tasting cellar – as if it were plopped in
the middle of the vines – one's gaze drifts to the hillside and, in the distance
to the left, the roofs of Ribeauvillé. The Kientzlers work almost 11 hectares,
3.7 of which are planted with *grands crus*: Osterberg, Kirchberg, Geisberg
and, very recently, Schœnenbourg. The reigning varietal in this family, as in
much of Alsace, is Riesling. One of the distinguishing features of the
domain's favorite wine is the marl soil and the exposure of the hill, providing
the necessary hardship to create wines that deliver their full power after ten
years of cellaring.

# MEMORIES

The most delightful pairings with the Geisberg Riesling were made during our annual supper at Thierry's house in February of 2007. That year, we had asked Bernard Antony, one of our outstanding cheese suppliers at Le Cinq, to send us a spectacular *choucroute garnie* on the appointed day. What he had delivered to us was beyond our wildest expectations: fermented cabbage and white turnip, smoked landjäger and Montbéliard sausages, wienerwurst and knackwurst, smoked and braised pork shoulder, and farmhouse bacon from Gérardmer.

At the same time, we had called up the Kientzler family in the hope of acquiring two magnums of the Geisberg of their choosing for the occasion. They too went above and beyond our expectations by proposing a magnum of 2004 Geisberg Riesling and a magnum of the 2000. It was an indulgent pairing, carried by the freshness and forthrightness of the Geisberg Rieslings.

More recently, the day after our visit to the Kientzlers in 2013, we had lunch with Nicolas de Rabaudy, Florent Martin – one of the up-and-coming young members of the team – and Thierry Hamon at Auberge de l'Ill. You simply must visit this large and wondrous house run by the Haeberlin family for generations. Imagine, three Michelin stars for more than forty years. As I wrote to them upon returning home to Le Cinq: a passion for hosting, elevated to an art form, was undoubtedly the elixir of youth for Monsieur Jean-Pierre, who left us in 2014. What a character! He was at once touching and admirable, an example for restaurateurs and many others. He was such a remarkable ambassador for our way of living! Our service professions are uncertain because they depend on those who do the honors – illustrated by the way the Auberge has mastered the art of "handing down" this art of hospitality to the successive generations that have passed through its walls. Exceptional.

Just hearing the name of certain dishes opens the door to an indulgent reverie. One such dish from that day was an exquisite partridge cutlet "Romanov" with a *Périgueux* sauce (a deboned young partridge stuffed with black truffle and goose foie gras), accompanied by a 2004 Vosne-Romanée Premier Cru Chaumes by Jean-Nicolas Méo. What joy! Especially when prepared by my friend of thirty years, Serge Dubs, the tireless sommelier of the establishment who, over the years, has become what he refers to as a "merchant of joy." He came in as an apprentice and went his entire career without ever leaving the Haeberlins, where he met his future wife and coach during competitions. Though he is now retired, Serge is still at the ready as soon as Marc or Danièle Haeberlin calls for him. An example for any budding sommelier, amongst others.

And yet, it was actually the dish that preceded it that held my attention. A poached egg placed delicately on a *vichyssoise* (a soup of potatoes, leeks and chicken stock), generously blanketed with shaved white truffle. It was accompanied by a 1990 Geisberg Riesling by the

Kientzler family. The most complete expression of two aromatic paragons. It was Serge who made that selection. I insisted that he serve us himself instead of delegating the task to an assistant, opening the bottles at each table in his section, with a few words or a kind thought for each and every one.

As I mentioned previously, every time he won an award at the national or international level, he was right back at his post at the Auberge de l'Ill the next day with the same enthusiasm. What humility, and what a lovely testament of loyalty to a family! In our trade, when we're amongst ourselves, the discussions about our former employers are merciless. Especially when they come up in the staff dining room during the family meal around 6:30 p.m. before service begins. Well, I know at least one exception: the Haeberlin family! Never once have I heard someone in the dining room or the kitchen say a single negative thing about them. There are very few in this category, and to understand, one simply has to visit the unique estate that is the Auberge de l'Ill.

ALSACE
Domaine André Kientzler

## The Wines

2010 Muscat Ottonel. *Delicate, light, subtle, floral. It is the antithesis of what we often expect from an Alsatian muscat. A wine perfect for enthusiasts during the green asparagus season in Luberon. Every year when it appears on the Chef's menu, we prepare the Kirchberg Muscat grand cru by the Kientzlers. There exists a natural affinity between the two. Here, the finesse and fragility of this varietal, in aromatic and gustatory ranges unlike a typical muscat, manage to rein in the vegetal aromas of the asparagus without dominating them.*

2012 Riesling grand cru Osterberg. *One of the family's historic grands crus. Fruity, delicate, fresh nose. Already pleasing. A light-bodied wine. Successful.*

2012 Grand cru Schœnenbourg. *Broad. Rich. Sweet almond.*

## Vertical tasting of the Geisberg grand cru, in October of 2013 at the domain

The family grows 1.5 hectares of Geisberg. Soil composed of limestone and marl. Ideal exposure due south.

2012. *Intense, remarkable, wide and deep. Very harmonious. An excellent wine.*

2011. *Delicate, discreet, reserved nose. The mouth is tense, very distinguished, with a saline finish. Lively.*

2010. *Discreet, narrowed. Nice fruit; austere at this stage. Time, give it time.*

2009. *Open, heady, rich, big. The mouth is wide. Ripe. Notes of white and yellow fruit like Mirabelle plum. Also aromas of white flowers, magnolia. Heady impression of excellent maturity, with the tension of a Geisberg.*

2007. *Expressive nose, tertiary bouquet, candied lemon, flash of schist. Mouth feel is hard and tense, thirst-quenching. Lovely retronasal aromas reminiscent of bitter almond.*

2004. *Open, sensuous, notes of beeswax, parmesan, roots, stewed tubers, parsnip. Supple mouth feel, mature, ready to drink.*

2002. *Sappy, deep. Orange zest. Fairly rich. Full-bodied, harmonious. Excellent bottle.*

1993. *Expressive, note of candied citron, golden color. The attack is very sensuous in the mouth, quickly followed by a bracing acidity. A mature Geisberg, superb.*

# Domaine André Ostertag

## Between the Fruit and the Root

**T THE BEGINNING OF MY CAREER,**
I WAS FIRING ON ALL CYLINDERS,
and in the mid-eighties I became convinced that what I needed
was to spend all of my time walking the vineyards and meeting
the men and women of wine in order to better understand
them. Certain winemakers were rebelling against the forms of order established by their elders. They dared to challenge the principles of cultivation and
vinification inherited from progress in both agriculture and œnology. One such
dissident who refused to perpetuate these agricultural practices was the imposing and tempestuous Didier (Dagueneau) from Saint-Andelain. In Epfig, I
met a slightly more level-headed version: André (Ostertag).

His choices hit the Alsatian elite like an asteroid. He inveighed against the
yields at the time – authorized by decree – and the excessive treatments used
on the vines. He was ready to take flight, like Icarus. And he was right to be
so bold – what a beautiful ascent! This was in 1988. When someone is driven
by a passion (for wine, in this case) and when that passion is the source of their
professional commitment, then it is important to shift into high gear to
quickly absorb as much knowledge as possible, but also to eagerly visit the
regions and meet the young winegrowers, who are themselves moving at the
speed of change, with visions that differ from those of their parents. The same
is true for each generation of winegrowers and sommeliers. In this respect,
André Ostertag has tirelessly delved further into his research, keeping metic-
ulous notebooks year after year on the results of the choices he made, and
what the climate and the terroir allowed him to harvest. Among his hall-
marks, I must mention his A360P Pinot Gris, which has been written about
extensively by his supporters and critics alike. The name of this vintage is
actually related to the quote featured on the label: "Solitary but free, like an
old oak in the middle of the pink sandstone." This motto describes the unique
nature of the vintage, which originates from a limestone vein that runs
through pink sandstone and volcanic rock. These 5,000 square meters of
Pinot Gris are listed in the land register as A360P, which became the name
of the vintage after it was refused the right to be called a *grand cru*.

Another of André's idiosyncrasies is his preference for maturing his wines in
*barriques* – smaller barrels like those used in Burgundy – instead of the larger
*foudres* typical of the Rhineland. Thirty-four harvests later (he started very

early), André Ostertag is still there. With the passing of the seasons – both the seasons of the year and of his life – he has acquired an incredible sense of peace and tranquility. With the sculpted body of a mountain climber (he reminds me a bit of Vincent Dauvissat), he is willing to endure hard work, to push himself past his limits. Always wondering and asking questions. A sculptor of Rieslings!

# MEMORIES

Beyond the inherent quality of the following pairing, it is more importantly an emotional memory for me, because of the kind of father I am. There was no indication that our son would pursue a path in the restaurant industry after finishing his studies in Classics, and yet...! Not content with serving in the dining room, he chose to specialize in... *sommellerie*. Not an easy choice. I remember what Sacha Guitry said regarding his father, one of the best-known actors of his time on the stages of Paris and Europe: "I already had a last name, but I had to make a first name for myself!"

Of his earliest engagements, I fondly remember when he entered and was subsequently selected in a competition for students in the restaurant industry. One of the challenges was a cooking exam. The required subject was a salmon tartare, to be prepared from a selection of available ingredients. He had the chance to practice ahead of time at home – we ate so much salmon tartare! During one of his trial runs, I had the idea to pair it with a 2011 Muenchberg Riesling, which I brought up from the cellar. The pairing proved to be absolutely remarkable. Muenchberg continues to be an example of a superb Alsatian Riesling, thanks first of all to its dry balance, and secondly to its bouquet reminiscent of lemon zest. The savory texture of the Riesling is critical to match a raw, fatty fish. Especially with the choice of Norwegian salmon, which is often quite oily. The other unforgettable element was prepared by his sisters: toasted sourdough bread which we procured from a bakery close to the house called Le Blé Sucré, run by a former pastry chef from Bristol. These toasts were important, as they brought a crunchy element to the dish, something to chew on. Later, Baptiste was able to finalize his preparations under competition conditions with one of our friends from the kitchen, David Bizet, and of course we did not miss the opportunity to repeat that indulgent pairing, which the two of them shared.

## ALSACE
## Domaine André Ostertag

These moments are among my most wonderful memories from the George V. I must confess, I am proud of Baptiste. Though he and his sisters were born into a family environment that encouraged a love of wine culture, the arts of the table, and quality products, that it does not make it any easier to break into this career path – fascinating, of course, but oh so demanding! And, just this once, I'll give André the floor to conclude these pages dedicated to his domain. From his 2015 New Year's wishes: "Wine is the Water of the Sky mixed with the Salt of the Earth, a great deal of Love and quite a bit of Work. Wine captures Life in a blend of living droplets carried by the passage of Time. All of those droplets combine to bring together those who drink them and allow them deep into their hearts, into their innermost dreams. Wine heightens our lives."

During my last visit to André in 2013, I was accompanied by Nicolas de Rabaudy, Florent Martin and Thierry. Before we even passed through the imposing double doors of the home, André's father came out to meet us. We spoke about the current harvest, though we mostly listened to him speak with all the wisdom of a man of the land, unconcerned by the drizzle that had been bedewing our shoulders for the past few minutes. What a joy, what kindness! Eventually, he led us down to the cellar, where André was deep in contemplation in front of a tank. He calmly makes sense of the vinification in progress and the wine to come.

Before I go any further, first a few words about the *grand cru* of Muenchberg. It owes its name to the Cistercian monks who planted vines on this hillside beginning in the 12th century, hence its meaning: mountain of the monks. It is a natural amphitheater on a hillside facing due south, in a valley at the foot of the Vosges mountains in the village of Nothalten, with a soil composed of pink Vosges sandstone, volcanic sediment and a bit of limestone in the east. In Alsace, there are a myriad of different terroirs, each of an incredible complexity.

What a delight to see André again in Epfig for an unbelievable tasting, in which you could recognize the man and his evolution. The property is managed like a garden made up of a multitude of micro-parcels spread throughout five villages, including Epfig where we are now. The property has 2 hectares of the famous Muenchberg. How time flies! To think that I first came here in 1988!

The domain has practiced fully biodynamic viticulture since 1998. André often cites Rudolf Steiner – a man who, incidentally, rarely drank wine. But to produce a great wine, one has to drink it. Which is not to suggest that one should become inebriated! Wine should allow thoughts to come alive and dialogue to be established, and should find its place at the table in sophisticated pairings.

In this regard, André has always defended the notion of the "digestibility" of a wine. This is a factor that I am very fond of, perhaps even more so as time goes by. This process manifests itself at the domain in the efforts to not push maturity too far. The presence of residual sugar can sometimes seem like an embellishment that dulls the precision of the Riesling aromas.

Note: the wines were served together and tasted one after the other. Delightful to "go back," switching from one to another.

ALSACE
Domaine André Ostertag

# Vertical tasting of Muenchberg Riesling grand cru

October of 2013.

**2012.** *Nose is floral, subtle, precise and dense. The mouth is wide, harmonious, spicy, the Muenchberg style. Will need at least five more years to reveal itself.*

**2011.** *Open, expressive, hint of citron, honeysuckle. Refined, dense. The mouth is sunny, wide and big. An intense moment when a new bottle arrived — surprise! It was a Muenchberg micro-vintage, but even denser, deeper, purer. And what a nose! Made from ungrafted vines! This wine exudes a life that no other wine we tasted possesses.*

**2010.** *Nose is closed off, backward; concentrated, somewhat milky. A rough patch in the life of the wine. Needs to wait.*

**2009.** *Sunny, harmonious, orange chutney, rich, waxy. Similar to the 2011, but more powerful. Need to give it time for this richness to blend into its balance.*

**2008.** *Pure, open, clean. Tense, note of verbena. Finish is floral, with young lemongrass. Very classy. Mouth feel is full-bodied and tight. Very balanced. Great length. This is how I like Muenchbergs.*

**2002.** *Here is a Riesling grand cru with 15 grams of residual sugar, but the wine has "eaten" its sugar, making it so the sweetness is barely discernable. This makes the wine opulent, big,*

*harmonious. The mouth is spherical and long — a wine to contemplate. A great Riesling to pair with seasoned and spicy dishes.*

**1988.** *One word right away: mineral (even if it is part of the pantheon of terms that are difficult to translate). This impression certainly arises from the volcanic sediments in the sub-soil of the Muenchberg grand cru, evoking flint and hot stone. At least that's what the nose and the mouth alike express as a whole. The nose is subtle, open, with ever-present notes of citrus. The mouth feel is fully developed. Nobody would guess its age. Enduring proof of André's masterful vinification at the time.*

**2007.** *Late harvest. Pale color, 98 grams of residual sugar. Rich, deep nose, exceptional liqueur. Long and opulent. Very nice length.*

*To conclude this tasting, I want to highlight something significant: André has maintained a long-term skill for harnessing the energy of his terroir, like those ungrafted vines in one of his "gardens" of 70-plus-year-old vines that I so enjoyed tasting, without being filtered through the rootstock. In them, I felt all of the energy that one finds in Didier and Louis-Benjamin's Astéroïde.*

# Domaine Michel Pichet

*Savagnin Defies Chronos*

**T THE EDGE OF THE FRENCH ALPS,** time is the medium of the finest watchmakers who work tirelessly to keep it, protected in precious casings and set in rare metals. On the slopes of our Jura, a wine that is truly one of a kind dances with the years. For if there is one French white wine that fares the best against the ravages of time, it is *vin jaune*! I discovered the *grands vins* of Jura while taking courses in Beaune. Let's just say it was long before the recent infatuation with these very "natural" and organic wines. When I received an offer to go meet one of the masters of Château-Chalon, in the person of Louis Florin, I jumped at the opportunity. Since then, I have always worked with the wines of this region. Whether it was with the Macle family or the Bourdy family, and their collection of more than a century's worth of Chalons, we have had up to fifteen vintages of Chalon on the wine list, from 2004 to... 1911. We have opened twelve bottles of it in seven years. Each one offered an unbelievable freshness, intensity and longevity, not to mention an impressive complexity. The gauntlet has been thrown down to Chronos!

Amongst our suppliers, I must include my friend Jacques Puffeney, with his subtle and oh-so-delicate Arbois. He, like his wines, is charming, sweet and kind. Not far from him, we had for a time a few bottles from Lucien and Vincent Aviet. They supplied us with old 1990 Cuvée des Géologues Arbois-Trousseau. A surprising, subtle, delicate wine, which is not dissimilar to the Volnay from Lafarge. In 2008, we served this Trousseau blind to friends at Le Cinq, who were astonished to taste a wine that showed such stunning evolution. This region is overflowing with hidden gems and rare wines. It is the only region in France that produces such a diverse array of wines: sparkling wines, dry white wines, *vins de voile* (matured under a film of yeast called a "veil"), straw wines, red wines, a *mistelle* (a sweet wine fortified with brandy) called Macvin, not to mention the *eaux-de-vies* and the *marcs*...

We have been close to Michel Pichet for many years now, even though things were rather complicated for him and his uncle, Louis Florin, during the transition. Nowadays we serve their *vins jaunes* by the glass throughout the year at Le Cinq, alternating with those from Jacques Puffeney. During my most recent visit to Michel with two of our sommeliers (Mickaël and Florent for this particular expedition), we were able to go out and see his vines. Imagine our surprise when Michel Pichet, who is always on the lookout, pulled a scallop shell from between two rows weighing 1.2 kilos (we weighed it when we got back to the cellar) and dating from the Early Jurassic period, or roughly... 155 million years old!

This terroir is composed of limestone and a mille-feuille of striated blue and gray marl, similar to what you see in the *lieu-dit* Beaumont, in Ménétru-le-Vignoble. Here, the south-southwest exposure is ideal to allow the grapes to mature to the optimal point of over-ripeness. The whole vineyard is set out in splendid terraces. This terroir exudes an unbelievable feeling, a telluric power. Everything here contributes to the creation of a rare wine, including the Continental climate, with its harsh winters and temperate warm days.

The rootstocks of Savagnin (also called "naturé") are more than sixty years old. Savagnin is the most famous white varietal in the region, but Chardonnay, the other white varietal grown here, is quite sought-after, like the Pinot Noir that is co-planted with Poulsard (or Ploussard) or with Trousseau. Here though, it is the white wines that keep you coming back, with their unique style and slow evolution. Even if not all of the wines which take the veil develop the film that allows them to mature in casks for six years, they all have the signature "*jaune*" taste. The principle of aging white wines in old Burgundy-style casks relies on not topping up the casks during the maturation process. In a nutshell, when the wine begins to evaporate, contrary to custom, the winemakers do not top up the cask to fill the space left by evaporation and prevent oxidation. In this case, the oxidation is intentional.

Over weeks and months, a thin film develops on top of the wine in the cask. This fungus goes on to colonize the entire surface exposed to the open air, and in doing so, protects the wine against excessive oxidation. This very rare phenomenon exists on a smaller scale in a few French cellars, including the famous cellar of the Plageoles family in Gaillac. It is particularly well known in the sherry-producing region of Andalusia. Casks that develop a sufficiently thick veil allow the wines to continue maturing up until the legal age of a *vin jaune*: 6 years and 3 months in not-topped-up casks. They are always kept in "hot" cellars – more than 15°C – with relatively low humidity (precisely the opposite of a "classic" cellar, which is 11°C and 85% humidity). This explains why Michel Pichet's cellar is located behind Uncle Louis' kitchen, and has been for what must be more than a century. Over my many visits, I've been able to identify the casks that "give" the best *vin jaune*. My preference is always for the first on the left when you enter the cellar. This is because this cask, more than the others, is subject to the most extreme temperature fluctuations that are partly responsible for the style of his wines. Over the aging process, the wine acquires the distinctive taste of *vin jaune*. The wine chosen at the beginning of the process must be powerful, since it will have to tolerate a lengthy barrel aging without being topped up. And here, that can last from seven to eight years for the oldest wines. During this period, the wine will develop its golden color and signature aromas of walnut and hazelnut. At the end of the maturation process, the casks will be opened and racked off, called the "*Percée du Vin Jaune*." The wines are housed in special bottles called *clavelins*. The bottles hold 62 centiliters, representing what remains of 1 liter of wine after maturing in casks for six years and three months.

 EMORIES
The "oldest" vintage of Michel's Château-Chalon I have tasted is his 1988. It is not included in those mentioned above. It was opened in January of 2012 during our annual sommelier dinner at my home. The highlights of that evening were:

Skewers of Indian-spiced quail breasts
with the thighs fried in butter
*Magnum of 1997 Taittinger Comtes de Champagne*

~

Salad of black truffle and Belles de Fontenay fingerling potatoes
*Jeroboam of Krug Grande Cuvée*

~

Roasted leg of wild boar from Normandy, sauce Grand-Veneur
Coco de Paimpol beans simmered with truffles
*1998 Barbaresco Riserva Pajé de Roagna Magnum*

~

Marcel Petite Comté, aged 24 months
Cave-aged Gruyère from Verbier
*1988 Château Chalon from Michel Pichet*

A selection of caramels and chocolates from Jacques Genin
*1977 Niepport Garrafeira Port*

~

*1952 Vieux Clément Rum*
Cohiba Siglo V Maduro cigar

Even though the clock had long since struck three – a.m., that is – every-one fully appreciated the Chalon, which rivaled the Krug Grande Cuvée in terms of pairing precision.

One of us was particularly touched: Victor Petiot, our resident Jurassian, savored these moments. He confessed to me that he had not imagined he would ever experience such an evening when he came to the George V. That night, I told him the following story: It was in 1992. A bitterly cold January night. We were going to meet one of the greats, if there ever was one, Mon-sieur Louis Florin, already retired at that point. When we arrived that eve-ning, his maid greeted us. She led us into the living room, where we had the pleasure of finding Madame Florin. She was at her spinning wheel near the hearth, spinning wool to fashion socks for Louis. In a frame on the wall was a yellowed letter, signed by General de Gaulle, thanking Louis for the 1929 Chalon, made by his father, that was served to the great man when he passed through Arbois.

After tough negotiations to acquire a few bottles for La Poularde, Louis spoke to us about someone who, in his mind, remained one of the best rep-resentatives of the greats of the restaurant world: Jean-Claude Vrinat and his father (Le Taillevent, three Michelin stars at the time). Those two came every year to choose their vintage of Chalon. This was uncommon in the 1960s and 1970s, when those in our trade rarely traveled out to the vines! A lovely piece of Comté awaited us on the wax tablecloth covering the solid oak table, along with a few big slices of country bread with thick, brown crust and, most importantly, a 1982 Château Chalon. After finishing our snack, we followed him into the scullery so he could "introduce" us to some bottles wrapped in yellowed paper: 1947 and 1949! Such wines! A dream come true.

# JURA
# Domaine Michel Pichet

# Tasting of Michel Pichet's Château Chalon, at his home, in 2014

**2006. Château Chalon.** *Nose is discreet, mentholated, pleasant, with a note of Poire William. Mouth feel is supple, round, fat, spherical. Finish is slightly tannic, should soften a little, nice length.*

**2004.** *Pale yellow color. Nose is clean, subtle, floral, fruity, notes of white blossoms and white pepper. Mouth is full-bodied, tight, concentrated, nice length. Remarkable. The finish is flavorful.*

**1999.** *Golden color. Evolved for its age. Big, open nose reminiscent of apricot kernel, dry yeast, breadbox. Mouth feel is evolved, supple, enticing. Very sensuous.*

**1996.** *Golden yellow color, moderate intensity. Subtle nose is grilled, rich and aerated. Mouth feel is big and buttery. Rather spherical. Nice length, balanced, finish is spicy and very long. Very nice Chalon.*

**1991.** *Intense golden color, hint of evolution. Subtle, open, complex nose of walnut and celery, grilled, elegant. Evolved. Note of ethanol (fresh walnuts). Mouth is tight and concentrated, finish is long and slightly sour. Nice length.*

# Domaine de Souch

*A Big Dream for Petit Manseng*

IX KILOMETERS
FROM THE CENTER OF PAU,
at the end of one of those narrow, winding paths such as one
only finds in the vineyards of Jurançon, the Souch domain is
set against the backdrop of the Pic du Midi d'Ossau mountain.
It all began in the late sixties, when Yvonne and her husband, René
Hégoburu, purchased a small domain in Laroin that included a house and
25 hectares of land, half of which faced north and the other half facing south.
Their idea was to replant a few vine stocks, since the domain had already
been planted in the 18th century, but the undertaking was judged too costly
at the time. Following the death of her husband in 1985, Yvonne decided to
devote all of her energy to the project that they were not able to complete
together. She sought advice from friends and planted 6.5 hectares of vines in
1987, when she was 60 years old. Later, she enlisted the help of a sommelier
(who was the best man at my wedding, coincidentally) Christian Péchoutre,
a well-known professor of sommellerie in Tours who was awarded the title
of *Meilleur Ouvrier de France* in sommellerie. Another sommelier, Vincent
Debergé, served as an intermediary between the domain and the George V,
where he worked from 2005 to 2008. Today, he is Director and Head Sommelier of Beau Rivage in Geneva. He allowed us to offer Yvonne's wines at
Le Cinq.

From the very beginning, Yvonne wanted to work the land as respect-
fully as possible. In 1994, she chose to implement biodynamic agricultural
practices, and she characterizes her commitment as being "deeper" than
organic agriculture. Her goal is to help the land recover faster. The work-
load is considerable, given that there are four people employed full time.
One of her soon-to-be devotees was Didier Dagueneau (who supplied her
barrels for several years). At the time, the latter dreamed of taking over a
mythical vineyard in the appellation, Clos Juliette: 2 hectares of Petit Manseng propagated using massal selection and vinified according to artisanal
methods by Madame Migné.

For some time, another "character" had his eyes on this microterroir – my
friend Gérard Depardieu. The project didn't come to fruition for either of
them, but that didn't keep Didier from making his dream a reality.
Amongst those who gave Yvonne a chance to speak is the filmmaker

Jonathan Nossiter, who devoted a long interview to her in his celebrated film *Mondovino*.

Yvonne Hégoburu, both inspired and inspiring, is blessed with an immense amount of enthusiasm and an iron will. Now over 80 years old, she serves as an important lesson in humility. Her commitment was recognized at the national level in May of 2014, when Yvonne was conferred the rank of *Chevalier* in the National Order of Merit.

# M EMORIES

It was a textbook morning at Souch. We began with a long stroll through the vines with Yvonne and her cellar master. This step is essential in order to understand the vineyard and its tillage, to go out and breathe in the land. This was followed by the tasting, first from the tanks and then from bottles. Then – an extra delight – lunch with Yvonne, who had the wonderful idea to invite Mathieu Cosse to join us. Mathieu, in addition to being a remarkable winegrower, is a peerless taster and one of Yvonne's guardians. Despite the chill in the air, the weather was sunny, so we shared a carafe of 2004 Veuve Clicquot rosé on the patio with Yvonne's three Great Pyrenees at our sides. A few toasts with duck foie gras raised our spirits. But our next appointment forced us to shorten our aperitif – that quintessentially French moment – so we could continue at the dining table with fresh foie gras, this time shepherded by a 1996 Marie Kattalin Jurançon René vintage. This was followed by duck confit with potatoes cooked in goose fat, who met their match with the two bottles that Mathieu brought. First, a magnum of 2007 Le Sid Cahors, still young, with hard tannins and a lovely freshness. Then a 2005 Les Laquets Cahors – yet another very nice bottle. As I tasted it, I thought to myself that this wine was missing from the wine list at Le Cinq. Incidentally, the domain is still represented on the wine list in 2015. Yvonne, fearing that we might still be hungry, brought out a tomme of Ossau cheese which we matched with a superb 2000 Marie Kattalin.

## SOUTHWEST
### Domaine de Souch

DE SOUCH
Jurançon
APPELLATION JURANÇON CONTRÔLÉE
Marie-Kattalin
2010

# Tastings at the Domaine de Souch in March of 2010

Following an hour and a half spent out in the vines with Yvonne, Thierry and Édouard.

**2009. Sec** *(sur cuve). (from the tank). Nose is still secondary. Fairly short. Mouth feel demonstrates nice maturity, fairly short finish.*

**2009. Moelleux** *(from the tank). Lovely nose, fairly low sugar. 75% Gros Manseng and 25% Petit Manseng.*

**2008. Moelleux.** *60% Gros Manseng and 40% Petit Manseng. Very nice. Much more coherent and long. Superb. Lots of baked apple, lovely freshness.*

**2007 Moelleux.** *50% Gros Manseng and 50% Petit Manseng. Nose of ripe mango, long, precise, chewy. Balanced. Superb acidity. The finish has a bitter hint of pink grapefruit skin. A wonderful success.*

**2006. Moelleux.** *Light, reduced nose. Fairly cold year, the wine is rather sluggish and unstable. Short. Green walnut on the finish.*

**2005. Moelleux.** *Very strong pastry notes. Nose of calisson, melon, almond paste. Very pleasant. This year has less acidity. Finish has already evolved.*

**2009. Moelleux Marie Kattalin vintage.** *This vintage is always produced from 100% Petit Manseng. Very ripe, balanced. Subtle and long. Superb. Notes of mango, baked apple and lemon.*

**2008. Moelleux Marie Kattalin vintage.** *Very acidic vintage. Decadent, lemon-drop finish. Fresh and long. Very nice bottle.*

**2007. Moelleux Marie Kattalin vintage.** *Superb. Still in the making. Superb bottle. Very young. Truffle gas. Lovely freshness. Balanced. Notes of white peach and stewed apricot. Very long.*

**2006. Moelleux Marie Kattalin vintage.** *The wine is currently closed, reserved. It needs more time. Will try again later.*

**2009. Vendange Tardive.** *Sublime, still in the making. Notes of candied apples and pears, long, distinguished. Powerful. Long finish. Notes of candies.*

*In conclusion, Yvonne Hégoburu's sweet jurançons, supported by the quality of the Petit Manseng, are of a remarkably high caliber. The warm valley where the domain is located in Laroin, near Pau, is ideally ventilated. The brilliance of the domain was to low-train the vines, contrary to standard practice in the region. Though they are more susceptible to frost, they are better able to nourish each grape cluster. The exemplary pruning work and vineyard management guarantee a perfectly ripened grape.*

## SOUTHWEST
## Domaine de Souch

# Les Jardins de Babylone

*Beyond the Ishtar Gate*

# T

## THE GARDENS OF BABYLON
### BEYOND THE ISHTAR GATE.

Welcome to the dream of Didier Dagueneau. This microscopic domain, covering just 3 hectares, is planted in tiers on the hillsides of the village of Aubertin, in the appellation of Jurançon. Didier had wanted for quite some time to make wine from these grape varietals that are unique in the French ampelographic landscape – Gros Manseng, Petit Courbu, Gros Courbu, Lauzet and Camaralet. When he found the place, he opened up about it to one of the devotees of his domain Saint-Andelain. The conversation went something like this: "Look, Guy, I found some land in a corner of the Jurançon appellation that is just begging for someone to take it over. A peaceful little corner for someone to retire in. And even better, I found that someone – it's you and your wife." To give you some background, Guy Pautrat was the first person to give Didier a chance when he found himself in a very difficult family situation as an adolescent. Guy took him in and trained him in what was, at the time, his profession: butchery. Guy believed in him. Later, it was Didier who asked Guy to join him. They would be forever united.

And so when we went to visit the Jardins de Babylone, it was Guy who was there to greet us. The man is larger than life, with a strong temperament; the type in a leather jacket, dark sunglasses... but a big heart. Nowadays, Louis-Benjamin Dagueneau is continuing his father's work. Guy is still there, the keeper of the flame.

When we arrived on that February day in 2010, I was first astounded by the scenery. Such a domain! What can I say? Didier's attention to detail was evident all around. And the view of the Pyrenees Mountains is magnificent. But there was another surprise awaiting us, one that made me wonder for just a second if I had overindulged in the Jurançon during lunch with Yvonne Hégoburu. Grazing here and there, like passengers from Noah's Ark, I counted... 1 llama, 3 donkeys, 3 sheep, 1 goat and 1 miniature horse. These trusty herbivores were doing their duty nibbling the weeds in the grass-covered alleyways between the terraces, which are not held up by walls here.

# M EMORIES

At the end of our day tasting in Jurançon, we set out on the road to Eugénie-les-Bains, the realm of the Guérard family. The journey was long, and I'll admit that, comfortably settled in the back seat of the Bentley, it wasn't long before I was lost in my thoughts. That evening, we were the last to arrive. Still, the *maître d'hôtel* invited us into the salon for an aperitif. We chose *Clicquot oblige*, a 1990 Grande Dame. The hors d'oeuvres were dainty and very welcome. To make things simpler for the kitchen, all of the guests agreed to order exactly the same dishes *à la carte*. The first was the famous soft pillow of morels and wild mushrooms in truffle sauce. It is one of Michel Guérard's signature dishes. He has managed to adapt it to each season, since he preserves all of the wild mushrooms in fall in order to be able to serve this dish year round. It was sensational, especially as I had chosen a 1995 Perrières Premier Cru Meursault by Jean-Marc-Roulot. Next was a roasted lobster served in medallions in its shell which had been smoked in the fireplace and garnished with fresh herbs from the "Priest's Garden" and melted butter, accompanied by a small plate of sweet and bitter endives preserved in coconut milk. Very impressive, and quite different from the one prepared by Philippe Legendre at Le Cinq. The meat course was yet another one of his classics: fillet of beef "*sur le bois et sous les feuilles*" (on the wood and under the leaves), with gravy and grape juice and both creamy and puffed potatoes. With this dish, we tasted a magnum of 1985 Château Pichon Longueville Comtesse de Lalande, which, I'll admit, was offered at a very reasonable price. What a bottle! Given the late hour, we decided to pass on the cheese course, but not on dessert – I absolutely wanted to taste one of the original Guérard desserts: his famous caramelized pear feuillantine with a coulis of Eugénie raspberries and pistachio ice cream. The fruit was as juicy as can be (preserved the previous summer). We then retired to the cozy comfort of the salon and a toasty fireplace to enjoy a 1973 Domaine de Gaube, a fantastic Bas Armagnac taken over by the Darroze family. This is a brandy that I had first loved when the former owner came to Montrond to present his 1973 vintage. At the end of this dinner, I promised myself that I would come back with Marie. It is true that I waited for quite some time to rediscover this region, and even though I knew the terroirs, the grape varietals and the wines, it was essential that I come and walk through the vineyards and taste the wines within their proper regional context. It is critical, and so enriching.

# Les Jardins de Babylone

The 2011 Jurançon sec was tasted in 2014 at Le Cinq. The following wines were tasted at the domain in the afternoon following my visit to Yvonne Hégoburu. At the time of that visit, the domain was perfectly autonomous. After successive manual harvests, fermentation occurred in barrels of varying capacities that Didier Dagueneau was fond of, including *demi-muids* and his cigar barrels.

**2011. Jurançon sec.** *50% new barrel and 50% stainless steel tanks. Varietals used: all included in the AOC* (appellation d'origine contrôlée) *except the Mansengs. Petit and Gros Courbus, Camaralet. Accessible, acidic, white fruit, exotic note.*

**2008. Sec** *(barrel tasting). Clean, fresh, lively. Nose of lemon, white grapefruit skin. What a wine! The best Sec I have tasted. Varietals: Petit Courbu, Camaralet, Lauzet.*

**2009. Moelleux** *(in a large wooden foudre made by Stockinger). Nose shows a hint of reduction, which is normal at this stage. The mouth feel is pure, clean, full and long. What a lesson! This is the third wine matured in this barrel.*

**2009. Moelleux** *(this time in a barrel made by Taransaud). Here, lots of fruit, very exotic, passionfruit, pineapple.*

**2009. Moelleux** *(in a "cigar" barrel). This time, the acidity is very present. Balanced wine. Nose is already subtle, note of blood orange.*

**2008. Babylone.** *Sour lemon candy. Very nice bottle. Full of life, with a remarkable length.*

**2006. Babylone.** *Fresh and long vintage. Complex nose. Clean in the mouth. Dramatic year for Didier, who lost 50% of his harvest because of a deviant cork. Dreadful.*

**2004. Babylone.** *Superb wine, clean, long, precise, and distinguished. Finish is still fresh, and such length!*

**2002. Moelleux.** *Didier never put this vintage on the market. The wine is in a traditional style, worthy of the old Jurançon. Didier didn't want any more of these wines. Once the harvest was finished, the grapes were vinified in Saint-Andelain.*

*There is another vintage that we weren't able to try: Ravaillac! Another affair!*

GERMANY P 450

ITALY P 460

SPAIN P 482

PORTUGAL P 492

HUNGARY P 512

UNITED STATES P 520

# Wines of
~
# Europe
# and the World

# WEINGUT EGON MÜLLER
## THE SWIRLS OF RIESLING

T he trip down the Moselle is very windy. The valley, especially at its midpoint, took our breath away. It is one of the world's most beautiful winemaking sites, along with the valley of Douro. With two areas - one in the north and one the south – the site truly represents the idea that great wines are born from places where the grapes must struggle in order to ripen. Steep hills full of charm dominate the scenery of this river and its two valleys dedicated to wine: the Sarr and the Ruwer. Because of their geographic positions (along the 49th parallel), the lay of these vineyards is crucial. The sun is of paramount importance here, even though for the past twenty years – perhaps due to climate change – the number of vintages making it to good maturity has increased substantially. (I recommend reading Egon's article in *The Magic of the 45th Parallel* by Oliver Bernard and Thierry Dussard.) The climate proves to be a key element, along with the slate-rich and acidic soils, in being very effective against phylloxera and draining. Next up is the Riesling from the third period, meaning thick-skinned and resistant grapes mature late.

The table is set. Now let us turn to the men, or to a family rather – a dynasty – the Müllers. Receiving us is Egon V, representative of the fifth generation of this family rooted in the Saar since 1797. For them, the eponym has been sanctified. You can see how their mark on this territory runs as deep as the vines thereof. As soon as you arrive at their property, it is always impressive. It is built at the foot of the Scharzhof. On a beautiful sunny afternoon in April 2014, Thierry and I finally arrived there – pretty late, as we faced complications in Luxembourg. Luckily, we were able to stop along the way for some sausage with slices of bread and a beer. Best be warned: when you have the distinction of being received by Egon, do not come on an empty stomach! It is not part of the custom to regurgitate the fruit of hard labor. Once we turned off our heavy-duty engine from the Ingolstadt company (my favorite builder), the peacefulness and quietude of the pace overcame us. The place is soothing here, which reflects the person walking up to us. Egon Muller welcomes us in his "gentleman-farmer" stance, with a soft and discreet voice. His French is flawless. The family library is full of first editions of Dante, Shakespeare, Cervantes and Molière, reminding us that, at the Mullers', the old tradition of the Grand Tour, as it was called in the 18th-19th century, is alive and well. His time spent on great domains both in France and worldwide bear witness. That being said, I could not say the same about my knowledge of the language of Goethe. After exchanging a few words about the latest vintage, our host leads us into the large vestibule of this beautiful residence. There, on a mahogany table, five samples of a 2013 vintage caught our attention, a glass next to each half-bottle. We are left to discover them at our own pace, our host there to answer our questions.

2013: one of the smallest harvests since 1945. The domain's yield averages 10 hectoliters per hectare. To make a domain economically viable, you want to count on 35 hectoliters per hectare for all wines. Thankfully, as Egon says, "our family can carry this type of vintage, but we cannot make it all too often." This vintage also experienced a disease formerly unknown to this vineyard: *esca*, a disease associated with parasitic fungi that cause very recognizable symptoms. Until recently, this ancient vine disease was mainly found in more temperate regions. Other diseases unknown to the region started appearing about ten years ago, diseases like black rot, originally from eastern North America, and this one too, a fungi-based disease.

As usual, we started the tasting with a current vintage, in the large vestibule. Before going any further, we need to mention that in Germany, wines are classified according to the sugar concentration of the musts. From driest to sweetest, the classification for Riesling is as follows:

– *Kabinett*, the driest, lightest

– *Spätlese*: signifies a wine from a late crop, the most full-bodied

– *Auslese*, wine with a high sugar content, from mature grapes

– *Beerenauslese*, very sweet, almost fortified, comes from grapes chosen for the over-ripeness, often reaching a noble rot

– *Trockenbeerenauslese* (abridged *TBA*), from grapes dried on the vine. The first *TBA* from Mosel was produced in 1921. The Müllers started theirs at Scharzhof in 1959 (the year Egon was born).

– finally, we have *Eiswein* (ice wine), with a sugar content between those of *Beerenauslese* and *TBA*.

Scharzhof Riesling No. 1: *Fresh, light aftertaste, refreshing.*

Scharzhofberger Kabinett No. 2: *Biting yet fresh. Comforting, a vivid citrus.*

Kabinett No. 3: *One of the wines at the Trier auction. Much cleaner, very pale color, with bright green reflections. A discreet nose, very nice depth and excellent body scope. A great wine, with tension, energy and density. The vines are* franches de pied *(not grafted onto rootstock).*

Spätlese No. 4: *Nice balance; fine, delicate.*

Auslese Lange Kapsel No. 5: *A denser color, rich nose, fresh, with a hint of candied grapes (confirmed by Egon himself who specified that this Aulese had been boosted with botrytized grapes). The body is full, rich and concentrated. The sugar is noticeable, a bit like sour candy with a long and dry floral note like lemon sours. It's a great half-dry in its own right.*

At the end of this first meeting, our host invited us to follow him to the cellars for another visit. For the first time, in this July of 2014, we entered it with Thierry. Once we passed through the large, old oaken doors to the cellars, the respect for tradition was noticeable. The horizontal press dating back to Egon's grandfather, who acquired it in 1910, still works. Right next to it is a brand new pneumatic press. It is used for their rare *Eiswein* batches.

Technology is welcomed here, so long as it does not encroach on the wines' soul. Every year, Egon and his team's goal is to find the best maturity levels on the Scharzhof, which covers an area of some 50 hectares. The Müllers own 8.5 hectares of prime wine real estate – at the heart of the hillside – with south-facing exposure and a fair amount of healthy ungrafted vines (*franches de pied*). The granite subsoil is topped with black and gray schists. The first Riesling harvests give rise to a batch of Trocken Riesling, and then, along with the concentration, the maturities go from *Kabinett*, *Spätlese*, *Auslese*, *Beerenauslese*, *Trokenbeerenauslese* and, less frequently, *Eiswein*.

The family also owns a second domain not too far away: the Gallais (still bearing the name of its former French owners) – 2 hectares near Wiltingen, all steep slopes of red schists. This warmer vineyard makes more voluptuous and easygoing wines.

Scharzhof, translated literally as "Black Hill," is a steep, serious, broad vineyard. This age-old vineyard, led with precise expertise, has in some years

OSEL-SAAR-RUWER
RIESLING
Product of Germany
Abgefüllt im
Keller zu Scharzhof
D 54459
by vol.

produced in some of the greatest fortified wine in the world. Considering the rarity of these great fortified wines, they are most often offered in half bottles. So they are typically ready to be tasted more quickly, and this format keeps a large number of wine lovers satisfied. This was our system for some time as it allowed us to give each sommelier of the team a chance to participate in a Trier auction. This gives them all the knowledge and passion needed to then offer them at Le Cinq. In regards to the *Trockenbeerenauslese* and *Eiswein*, these wines are fought over by collectors and amateurs worldwide, often for sky-high prices. *Vinum Rex Regorum*.

# MEMORIES

The ancient city of Trier is one of those rare old German cities that was spared from the terrible conflicts that ravaged Europe throughout the 20th century. It was one of the four imperial capitals of the Roman Empire, along with Rome, Constantinople and Lyon. Every year on the third Saturday of September, the city holds one of the most extraordinary auctions. For more than ten years, we have dispatched two to three of our sommeliers to represent us for this event. I myself go every four years, since the time spent there is so rewarding.

It all starts with a tasting. The morning of the auction, at 9 a.m. sharp, the room opens its doors to future bidders. Under the wing of our importer, my friend Bernd Kreis, we taste, with calm and order, every batch that will be offered for auction that same afternoon. Each domain is represented by its winemaker and/or one or more members of the family. The quantities served are abysmal but coherent enough, considering the density of most of the wines on the list. Everyone comes with a specific notebook wherein each batch is evaluated.

As 11 a.m. approaches, tastings stop. Traditionally, we find ourselves in the main hall connected to the auction room. And it is there, over several pints of local beer and snacks of sausage spread, black bread and soft pretzels, that we decide on the potential offers with a broker we rely on. This is the person who will bid for us in the auction. We sit ourselves at one of the tables in his row, right in the center, given that he belongs to one of the oldest

## GERMANY
### Weingut Egon Müller

auction houses in Trier. We evaluate the current offers with him, in accordance with the different purchase orders he has already booked or caught wind of from his colleagues, based on the current quotes. In total, nine brokers book the purchase orders for over 200 potential bidders, all registered beforehand. At 1 p.m., everybody meets back at his place. Every year we sit at the same table with Bernd, right behind the Italian restaurateurs who also work with our broker. Each of the nine rows of tables are perpendicular to the stage where the clerks, the president and the auctioneer sit.

At 1:30 p.m., the president of the auction, which had been Egon Müller for a long time, gives a few words on the crowd-favorite vintage. This auction is organized by a consortium of Moselle's best winemakers. During this time, the first wine to be put up for auction is served to all the bidders and then to the public, more than 300 people. This process is like clockwork, taking no more than five minutes with an army of seasoned waiters who only serve one to two centiliters at the most to everybody. The goal here being to have everybody remember the wine before the auctions start.

They start right after the batch is presented by the auctioneer. At that moment, the only thing that can be heard is the movement of his gavel as he slams it down calling out a new number. Suddenly, the speed of the bids dies down, and a broker, seated at the end of the table close to the stage, stands up with his sheets of grades, signs and totals. He approaches the stand, followed by one, two, three brokers, and the auction stops! They discuss among themselves, and, every so often, one of them will raise their index finger, and the auction will resume – and then stop once again. The broker looks at you: the limit to your bidding is about to be reached. What will you decide? A more or less noticeable nod of the head or a left-to-right motion, and it is all set.

The problem with this auction lies within the weakness of the batch put up for sale. As these are only sold in groups of three bottles, the demand very quickly exceeds the supply. So it comes down to knowing which bidders are more likely to acquire the bottles at a price higher than the price currently being offered. The broker with the highest number of clients who set the highest bids is the one who takes control of the auction. Next, he distributes the quantities set at the highest price, taking the part intended for his clients. If needed, the winemaker seated at the left of the auctioneer can be consulted, since he sometimes keeps an extra microbatch of the current vintage. He can provide twelve, twenty-four or even thirty-six half-bottles more, and the brokers can validate the desired quantity, or at least a part thereof. For this auction, we grab thirty-six to seventy-two half-bottles, including the *Auslese* and *TBA* and somewhat less of the *Eiswein*.

This system is complex, but it helps regulate the sales and prevents too high a demand from monopolizing an entire batch through the lack of a bidding ceiling. Unfortunately, the prices increase every year, and new amateurs from the East tend to grab more and more batches. Price does matter to them. For the first time in 10 years, after the 2014 auction, nobody from the team went there. Even our importer Bernd Kreis could not get anything. However, the goal of the auction has always been – or *was* perhaps – to allow amateurs and collectors to walk away with a few bottles. Truly, the greatest expression of German Moselle wine is displayed at this auction. At Le Cinq, 80% of our wine from this region are wines from the yearly auction. It is a perfect example of winegrowing excellence.

The wine produced by Egon Müller are great wines with a balance as fragile as crystal, both airy and dense. They are excellent depending on their degree of concentration over multiple preparations. The difficulty resides in the pairing that must be created. It requires the perfect frame to highlight this diamond of unparalleled purity. It works even better if the pairing is organized for a guest who will be sensitive to it. It turned out that at the end of a dinner at Le Cinq, one of our clients, already a regular at that time (2002), asked me to amaze him when dessert came. He was from Chicago, one of the most notable businessmen in high-quality olive oil for North America. He had a sharp palate, and that night, he went with a 1998 Montrachet from Roman Romanée-Conti with royal langoustines roasted in coconut milk, then a 1982 Château Latour to accompany his hare de Beauce à la Royale, in a Périgord style. Before the cheese cart made its way to him, M. B. said to me, "Tonight, Eric, amaze me!" In general, he goes more towards a 1967 or 1937 Yquem, maybe even a 1947 Foreau Vouvray, all available in the cellar on that evening. After a little dealing with the pastry chef, the charismatic Laurent Jeannin, we agreed on a lemon soufflé. Then I called up a half-bottle of 1996 Scharzhofberger Trockenbeerenauslese Riesling from Egon. Chilled to perfection, I serve the nectar with contrition after

GERMANY
Weingut Egon Müller

456

tasting it. The Riesling's intensity was so much that Mr. B. and his wife were amazed. They had never tasted wine like this before. This Riesling had a baffling bite to it. The alcohol density was huge, but the balance mesmerized. And what a length! Impressions of a sour candy of infinite complexity between citrus zest, honey flower and icy mint. It was one of those sublime moments when nobody speaks. Because the wine occupies all the space.

Following this tasting, Klaus wanted us to have dinner with our wives in a great Parisian restaurant of my choice. Since then, we have become very close friends, and it is through him that each year we go to Tuscany or Sicily to develop our vintage oil blend to be served to the guests at Le Cinq for the following year. It was the 1996 *TBA* from the Müller family that allowed this relationship to happen. The power of wine develops friendship. Egon, I thank you!

# The Wines

After this first overview of 2013, we visit the cellar and vaults for the reserves. Back in the living room, we enter the second part of the tasting. The living room where in the past we tasted collector wines is connected to the library. Calm, relaxing, peaceful. The chirping of birds can be heard through an open window. It is warm, a beautiful day – early for the season.

**2007. Kabinett.** *Great year, in an opulent style. This pale-colored Kabinett has a discreet nose and average intensity. Its minerality is noticeable on the attack. Truly thirst-quenching, reminiscent of grapefruit rind. The finish on the mouth is spiced and lingering. A perfect pairing with smoked salmon.*

**1990. Kabinett.** *The golden color and open nose of this wine recalls candied lemon zest, dry floral and truffles. Very pleasant. Full-bodied mouth, rich, seductive and complete. The gas is still noticeable, but the whole is wonderful. I imagine it would be very nice with shelled scallops and lemon confit.*

**1999. Auslese** *(Trier auction). First glass (straight from the bottle. What remains is decanted so as to compare how the two evolve). Superb, fine, delicate nose, racy. Very dense! Not much deviation. Tense with notes of citrus confit. The mouth is savory, almost salty. Almond paste.*

*A year with noble rot, there is in this one. 1999 is one of the greatest years harvested and vinified by Egon to date.*

*Between these two glasses, Egon's wife greeted us with their son, Egon VI Junior, both of them carrying platters with little "rescuers," which our stomachs welcomed with pleasure. These tastings and our brief stop on the road stimulated our appetites.*

*Second glass (this time from the carafe): the wine is way more open. What finesse! The color is dense and pale yellow. The nose is tight and extremely concentrated. Rich mouth, with a sweet balance, thanks to the noticeable acidic structure. Long finish with a complex retro-olfaction, toasted, reminiscent of blonde caramel. No bitterness.*

*At this point, our host took out a ringless corona from a Havana cabinet with gleaming capes (caps). While listening*

## GERMANY
### Weingut Egon Müller

to us, he lit the cigar and, after letting out a few blue billows of smoke, he shot up and said, "I'll be back." A few minutes passed, and he reappeared again with two bottles.

**1971. Beerenauslese Eiswein.** *The color is a deep topaz, very amber. Nose is complex, rich and fruity. Dry floral notes reminiscent of a linden infusion, lemongrass, tea and honey. The rich and lasting mouth begins to loosen up and becomes slightly more fluid and light. With an impression of light moistness but with a beautiful length. This was truly a good year. Notes of bitter orange confit, orange chocolate, sweet spices, with a hint of resin and pine, stand out after a few minutes. A marvelous wine. This wine is the result of two processes on the same vine. The first part was cut in November (more of a Beerenauslese style), then a second section was cut in January (for the Eiswein).*

*The first TBA was produced in 1959 at the domain (the year Egon was born). The great years were 1959, 1971, 1975, 1976, 1989, 1990, 1994, 1995, 1997, 1999, 2000, 2001, 2003, 2005, 2007 and 2009. And the first Mosel TBA was produced in 1921.*

**2011. Trockenbeerenauslese.** *5.5 % vol. (Really grand year, like the 2005). Vivid topaz color. Highly concentrated nose, candied fruits, exotic: mango, roasted pineapple. Stunning, fresh. An indescribable mouth, full and wide. Very long-lasting and persistent. Very candied notes. Difficult to describe as it is so intense. Will be aged for over five years. Northern ambrosia. 100% extra-dense botrytis, trimmed for the time. Here is a wine on the level of those at the annual Trier auction.*

# BRUNO GIACOSA
# THE PATRIARCH OF LANGHE

**B**runo Giacosa is based in the village of Neive, where he was born in 1929, to the east of the Barbaresco vineyard. Today, he is a patriarch respected by everyone. His health does not allow him to receive guests as regularly as he would like to; it was his cellar master and enologist, Francesco Versio, who received us for our 2014 visit. He started working at the domain in 2011 and was preceded by a famous enologist who signed several magnificent wines from this domain between 1991 and 2008. Francesco is impressive, and I would love to see him again in the future. I was accompanied by Gabriele Del Carlo, the maitre d'hotel and sommelier at Le Cinq. In the early 1960s, Giacosa was one of the best traders in Barbaresco, alongside Angelo Gaja. Both are responsible for the reputation of the appellation that they brought up to the level of their great neighbor: Barolo. In 1967, he managed to create his own domain. In 1982, he bought the famous Falletto plot, in Barolo, and in 1996, the parcels of Asili and Rabja in Barbaresco.

Today the domain covers 20 hectares between the various appellations represented: Barolo, Barbaresco, Barbera d'Alba and Dolcetto d'Alba. Generally, the Nebbiolo of Barbaresco are more accessible than those from Barolo and mature sooner, which is certainly due to the milder climate but also the sand and marl soils. So much so that the Nebbiolo are harvested on the Barbaresco terroir two weeks earlier than in the Barolo. Furthermore, the proximity to the Tanaro River, which separates the two appellations and flows into the Po River, is a wonderful thermal regulator for Barbaresco.

At Giacosa's, the grapes follow a simple vinification process. After being macerated in thermo-regulated stainless steel tanks, the Nebbiolo are kept in French oak casks, from Stockinger or Gamba, either 52 or 110 hectoliters (average age of the barrels: 25 years). These capacities allow Giacosa to store each cuvée in a single tank – and, with this principle, to create an aging homogeneity from the beginning. This takes between one and three years depending on the cuvée. Bruno Giacosa's precise maturing, which is applied

by their young oenologist, lends beauty to the elegance of their tannins. These wines have a medium color intensity, shining, and the bouquets are complex and refined.

Much like many complex, secret terroirs, the wines from the Giacosa family were added to my tasting memories just about 10 years ago. My palate had never understood this type of elegance and refinement until that point. My approach to these appellations focused on domains with more contemporary vinification and maturing processes. I was conflicted about these two schools for a while. It was modern versus traditional.

If it is for certain that a rustic, deviant style does not interest me, it's even more true for sensationalist wine. What I like above all is encountering new faces and discovering new approaches used on a terroir. This is why I often try to schedule a new winemaker I do not know during my tours. With this in mind, I ran into a young, talented and passionate winemaker from Barbaresco. He was already highly sought after, but until now, I had never tried his wines. Listening to him while tasting, I immediately felt what I love in wines: energy, delicacy and density; fresh fruit and depth. Upon my return to Paris, we introduced three wines from this winemaker, Mr. Luca Roagna, simply in order to share this complementary expression of our choices with our regulars and wine lovers. When a young Italian winemaker starts reciting verses from *The Love of Wine* by Charles Baudelaire, he cannot be all that bad. This domain, as with the one of Bruno Giacosa, was suggested to me by a client who has become a close friend over the years. Roberto is a man of taste. Originally from Padua, we first met at La Poularde. Today, he's a regular at Le Cinq.

It was in 2012, during a trip to Venice with Marie – without the kids – that Roberto had me try a Barolo, Le Rocche del Faletto Giacosa 1997, for the first time. The bouquet was marked with notes of black truffle, stubborn, with touches of wax. The mouth was slightly bitter, but it had such tension, such delicacy! I had not felt this sensation in a long time. This day remains one of the key moments in the evolution of my taste for Barolo. A revelation. The scene of this tasting also contributed to the perpetuation of this memory: Venice, with my wife and a dear friend, at the top of the terrace at Cipriani, with the lagoon reaching towards the horizon and, before us, a risotto with white truffle grated by the white-gloved maitres – the starchy suit, the jet-black gelled hair – all took me back to memories of *Summertime* with Katharine Hepburn.

EMORIES

At the end of the tasting day, it was not easy to find a welcoming, warm place to keep the day going with joyous libation along the way. Even though I often made this finding in France, nothing about it is the same in Italy. There are no villages worth making the stop for a bite to eat. I recall my first visit with the Emperor of Barolo, Angelo Gaja. The tasting was run smoothly. But I remember just as much, if not more, of the lunch that followed at the Trattoria Antica Torre, just a step away from the shielded domain of the illustrious winemaker. There, the family's sole specialty is *tajarin*. I remember a dish of this pasta, put into boiling water for just more than 10 seconds and then thrown into foamy butter with sage leaves. A few slices of Parmigiano grated right into the same platter, and then the magic happened... I'll come back to this one later.

A few kilometers from there, in the village of Serralunga d'Alba, we are off to the vinoteca set up in a small, hard-to-reach house. Once you cross the threshold, the shelves full of large, slightly dusty trophies indicate that one drinks good wines in this house. After a beautiful day between Barbaresco and Barolo, Gabriele, Roberto and I were happy to get to this haven of delicacy. Barely seated, we were served focaccia bread right out of the oven and thinly sliced, delicate charcuterie. Next up was a veal tartar lightly seasoned with just a dash of olive oil, chopped capers and freshly ground white pepper. We compared this delicacy to the *trois seigneurs du cru* of the 2001 vintage, a clash of the Titans:

– Barolo Riserva Monprivato Cà di Morissio from Giuseppe Mascarello: *A domain that I tasted that evening for the second time. Particularity: I had never been able to get there. A dream. At the opening, it had a feral side. Powerful, broad. With a few notes of reductions that dissipate with aeration. The tradition of strong character.*

– Barolo Le Rocche del Falletto Riserva from Bruno Giacosa: *A domain that I have been slow to discover. Even if I had been there a couple times, I had never met the Giacosas. Here the Nebbiolo is full of finesse, without being stripped of a certain strength.* Noblesse oblige.

– Barolo Monfortino from Giacomo Conterno: *I am familiar with this from serving it now and then at the George V and having tasted it at Conterno. Impressive, very fine-seed tannins, carried by the acidity, which is the wine's backbone. Finesse, length, raciness. The ultimate.*

There is a scent of mystery around these monuments to the Nebbiolo, a scent of secrecy that must be upheld. The wines of these winemakers remind me of guardian figures like the Foucault brothers or Emmanuel Raynaud.

The three wines and our conversations led me to accept with glee the *risotto carnaroli al dente* generously covered with white truffle offered us by

the chef, a jovial fellow. This dish allowed us to keep the comparisons going between these three great expressions, rare among the Nebbiolo grape. When the bottles gave their last drop, nobody felt the need for more. A *ristretto* and chocolate-coated dried hazelnuts met our expectations.

The night was beautiful.

ITALY
Bruno Giacosa

# The Wines

The situation at Falletto is remarkable. We were at Serralunga d'Alba. The hill has a southern exposure on a rocky outcrop called Le Rocche. The soil here is made of limestone and clay, which blend wonderfully and create that famous blue marl.

Before bringing up this rare wine, a few words are needed to better read Bruno Giacosa's labels. The first thing to understand involves the difference between a red label and a white label.
– The red label indicated Riservas, which are solely from Giacosa family vines, in other words, the best batches of Barolo and Barbaresco, and only those from the best vintages. Each choice depends on the patriarch's judgment. At the

bottom of the label, all you see then is "Azienda Agricola Falletto di Bruno Giacosa." But for wines made with the domain's winemakers that are not worthy of a red label, they go to white label, which only carries the mention "Azienda Agricola Falletto"!
– The white label: through a choice made in 1996, Bruno has distinguished his wines between those from his vines and those from bought grapes and musts, his main business activity. At the bottom of the white label, you see "Casa Vincola Bruno Giacosa."

# December 2014 Tasting at the Domaine

**2011.** Barolo Le Rocche del Falletto (white label). *Brilliant color, with a clear garnet. Woody nose, fine and closed. The mouth is full without deviance. Very structured, extremely long, racy with equally long tannins. Great maturity as well.*

**2009.** Barolo Le Rocche del Falletto (white label). *Garnet color with less intensity. A round nose, open, generous, fruity, reminiscent of Dalmatian cherries and licorice. It is young, but its signs of evolution are noticeable. Its body follows my impression. It creates a flat sensation without much depth. Disappointing.*

**2008.** Barolo Le Rocche del Falletto Riserva (red label). *Dark and shiny color, displaying a few notes of evolution. Closed nose, deep and complete. Very licorice-like, with soft sensations. The body literally stops the dialog. Very complete. The tannins are present but fine. The acidity is discreet, and the finish is long. To be opened in at least ten years.*

**2007.** Barolo Le Rocche del Falletto Riserva (red label). *Dark color, intense ruby. Open nose, flattering, fruity and woody. The body is creamy on the attack, and the tannins are buttery. The sensation of sweetness coats the palate. The chalky, sapid character returns in the retro-olfaction. Very nice 2007.*

# GIACOMO CONTERNO
# THE THUNDER OF TRADITION

I n 1990, with Marie, we took our first trek through the Piedmont. On a friend-of-a-friend's suggestion – through Gilles Étéocle, a restaurateur in Montescano, near Pavia – I met with a colorful character: Franco Colombani, restaurateur in Maleo, Albergo del Sole, near Cremona, between Milan and Parma, who ran the International Sommelier Association from 1977 to 1981. Throughout this trip, he introduced me to Nebbiolo tasting, in particular, to older vintages. This is where I discovered a well-known and often overused product, Balsamic vinegar. Among the rarities Franco had us taste, I remember in particular a drop of 1945 balsamic vinegar, in a coffee spoon with a *ristretto* (strong espresso). This pairing overturned my world. It did not have an acidic note, but instead an extraordinary sweetness, with notes of vanilla, a blend of times. He allowed me to accompany him into his aging attic. Since Franco Colombani matures his balsamic vinegars in drums for up to thirty years, the essence of the barrels' wood itself changes throughout the years. Each one enhances the vinegar with complementary aromas. He has drums from American oaks, sessile oaks (a variety of oak from the Tronçais forest), from chestnut, acacia. The choice of an attic was not without reason – temperature fluctuations play a helpful role in the maturation of bouquets and structures. The drums were not sealed by a bung. Nothing more than a flat rock placed on the opening kept the top sealed. The vinegar must breathe. Since this visit, I've never experienced anything like it with *aceto balsamico*.

At the same time, Franco Colombani told me about the Barolo and Barbaresco terroirs and opened me up to the great wines of Angelo Gaja. Back at La Poularde, I had the chance to order wines from the great winemaker of Barbaresco through a friend-importer based in Milan: Walter Pugliese. He was the one who organized the exceptional meetings that led us to Giuseppe Rinaldi and then Roberto Voerzio in 1995. The ancient and the modern! A shock of cultures, visions and tastes. It was rewarding. I was familiarized with the different approaches to the Nebbiolo. This rather fragile variety is found nowhere else in the world. During my journey across one domain to the next, I was overcome by the bucolic landscapes in these villages clinging to hillsides, clustered tightly around their churches. As it was winter, the famous local fog (*nebbia* in Italian) only allows us to see the summits of the hilltops, the steeples, the battlements and towers of very old fortified houses from time to time. These climate conditions reminded me very much of the Burgundy fog you see in February.

Here, the horizon goes all the way to the distant wall that is the Alps. Since we were at the foothills of this mountain range, the region is home to the perfect conditions for making an exceptional wine. Each seasonal cycle of this continental climate leaves a good annual frequency to the vines, from their dormant period to their awakening, up through their blossoming stage. These conditions are compulsory for regulating the grapes' maturity. The soils here, a mixture of calcium and clay with sandy outcrops that lick the hillsides in certain places are the signatures of a great terroir. All this gives the wines a refreshing acidity and imparts a unique aromatic blessing on the land: white truffle. This is the perfect setting for Nebbiolo, a period-three variety, which notably matures late, around mid-October. All these elements will be transcended with a long maturing period. As an example, in 2014 we started receiving 2008 Barolo Riserva. Six years of aging in total, first in barrels and then in bottles. Other subvarieties of this grape are also grown: the Michet, Lampia and Rosé.

During another tour of the Piedmont in 2007, I embarked on a journey enhanced with tastings and readings on this transalpine nectar. I was ready for other discoveries – especially considering that around me were Philippe Bourguignon and François Mauss, respectively, director general of the Laurent and president of the European Grand Jury. Two accomplished connoisseurs of these wines. It was during this trip that I would learn that the *Michelin* awarded us two macarons in their new edition! Long story short – we lost the third one. Upon hearing the news, which turned me pale, Phillipe, after comforting me, thoughtfully said: "Well, Beaumard, if they took the third from you, what else could they have in store?" Back in Paris, he called me to tell me that the Laurent actually went from two stars to one! A tragedy for Phillipe. But his customers remained loyal to him despite the obstacles. Despite this news, it was by their sides during this trip that I improved my comprehension of the major terroirs of Barolo, thanks to the villages of La Morra, Castiglione Falleto, Serralunga d'Alba and Monforte d'Alba. These villages represent the heart of the 1,300 hectares known as the Barolo appellation.

This was notably my first visit to Roberto Conterno's, the place where Monfortino was born – the saint of saints, the Rayas de Barolo. The place, the character that is Roberto – composed, reserved, austere – created a monastic atmosphere. To fully understand the Conternos the same way that applied to the families of Burgundy, one must follow both the family trees and the land registry in order to grasp all the subtleties. Roberto is the grandson of Giacomo Conterno. He was preceded by his father, Giovanni. His cousins are both descendants of his uncle Aldo Conterno. In 1969, the two brothers, Aldo and Giovanni, could not come to terms on how to handle their father's domain, which they inherited in 1961, so they split up. Aldo founded his own domain, while Giovanni continued his father's work – based on the respect of a centuries-old tradition. Then, in 1974, the latter acquired the terroir of Cascina Francia in Serralunga d'Alba: 14 hectares of Nebbiolo and Barbera. In 2004, he passed away at the age of 74. His youngest son, Roberto, who had been at the domain since 1988, would ensure his father's succession.

Thus, Roberto received us. Visiting the site, the fermenting room, the storeroom with its immense tanks and seeing this man's manic cleanliness and attention to detail, got me excited for the tasting. The choice in tasting glasses for the wine was the fruit of a long and patient labor of comparison and research. I was amazed at the glasses he used. It was a glass from the Zalto house in Austria, their *Bourgogne* model. It has to be the lightest glass, the finest one I know. The rounded corners and the chalice's outline make it perfect for Pinot Noirs and Nebbiolo. It was a revelation. Back in Paris, I was finally able to offer the first exemplars for Le Cinq thanks to Jean-Nicolas Méo and a bit of looking around. Simply opening a bottle carries a significant importance for Roberto. He stares at the neck for a while, the back of the cork which he just pulled out before serving the wine. He is right, for this cork still has a lot to teach us about its life in contact with the wine. Throughout the years, I would often come across stoppers from his

Monfortino or his other vintages showing no alteration, even with wines aged for ten to fifteen years. After tasting his wine, alone, he talked about it while serving us with an air of reverence. He develops his phrases as if he were thinking aloud – and woe to he who dares to interrupt him. For he would break this spell and seriously cut into the tasting time. Then we take turns evoking our feelings about his Monfortino from the Cascina Francia terroir. This batch is only produced three to four times every ten years. It takes seven years before Roberto decides to take out the Monfortino or not. Seven years of aging in barrels.

A year later, in February 2008, I had the pleasure of returning there, this time with Matteo Ghiringhelli (Best Sommelier of Italy and bronze winner of the European sommeliers at 24), Cédric Maupoint (head sommelier of Shangri-La Paris) and Thierry (Palm d'Or for competition management… coincidentally). Matteo is one of the best sommeliers that we have had at George V. After he left us in 2005, we tried with Thierry to get him to come back to Le Cinq, which did not happen. He continued his career in Italy. Then, as soon as we were able to, we met back up in the vineyards or over a drink at Le Cinq's office at the time of his leaving. Having Matteo here for the second visit allowed us to get closer to Roberto, who, that year, had made a beautiful acquisition: the vineyard of Cerretta, 3 hectares to the north of Serralunga d'Alba.

EMORIES
In the beginning of 2009, a client of the George V, a New York banker and a great wine lover, organized a prestigious dinner for his "colleagues" at his property in Long Island. He wished to include me, and I accepted the invitation provided my wife could join me for the trip, a request that was received with joy.

Arriving the day before, we were able to rest and visit a friend, Pascaline Lepeltier, a passionate sommelier, energetic, with expert eyes. She led us to a famous restaurant, the Rouge Tomate, on the Upper East Side. The place, very well known, was the first in New York to apply a very specific nutritional charter combined with a menu of very biodynamic wines.

The next day, in the late afternoon, Marie and I arrived at the home of a friend of ours to go over the details of the party. Led by a butler, I went from the lounge to the dining room. Everything had been carefully thought out. The glasses were from Riedel and complemented the Christofle silverware and English porcelain from Royal Albert. The mahogany tabletop was gleaming. The bisque porcelain centerpiece decorated with *putti* was garnished with seasonal fruits and flowers. Like the house, the dining room gave off a very Victorian atmosphere. Then I checked the wines: nothing but greatness and all in magnum bottles!

At night, six couples – the women in long gowns and the men in tuxedos – gathered in the lounge to share a magnum of a 1997 Taittinger Comtes de Champagne. Then dinner was announced, and everybody returned to their seats. The supper-tasting could finally begin. Upon the request of our host, the butler served each wine in a decanter and blind. None had been listed on the menu.

To accompany the roasted Maine lobster, served in a salad, most guests easily picked up the trace of a great Chardonnay from the Côte de Beaune. Everybody was thinking of a great vintage – more rare were those who came up with the name: Chevalier-Montrachet, and the year: 1992. Only two went as far as to say the name: Domaine d'Auvenay. Which it was!

Then came the Argentine lamb racks with rosemary. Accompanied by a truffle macaroni, keeping with the spirit of Éric Fréchon's famous Le Bristol recipe. For this dish, and the aged Gouda that would follow, the five red wines were served at the same time, without my knowing which wine went into which glass. Each went from one to the next, all while we enjoyed the dish before the conversation resumed on the endless merits of each wine. The only clue we were given was that it was all from the same vintage. It was quickly targeted and defined: 1990. For quite some time, the opinions differed on the origins of each glass. Two were outed quite quickly, discovered by three of the guests. First was the 1990 Lafite Rothschild, then a 1990 La Mission Haut-Brion. The 1990 Latour and Pétrus underwent a second round of questioning. Then came the last of the glasses, held not for its inferior quality but since it stood out from the rest. Nobody knew how it fit in, though most were aware of its having been tasted before! It was a 1990 Barolo Riserva Monfortino from Giacomo Conterno. The Monfortino did

ITALY
Giacomo Conterno

well among these renowned Bordeaux wines. The level of the glass of the grand Nebbiolo was not the last to touch the bottom of the chalice.

As for me, I succeeded in placing the name of each vintage on each glass without mistake. As a sommelier, I had to live up to the reputation people placed on me. Then, as a Frenchman, it was the least I could do, surrounded by this Aeropagus of New York wine lovers. These businessmen, all of them surrounded by the world of international finance, constantly under stress, counting the seconds to their meetings and leaving nothing to uncertainty, knew to let their feelings do the speaking for that party. They recalled their tasting memories and debated over their impressions. What an atmosphere! It was far from the contingencies that governed their daily lives. It was not meant to be a match where a judge keeps tabs of who succeeded at recalling wines blindly. The idea was simply to share the wines, which had certainly become expensive over the years.

Upon arriving back at our hotel, thinking of the wines we tasted over the course of the dinner, I could not help but say to Marie, "Doesn't tonight remind you of our dinners at Saugues?" It was not all that long ago that we had a night like this at one of our veterinarian friend's in Haut-Loire. The wines offered already represented a decent budget, but he still found the room to bring up a few more bottles from his cellar. Twenty years later, it is thanks to my friendship with this very wealthy amateur that I tasted these exceptional wines based on their qualities, their aging potential, their charisma and, most importantly, their capacity to keep intact the flavor imparted to them by the lands that give birth to them through man's passion.

# The Wines

The Monfortino is an icon of Barolo and one of the greatest wines on the planet.

**2010. Barolo Riserva Monfortino.** *An intense, bright garnet color and a tight, precise nose of berries and Dalmatian plums come together with notes of oriental wood. The mouth is full and has a tannin-like and highly sensual structure (which is extremely rare). The length is lasting with a spherical finish on the body and a lightly salted finish that highlights its minerality.*

**2008.** *In a register just as flattering but with a slightly weaker density, this Monfortino remains racy yet discreet. The notes of truffles, spices, wood and gentian rhizome give it wonderful character. A great finesse and a refined, subtle hint of velvet reside within it, which is what Roberto wanted.*

**2006.** *While still closed and deep, notes of graphite and macerated fruit highlight the nose, resulting in a serious bouquet. The body is full and tannic, very complete. The austerity doesn't disrupt the tannin balance, which stays relatively well integrated. One of the great-quality wines from Roberto Conterno.*

**2000.** *(Tasted in September 2014). A deep ruby color, red tile and luminous. Open, fine and complex nose. Macerated fruits, notes of cedar and sweet cherries are present. The 2000 is a classic great Nebbiolo – racy and intense on the whole – with a full mouth that is concentrated and structured with fine, bold tannins. All of this is enhanced with a discreet acidity. A very high-class body with impressive volume and a woody retro-olfaction without violence. Great wine. It's ready to be appreciated now and with much happiness over the next twenty years. Think of a risotto with Alba truffles.*

# VOLCANIC PEACEFULNESS

**W**hen I was studying these islands from the books I devoured around the time of the contest deadlines, I found myself daydreaming about traveling from island to island, at the helm of a majestic sailboat like Alain Delon in *Plein Soleil* (*High Noon*). With Marie, we swore together that after the world contest – whatever the outcome might be – we would go for a trip around those lands bathed in the sun and cloaked in the winds and scents of the deep sea. Those waters do not hide the Aeolus island like Homer in his *Odyssey*. We would have to wait a few years more. An encounter with our friend and neighbor Giuseppe Lo Casale, a Naples native – architect and a cook of utmost excellence – made our dream a reality.

After traveling through the Neapolitan coast, we boarded and sailed with Giuseppe and his wife toward Stromboli for our 2006 summer vacation. We rented a villa on the hills of Ginostra, far from the city, the antipode of the consumerist universe we were ceaselessly trudging through in Paris. This was a rebirth, a return to the elements: earth, water, wind, fire. This first voyage was followed by numerous others, as each year we were drawn by a craving for the energy oozing from these powerful sites. Over the years, we explored every corner of the island, even the most remote ones. Our walks were much like pilgrimages through those sometime arid desert landscapes, where only Barbary fig trees, caper bushes, olive trees, myrtle and vines can survive. Thank God, some of those paradise islands still exist in the Mediterranean, such as the Aeolian islands, surrounded by a turquoise sea, with dark soils and a worrisome, mysterious and almost hypnotizing aura, as was the case in Roberto Rossellini's movie *Stromboli* with Ingrid Bergman, screened on the white wall of a Ginostra house in the evening, which was dominated by the scarlet aura of the eponymous volcano in the distance.

Even though we rested on Stromboli, the best island for visiting the Aeolian Islands is without doubt Salina. From there, it is easy to head for Panarea and, especially, to Lapiri and Vulcano to the south with a sulphuric atmosphere. Winemaking sites are all around Lipari, which was the flagship of the Malvoisie in the 30s. Nowadays, the island has around 70 hectares of vines, with 30 more hectares spread across the other islands of the archipelago. It is Salina where the Malvoisie is most balanced. As its reputation increased, financing and technical resources began to appear, and production felt this advancement, both qualitatively and quantitatively. My closeness to those wines developed further through my encounter with Antonio Caravaglio, thanks to his stepbrother Mario, an excellent restaurateur with an islander mind, a strong-charactered Sicilian.

On those islands, if you are not introduced by a member of the family, you will not be doing much of anything. These people perfectly mirror the elements of these islands. Arid and strong on the outside, tender and warm within. One summer, Caravaglio told me about his dream of vinifying a Malvoisie on Panarea. He got his hands on a small parcel in the village, San Pietro. This island is one of the archipelago's smallest – in between Stromboli and Salina. He wanted to harvest it and vinify it in amphorae. And he did exactly that! In 2012, albeit with a few logistic issues, we were able to find an importer who would handle getting this Malvasia Candida de Panarea to the George V, which we served with roasted langoustines with sour oranges. Beyond the success of the pairing was a journey we gave ourselves each time through this wine. Then, my winegrower friend started a complex task: growing a few acres of Corinto Nero vines in the crater of Panarea and, of course, ungrafted. Then again it was done and, four years later, there we were enjoying this red wine at Giuseppe's restaurant next to Saint-Nicolas Street, Assaporare, in Paris's 12th arrondissement. In regards to the Malvoisies from grapes dried on the vine, they were heady, with a smooth fruity flavor, the perfect wine for almond pies and citron confit.

At night in the Strombolian summer heat, it is good to enjoy a glass of Malvoisie *flétrie sur pied,* liqueur made from grapes ripened on the vine. It is slightly sour, delicious and refreshing, especially with almonds and a Stromboli lime granita. Here, all the products are worthwhile. After the fast-paced rhythm of Paris and the never-ending stress of the George V where expectations are always high, I savor this calm and peaceful flow to life. In the morning, around 8:30, I buy some vegetables from the grocers of Ginostra, Marco and Enzo. The whole time, I enjoy the smells of the

scrublands: wild fennel and myrtle. Time flows to the rhythm of walks, dinner preparations, the long-awaited nap and nighttime hikes. Every time I visit this island, I like to climb the slopes of the Stromboli volcano, after a five-hour climb in the falling night. To be welcomed with a guide to one of these majestic eruptions. I could not forget to bring two glasses and a bottle of Salvator d'Amico Malvoisie to better take in the moments where scarlet streams of lava from the core of the volcano seem to ignite the topaz color of the wine. The volcano on this telluric islet erupts every thirty minutes. It gives me an incredible amount of energy and alerts me to the nature of things. And I feel microscopic surrounded by the power of these elements.

From the moment we traveled Ginostra with Marie on the other side of the volcano, I was able to get more familiar with the winegrowers who, year in and year out, continue to keep up their vines on the slopes of this island. Our reunions are always a good opportunity to open a few bottle from their cellar, made from Corinto Nero, Malvasia and Bianca Candida grapes. Stromboli also offers me the pleasure of a Cohiba *Behike* with a drop of 1929 Bally rum at night after dinner, on a terrace, the view lost in the glare of the setting sun. During these travels, I often plan a trip to the island of Salina, in the volcanic theatre of Pollara where *Il Postino*, starring Philippe Noiret as the poet Pablo Neruda, was filmed. This island produces one of the most majestic Malvasia Passitos.

# A PAGE OF THE SICILIAN STORY AT THE GEORGE V

### The Story of the Marsala 1860

On a morning in November 2010, Gabriele Del Carlo (maître d'- sommelier at Le Cinq), Thierry Hamon and I were preparing the bottles we would serve for the evening at M.P.'s table, a famous gastronome from Northern France who was among our hosts. The dishes and wines had – throught the duration of the entire evening - been assembled painstakingly, as much by their rarity, the quality of their harmonization and even their succession. The party of guests: six gentlemen and gastronomes, were waiting at the table. When suddenly, I glanced at the label of this majestic Marsala wine and noticed something missing: there was nothing stating if it was dry or sweet. What do we do now? We had to know, because we were to open it at the end of the dinner, along with the dessert made with nuts from the Piedmont and caramel made with salted butter. There was only one solution: We had to call the Azienda Samperi, the famous house of the grand De Martoli family, located in Marsala. After some research, we managed to get a hold of a shaky-voiced secretary with a rather heavy Sicilian accent that took our employee quite some time to understand. "What did you want? Is the 1860 vintage dry or sweet?" We could hear this lady walking for an eternity, first on marble slabs, then across a creaking wood floor, and then onto thick carpets, and each time we heard the sound of her steps change, it was preceded by the sound of heavy wooden doors grinding along their ancient hinges. Then we heard three sharp knocks followed by a rather unfriendly "Si." To this she asked, which I am translating here, "Signore De Bartoli of the George V in Paris is on the telephone. They would like to know if the 1860 they are about to open tonight from your grandfather is dry or sweet?" A few moans and groans later, followed by the sound of a thick binder that some would have taken off the bookshelves only to open after a long sleep, the answer was revealed.

"It must be sweet ... or semi-sweet." We had our answer and were ready to prepare this wine in total peace.

At the end of the dinner, at the set time, we brought forward the pedestal table and, almost solemnly, opened the bottle. It was indeed semi-sweet and went perfectly with the dessert we created for it.

### The 1860 Vintage
Before opening the wine, which was a decision with which the host entrusted me, I allowed myself to offer to our host a DVD version of *Guépard*, a Luchino Visconti masterpiece. Well, it seemed that this masterpiece, based on the novel by the Prince of Lampedusa, from an old Sicilian family, recounts the life of an aristocratic family, headed by the Prince of Salina, in a magnificent fashion. The story takes place in 1860, the year Garibaldi and his "Redshirts" disembarked in Marsala, after their numerous victories we know against the Royal Neapolitan solders. Shortly after, Italy would be unified into the country we know today. My idea was that, after drinking this wine and engraving it into his memory, our friend and client

could, once back at his residence, discover this masterpiece while enjoying the privilege, the rare feeling of being a part of the story since he himself had tasted a wine from the same year, vinified by people who lived in that same period. That's what happened – the memories coupled with those images, aromas and tastes were etched into his soul for the rest of his life.

## White Wines

### Aeolian Islands

Malvasia L'Insolita from Nino Caravaglio. 2012. *Nino's choice to develop this dry Malvoisie is testimony to his temperament since the Malvoisie is all sweet in this area. The Panarea Island is an example. The man didn't speak to me once during my 2010 summer vacation. The aroma is unique, one of the few dry wines lost in these Aeolian microterroirs. The only Malvoisie on this small island, with a unique charm.*

*Intense golden color. Open flavor, fine, fruity, reminds me of orange flowers, linden, and exotic fruits. A nose slightly warming, yet remaining relatively complementary. The mouth is full and generous. A discreet, salty freshness and a weak acidity fit well with the salty notes. The finish is smooth with an exotic flavor reminiscent of a famous candy: Calissons.*

### Sicily

Etna Pietramarina from the Benanti family 2004. *A vintage from the local Carricante vines. It has a great ability to withstand the strong heats of the Sicilian weather. It needs volcanic soil. There, it can reach its full potential. The Benati are the vanguards of a young winegrower movement who are motivated to enhance the level of wine made from Etna terroirs. They are aware of the majestic geological and geographical environment they have been given for maintaining and developing native varieties, sometimes endemic, of Sicilian grapes grown at an altitude of 500 to 600 meters.*

*The wine has an intense golden-yellow color and a rich and generous, yet strong, nose with a mature bouquet of wax, honey and dried verbena. Aromas that spell maturity. Notes of citron and medlar peel underline a great sunshine. Full-bodied. Getting tighter mid-palate. The finish carries citron notes.*

Catarratto Porta Del Vento of Marco Sferlazzo 2007. *Intense golden-yellow color. Just a little gas is present on opening. The nose is open, waxed and lemony, slightly smoked and mineral. Once opened, a roasted note suggests maturing mostly in barrels. Notes of pharmacopoeia and camphor bring a touch of originality. The mouth is dry, tight, slightly thin and astringent. This variety is one of those created for Marsala. Mirroring other varieties of white grapes from the south of the peninsula, we can feel some almost astringent touches that bring a savory freshness to the wine. This description brings me back to local pairings of rockfish carpaccios with just a spritz of citron and a dash of olive oil.*

ITALY
### The Aeolian Islands and Sicily

# White Wines

## Sicily

**2011. Salina Nero du Munti of the Caravaglio Domain.** *Intense ruby color with signs of evolution. Open nose, intense, fruity, candied, licorice and spicy. A pleasant and pulpy nose. The mouth is structured and fresh with energy. What troubles me about this wine is its production site: the bottom of a volcano in Lipari. Here the Corino Nero vinestocks are non-grafted. Such intensity in these volcano gardens! Access is very difficult but necessary to behold this vineyard, planted in the amphitheater of this volcano. More of a tribute to Vulcan than to Bacchus.*

**2009. Salina Nero du Munti of the Caravaglio Domain.** *Fairly light ruby color. Open nose, cherry, slightly spicy.*

*Soft mouth, minty, gourmet and simple; the tannins are soft and fat. It is a reflection of this extreme climate. I can't imagine how this vine withstands these harsh climates.*

**2005. Etna Rovittello from the Benanti family.** *Deep ruby color, red reflection. Open nose, intense, fruity, animal notes, generous, woody with truffled notes. Overall, an original nose, full and fine. The attack in the mouth is sappy and structured. Discreet acidity, present and fine tannins. Some depth, great interpretation of Nerello Mascalese and Nerello Cappuccio. I praise these winemakers who defend their heritage and fight against Cabernet Sauvignon at all costs. These varieties have a trump card in terms of authenticity and diversity.*

# Sweet Wines

## Sicily

**2011. Malvasia delle Lipari Il Sapore dell'Isola from Caravaglio.** *Sustained topaz color, brilliant, luminous. Fine nose, open, fruity, rich, candied. Notes of bitter orange and marzipan with a touch of saffron. Wide mouth, caressing and creamy. Nice length. The retro-olfaction is very honeyed. Slight lack of acidity but the whole is consistent. A beautiful Malvoisie. A reflection of these hot islands.*

**2010. Malvasia delle Lipari Il Sapore dell'Isola from Caravaglio.** *The color is a clear topaz hue. Intense nose, rich, notes of candied citron, fresh almond, bitter orange. The mouth is sensual, marked by a balanced sweetness, slightly saline in the finish. Very good length. Reminiscent of bitter citrus. A perfect wine with a Madagascar vanilla and candied kumquat millefeuille and an apricot soufflé.*

# BODEGA VEGA SICILIA
## THE BEST OF SPAIN

I n the late 1990s, I showed up at the gates of this domain, without an appointment, where I could only catch a glimpse of the site behind the high walls and the guarded security station of such a stronghold. I retained a painful memory of it because I drove two and a half hours from Madrid to reach the Ribera del Duero vineyards (here the vineyard is located near the Duero River, which means "gold"). Admittedly, I was then able to visit other surrounding domains, but Vega… I would have to wait until June 2003 to take advantage of an on-site visit. There were three of us: Marie, my wife; René Millet, a true gourmet from the Club des Cent, and myself. At the time, Mariano García, house oenologist since 1968, received us. It was moving; he showed us his life's work. He had passed on the reins to his successor but continued to fulfill his duty of remembrance.

This Spanish journey was very significant for me because René was a prominent art dealer, possessed a fine palate and was a seasoned wine enthusiast. With him, we discovered back in Madrid the Thyssen-Bornemisza and the Prado. He spoke to us about works with such fluidity that, there, I could not help but see a parallel with wines. Without him, we would have only seen a small portion of these masterpieces. With his commentary, we were able to memorize and understand certain paintings. It is the same with wines when a sommelier explains them to neophytes.

This visit to Vega in 2003 was followed by another one nearly ten years later. In fact, in 2014, for the second time, I came back to the Bodegas Vega Sicilia. The domain was celebrating its 150 years. This time, the appointment was made (as it should be), and it went a lot smoother. Meanwhile, the George V had brought us much closer to the Vega Sicilia owners.

In the mid-2000s, at the meeting taking place every evening before dinner with the dining room staff and, usually, a member of the kitchen management, one of the maitres d'hotel would announce each table and name the invi-ting hosts. One night, the name Álvarez was announced. I immediately checked the customer's record. He came down to the George V with Madame – without giving any more details. When the couple arrived at Le Cinq, I welcomed them and, naturally, led them to their table. I then extended to Monsieur the wine list, incidentally opening it to the page exclusively containing three references to the most famous wine of the Ribera del Duero: Vega Sicilia Unico. Immediately, Monsieur pointed to his wife and told her, in the language of Cervantes: "You see, we are on the menu." It was indeed "the" Álvarez. Brought to my attention, the director general decided to offer them a stay, announcing himself at the time of their departure. As of this evening, we could envision a broader view of Vega Sicilia's visibility on the wine list. As of February 2015, we had sixteen Unico vintages between 1942 and 2000. Some were allocated to us on an exceptional basis by the Álvarezes through their sole French distributor. This is again a particularity of the domain: a single importer per country, knowing that production is acquired at 65% by one of the lucky recipients of Vega Sicilia, 80% of whom are individual customers.

Here is a wine that truly lives up to its name. Everything about it is unique, set apart, starting with the domain name which novices often associate with a hypothetical Sicilian vineyard. However, this is a distant historical heritage. In fact, from the fifteenth to the seventeenth century, the golden age of the Spanish Empire, the kings of Spain had possession of the kingdom of Naples, including the portion south of Naples in the Italian peninsula, Sardinia and Sicily. It is also a unique wine by the size of the domain: 1000 hectares, 200 of which are vineyards. About 100 hectares of vineyards are devoted to l'Unico, nearly 100,000 bottles per year. The other part of the vineyard is for the production of Vega Sicilia Valbuena and the Alion cuvée. Six hundred hectares of forest were planted (over 100,000 oaks) after the Álvarez Mezquiriz family acquired the property in 1982 (the A and M intertwined on the coat of arms on the label). The previous owners, the wealthy Herrero family, had raised the Bodega wine in the same spirit as Aimé Salon in Champagne. A wine for their friends, their families and, where appropriate, a chosen few. The myth was born. When you wander around the property, in the hills, it is reminiscent of another rare wine, but for different reasons: Château Rayas, in Châteauneuf-du-Pape (property of 80 hectares, 40 of which are vineyards and 40 are forests and pine forests).

There, like here, the canopy of trees is wholly integrated into the identity of the wines.

Upon purchasing, Pablo Álvarez's father entrusted the management of the property to his son. Work was undertaken throughout the years for the completion of a new wine cellar, a model of its kind that is visited world-wide. It has been in operation since 2010. It is equipped with isothermal vats, the same inertia as cement as soon as you connect them to the ground to vent electricity. The whole is both technical and practical, easy to navigate and manage. A small vertical press, for example, to facilitate the parcel pressing (the vineyards have nineteen different soil types, all harvested and revitalized separately). The domain also has its own cooperage at its disposal, where it produces parts from dried staves within the domain for three years (two years outside, one year covered). There are three full-time coopers. They prepare the barrels with staves of American oak. To this production must be added 2,000 to 3,000 barrels of French oak. They are, themselves, deliv-ered by French coopers every year. At Vega, there is parity between French and American oak. We enjoyed all the facilities during our July 2014 visit, with Thierry and Christophe, a Genevan friend, lucky beneficiary at Vega and great consumer of the domain's wines. The visit took place with Xavier Ausás López de Castro, who joined the domain in 1990, becoming technical director and cellar master in 1998.

When I remember, however, my tastings of the 1942, 1953 and 1970 (for me the greatest red wine in the world in this vintage, tasted for the first time at La Poularde in 1995), for which these facilities did not exist, I cannot help but think that great wine is born in the terroir and not in the cellar. These considerations are all even truer in Vega Sicilia. For here, as our guide explained to us throughout the visit, the wine follows a unique path through-out its maturing at the end of vinification:

– The first stage in maturing here is called "ratification." It takes place in casks and aims to define which batches will be able to continue the cycle to become l'Unico. Others will join the Valbuena cuvée. Throughout this first breeding, the wines will be tasted regularly. Only those who possess the characteristics required will continue on the course for l'Unico.

– Second stage: this is the bodybuilding stage of the wine in new oak barrels (partly produced in situ, completed by purchases of French oak).

# SPAIN
## Bodega Vega Sicilia

Period lasting one year to eighteen months or more, depending on the vintage.

– Third stage: the wine is racked into barrels that have already seen several vintages. It is a passage called "education."

– Fourth stage: the wine continues its existence in casks. It is also the preassembly stage before bottling. A resting stage.

These different breeding installments may take six to nine years for l'Unico. The last stage, the bottle's aging, can last three to six years before being placed on the market. This method is unique in the world! Especially since all these steps are performed by gravity without the wine being pumped. For Valbuena (the name of the first domain owner, the Marquis de Valbuena), another cuvée of the domain, the whole cycle is reduced to five years, or three years in wood and two years in bottles, before being placed on the market.

Following these explanations, we received the grand tour of the domain and vineyards. The morning sun radiated the dense, clayey hillsides of white limestone and revealed to us the protected landscapes, slender cypress and bright green, thorny thickets. The hills peak at 780 meters. The vines are pruned in a goblet shape, facing north. Here, the tinto fino, tinto del país or tempranillo reign supreme. Ideal variety when the weather suits it. However, this latitude makes us forget that here, in this part of Ribera del Duero, it is as cool as in Champagne (nearly a hundred days a year with temperatures below 0°C). Other planted varieties representing a total of 20% are complementary on the domain and enter a small percentage in l'Unico (Cabernet Sauvignon, Malbec and Merlot). Over the years, the cultivation manager has identified the best parcels of Vega hillsides to produce l'Unico. Other midslope parcels may enter into the l'Unico blending but are usually reserved for the second wine: Valbuena.

Below lies the alluvial plain. The wines produced here are cheaper. Therefore, Cabernet Sauvignon and Merlot are represented, as well as a small percentage of Malbec. Merlot is used for the Alion cuvée, the latest addition to Vega Sicilia. At present, these vines are planted alongside plantings of cork and holm oak. There is another cuvée, the oldest of its tradition, the cuvée Especial. This comes from the blending of three different vintages – that's why it has no vintage. Originally, this wine was intended for family

celebrations and special occasions, to create a wine representative of that which characterizes l'Unico. In a way, this philosophy is similar to that of the Krug family with its Grande Cuvée, namely, the power, finesse, balance and maturity coupled with a complexity ensuring we enjoy it immediately. The production of it is very limited and maintained at the will of Don Pablo and his family. At Vega, tradition and modernism are intertwined.

By the time we finished the tour of this domain, where more than ten vintages were in the process of aging, we had gained a better understanding of why there was a need to maintain a high-security perimeter around the area.

# MEMORIES

After visiting Vega for three hours on this beautiful summer day, we found ourselves in an unusual location, Zurita, in Tudela de Duero near Valladolid. Even the most gifted of navigators would have had difficulty finding this place. Our chauffeur, a Madrid native, held tight to not lose sight of Xavier's vehicle leaving Vega Sicilia. As good French workers of the restaurant industry, Thierry and I were a tad embarrassed to enter the tavern with the clock showing 2:30! At Le Cinq, at this time, it is extremely rare for a table to be available. Through a discreet door, a young woman accompanied us to a large round table in a cool room, shaded by Venetian blinds, the air stirred by indolent fans. Only two other tables were occupied. Damnation, all the clients must have already finished lunch! The tables were even re-set. We had to be pretty darn late. No sooner had we ordered than the room began to fill up. At 3:00, it was full!

We had the pleasure of discovering simple, high-quality products. First: white asparagus from the banks of the Duero, served tepid, with olive oil and chorizo chips. This fine root, the head barely tinged with chlorophyll, recalled those of Vineuil on the Loire. This entrée was served promptly to refresh the palate. With a 2011 Alion (the first Alion vintage was produced in 1991), dense, warm, powerful, we devoured a delicious dish of Murcia. A kind of pork blood pudding with chorizo spices and wine vinegar, served piping hot in a flat bowl of glazed terracotta with croutons rubbed with young garlic. Then a 2010 Vega Sicilia Valbuena, the other Vega wine produced in the parcels at the bottom of the hillside. For this wine, the innkeeper brought a young lamb cooked in a bread oven, wonderfully roasted, leathery skin, crisped to perfection, without the harshness sometimes found. Simply accompanied by a crisp salad, peeled tomatoes and a spring white onion in olive oil. A dish of exquisite finesse with a rare economy of means. Its success lay in the quality and freshness of the products and not in the complexity of the preparations. The end of the dish was enriched by the arrival of a bottle of 1994 Vega Sicilia Unico. The tasting was prolonged by the serving of a tomme of Manchego cheese (100% sheep), not too chalky and quite soft.

During the coffee service, I felt a buzz in the room. Upon the passing of a man who had just entered, the men at the tables in his path stood up to greet him. Don Pablo Álvarez Mezquiriz made his entrance. In turn, we all stood up at once, a chair was brought to him, and his coffee was immediately served. The conversations were resumed with vigor. An impressive man. As we chatted about our visit, we came to discuss the approaching dinner. We had to go back to Madrid for the night… and none of us had thought to reserve a table. Among the great two-star restaurants of Madrid in the Michelin Guide, there was one that particularly caught the attention of our Genevan friend. However, to get a table there at the last minute was out of the question. Don Pablo then took out his phone, dialed a number and gave some instructions. Within minutes, he received a call back – a table had been reserved for us at 9:30! No problem.

Back in Madrid, after we had freshened up with a cold beer at the hotel, we made our way to the two-star restaurant, long overseen by the late Catalan chef Santi Santamaria, slayer of molecular cuisine. We were going to dine at Santceloni. Our friend, content with the day he had dreamed about for years, wanted to thank me for allowing him to return to Vega and, especially, to better understand its inner workings. To begin, he chose a bottle of such rarity that we had sought after all day: a 1997 Champagne Salon. A wine that is refined and stretched with time, notes of menthol, citrus, fine. Served at a very good temperature, chilled but not iced. A nice harmony with the sea scallop tartar.

SPAIN
Bodega Vega Sicilia

We chose the dishes; Christophe, our host, chose the wines. I was consulted for some vintages, but the framework was centered on a Vertical Vega Sicilia Unico. In hindsight, I recognize that the service order was not the smartest choice, as we began with the 1991 l'Unico. A great success for Vega. With this wine, we made the choice of empty potato shells stuffed with a fine and savoury mince. The 1987 l'Unico following it was a bad choice on my part. It was a vintage we had tasted at the George V, but in double magnum! There, in the bottle, the nose offered a certain complexity but the mouth was disappointing, gaunt. It was maintained through the acidity. A character trait of the Vega Sicilia wines: their ability to retain this acidity preserves them throughout time. We then tasted the 1981 l'Unico. This time much more complex with a delicate mouth and a long finish. Both vintages were served with the main dish, the specialty of the house: braised veal shank, succulent, very tender.

Then came the climax: the 1965 l'Unico. Incredible. We didn't have it decanted so as to appreciate the flavors from the opening to the evolution in the glass. The Manchego was present, but let the wine speak without bullying it.

Back at the hotel, where a few short hours of sleep awaited us, we did not stray from our usual routine with Thierry; we met in one of our rooms – with a large bottle of water – to go over the best moments of the day. It was made possible by a combination of factors, at the heart of which stood the George V! For, if we can serve these wines, it is because of our customers who order them or who are willing to accept our recommendations. It is a luxury, a pleasure, of which every time we feel its importance.

# The Wines

Tempranillo is a third-period variety (late-maturing variety). It is perfect on these limestone soils. This variety has a high acidity, giving it a unique aging capacity. It is pruned in goblets in this area. The port is low and develops pretty strong wood. The advantage of goblets in hot climates is that the règes, when falling, protect the grapes from the sun. Here, the planting density is low given the extreme condition of this vineyard, with scarce water: 2,200 vines per hectare.

# Tastings carried out the day of the visit at the domain

**2004. Vega-Sicilia Unico.** *The youngest (released in 2014), deep color, ruby. Open nose. Beautiful density, spicy, woody. For now, the breeding is felt at the nose. Forthright mouth, ample, very concentrated, very young. To be revisited.*

**1994.** *Evolved color, always brilliant, open nose, floral faded pink. Delicate. Slightly acidic. Full-bodied, generous, without heaviness. The freshness reappears on the mid-palate. Fine tannins. A lot of elegance, to drink now.*

**1991.** *Incredibly clear color. Very bright. Unsettling nose with a fresh and spicy character. I could imagine a red hermitage, some cedar notes make the whole more complex. The mouth follows the nose in this refinement and complexity. Very good length. Mellowed tannins, everything comes together. Great wine.*

**1987.** *Surprising vintage with a constant aromatic mark appearing in Vega: acidity. Dominant in this vintage. I tasted the wine better in double magnum two years ago. The nose is rather tart, slightly metallic, without the generosity and pulp of Vega. The mouth justifies the nose by a very angular character, making the wine thin, even fine. It loses its thickness, making it austere and rather monolithic.*

**1981.** *The wine is now ready, perfect, elegant and calm, complex. Combines small red fruit such as candied cherry with notes of cedar, associated with this type of breeding, long. The very elegant, sensual mouth, without asperity, gives us all the delicacy of this high-altitude terroir. The acidity preserved this great wine for many years.*

**1965.** *Still incredibly dense color, brilliant, evolution towards orange reflections; complex nose, woody, cigar box, cedar, macerated fruit; dense and precise nose. Milk chocolate, cocoa. Candied fruit. No deviation. The mouth seems almost more concentrated than the 1981 tasted just before. Unbelievable. Certainly from low yields. The wine has not lost its power and concentration. A lesson and, above all, one of the finest bottles from a miserable year in France for this 1965 vintage (the bottle to be had when turning 50).*

**1942.** *(Tasted in September 2014 at Le Cinq). Surprisingly dark color with brick-red reflections and a high-gloss appearance. Open nose, concentrated and dense, with a fragrance of dark fruit compote, candied. Candied black cherry.*

*Spicy, camphorated, cigar box. The olfactory whole is incredibly deep and still has potential. The depth of taste and structure are visible in the attack and gain power after an hour of decanting. A mid-palate with thickness and sensuality reveals retro-olfaction of camphorated spice. A great length completes the 1942, making it a legendary bottle. The wine is well balanced with a soul, giving it exceptional longevity.*

*PS: I tasted the dregs at the office after the service, and it was like tasting an aged Côte de Nuits Pinot. Kirsched cherry aromas, dried rose. Delicate.*

# QUINTA DO NOVAL
## AT THE HEART OF A
## WONDER OF THE WORLD

Every year, I have the pleasure of flying to Porto. The huge airport, empty, surreal, reminds me of *Playtime* by Jacques Tati. I often find myself imagining the unforgettable M. Hulot wandering, lost, among the endless corridors. However, it was when the car approached the vineyard that I began to dream. Several options for getting to the great domains exist; I take advantage of both. First, the train, winding along the Douro, revealing the Pharaonic work undertaken, not only on each side of the river, but also on those of its tributaries. The other takes a bit more time and requires some people skills, but it is the most delicious: travelling up the river. I have been able to do this three times, on board a beautiful yacht, in the same vein as Jean Gabin's in *Le Baron de l'écluse*. By this fluvial means you can, while enjoying a Colheita, appreciate even more profoundly the extent of peaks and the different types of vine growths on the hillsides. Man has achieved, over these 40,000 hectares of vineyards, a mammoth task. Over the hills, shale terraces see the growth of a considerable number of varieties: there are nearly ninety. Five varieties, however, dominate the plantings: the famous Touriga Nacional, Tinto Roriz, Tinto Barroca, Touriga Francesa and the Tinto cão.

These vineyards are governed by ancient boundaries, since it is from 1756 that Sebastião José de Carvalho e Melo, Comte d'Oeiras and better known by his last title of Marquis de Pombal (1699-1782), undertook to regulate port wine trading. The Douro production zone was formally demarcated by 335 granite landmarks, called *marcos pombalinos,* which are still visible today. During the following year, a detailed classification of *quintas* was established, for it was as much the domains as the terroirs that were classified. For the record, the brokers from the Place de Bordeaux took a simpler route when, in 1855, they created the Crus Classés of Médoc and the Sauternais, as requested by Napoleon III. Classifying châteaux and not the terroirs allowed, and still allows, developments and modifications through sales or acquisitions of properties without requiring a revision of the classification.

In the Douro, at the time of the classification's inception, the vineyards producing the best wines, called *vinhos de feitoria*, had the right to sell their products for export at higher prices, the *quintas* of this category being ranked A and B, while those offering wines of a more modest quality, the *vinhos de ramo*, were confined to the domestic market, ranked from C to F. Many parameters are involved in the ranking: altitude, yields, soil type, age of vines, geographical area, orientation and inclination of the slopes…

The entire demarcated area of the Douro covers 250,000 hectares. The vineyards appear at the level of Barqueiros, sixty-five kilometers upstream from Porto, and continue up the river to Barca d'Alva, two hundred and twenty kilometers away. The finest terroirs generally occupy the steep slopes lining the Douro River. About two thirds of them extend to slopes greater than 30°. This whole is divided into three parts: Baixo Corgo, Cima Corgo and, further east, Douro Supérior. Many historic *quintas* are located in the middle part of the vineyard, the Cima Corgo, still the heart of port production. These domains line the steep slopes of the Douro and its tributaries, the main ones being the Távora, the Rio Torto, and the Pinhão. It is also in Pinhão that you either dock or get off the antique train. On its own, the station is worth a stop to behold the *azulejos* (earthenware tiles richly decorated and glazed, typical of Portugal).

To reach the object of our destination from the station, you take a winding road and go back from Pinhão to the Quinta do Noval. After thirty minutes up a hillside, you arrive at a narrow, granite-lined road, fully shaded by seasonal pergola vines. This is the entrance to the *quinta*. It still takes five minutes to climb this peak, which commands a breathtaking panorama. The massive historic *quinta* forms a sort of hamlet with its cellar, farm buildings and domestic outbuildings. The building even has an old chapel, confined to the heart of the house. Several times have I stayed there, visiting both sides and up and down the property. I was able to soak up the tranquility that prevails over the terrace in the late afternoon, under the venerable Lebanese cedar. This majestic tree, as it hangs off a cliff, has been a privileged witness to all the highlights of Noval. From the passing of prestigious guests to coy lovers, not to mention lovers of pétanque, all basking in its generous shade.

During visits to Noval, as with every great *quinta*, you must visit – especially during harvest season – the winery and its *lagars*. These are huge granite troughs in which the grapes are crushed by the pickers. The goal is to release the juice and the coloring materials without crushing the seeds. The soles of the feet are the only way to achieve a uniform result. I took this risk once during a visit with our guide, Vincent Gournac. Very interesting experience because you feel the presence of seeds in the juice without crushing them (which would release the oil they contain). It is exhausting work – it lasts for hours. Modern techniques have once again replaced man, but this winemaking legacy of two centuries remains alive in the development of vintages. From these whole grapes, a purée of grapes is obtained, which, after the start of the alcoholic fermentation, is stopped by the addition of wine spirits. Very different aging processes will follow, depending on the types of port desired.

One of the most dramatic gestures at Le Cinq for serving wine is the opening of a Vintage Port with tongs. We at Le Cinq are among the last to keep this technique alive, which consists of cutting the neck of a port bottle below the cork with a pair of wrought iron tongs, white-hot from the kitchen burners. The neck is clamped firmly for several minutes. As soon as you release the grip of the tongs around the neck, an assistant tightens iced linen around the precisely heated location. The thermal shock is so violent that the glass is cut apart, leaving no piece behind. To achieve this opening, it is best to place the bottle upright at least two hours in advance to allow the sediment to settle in the bottom of the bottle. The major interest is to not use a corkscrew to extract the cork. In fact, with Port wines, being powerful and generous in alcohol (between 19 and 20% vol.), the corks are often damaged and crumble upon opening. Don't forget that these vintages are bottled after only two years in the barrel, keeping a lot of color within them and, as a result, a lot of sediment after twenty to thirty years of aging. That is why, when using a traditional corkscrew, it is often necessary to then use a funnel equipped with a cotton cheesecloth to filter the wine and remove impurities. In doing so, the wine turns irreparably cloudy and you lose the transparency that is ideal for enjoying the nectar. It is also a way to bring life to the dining service.

PORTUGAL
Quinta Do Noval

# MEMORIES

In 2013, the annual dinner of the Mad Waiters Wine of the World was held in Noval. After a tasting of white and red wines – very quiet – in Douro, in a word, non-fortified wines, a symbol of the evolving consumer market of ports that has been in decline for many years, we started the ports with the Colheitas de Noval.

Two newly bottled vintages were presented: 1971 and 1976. These vintage ports are stored in barrels almost indefinitely until a potential buyer comes along. They were served with cured meats from an artisan's shop in Pinhão, a character who could well have descended from Raimu, at whose place, the year before, we had experienced an intense tasting of nearly an hour and a half amidst the smoke of his brazier, where sausages and bacon fat were grilling in diaphanous slices. While he entertained us, his two sons chopped up pig segments in a sustained rhythm. It was a Friday – a busy day. One of his sons was gruff, with bushy eyebrows, and a bright and a precise gesture. His brother seemed more brusque and taciturn. We had to change before dinner, as we smelled of smoke and roasted pig. The meats were splendid but the white wine, from their domestic production, was "special."

After these preliminary sharings in the salon, the Vintages made their appearance along roasted goose surrounded by garden vegetables and Noval rum raisins. Two vintages were opposed in the pairing, from the same year. Two 1970 wines. The "classic" Vintage and the Nacional. The classic Vintage, compared to the Nacional, had some difficulties. The latter reigned over all its subjects, but the pairing was fantastic with the grilled goose flesh and the red cabbage, candied with raisins. The succulence and persistence of the goose resisted the assaults of the two ports.

The next dish was reminiscent of the *collège de sommeliers*, assembled around a large mahogany table. A scene also worthy of a gathering orchestrated by Coppola filming the *Godfather*, but with swim fins instead of popguns, a signature Uderzo setting and Goscinny dialogue. There was Signora Chantôme, representative of the Grande Famille des Sommeliers; Dogña Patricia, Pax Europa plenipotentiary ambassador; Dac and Blanche de Bruxelles (better known under the names Wouters & Boschman); Maestro Kreis de Stuttgart (a Goth of the Rhine flute); Sir Édouard de Champagne

(yellow anchor jersey); Ruet la Cervoise, a.k.a JC a.k.a "Lutèce/Lugdunum," the irreducible Poussier de Paris and his Consigliori Martray de Savoie; Beau Marc I, known as "Class" and his aide de camp, the battleship Hamon, not to mention the one who received them into his stronghold, the Pires du Douro. All in standard tuxedos… more fins. They were surrounded by representatives of the *quinta* and servants, laughing.

The fare arrived, carried at arm's length by robust cooks of the *quinta*: *cocottes lutées*. Their opened lids, once on the table, released perfumes of truffles, foie gras and garden herbs. It was yellow lentil cooked in juice with black truffles and duck foie gras. The dish was accompanied by the famous 1963 Nacional! A legendary bottle. I had only tasted it twice before. A tremendous pairing with this dish. The flavors and aromas intermingled. The uncompromising, extremely dominant, chastened and intense fruit of the 1963. In fact, the great vintages stay young when sealed for many years. The 2011 vintage will evolve in this direction.

To finish, it took only a few clacks of the fins to rejoin the salon and enjoy a Cohiba *Behike* 1956 with a 1976 Colheita. By lantern light, some ventured outside on the terrace to breathe in this softness – a great plenty.

# Tasting at la Quinta do Noval, Winter 2014

With Eric Boshman, Marc Monrose (director general of la Quinta do Pessegueiro), João Nicaulo de Almeida (cellar master at Pessegueiro) and Thierry. João confided to us that this was the first time he had tasted the Nacional and, moreover, in Noval.          .

During this tasting, we enjoyed the quintessence of the domain's production. The Nacional, the Vintage, the LBV and the Colheitas represent only 20% of production in Noval. Most of the wines from the quinta are represented by Ruby (60%) and Tawny (20%) port wines. It has been several years that red wines produced under the Douro appellation have been part of this production.

**2011. Porto Vintage.** *A lot of power, dense, long, black currant, blueberry, great strength.*

**2003.** *At this stage, marked alcoholic notes. Very ripe, heavy.*

**2000.** *Dense and large vintage, some astringency in the finish. Ripe. Notes of fruit jam, blackberry.*

**1994.** *Long, large, fine and sophisticated. The alcohol is well integrated. Charming, good length.*

**2004. Porto Late Bottle Vintage.**
*This port aged four years in barrels before bottling. The wine is dense with a nose of black cherry. It is ready to be served. At the George V, this wine is offered during the fall-winter season as a welcome gift upon the arrival of our residents to their suites, along with Jacques Genin caramels.*

## The Nacional

*In Noval, a small parcel tolerates phylloxera with more resistance than any other in the domain. On average, a vine reached by the aphid can resist for a decade, but in this parcel of Touriga Nacional, the vines live almost thirty years. This makes the cultivation possible. Therefore, this area is planted without American rootstock, giving the wine an original style.*

*The wine from the non-grafted vines is the darling of the domain. The first to be produced was the 1931. The Douro is one of the crucial vineyard discoveries for any sommelier. Tasting the Nacional is one of its crowning jewels, both for its aging capacity as well as its delicacy.*

**2004. Porto Vintage Nacional.** *More power, density and width, but also more restraint. It has a very fine seed finish. 2004 is not considered a great Vintage year. Yet, there was still a Nacional.*

As a whole, the valley declared few Vintage wines in 2004. Grains of polymerized tannins, with great tension in the mouth. No element overwhelms another in the balance. Neither sweetness, nor alcohol, nor acids. And such tension! Slightly spicy, fine, immense.

**2003.** *As always with the ungrafted Touriga Nacional, it is the power that dominates. Complex, long, slightly mentholated, violet liqueur. The mouth is dense and sophisticated. The tannin grain is sublime. Fine. The finish is educated. No alcoholic notes.*

**1970.** *(Tasted in Noval in 2012). Deep ruby color, luminous with orange reflections. The nose is open, dense, fine, marked by notes of macerated fruit, slightly kirsched. Several minutes after opening, they mix with touches of dried fruit, sweet spices, woody licorice . The whole creates an oriental impression. The mouth, through its body and delicacy, emphasizes the great balance of this wine. The touch of liqueur is discreet and reveals fruit and elegance.*

**1963.** *(Tasted in Noval in 2012). Intense ruby color, concentrated. Open, extremely dense nose, tertiary. Same*

impression when tasting a Taylor's 1945. Note of burlap candied cherry, orange peel and sandalwood. A flamboyant nose. In the mouth, the power of the attack reveals a remarkable creaminess. The wine makes its mark in the finish, where the cream of the blackberry harmonizes with the notes of brown cocoa and dried fig. The level of this Nacional illustrates the great rare wine it is again today, as in the 1970s and early 1990s. A lack of density was noticeable in the Nacional.

After this wine, we entered the chapel of the domain which, in fact, is adjacent to the tasting room via a backdoor that allows the homeowners to attend mass from the upstairs of the chapel. The people of the domain, called by the bell, are seated below and enter through the courtyard. The chapel had a quaint charm. Its stained glass was understated and beautiful. The light reaching us was softened by the thick branches of cedar.

After the tasting, we also went under the cedar to enjoy the view with a glass of 2004 Nacional in hand and roasted, salted almonds from the quinta's almond trees placed in cups, awaiting our gluttony.

# MADEIRA BARBEITO, BLANDY'S AND D'OLIVEIRAS NEVER DIES

**A**s a genuine vineyard globetrotter, I have knxocked on the door of every continent where vines grow. Some sites are less accessible than others. If there were one flight from our travels that my wife and I keep a powerful memory of, it would be without a doubt our first landing in Funchal, the capital of Madeira. The flight went off without a hitch until the pilot proceeded to make the "final approach" of the plane to position itself on the center runway. Being at the window seat, I had plenty of time to observe the airport's configuration and its sublime runway – unique – ending, like the flight deck of the *Charles de Gaulle*, with the gaping ocean! On seeing this sight, we had the peculiar notion that we had arrived at the vineyard that was located at the very ends of the earth. As the wheels touched the tarmac, a brave woman next to me was praying, her hands folded. As for my wife, I bore long marks from her nails in my forearm. Once stopped, everyone applauded the pilot fervently. Turning to the window, I saw only the sea below. The runway edge was "very" close.

Finally, as it must have been for the great navigators in the past, this stopover seemed like an oasis upon landing. Here, everything was exuberant. The fragrant and colorful flowers carried a perfume of paradise to the island. When we entered the cellars, it was another dream, transported through the centuries to carry on… and on… But before indulging, let's first peruse the rich history of this archipelago. These islands are located 600 kilometers off the Moroccan coast. The islands of Porto Santo and Madeira are inhabited, while the Desertas and Selvagens islands are uninhabited. These islands are the summits of a submarine volcano 4,000 meters in height. The volcanic soil, combined with a subtropical climate, ensure that these islands are very wooded, very steep and impenetrable. The island of Madeira remained uninhabited until 1425, when João Gonçalves Zarco began its colonization on the authority of King João I of Portugal. The first Portuguese settlers were soon joined by entrepreneurs hailing from Italy, France and Flanders with a thirst for adventure,. The island was then entirely covered with forests (hence its name, *madeira,* meaning "wood" in Portuguese). In 1433, due to fires caused by earthworks, most of the island was deforested. Then followed the creation of a vital irrigation canal system, the *levadas*, dug by North African slaves, which is still operational today.

One of the first great figures to make his mark on the archipelago was Christopher Columbus, during a stay in 1479, when he married Filipa Moniz, daughter of Bartolomeo Perestrelo, captain governor of the island of Porto Santo. From this union a son was born, Diego Columbus. His wife died shortly after childbirth. Legend has it that Columbus perfected his knowledge of navigation with the maps that his wife brought as dowry, maps of winds and currents of the Portuguese possessions in the Atlantic, which, perhaps, belonged to her father.

At the turn of the sixteenth century, sugarcane plantations experienced tremendous growth. In 1508, the capital, Funchal, already had 5,000 inhabitants. Soon, however, diseases and the overuse of agricultural land, combined with the large-scale development of sugar cane in newly conquered Brazil, caused a radical change in cultivations. Henceforth, it was the grapevine that occupied most of the available land, combined with food crops. The first wine exports – non-mutated – began in 1537 to Great Britain. In 1590, the first British buyers landed. In the late seventeenth century, the wine became an export of vital importance to the archipelago, especially since it was a valued commodity for all types of buccaneers stopping in Funchal. They were the first to spread word of the Madeira wines to the rest of the world, making them famous. In 1768, James Cook stocked up for himself and his crew, carrying the wines away to his homeland. In turn, the British swarmed in numbers to Madeira. It did not take long for tourism to become the primary source of income for the island.

Throughout the eighteenth century, exports to Europe and the Americas burgeoned. Madeira was so famous that George Washington chose it for his inauguration in the city to which he would bestow his name. This boom lasted until the mid-nineteenth century. From this period on, the island suffered a serious crisis due to fungal diseases, such as mildew and

phylloxera. By the end of the century, of the seventy English trading houses that included Funchal, only five had survived. Tourism, however, had not weakened, and in 1891, the famous Reid's Palace opened its doors to travelers worldwide. It still remains a reference, a key venue, as I discovered myself.

Early on, I was fascinated by the history of Madeira wines, through works that I had devoured in my competition preparations. Then I met, through a Flemish friend, the Smeyers, a couple from Antwerp who shared a passion for these wines. At their home, I found some rare gems. When Thierry would call them to order Boal 22, Raymond and his wife would always ask, "You want Boal 22… but what century?" At their home, it was possible to go back to 1795, with hardly missing a vintage. Unique in the world. How many hours have we spent dreaming of serving these timeless vintages: 1875, 1895, 1900, 1922… We would not hesitate – and this is still the case at Le Cinq – to open some bottles weeks in advance. A true challenge of common sense for any sommelier, whose obsession is often oxidation.

Yet, the regulars at La Poularde were not sold, as the image of Madeira then and for more than a century has been prominently placed among the so-called "cooking wines." Remember the communion banquets of old, serving a good beef tongue in madeira sauce between the roast beef and roasted poultry… It was a whole era. In Montrond, nothing to that effect. With Étéocle and the kitchen brigade, I would compose dishes to pair with these venerable wines. For example, a Madeira Verdelho with an oxtail double consommé, or even a Madeira Boal 1922 with a dark chocolate shortcake.

Upon my arrival at the George V, the Smeyers followed me and, with them, a myriad of fabulous vintages. The only down side to which we did not have a suitable solution: the service temperatures of these Madeiras. Sometimes too cool when we took them out of the wine chillers at the last moment, sometimes too hot if they remained too long in the dining room. It took us several years to design and implement a solution. With the sommellerie team and a master Parisian silversmith, we designed a uniquely-shaped horseshoe object, pierced with seven air sacks in which crystal carafes were embedded. A clever device that keeps the carafes between 14 and 16°C in the room. I realize that you would need to serve in a palace to really see this project take hold, considering the cost of such an item, but the result lives up to our expectations and those of our guests.

**M**EMORIES
Le Cinq, 2:00 in the afternoon. One of our regulars, who became a friend over the years, called me, freshly off his jet. He was starving and aware that in the time needed to get there, the kitchens would be closed. What to do? Not to worry, we took down his order over the phone, remembering his usual, two, three bottles of his favorites. Forty minutes later, he was there with two American colleagues. Lunch could begin. Everything was coming along. Good humor reigned over the table, when suddenly he asked me to prepare him something special before coffee service. It was July 4, 2012, a national holiday in the United States. Several wines came to mind, and, with Thierry, we looked at each other and both said, "How about a '92'?" It was, after all, in 1792 that Columbus Day was celebrated for the first time in the United States to celebrate the 300 years after the arrival of Christopher Columbus in the Americas. This was also the year of George Washington's reelection.

Deep in the cellars of the George V, among other treasures, rest the Madeiras of this vintage. One of more than 200 years present in the George V cellars comes from a batch of 1,228 bottles of Malmsey Extra Réserve Solera 1792 from Blandy's, bottled in 1957 on the occasion of a private visit from Her Majesty Queen Elizabeth II and His Royal Highness the Duke of Edinburgh to the island of Madeira. Here is the extraordinary story of this Madeira.

On August 7, 1815, Napoleon boarded a British warship, the *HMS Northumberland*, for the island of St. Helena, as decided by the great powers. The vessel stopped in Madeira to stock up on water and food, as was then customary. Among the stocked barrels was a unit of 1792 Blandy's Malmsey Madeira. Unfortunately, for health reasons – his stomach – the Emperor's doctor forbade him from any consumption. The barrel therefore remained intact in the cellars of the Longwood residence. Upon the Emperor's death, in 1821, following a regulatory problem, the barrel was returned to Madeira and stored at Blandy's until 1840. That year, 200 bottles of this unit were

## PORTUGAL
### Madeira Barbeito, Blandy's and D'Oliveiras

racked for wealthy amateurs. Thus began the second life of this wine. As of this date, a *solera* – based on the remaining 400 liters – was established. A first bottle of this 1792 *solera* was racked for Sir Winston Churchill in honor of the Nobel Prize in Literature he received. Therefore, between 1840 and 1953, more than a century of vintages enriched the *solera*, offering it eternal youth. When we presented this rare wine to the Prime Minister of Her Majesty, he wanted to serve it himself, interjecting to the guests, "When the first vintage was vinified, giving birth to this wine, Queen Marie-Antoinette was still alive!" Indeed, in August 1792, during the height of the Reign of Terror in Paris, Louis XVI and his family were arrested and imprisoned. Some time later, they would meet their historic end. This is one of the bottles that was returned. There was a moment of palpable emotion at the table. The cork was not to be extracted without resistance. We could not expect less. The color showed some turbidity which remained after opening, the nose, tenuous at first, developed slowly to fill the entire crystal chalice containing it. Perfumes of amber, incense, sweet spices and candied fruits permeated from it. The mouth also needed time to approach. But once again, the wine was still there, alive.

Another bottle, still within the George V cellars, witnessed a rare scene. On the occasion of a visit to the cellars by His Royal Highness Eudes d'Orléans in 2014, Thierry pointed out this bottle, among other bottles from the eighteenth and nineteenth centuries, on a shelf. The prince had a moment of stupefaction, then asked if he could hold it. After a few moments, emotional and distant, he replaced the bottle, thinking aloud that his distant ancestor, Louis XVI, had also held this bottle in his hands! The magic of the wine, transcending time and space. Madeira is the product created by man, outliving him, improving with age. The wine that never dies!

# PORTUGAL
## Madeira Barbeito, Blandy's and D'Oliveiras

# The Wines

Madeira has an impressive number of varieties. However, of the 450 hectares of the DOC Madeira, 85% are planted with Tinta Negra mole, a hybrid of Pinot Noir and Grenache. Most of the Madeira labeled three years in age, sometimes five, or even ten years in age are made with it. The most prestigious group has only four varieties with well-defined characteristics: Sercial (vinified dry), Verdelho (semi-dry), Boal (semi-sweet) and Malvasia (sweet). To this list we must add two more rare varieties: Terrantez, almost non-existent today (it is sweeter than Verdelho and less sweet than Boal) and Moscatel (sweet), which is no longer grown. It is these latter varieties which interest us. As we know, the wine of Madeira began to be exported worldwide in the eighteenth century. The weather conditions of Madeira are not always conducive to obtaining the optimum ripeness of grapes. To soften these acidic and astringent wines, the addition of cane sugar was resorted to, which is easily produced in the island. These bitter-sweet wines were initially used, in part, as ballast on ships. To preserve it from the passage at the equator, a consequent dose of cane brandy was added.

These casks of wine transported by ships were subject to countless temperature variations before arriving at their destination. The unsold wines would return to their point of departure. Once back on the island of Madeira, it was found that the wine had acquired more complexity. From this fact, 1,730 barrels of Madeira began to be sent on long expeditions with the goal of obtaining better quality. In the early nineteenth century, producers started studying different ways to reproduce the warming and cooling phenomena that the wines encountered on the high seas in order to improve the quality of Madeira wine. Two processes were then favored.

– The first, *estufagem*, where the wine is heated in a container for three months. Take note that a three-month stay in *estufa* corresponds to five years of maturation in *canteiro*. This is a relatively quick and economical process and is used for less complex, lower-quality wines. This is a production method designed in France for cooking recipes.

– The second, *canteiro*, where the wine is placed in oak barrels positioned just below the cellar rooftops to accumulate more heat and sunshine, while subject to the oceanic rigors of winter. The best wines are stored in pipas of 418 liters, where they will spend years. Before this, the wines will have undergone an addition of alcohol during the fermentation process and at specific stages, depending on the variety and style of wine desired. Therefore, Malvasia is fortified shortly after the start of the alcoholic fermentation to obtain sweet wines (more than 60 grams of residual sugar). For Boal, it takes between two to three days of fermentation before fortification to obtain the semi-sweet (40 to 60 grams of residual sugar). Verdelho will require four to five days before the addition of neutral wine brandy at 96° for semi-dry wines (between 17 and 40 grams of residual sugar). Finally, for Sercial, fermentation can continue for one week, since a drier Madeira is sought here (less than 25 grams of residual sugar). The Madeiras, which then age for twenty years in barrels and are produced from a single varietal, then have the right to the "Frasqueira" or "Vintage" title. They must also be kept two years in bottles before being put on the market.

This additional conservation is used primarily for wine to adapt to its new environment after spending decades in barrels.

Recently another category of Madeira wines had arrived: "Colheita" wines, produced from a single grape variety, still younger than the "Frasqueira."

# Tastings at the George V, in 2014
(except for those whose dates are specified)

1910. Madeira Berbeito Sercial. *Intense topaz color, bright and luminous. Fine nose, complex, intense, chiseled. Honey notes, generous, dried fruit, dried floral, pits, dried almond, licorice, vanilla bourbon, coconut. The mouth is full, very quickly stretched, intense, very long, the aromatic plume is exemplary, like the nose with extra orange, bitter curaçao, dark chocolate powder, candy and licorice. All this with an incredible energy. A wine brought to its harmonious peak paired with a dish by Philippe Legendre: leeks tied with string, stuffed with truffles and pine nuts, served with a double consommé and warm vinaigrette.*

*I would like to pause here to discuss an iconic French dish which, upon tasting, I can't help but associate with the famous 1910 Madeira Sercial. It is the famous VGE soup of M. Paul. There are, in this dish, all the elements that pair with this wine: strength, flavor, power, character. Adjectives that also describe the creator of this dish. When I tasted it at Collonges for the first time, I couldn't help but consider this sublime pairing.*

1962. Blandy's Madeira Sercial. *Intense topaz color, cloudy. The nose is open and powerful, recalling nuts and parmesan (lactic). Note of intense woodiness, vanilla; the whole is complex, notes of spices and candy further emphasize the incredible nose. Intense mouth, reasonably smooth. Dry and tannic finish. Very aromatic retro-olfaction, cedar, candied fruits and slightly salty. Remarkable Sercial.*

# PORTUGAL
## Madeira Barbeito, Blandy's and D'Oliveiras

**1862. Madeira Sercial D'Oliveiras** *(opened in autumn 2013). Opened several days prior for the inviting host, who tasted it before the bottle was put back in the cellar. Dark amber topaz color. Nose is not very expressive at the beginning, but quickly becomes complex and intense with a hint of poultry and parmesan, slightly lactic. It will be clearer and more precise next week. Very dense mouth. The attack is relatively sharp for a Sercial. Nice length and impressive retro-olfaction. Recalls dried fruits, dried figs, sandalwood and cinnamon. A unique bouquet.*

**1981. Madeira Verdelho Frasqueira Barbeito.** *Clear topaz color, slightly cloudy. The nose is open, expressive, fruity, recalling date and apricot. Slight note of aldehyde gives off caramelized sensations. The medium-bodied mouth is quite supple. The attack is tighter. Good length in the finish. Notes of dried walnuts. Between December 2014 and January 2015, we served this Verdelho by the glass, pairing it with a preparation of truffled onions au gratin by Christian Le Squer, who gained unequivocal acclaim with this pièce de resistance.*

**1984. Blandy's Madeira Verdelho** *(bottled in 2010). Intense topaz color, very clear, recalling an aged cognac. Open nose, aldehyde, notes of grape marc, woody, rancio. Very forthright, exhausting. The alcohol is dominant. Frank attack, sweeter than the Sercial. A touch of poultry refreshes and makes the bouquet more open and warm. In the finish, it is a semi-dry Madeira that blends perfectly with a Roquefort Carles cheese accompanied by celery or a chocolate and tonka bean soufflé.*

**1959. Blandy's Madeira Boal.** *Walnut stain color, intense, brilliant (almost black), nose recalling baking, a bowl of plum jam, molasses, controlled oxidation. There reigns an impressive concentration of sensation. The mouth is sensual, round, without aggression or heaviness. The length is incredible. The retro-olfaction evokes toasted cashews, cocoa and greengage jam. Note of Antésite. This is a great Boal, begging for a Havana of great breeding and perhaps a Pu Er tea of the same vintage, as master Tseng prepares it in his Maison des Trois Thés.*

**1968. Madeira Boal D'Oliveiras.** *Golden amber color, brilliant. Open nose, very intense, woody, licorice with generous notes of fig. Marked volatile acidity upon opening (tasted again a week later, the volatile notes will be gone). The nose recalls an aged cognac with its precious woody bouquet, mocha and notes of English orange marmalade. The mouth is full, concentrated, smooth and syrupy. The finish is quite tight, the liqueur is not tiring. The balance of this Boal is instead based on energy. It's perfect for chocolate and caramel sticks.*

**1950. Madeira Terrantez D'Oliveiras.** *Brilliant amber color. Open, exhilarating and fresh nose, very intense. Notes of mocha and orange. The rancio appearance brings elegance. The mouth is full and smooth with some relief. The finish is dry, even tannic. Retro-olfaction; woody and resinous, mentholated, notes of citrus, zest of candied lemons, caramelized.*

**1795. Madeira Terrantez Barbeito** *(tasted in 2008). This was a rare half-bottle that the Smeyers, our importers from Antwerp, offered me. I kept it in my personal cellar in Paris and took it out on the occasion of a sommelier dinner at Le Cinq in January 2008. Thierry had planned a double consommé of game birds served with partridge dumplings and truffles. I had taken the precaution of opening the bottle in the cellar several days in advance. The color was a deep mahogany, intense and brilliant. Complex, dense nose, marked by notes of light caramel, dried raisins, amber and incense. The mouth was tight, with an incredible length, timeless. For a long time, there was not a sound coming from the table as the wine spoke. Far from being blown into oblivion, every minute seemed to unveil new facets. The glass empty, several hours later, the soul of the wine still clung to the walls of the chalice. For all the young people around the table, and for me, it was a unique experience.*

**1900. Madeira Malmsey Barbeito** *(bottled in 1996). Dark topaz color, bright and clear. Open nose, complex, rich and fruity. With notes of cocoa and Solies figs in wine. Stone fruits such as candied apricot, caramel and frangipani. An incredible youth. Sensual yet stretched mouth. No sluggishness, extreme length. An exceptional bottle.*

**1907. Madeira Malvasia D'Oliveiras.** *Mahogany color, brilliant. Open nose, rancio. Upon opening, the volatile acidity is marked. But what intensity! The mouth is ample, rich, heavy perhaps, and long. It reminds me of the famous Liège syrup. The finish is exemplary. Lush, complex, with notes of baked plum, mild tobacco, mocha, cigar box, cedar. It called for a rare cigar: the Partagas Salomon… fullness and bliss, harmony and softness.*

**1875. Madeira Malmsey D'Oliveiras** *(last bottle tasted in 2013). The last bottle of this wine opened at Le Cinq was for some rare customers: a small group of people from Hong Kong who visit the George V twice a year. Their peculiarity lies in the fact that they send an email to Thierry to give notice of their arrival two weeks in advance. They ask him to open a particular bottle in anticipation of their arrival – a bottle which they took the care of paying for during their last stay. They only come for one dinner! They arrive the morning of the set day,*

# PORTUGAL
## Madeira Barbeito, Blandy's and D'Oliveiras

*are joined at dinner by two couples, one from London and the other residing in New York, and take a flight out the next morning! For the choice of dishes, they trust us. The last time they came, we prepared a feuilleté of game birds with a turning coated in chestnut honey and autumn fruits. Great classic by Éric Briffard. The wine was a deep mahogany color. It proved to be much more complex than when opened a week earlier. The mouth was wide and drier than I would have thought at the beginning. The finish is almost dry. Extraordinary length. It was a silent pairing shared by the six guests.*

**1907. Madeira Moscatel D'Oliveiras.**
*Dark, almost black color. Brilliant. Intense, open nose, compote, candied with notes of bitter orange marmalade. A lot of richness and sweetness. Soft mouth, generous and creamy. Raisins, honey, sensual mouth, slightly heavy. Touch of bitterness in the finish. Interminable length. This wine reminds me of the Rutherglen liqueur Muscat in the State of Victoria. Must be appreciated with a Christmas pudding with my friend Gérard Basset in Hampshire.*

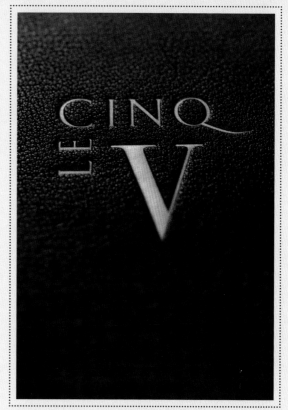

# DOMAINE DISZNÓKÖ
# THE GOLD OF THE MAGYARS

I t was through Jean-François Ragot that I discovered the wines of Tokaji in the mid-1990s. A charismatic manager, an incredible braggart from Dionis, in Orliénas, at the door of Lyon, he was one of the few in France to promote the great sweet wines of Europe and the Southern Hemisphere. He led me to discover the Noble One from the De Bortoli family in Australia, as well as the Vin de Constance from Klein Constantia in South Africa. He particularly specialized in sweet wines from Burgenland in Austria and Tokaji from Hungary. Through many tastings in his vault, the idea came to us in 1995 to acquire some vines in the Tokaj vineyards. Since 1992, the Hungarian government has allowed foreign investors to acquire great domains. Several large French and European businesses have taken over illustrious properties. In 1993, the Álvarez family, owner of Vega Sicilia, purchased Oremus, one of the jewels of Tokaj.

In order to realize our project, I went to Hungary several times. These vineyards are located in the foothills of the Zemplén mountain range, northeast of the capital, on the borders of the Slovak Republic and Ukraine. It took four hours and a considerable number of stops to cover the 200 kilometers between Budapest and the village of Tolcsva, at the heart of the vineyard. There, Jean-François, who was waiting for me in an old Renault 19, led the way.

Our first actions were to heed the advice of one of the vineyard pillars, Tibor Kovács. He was and still is the cornerstone of Domaine Hétszölö. At 6 foot 2, he is a strapping man, calm and powerful. Armed with recommendations and addresses, we roamed the hills north to south along the Bodrog River with Jean-François. I was overwhelmed when I first visited these vineyards; interspersed with stone walls and hedges, the farms and the villages seemed to have escaped the industrialization of the twentieth century. What surprised me the most, however, were the labyrinths of cellars, dug by hand in the volcanic rock. Their existence dates back to the reign of King

Kálmán I, in 1110. They have the distinction of not being attached to the wine buildings or domains and are instead scattered throughout the vineyards and hills, almost invisible to the eye. Only the entrance, protected by a heavy wrought-iron gate or studded oak door, emerges from the hillside, like a Hobbit house. As early as 1561, there is a reference to Aszú wines being produced in these cellars. In 1700, fifty-six years before the demarcation of the Douro vineyards by the Marquis de Pombal, the Rákóczi princes undertook the first classification of terroirs of the Tokaji region. This family ruled over this region from the twelfth century on. One of its illustrious members, Prince Ferenc II Rákóczi, was the one who presented the Tokaji at the court of Louis XIV, thus ensuring the renown of its production throughout Europe. In 1804, more than fifty years before the Médoc, a comprehensive ranking of the vineyards of twenty-eight villages composing the wine region was created. The result was a hierarchy organized into grands crus, premier, second and troisième crus. This classification would endure until the end of the Austro-Hungarian Empire. For many years, the Hungarian production of quality wine would be synonymous with Tokaji.

Today, the entirety of this wine region, unique in its kind, has been a Unesco World Heritage Site since 2002. This classification contributes to the revitalization of this once extremely prosperous vineyard, first swept away by phylloxera and then by the conflicts of political events in the twentieth century. When the country was toppled during the communist era, the vineyards covered more than 5,000 hectares. The domains were combined into a single state entity, and the production was intensified and managed by immense cooperatives, also regulated by the state. These wines were exclusively exported to member countries of the Comecon (the common market of countries allied with the USSR). With Jean-François, we all felt the weight of this system in place for decades. We were passionate about this vineyard to the point of wanting to buy, in the heart of Mount Tokaj, a parcel of the melegoldal grand cru's terroir, but the sprawling and complex system of the former Communist administrative regime eventually dissuaded us.

It took time for us to choose the domains seriously, to understand them, before finding the desired wines. Disznókö was not my preference. Axa, purchasing the domain in 1992, had wiped the slate clean with large investments. The first vintages saw the light in agony. We steered towards other wines. These trips led me to quickly develop a cup service of Tokaji Aszú at La Poularde. We created, with chefs Bernard Barret and Philippe Sailly, entrées calling for these wines. Jean-François devised his own cuvée from wines selected from trusted domains under Château de Sárospatak, named after a village located in the Tokaj vineyards.

A few years later, the Tokaji wines were the first to be delivered to the temporary offices of the George V in June 1999, then on Avenue Pierre-I$^{er}$-de-Serbie. It was a selection of several vintages of István Szepsy Tokaji Aszú 6 Puttonyos. I met this great figure of the Tokaj wine revival during a visit. It was he who first showed me the principle of extraction for the essence of Tokaji. An open tapered barrel is filled to the brim with Aszú Furmint grains. A keg key is placed and left open under a terracotta jug. Drop by drop, under the weight of the grains, a dense and dark juice flows out. This natural extract of candied berries by *Botrytis cinerea* or *passerillées* will then ferment for years to finally titrate at 2 to 3° of alcohol and be stored in cylinders, indefinitely, as needed. With István, I found in this responsible and passionate man all the possible emotion that the independent winemaker could possess.

For years at Le Cinq, I have been able to serve, with Philippe Legendre's cuisine, Château de Sárospatak and Szepsy wines. We created a dish with the chef that has been a classic at Le Cinq for almost ten years, an association of both the barnyard and the sea: a Bresse chicken and Breton lobster stewed with tarragon and spices in an added consommé of iced lobster, served in a luted copper casserole dish. The delicately reduced nage is whisked in lobster sauce, with an added dash of Tokaji. A delectable dish.

Some time after the arrival of Éric Briffard, a new era of my relationship with this vineyard was born. In 2010, I met Vincent Gournac, in charge of the marketing of Axa Millésimes wines. He introduced me to a new kind of cuvée. It was the 2005 Kapi Vineyard Tokaji. From the start, I was seduced by the luminosity of the color, the freshness of the flavors, the sharpness in the mouth. I was not expecting the work undertaken at Disznókö to achieve this quality (the domain covers 104 hectares of vineyards). Soon, we began to serve this cuvée made from a single vineyard, with only the Furmint variety. This rediscovery inspired me to return there. So, we set a date with

# HUNGARY
## Domaine Disznókö

Vincent Gournac. In early autumn 2011, we were ready to go. For the first time, we would be travelling to a vineyard with Marie, my wife, Thierry and Nicolas, his partner. It was important to experience these moments together. We can never thank our partners enough for their patience in the pursuit of our interests. All six of us (Vincent's wife was also able to join us) met in Budapest. Serving at the George V provides some nice amenities, like being received in the most famous hotel in the capital, Gresham Palace, under the Four Seasons. Our arrival was even more momentous when, on the palace piazza, I recognized the director general, Yves Giacometti. He was, for many years, director of the George V, chaired by Didier Le Calvez.

The Four Seasons Gresham Palace Hotel is located on the banks of the Danube on the Pest side, opposite the Széchenyi Chain Bridge, or, in French, the "Pont des chaînes Széchenyi," named for the man behind the project in 1839, Comte István Széchenyi. We had the advantage of rooms opening, on one side, onto this work of art and, on the other, the high city of Buda. We began with a visit to Pest's huge indoor market. The belly of Budapest, like the one in Paris before it was demolished… there we enjoyed a pint of draft beer, bitter and refreshing, at a counter while munching on salty, hot and delicious waffle fries. Then, with lunchtime approaching, we took Yves's recommendation and trekked the uplands of Buda to the Café Pierrot. A table was given to us in the small inner courtyard with a lush and relaxing garden. The wine list offered a 1998 Veuve Clicquot Grande Dame, conveniently located at the end, which I ordered once again.

For the goulash, savoury with a beautiful paprika hue, we bypassed the wine. However, the deer fillet from the Germenc forest, with black salsifies, called for a red wine of character. My eyes fell on a reference that I did not expect to find there: a 2006 *Domaine de Villeneuve Chateauneuf-du-Pape* by Stanislas Wallut. The Châteauneuf domain, available at Le Cinq, has the distinction of being planted with the Grenache, Syrah, Mourvèdre, Cinsault and Clairette varieties, which compose its assembly and are planted together, pruned into a goblet shape. Stanislas particularly succeeded with this vintage. It paired perfectly.

Only one option remained after this time on the uplands: a journey through the Széchenyi baths, one of the largest historic bathing sites in Europe. After several hours of ablutions and, not to mention, changing into a suit, we were ready for dinner. In remembrance of my first visit to Budapest, I wanted to share a particular landmark of the capital: the Gundel. The place had not changed, with the same decor, the same atmosphere and the same dishes, which I recognized as they left the kitchens. Looking around the room, it was easy to imagine at the tables actors from the film *Le Serpent* by Henri Verneuil, with the academician shouting "Action!" We chose hearty dishes, the height of which was the house specialty, a kind of pancake typical of Central Europe: a palacsinta cream with nut filling, flambéed with cognac.

The evening was punctuated by Hungarian rhapsodies and international hits, which were selected based on the nationalities of the guests present that night. The site's Gypsy orchestra, composed of violinists, a bassist and a cymbalist on a very intricate cimbalom, was the image of this breathless place. A timeless day full of laughter and gluttony. And, most importantly: we were together!

The next day we boarded a train for Tokay, taking a lot less time than I remember to reach our destination. It was László Mészáros, director of Disznókö since 2000, who greeted us. It was he, with considerable resources at his disposal, who was the source of the qualitative acceleration taken by the property. Under his leadership, we began with a tour of the vineyard with clayey limestone slopes, before commencing a wonderful tasting.

HUNGARY
Domaine Disznókö

# Tasting at the domain, in October 2011

2010. Furmint Sec *(screw cap)*. *Crystalline color, fresh nose, lively, still fermenting. Balanced mouth, quite fluid, saline. Light bitters in the finish. This wine produces up to 30,000 bottles per year. It is offered for about 5 euros on the French market! This cuvée is the result of the changing consumer market. The lower demand for sweet wines has led to a preference for dry wines.*

*This allows the domain to continue to operate and, at the same time, to concentrate on the production of more elaborate, better defined and more precise sweet wines. To some extent, this evolving market is parallel with that encountered in the Douro with Port wine and, to some extent, our great sweet wines of Sauternes.*

# Tasting of Tokajï Aszú

2007. Tokajï 5 Puttonyos. *Tokaji Aszús are made from Furmint, Zéta (cross between Furmint and Bouvier) and Hárslevelü. Pale yellow, exotic nose, fresh pineapple, vanilla. Wide mouth, very present liqueur. Long.*

2006. Tokajï 5 Puttonyos. *Wine with beautiful definition, yellow peach nose, candied citrus. Mouth has a nice balance.*

2003. Tokajï 5 Puttonyos. *(145 grams of residual sugar) Solar Vintage, very well maintained. A rich wine, complete, long.*

2002. Tokajï 5 Puttonyos. *(150 grams of residual sugar). Deep yellow color, brilliant. The nose is discreet, dense, complete and fine. Notes of apricot and honey. Tangerine peel. Great density in the mouth. A rich attack, tight, and a full and dense mid-palate. Long and persistent finish. A superb 2002 with very nice evolution.*

2000. Tokajï 5 Puttonyos. *Intense yellow-gold color. Confectionery nose, a solar vintage, wax, forest honey. The mouth is dominated by the liqueur. Here, more than 180 grams of residual sugar. Quince paste, yellow fruit jam.*

1999. Tokajï 6 Puttonyos. *Clear topaz color, luminous. Open, intense nose, aromatic honey and candied apricot. An intense olfactory sweetness showing great concentration. Notes of quince and medlar jam. Medium-bodied mouth. The balance is fine, created by a well-preserved acidity. Nice length with a half-body style.*

HUNGARY
Domaine Disznókö

**1997. Tokajï 6 Puttonyos.** *Intense amber color. The relatively low acidity in this cuvée slightly relaxes the mouth, softening it.*

**1993. Tokajï 6 Puttonyos.** *First vintage after Axa's takeover. Topaz, dark amber color. Very candied nose, very cooked bitter orange jam. Light oxidation notes. The mouth is doughy with a butterscotch and baked potato aftertaste. A style belonging to the past.*

**2006. Tokajï 6 Puttonyos** *(recently bottled). Cuvée exclusively developed with Furmint. Although marked by breeding at this stage, the wine has a lot of energy and richness. Balanced. Foretells a beautiful future.*

**2005. Kapi Vineyard Tokajï 6 Puttonyos** *(production limited to 5,600 bottles). This wine is 100% Furmint. Pale yellow-gold color, brilliant. The nose is fine. Sweet, intense aromas. The sharpness is interpreted by floral and vanilla aromas. Mentholated notes, verbena, lemon grass, remarkable delicacy. Notes of juicy Bergeron apricots. Wide mouth, dense and complete. Great purity, long and elegant finish. Congratulations for separating this Kapi cru, which is distinguished by its brilliance and sharpness. I look forward to the 2011.*

**2005. Eszencia.** *Two figures: 600 grams of residual sugar and 2° alcohol. This is not a wine but a syrupy sweet wine which permeates. The most impressive element lies in the incredible freshness of the essence of Tokajï. The color is an intense gold, deep, slightly opaque. The nose is a cornucopia, overflowing with lemon bergamot, candied bitter orange peel, propolis, porcini powder. It is a concentrate of life.*

# Legends of the Tokajï Essence

*This nectar was so coveted in the nineteenth century that the Russian Tsars had it escorted to St. Petersburg by a regiment of Cossacks. Legend has it that, at the imperial court, when a family member asked for the Sacrament of Extreme Unction, a butler would serve them a glass of Tokaj to extend their life until a priest could arrive. Lastly, regarding this wine, Voltaire spoke of it in these terms, "The Tokaj Aszú is an amber beverage of brilliant colors, weaving the golden threads of the mind and making the most spiritual words sparkle."*

# MARCIANO ESTATE
## THE STUFF OF DREAMS

T**he friendship binding me to the Marciano brothers was born at the George V. Gradually, throughout their hotel stays and dinners at Le Cinq, we came to know one another. That was how I discovered their interest in the great wines of Bordeaux and the importance of their collection, albeit with one slight difference: the treasures they collect are consumed! For them, it was out of the question to simply purchase them for the sake of ownership. They acquired wines so that, one day, they would serve them at their table and share them with friends.

This love of wine inevitably led to their purchasing a wine domain. A very distant choice from their professional world, centered on fashion and haute couture, yet similar through the concept of creation, movement and the cycle of seasons.

They chose Napa Valley and the Village of Saint Helena, known for its high quality of wines. Maurice Marciano acquired an old property built by Franciscan monks in the early nineteenth century. They started from scratch, beginning with the vineyard, in very poor condition. After extensive work in the parcels, the first vines were planted in 2005. They could count on an important talent to advise them in what was required in these vineyards: David Abreu. For the management of the vineyards and cellar: Andy Erickson.

This creation of a domain and vineyard, which I was able to witness, was an amazing experience for me. It is very rare to discover terroirs in Europe, where the vineyards date back centuries or even millennia. In Napa, however, it is still possible to create, from a fallow terroir, a burgeoning vineyard. It is inspiring! I was able to be present for each stage of this creation:
– The choice of terroir in the appellation area.
– The selection of the best exposed and facing hillsides.
– Clearing and soil preparation.
– The implementation of a water drainage system in certain sites.

UNITED STATES
Marciano Estate

– The choice of varieties, vine management and sizes.

There were so many discussions and tastings! Plans also needed to be drawn up for the winery, cellars and technical systems. This led to the choice of fermentation vats and systems ensuring optimum winemaking in terms of technicalities and grapes.

Late at night, I would respond to emails from Maurice and David, asking me countless questions. The work, from the beginning, had been both healthy and energetic with the arrival of Andy Erickson, head of cultivation and cellars, who had earned many accolades in the region. He was joined by Stéphane Derenoncourt, offering further expertise.

Not being a native of Napa, although having visited many times since 1996, I only began to understand the climate of the region after an airship flyover in 2012. We left early in the morning from Maurice and Andy's property with the pilot. We ascended to 350 meters. For three hours, we witnessed the topography of these fantastic landscapes caught between East and West, and two mountain ranges, Howell Mountain, northeast, and the Mayacamas Mountains, southwest. Most mesmerizing, however, was that in the middle of the valley, a cloud layer withdrew in the direction of the San Pablo Bay. Then, appearing on the hillsides, in golden waves, the rays of the rising sun. While nature offered us this vision, every day renewed yet different, we received a lesson from the air, lectured by Andy, on the surrounding vineyards. He explained that the sun can be disastrous if too powerful. Also, here the clouds have a beneficial effect as they protect the grapes from sunburn. This microclimate is barely visible in the valley. In fact, the cold Alaskan current laps at the California coast. It is not uncommon to find elephant seals on the coast of Monterey. The great San Francisco Bay sucks in all the cold air coming towards the valley. The closer the vineyards are to the bay, the cooler they are, and vice versa.

Another particularity of Napa: the alluvial soil of volcanic origin found around Maurice's home. These volcanic movements occur in the region of Saint Helena through the appearance of sporadic geysers.

The harvest of this first vintage, 2012, took place at night to preserve the freshness of the berries and to bring in fresh grapes to the cellar. Here, to curb the natural power of the climate, and sometimes even the heat of the afternoon, 10% of the most fragile vines benefit from a drip irrigation system.

The choice of grape varieties planted took time and was well planned. The investment was considerable. Only 5 hectares of vineyards planted to date in a total plantation estimated at 50 hectares. The parcels consist of Cabernet Sauvignon (90%), Cabernet Franc (7%) and Petit Verdot (3%).

In March 2014, I eagerly flew to Napa to attend the assembly of the first cuvée from the first harvest of the Maurice Marciano domain. Paul and Armand, Maurice's brothers, but also Andy and Christian Navarro (in charge of the domain's activity) were all there for the 2012 birth. At many tastings, we were tempted to add more Petit Verdot to brand the area's character. We tried to recreate, with Maurice, a wine closer to his Bordeaux aspirations. The first wine, with an intense garnet color and shapely legs, at once silky and velvety, could be displayed in its glass case, dressed in its colors, donning a collar clamped around the neck ring. Soon, it was paraded to the tables. We celebrated this birth on the property where Maurice and his brothers reside. Everything here is locally produced: vegetables, fruits, olive oil, honey and flowers arranged in the bedrooms and salons. This is a haven of peace, serenity, love of life, good wine, women and thinking, respectful of a lifestyle to which they have always dedicated themselves with passion.

## UNITED STATES
### Marciano Estate

# MEMORIES

If I had to define Maurice Marciano in one word, it would be: generosity. Rarely would a passionate aficionado of his stature allow me to taste and discover such rare, high-end wines in such abundance. One of the last dinners he invited me to was, in every way, worthy of my praise. During this stay in 2014, I was at the Four Seasons Beverly Wiltshire, thanks to the benefits offered to Group employees worldwide. Maurice and his brother Paul awaited me. They had prepared a lunch, among friends, as well as a blind tasting. Despite this fact, there were some elements that were known to me. In fact, Maurice and Paul almost exclusively consumed mature Bordeaux crus.

Lunch consisted of a single dish: grilled Wagyu rib steak and a large salad of crisp greens. For the first wine, consumed while conversing, they made the blunder of mentioning it to me. It was a bottle of 1990 La Mission Haut-Brion. An amazing achievement of La Mission in this vintage. It was at once creamy, pulpy, woody and fine, with licorice. With a full mouth, spherical. Delicious, such charm!

The second wine had a ruby color, with orange reflections, luminous. Maurice asked me, without awaiting more description, "What do you think?" – "To me, we're in the 1970s." Correct. So, it remained either 1970 or 1975, the other vintages not really surviving today. The nose, however, seemed a bit faded, with notes of graphite, mineral and fruits in brandy. The acidity was marked, the attack full, and the tannins blended. If it were a 1975, it would have had a heavier finish and a less evolved nose. By the graphite nose, I immediately thought of Latour. Stroke of luck, it was a 1970 Latour!

This unexpected tasting was followed several days later by a special dinner at their estate, during which they served:

– A 2003 Dom Pérignon Rosé, still incredibly fresh and full-bodied. A great wine. With poached eggs and caviar and lemon sour cream.

– A 1990 Château Margaux, with an intense ruby color, delicate floral nose of dried violet and a touch of cedar. Without maturity or deviation. Remarkable body, great balance. Very straightforward, great length, supreme elegance. Very nice with poached lobster, herbs and truffle mousse with hazelnut butter.

– A 1982 Château Lafleur, certainly one of the finest 1982s at the moment. Dark color, intense, deep nose, very concentrated, black fruit and truffles. Vibrant. Smooth mouth, full, without troughs on the mid-palate, very long, still young. Admirable retro. Nice harmony with chicken stuffed with summer truffles, green asparagus and Albufera sauce. Very velvety texture. Fits perfectly with the poultry meat.

– A 1961 Château La Mission Haut-Brion: upon opening, it seemed a bit cloudy. It was carefully decanted. Do not interpret these notes as cork; some time after opening proved me right. Nose of cigar box. The mouth had an exemplary concentration with touches of candied fruits, balsamic notes, cypress wood and Landes pine. Slightly camphorated. We tasted it by itself in the extension of the dish, without asking for anything but time.

That evening, like the lunch they organized for me, was once again testament of their friendship and rare generosity. For any amateur, for any passionate sommelier, the opportunities to taste these wines at their full maturity are always so rewarding.

# HARLAN ESTATE
## FRENCH INSPIRATION

T he first time I met Bill Harlan and his wife Deborah, it was at Château Latour, in 2001, during a Vinexpo dinner. On my first trip to California, I did not dare knock on the door of this prestigious domain. It was upon speaking to them, at the table, that we agreed on a meeting. It came to fruition the summer of 2002 during a trip with Marie and the children.

The iconic nature of the Harlan estate began with its progenitor, William Harlan, called Bill. He was a quiet man, composed, pragmatic and visionary. The place was simple, human-scaled. Compared to our famous domains, the Harlan Estate is a spring chicken. The idea of buying an estate took root for Harlan in the early 1970s during a meeting with Robert Mondavi. In 1979, a project led him to take up the Meadowood domain, which was, firstly, a renowned golf club. Instead of planting vines on the greens, he developed a hotel, now a member of Relais & Châteaux. In this lush setting, the same Mondavi suggested creating an association of winemakers in Napa Valley. This association now has over 500 members. Every year a huge gala – a "paulée," as they say in Meursault – brings together more than 1,000 people. It was from this association that Bill decided to establish a large, annually held auction, modeled after the Hospices de Beaune. To this end, he undertook a six-week trip to France, split between Bordeaux and Burgundy. In this journey, he was accompanied by his mentor, Robert Mondavi.

From this trip, he developed a profound connection to the Bordeaux varietals and a reverence for these Burgundian parcels, lovingly maintained by generations of winemakers. It was in this direction that he started to look for an estate. In his research, he understood that, since the arrival of the first European immigrants in the mid-nineteenth century, it was in the Rutherford-Oakville area that the best wines were produced. It was the pioneering era of Magyar Agoston Haraszthy's work (called "Count Haraszthy" by the Prussian and Austrian settlers of California), considered a viticultural innovator. This aristocrat was the first Hungarian to permanently immigrate to the US. In 1856, he settled in Sonoma after carrying out varietal planting trials in the San Diego area. A year later, he founded his first vineyard – Buena Vista – and hired, as a winemaker, Charles Krug (no relation to the Champagne-based family, other than his Rhenish origin). The latter created his own winery in Saint Helena in 1861. In 1943, the Mondavi family purchased the winery. It was here that Robert would establish himself before creating his own winery in Oakville.

In 1858, Haraszthy wrote a nineteen-page report on grapes and wine from California, now considered the first treatise dedicated to the subject. He traveled through France, Germany, Switzerland and Spain before returning to California in December 1861, with over 100,000 cuttings of more than 350 vine varieties. Several years later, Sonoma, and then all of California, were affected by phylloxera. The insect was first described in 1855 by Asa Fitch, one of the most prominent American entomologists. The proliferation of this insect was circumvented by the use of a resistant rootstock, also discovered in California. Despite these advances, the vineyard suffered the devastating earthquake of 1906, and the enactment of Prohibition annihilated all efforts in the 1920s. It was not until the 1950s, with the arrival of the Mondavis, that quality wine-making was revived in Napa Valley.

Armed with this knowledge, Bill Harlan had the intuition of settling on the uplands of Oakville, in the hills, well beyond other, established domains. Making this decision, he was one of the first to understand the qualitative factor of the Napa hills. This man, starting out in wine, had previously built his fortune on real estate in San Francisco. After his visits to France, he understood the importance of the domain's location. He acquired his land in 1984 and began to clear and plant the following year. At the time, Napa had no more than twenty-five domains. The first vintage was produced and marketed in 1990, but, rare in California, it was not placed on the market until 1996. The lower production of this wine made it rare from the start. It was then put up for a charity auction by the association he had created of winemakers from Napa to Meadowood, adding to its prestige. When, in 1994, Robert Parker ascribed to it a supreme grade of 100/100, it was an absolute consecration! This grade was again attributed to the vintages of 1997, 2001, 2002 and 2007. Today, it is one of the most sought-after and popular wines in Napa Valley, only surpassed by the wines of Screaming Eagle.

The property is located on the west side of the valley, in the Oakville area on the east. It extends over 100 hectares. Only 17 hectares of vineyards are planted, with 70% Cabernet Sauvignon, 20% Merlot, 8% Cabernet Franc and 2% Petit Verdot. The soil is volcanic in places and, for the most part, with rather clayey parcels.

If today the domain is equipped with technology at the forefront of modernity, it still remains traditional in its use of conical vats, like those of Château Margaux. The wines are aged twenty to twenty-four months in Bordeaux barrels. The current cellar was inaugurated in 2002. It integrates perfectly with the landscape of surrounding hills, vineyards, olive groves and forests crowning the hills.

# M EMORIES

One of my fondest memories associated with Harlan remains a dinner organized in 2007 by Maurice Marciano, in Los Angeles. Around the table were Christopher Norton, Maurice, Bill and Deborah Harlan, and Ann Colgin and Joe Wender. The meal was prepared by Thomas Keller, culinary star in the US with three Michelin stars at The French Laundry in Napa: Yountville. A friend of the Marciano's. The entrée consisted of velvety Holland asparagus, crispy quail eggs and garden radishes with herbs. To accompany it, Maurice opened a 2006 Araujo Sauvignon Blanc: always aromatic, slightly reduced, a bit exotic with a nice tension. A feat for the Calistoga cru, the hottest region of Napa Valley.

The chef then prepared his fresh tagliatelles with truffles, with a very dense and powerful 1997 Colgin Cariad. A wine made to last. Then, grilled Angus beefsteaks and potatoes with black trumpet mushrooms, bordelaise sauce and, like a fresh bouquet, hearts of lettuce and romaine with crisp beans.

Bill brought us a 1994 Harlan Estate: very deep, even opaque color, dense, generous nose, stewed black currant, black olives, spicy. Very dense, tight. We were a bit reluctant with the alcohol. The mouth was very full, with a

soft sensation. Open structure. One of the famous 100% grades by Parker. Always a wonderful moment to taste these wines in abundance, with their owners, and, outside of commercial parameters, to ask questions no one usually dares broach. The wine, simply, by itself.

## UNITED STATES
### Harlan Estate

# Tasting at the domain, in 2013

Both of Bill's right-hand men were present during the tasting: Don Weaver (director of Harlan Estate) and Bob Levy (head of cultivation), both a part of the endeavor since 1981.

In the 1990s, the vineyards were placed in the capable hands of David Abreu, always present during the harvests. They are then grafted to the liking of Cory Empting, the young cellar master. He embodies the succession and patrimonial transmission of Bill Harlan. For him, there is no success without transmission, also a lesson learned during his stay in France. Hailing from our country is also the consultant – the flying winemaker – of the domain since 1988: Michel Rolland.

Although not responsible for tasting, we must recall the 1999 creation of the cuvée, The Maiden, another wine produced at the domain on a basis of 75% Cabernet Sauvignon, completed with Merlot, Cabernet Franc and Petit Verdot. Another "Harlanesque" project in the works: Bond. To be continued...

**2012.** Harlan *(in barrel). Opaque ruby color, open nose, notes of black fruit, elegant, full mouth without excess, touch of delicate tannins. The mouth is smooth. The whole is consistent. This is a more elegant than powerful Harlan.*

**2010.** *Deep ruby color. Dense. Powerful and generous nose, woody. Full attack, licorice. At this stage, the wood marks the blend a bit. The tannins are tight. The wine is heavy, slightly austere.*

**2009.** *The nose is open, fine, woody note of cedar and cigar box. Attack in the mouth thinner than 2010, slightly flowing mid-palate. Slightly dry finish. It's a rather soft Harlan.*

**2008.** *Open nose, fresh, fruity, recalling vine peach. Great fullness in the mouth, it is elegant, the level of freshness is optimum. Delicate tannins still rather tight. It is a balanced wine without the excess of 2010. It is more dynamic.*

**2007.** *Very dense color, open and powerful nose. The black fruit is marked, vine peach, licorice, intense. Very wide attack in the mouth. Profound and complete mid-palate. Finish of sappy tannins. A great success.*

**1997.** *(In magnum). Very rare! Black color, intense, concentrated nose. Still closed, incredible. Full-bodied, present tannins. I found the tannins present, austere even. Related to the container preserving the wine, with rapid evolution. It needs a few more years of aging, perhaps more than ten years, before reaching its potential. However, there were only 300 magnums in this vintage. How many are still sleeping, awaiting a more favorable hour for their stirring?*

DOMAINE BOINGNÈRES P 534

DOMAINE DE SEMAINVILLE P 541

LA GRANDE-CHARTREUSE P 548

CHÂTEAU HAUTEVILLE P 559

ÉRIC BORDELET BRASSERIE CANTILLON P 564

# Spirits Liqueurs Ciders and Beer

# DOMAINE BOINGNÈRES
## THE MUSKETEER
## OF LANDES

T he world of brandy is often associated with men. However, it also includes women – and one of them, who has a strong disposition (it should also be noted), is Martine Lafitte. I am taking you to the confines of the Landes and Gers. It is a region without a highway (well, nearly) – a region with green hills, dotted with vines planted on gentle slopes. Here and there, the vineyards are joined by fields of wheat and corn… a lot of corn. These fields are often bordered by rivers and streams with tawny sand beds. And, then, there are farmhouses that demand our attention, ones with marvelous names such as: Labastide d'Armagnac.

Evoking the name, I remember the poem *The Flute of Bertrandou* by Edmond Rostand, found in *Cyrano de Bergerac* (Act IV, Scene 3), particularly the last stanza:

"Listen, Gascons… It is no longer, under his fingertips,

The piercing fife of the camps, it is the flute of the woods!

It is no longer the call to combat, on his lips,

It is the slow galoubet of our goat-herders!…

Listen… It is the valley, the moor, the forest,

It is the dusk of unripe sweetness on the Dordogne,

Listen, Gascons: it is all of Gascony!"

Since the time referenced in these verses, this beautiful village built around its square plaza, with its stone archways and classified facades, has not changed,. Of course, today it is lovingly maintained by… the English and Dutch who vacation there.

I've often had the opportunity to defend this region, such as in a competition held for the title of 1992 Best Sommelier of France and that of the 1994 Best Sommelier of Europe. At the time, competitions already made it necessary to know all spirits and liqueurs of France and Europe. This essential knowledge has since been extended to the world. That is fine with me. For after all these years in the midst of competitions, I know better to appreciate the intricacies of our great French brandy. On this occasion, beyond the fact that I won the title of Best Taster of Armagnac, I had the pleasure of meeting great people, ones who ardently defended their terroirs and their unique brandies.

The late 1990s was the last time the restaurants of Paris and the provinces eagerly supported the producing regions, including Normandy, Cognac, Landes and Gers. Today, eating habits, hygienists of all sorts and regulations work against the tasting of these products that contribute worldwide to France's image and stature. I remember being in Montrond with Thierry at the end of 1995; we were still opening Gascon bottles from the 1930s, well protected in their wooden casings, during memorable family meals of thirty to forty guests in a private, indoor room. I fear this era has been expunged. It was during this time that I discovered the great Bas-Armagnacs of Martine's father, who would come himself to deliver them to M. Randoing at La Poularde in the 1980s, a beret on his head.

More recently, in early 2000, I was able to participate in some sessions of an association created by die-hards: The Five Legendary Crus. It included important families, such as the Laberdolives, the de Luzes (Château de Briat), the Grassas (Domaine du Tariquet), the late Comte de Boisséson (Château de Lacquy) and Martine Lafitte. These meetings were great for amateurs to attend because we could go on forever about the benefits of a given choice within vine populations – for or against the use of Baco, for example. While on the subject, it should be noted that this hybrid results from a cross between the Folle-Blanche of the *Vitis vinifera* strain and a grape variety of the *Vitis riparia* strain, a unique case in French viticulture. During these verbal jousts, some would also broadcast their opinions on whether or not to use new barrels. There were fierce defenders of the tradition, tenacious and reassuring, and on the other side, there was a throbbing desire to change the habits of empirical, ancestral knowledge. We met around a good table after sharing a hearty morning snack, while a trickle of white brandy flowed clear from the alembic, to be lodged in a barrel. The distillation room, around the alembic tray, was filled with unique scents, floral and fruity. What an atmosphere! And these songs in Béarn, what a life!

With Thierry, we stayed at the Château de Lacquy with the Boissésons. To get there, we had to get off the municipal road and, after several minutes on a logging road, we reached the sublime residence. The Comtesse was in the library, comfortably seated in a broad armchair covered in garnet velvet with an upholstered back, surrounded by books with antique bindings. A nice fire crackled in the fireplace – she had a Simone de Beauvoir way about her. We chatted for a few minutes and then took our luggage to our rooms. I was always on the noble main floor. Thierry found himself in the attic, which at another time would house domestic servants and which now is reserved for younger family members visiting relatives. From there, the morning view of the surrounding lands, in the morning mist, was magical. The silence was absolute, broken only by the flight of a few pigeons and the graceful jump of deer. These blissful moments were interspersed with round trips to various cellars.

Nonetheless, it seems that these passionate debates remained no less vain. It is true that this appellation does not benefit from a common strategy in terms of communication, marketing or distribution. There is no high-visibility brand for these brandies, no locomotive to draw in key qualitative players of Armagnac. Of course, the different sub-regions (Armagnac, Bas-Armagnac, Ténarèze) are fragmented. The properties, folded over themselves. So many elements, while at the same time, each one preserving its uniqueness. This is also what draws me here. But is it enough in the ambient business environment? Regardless, I hope with all my heart that people like Martine will long be able to offer us brandies such as the ones I now describe to you.

# SPIRITS
## Domaine Boingnères

Folle-Blanche produces especially lively and rustic wine, enhanced by the alembic's alchemy. To do so, the size of the brandy depends on the dexterity of the distiller. Martine maintains her father's method. The alembic is also of his making. It optimizes the hearts of distillation, properly removing the heads and tails. This is also called the "petites eaux," namely, the first trickles of the brandy that come out of the alembic and the last, both of lesser quality, are removed from the heart of the heating, the finest brandy. She does everything to conserve the soul of this domain of which today she is the guardian and owner, as well as the custodian of a legacy. For, among the Lafittes, time is important. It is conserved and protected by the work of two generations.

The geographic area of the Grand Bas-Armagnac is characterized by outcrops of clay-siliceous soil on tawny sands and boulbène (hard clay loaded with concretions, also called *terrebouc*). These geological features are associated with unusual varieties, an oceanic climate and a unique method of continuous tray distillation molding the occasionally sharp character of this brandy (but one certainly not lacking in charm). The purest, the one that claims my preference, is the one from the Folle-Blanche distillation! It is impetuous, direct and terribly spicy. A true character.

We serve both older and newer vintages daily at Le Cinq. It should be noted that each one still includes the date it was bottled. For example, the 2001 was only bottled in 2013! The time is extended as much as possible and if the maturation is "quicker" than other vintages, it is evidence of Martine's wish to preserve the tonic freshness of its Folle-Blanche. Here, the Bas-Armagnacs always titrate around 49-48% vol.

# M

## EMORIES

The greatest table moment with Martine was a lunch in her home on a beautiful summer's day in 2008, with Thierry and Nicolas, his friend. We had a morning tasting in the cellars, but an untimely delay led us to the property at cocktail hour. Meanwhile, Martine had taken the lead: a Bollinger Special Cuvée in an ice bucket was waiting for us in the salon, along with small, broiled, smoked sausages and flute glasses. This salon, adjacent to the dining room, emanated tranquility and a sweetness of time, recalling the setting conveyed in the splendid descriptions of Henri Troyat in *Viou*, which I read near the end of my schooling. The floors exhaled beeswax; the room, plunged into semi-darkness, remained cool in this month of August, thanks to the bay windows overlooking the garden. The large table was covered with an immaculate linen tablecloth, the napkins – huge – with the monogram of Martine's mother alongside beautiful Limoges china and silverware that had served several generations of gourmets.

The faithful housekeeper announced that we were served. We sat down to enjoy a lobe of semi-cooked duck *foie gras*, cooked in a cloth, accompanied by country toast with a thick and fragrant crust. It was simply joined by a Jurançon Moelleux Pour René from our dear Yvonne Hégoburu from the Domaine de Souch, in a 1996 vintage. A superb vintage wine, thanks to the *Botrytis cinerea* of an exceptional purity.

Following which, to this day remains my most memorable savory dish, a salmi of pigeon. The ragout had long simmered in its glazed earthen casserole dish in the corner of the furnace – we gave in and took three helpings! Especially since the harmony was perfect with the 1990 Château Montus Cuvée Prestige, a famous Madiran cuvée by Alain Brumont, great defender of the Tannat, the king grape variety of that appellation.

After this delectable dish, magret and confit duck legs grilled and crusted to perfection, without any sauce, arrived from the kitchen, simply accompanied by a frisée with walnut oil and a few drops of lemon juice, the bowl rubbed with garlic. The dish was accompanied by a beautiful Pomerol, the 1995 Château La Conseillante.

At this point, I admit that we were slouched in our chairs and fairly well sated. However, we still did the honors with the tomme (cheese) of sheep's

## SPIRITS
## Domaine Boingnères

milk from the Ossau Valley. Then came the final blow – toasted, like us – in the guise of a warm croustade (cobbler) landaise with Armagnac. This specialty is based on crust as delicate as a veil. It requires a rare and elegant dexterity. Generous specialty with Chanteclerc apples. With this, you must choose a young and impetuous Folle-Blanche, full of fruit and life!

The coffee served, we took to the cellars where Martine's sharecropper awaited us to open the paradise of Lafitte… The tasting that followed was intense, despite lunch, or perhaps thanks to the dishes shared. We could go back in time to the Bas-Armagnacs of Martine's father, some of which were still in barrels: the vintages of 1966, 1967 (exceptional) and 1968 of noble grape variety.

The afternoon's end was approaching. The sun was dipping. We had to leave these welcoming places, the warm smile of our hostess, this sweetness of life, championed by our friends of the Crus Légendaires, true descendants of the Gascon Musketeers!

In late winter of 2014, Martine had resolved, for lack of succession, to consider separating from the domain for which she had fought all her life, especially since the death of her father in the early 1990's. With her, an important page of Bas-Armagnac will be turned. At the same time, the appellation was revoked on December 28, 2014. Now the Appellation d'Origine Contrôlée (AOC) is unique: Armagnac. The five existing hitherto – including Bas-Armagnac – have been relegated to "complementary geographic denominations" of the AOC Armagnac. Heartbreaking for Martine and all those who maintain the expressive identity of their terroirs.

# Tasting at the George V, Spring 2014

**2001. Folle-Blanche** *(bottled in June, 2013)*. *Amber color with dry, floral nose, fine, stretched, citrus notes. The woodiness is present on the attack. More power in the finish. The wood should be better assimilated – it deserves it.*

**1999. Folle-Blanche** *(bottled in September, 2012). Amber, dark topaz color. Notes of camphor, mild tobacco. Then progresses to rancio, cocoa, vanilla. Wood is better integrated. However, the finish is still hot. The whole remains very attractive.*

**1985. Cépage noble** *(bottled in 2012). Dark topaz color. Rich and broad nose. Less woody than the Folle-Blanche. Open nose recalling orange, quince, sweet almond. Buttery and rich mouth. Rather sharp in the finish, to be enjoyed with a good cigar, such as a Cohiba Behike 56.*

**1984. Folle-Blanche** *(bottled in October, 2011). Amber color, delicate nose, touch of saffron, great delicacy. The mouth is stretched and nervous in the finish, remarkable.*

**1981. Folle-Blanche** *(bottled in 2012). Complex nose, spicy, citrus, complete. After aeration, the "rancio" appears, sandalwood, fruity notes, recalling baked apple. With twenty years of aging, it has acquired a patina. The length is remarkable.*

**1975. Cépage noble** *(bottled in March, 2012). Intense color with shades of light amber, brilliant. Fine nose, velvety and smooth. Combines dried fruits and stone fruits. The wood is very delicate, not aggressive. The "rancio" appears slightly but is not dominant. The creamy mouth is round, underscoring a spicy finish, precious wood, toasted almond, light caramel. A Bas-Armagnac to enjoy sitting in an old Chesterfield.*

## SPIRITS
## Domaine Boingnères

# DOMAINE DE SEMAINVILLE
## THE RESPECT FOR TIME

The day that I took my job in Paris, I felt that I was leaving the vineyards. I thought it would be more difficult for me to join the winemakers across France. Fifteen years of Parisian life have allowed me to say that I was wrong. From the capital, it is easy to reach any point in our country, like our vineyards – by air, railway or roads.

Passionate about mechanical wonders, I love major highways. They take us away from the buzzing of the cities and play for us the film of our landscapes. We become spectators of the upheavals of our countryside, discovering the silent, sometimes lifeless expanses devoted to the intensive cultivation that alone limits the horizon. This has not always been the case. After the Second World War, a political decision would profoundly mark our regions: the notorious land regrouping. Its application had the immediate effect of eliminating slopes, sunken roads and other groves, which, for centuries, had demarcated each piece of land. This redistribution was intended to improve the productivity of our operations. This overhaul of the fields particularly accelerated the shift towards "surmécanisation" and, consequently, led to the arrival of tractors, as powerful as tanks, which previously had been unusable in our groves of true monochrome palettes, knitted by centuries of labor. When I was a child, alongside my father, I discovered damage around every farm caused by a shortsighted system. He was an inseminator in the Louvigné-du-Désert country, and on board one of his Citroën 2CV – of which he had accumulated sixteen models – I could breathe in the countryside.

Sometimes, like here, in the heart of the Norman bocage, no cadastral concession came to modify the property, preserved by this stubborn family. For those familiar, envision these winding roads of endless turns, the edges of which stand proudly atop high banks, venerable barriers of dark ivy, especially these trees, the souls of our landscape. With a bit of light mist and the cool of an autumn morning, as was the case in late September of 2013, for me it was like the setting of the *Grand Meaulnes* by Alain-Fournier.

When you enter the Camuts', you cannot remain untouched by the picture before your eyes. Furthermore, on this day, we stopped the sedan (despite already being late for the appointment) to admire this gravel road upon which stood a Norman half-timbered house dating from the eighteenth century, right out of *Trou normand*, a film starring a child native to the country, the great Bourvil. Continuing on… the wheels screeched on the driveway. To the right lay a beautiful orchard with soft green carpet, further away, a second one was fenced off to keep around the ancient cellars the guardians of the domain, the same as in the Capitol: geese! Welcome to the Domaine de Semainville, with the Camut brothers.

They are three of them – big-hearted giants. From their grandfather Adrien and their father, they inherited a very strong sense of quality research. They know the limits of their production capacity within the defined framework that is their own: their orchards and time. Here, it is only known that time does not like what transpires without it. The pace is not always that of a slow and rational production. The global market no longer has time. The era of industrial Calvados is in full swing, supplying the high-demand US market. The reason is historical. The day after landing on the Normandy beaches, American GIs, duty fulfilled, returned to their counties in the United States. Some never returned. Others wanted to maintain the common thread to this lived experience. They found it in Calvados, in its apple brandy, with which anyone could, by consuming a mouthful, remember those difficult hours. The years passed, the heroes died out, but the brandy remains, more than ever, this is the link to their ancestor who landed here. This is one reason for the popularity of this brandy.

Respectful, the Camuts are among the few frenetic defenders of an ancestral knowledge. At the heart of this family are their 45 hectares of apple orchards (twenty-five varieties in total), all tall stocks and planted at very wide intervals. In short, here we are far from the densities of planting and yields found in an industrial type of orchard, as the total production of the Domaine de Semainville corresponds to that of 5 hectares planted on short stocks with planting densities pushed to the extreme. At the very least, one could say there are many apple varieties present: sweet, bitter, and acidic. Some mature early, others later, since the harvest stretches from the end of the summer until the first days of winter. Some have an intense color strength, others a delicate skin with succulent flesh… All of these varieties, often rare, sometimes forgotten, fragile, take part in the complexity of ciders and, later, of brandy.

The bucolic nature of the Camut orchard is not only an idyllic picture but also shows a deep respect for the fruit in its sustainable development. This ecosystem is also based on the action of "mowers." In fact, good Norman cows, unfettered in the orchards, peacefully graze the grass between the trees. They also play a role in the fertilization of the orchards. Watch where you step – I made myself and my Berluti shoes remember that! Moreover, rubbing against the trunks of the apple trees, they make the worm-eaten fruit fall before harvest-time. Their gourmandise leads them to nibble on the lower branches, pruning them. They are essential, like the family's maintenance of beehives, maximizing pollination during flowering. Keeping the Normans in the orchards is not the result of folklore but of necessity.

Once the cider is fermented, the alembic comes into play. Here, an original idea of Adrien's was to patent an alembic through which the brandy would come out weaker than usual (52% vol.). This is commonly called "ma bonne chauffe." Adrien noticed that when the brandy would come out at 70% vol. from the alembics, it would "burn" the staves of the barrels, limiting exchanges between the inside and outside of the barrels. With his innovative process, Adrien favored the breathing of his brandy in the early months and facilitated the easing and complexity of the bouquet.

The size of the barrels is also important. They are imposing and, surprisingly, never completely filled, instead kept at two-thirds capacity. The reason: to promote the brandy's contact with air as well as the evaporation of the more volatile esters. Add to this the fact that the cellars are not air-conditioned and are therefore subject to the annual climatic variations of seasons. This contributes to the evaporation of the strongest esters. The sharp and aggressive ethanol has almost disappeared after fifty years of barrel aging. Here, between 4 and 5% of annual evaporation is allowed, while for Calvados from major groups, the rate is reduced to 1% maximum!

Calvados
Pays d'Auge
Réserve d'Adrien
Assemblage de Calvados
provenant exclusivement de la propriété.
Adrien Camut

# M EMORIES

December 2013, the night before Christmas Eve.

We arrived with Marie, Margot and Baptiste from Paris. For their part, Thierry and Nicolas, leaving Saint-Brieuc, veered towards Cancale, to stop at the Grain de Vanille, Olivier and Jane Roellinger's bakery. A place of gourmet perdition. This detour in their itinerary caused them some delay. Waiting for them, we traversed the domain with the Camut brothers. The cellar where apple fragrances emanated from the press. The vast barrels where Calvados vintages patiently age. We then entered the ancient building housing the stills patented by Grandfather Adrien, still working! In one corner, a large pot was kept on a wood fire (pearwood, since the combustion is slower) containing apple juice, which reduces slowly. The room smelled of *tarte Tatin*, vanilla, cinnamon, light caramel and candied quince. The results lead to the realization of their very rare and private apple vinegar, *versus* balsamic, after long years of aging.

Finally, the stragglers arrived. We stopped by the timbered house where the grandfather lived. A good fire awaited us in the dining room. A magnum of champagne from the Maison Lanson came to enliven us, subtly paired with elaborate canapés, evocative of Norman heritage.

At the family table, sliced scallops, remarkably fresh, lent their softness to a magnum of 2007 Puligny-Montrachet 1er Cru La Truffière 2007 by Jean-Marc Boillot. Then came the dish we were all waiting for and the very purpose of this reunion: roasted goose on a spit in the fireplace, in two services. There, a beautiful 2001 Vieux Château Certan was appropriately revealed. To complete the pairing, we shared a drop of Prestige Calvados for one of the geese who had passed on. His life spent standing guard over the cellars. He needed to be honored.

Then, preceded by their smell, two great Norman lords announced themselves. First, a rare Camembert from the Héronnière farm. This cheese is the last of its kind to be produced by François Durand at his parents' farm in Camembert, which he took over in 1981. The raw milk – unpasteurized – comes from the sixty dairy cows of his herd, which his brother, Nicolas, cares for. It has become a luxury to taste this cheese at its heart of maturity, soft, airy, much thicker than its counterparts. A good consistency!

The other ambassador was an unforgettable Livarot cheese from the Saint-Hippolyte farm in Saint-Martin-de-la-Lieue, near Lisieux in Pays d'Auge. Likewise, it was from the last remaining Livarot farmer in Normandy to use solely the raw milk of his own cows, hence the term "Farmer Livarot."

All that was left was to taste the best *tarte Tatin*, accompanied by a fresh cream that carried us away in gluttony, especially with the family's Prestige Calvados.

This was a moment of joyous gourmandize. Also, it was the first time we found ourselves in a domain for a tasting with the family. Only our youngest, Lisa, was missing, an additional reason for us to return.

# SPIRITS
## Domaine de Semainville

# The Eaux-de-vie

At the Camuts, the first Calvados put out on the market are six-year-old brandies. The Calvados needs time to interact with ambient air to become civilized. In terms of age calculations, they have decided to not pursue vintage production. They now favor brandies with defined assemblies according to Calvados's principal stages of maturity. The total cuvées come to approximately 20,000 bottles a year, which, considering global demand, is minimal. Thus, La Réserve d'Adrien, issued from brandy twenty-five years old on average, corresponds to adolescence with all the energy and passion that it entails. Then, there is the Camut Prestige, made from Calvados with forty to fifty years of barrel aging. Here, we are in the prime of life, mature, complex and intense, without losing sight of the result. I admit – I recognize myself in it! Finally, the Rarity cuvée. This time the Camuts call on their "paradise" to form this rare wine, which consists only of Calvados seventy to eighty years in age. It is the memory of the domain through the generations, with the wisdom and restraint acquired over time.

**Calvados, La Réserve d'Adrien.** *The topaz color is clear, intense and luminous. The nose is fine, straight, open, very fruity, recalling apple compote with touches of soft vanilla. The mouth is smooth and slightly rich with elegance and length, with floral notes of rum raisins. The finish is slightly hot. It is a tonic brandy, direct, very fine.*

**Calvados, Prestige Camut** *(in magnum). Amber color, very intense mahogany. Open nose, powerful but not aggressive. Notes of caramelized, candied apples mixed with woody notes, licorice and a touch of cinnamon. A brandy of great generosity. The mouth is voluptuous, rich, embracing and fleshy. Very dense with a finish of great elegance. Spices such as cocoa and vanilla emphasize an incomparable class. One of the best Calvados I have ever tasted. It brings together all the possible qualities of a great apple brandy. A tribute to Grandfather Adrien.*

**Calvados Rareté.** *Dark topaz color, very intense. The nose is fine, deep, complex. Notes of rancio and spices, dominated by aromas of mocha and cocoa vanilla. The fruit is discreet, but the concentration is extreme. The age brands the style. Attack in the mouth of great density and extreme length. Woody notes, fresh nuts and coffee coat the thoroughly caramelized fruit. An incredible taste fingerprint with the fruit fading into the meanderings of time. A meditation Calvados.*

# LA GRANDE-CHARTREUSE
# 400 YEARS OF FRENCH HISTORY

C hartreuse is, for me, synonymous with sharing. Whether at La Poularde, or later, the George V, I was always surrounded by Carthusian liqueurs. I do not remember ever having failed to present a VEP or a Tarragone des Pères Chartreux to customers or friends over lunch or dinner, where it was not a big hit. It was in Montrond where my visceral attachment to these liqueurs took root. We had the chance to serve the 1963 Chartreuse VEP Verte (the first of its kind) acquired by M. Randoing. When we would visit his home, to his rooms overlooking the Loire, he would go and get us a bottle that he kept under the sink in his kitchen, "where no one would think to look," he told us. Evoking this memory recalls an indefinable perfume of sweetness mixed with spices and fine pastries.

Throughout my twelve years spent at La Poularde, I was always committed to placing Chartreuse center stage. I long remember this day in Voiron in 1993, with Chef Étéocle, Patrick Henriroux and Jean-Claude Ruet (from La Pyramide in Vienna), and Gilles Hascoët (head sommelier of Georges Blanc at the time). We came to discuss with the directors of Chartreuse Diffusion and Père Chartreux the importance of keeping the secondary label on the Chartreuse VEP: vieillissement exceptionnellement prolongé. The Carthusians thought the vintage indicator on bottles spurred confusion among consumers. On the contrary, time proved that these VEP "vintages" were sought out by fans.

Another time, during the winter of 1996, I assisted, in an expert capacity, an auctioneer friend in Saint-Étienne for the evaluation of a most surprising lot of Chartreuse. He led me to someone's home, to an old coal and wood cellar. There, embedded in hollowed logs, were Tarragona Chartreuses, carefully stowed away during the Second World War by the former owners, as evidenced by the labels, and long since forgotten in this abandoned reserve. These bottles were impossible to extract from their wooden shells. Only the label was visible and the cork accessible. We did not, then, have at our disposal the fabulous work of Michel Steinmetz, *Chartreuse. History of a Liqueur. Guide for Amateurs* (Glénat, 2006) to date the bottles. However, we could still open one in the living room. The richness of aromas and flavors that I discovered would not reappear until 1999 during a "Chartreuse gala" in Voiron, with the successor to Fernand Point. I have long envied La Pyramide, in Vienna, for its inexhaustible reserves of Chartreuse. In the great age of Mme Point, very pious, she was sure to stock up, certainly with the objective of redeeming the gluttonous sin of her husband, the great Fernand Point. The faithful sommelier, Louis Tomasi, jealously safeguarded the treasure. At La Poularde, I developed a Chartreuse cocktail, which we served after dinner to the patrons enjoying their food. For the more experienced among them, we prepared a Royal! We rolled out, in front of the table, a pedestal containing the following:

– a carafe immersed in ice placed on a silver tray with a perforated grid
– a bottle of Chartreuse VEP Verte at 54% vol, brought out straight from the cold
– a bottle of Chartreuse Eau-de-Vie at 40% vol.
– frosted liqueur glasses
– tin measuring cup of 5 and 2 cl.

The recipe was the following: a 5-cl dose of VEP verte + a dose of 2 cl eau-de-vie per guest, poured into the icy carafe, upon which we would imprint a large twisting motion, allowing the two elements to mix. We would then serve the liqueur flowing from the decanter, like a trickle of amber with malachite reflections. It was "the" famous cocktail of La Poularde. It would help, after a big dinner, to keep everyone entertained and, proven fact, it also helped with digestion.

The liqueur used was a novelty in the early 1990's. We had found a supply of it in the cellars of Voiron during a visit with Jean-Claude Ruet. The monk who accompanied us had given us a bottle each. We did not hesitate to put it to use. It was a liqueur distilled by the Carthusian monks in their Aigues-Vives dans le Gard distillery circa 1941. Originally, it was used for the maceration of plants. The remaining product, aged in casks and bottled, had never been sold before. At La Poularde, to the delight of gourmets, it found one of its first opportunities. Here lies one of the defining elements of the liqueurs: their positive effects on organisms. Since the beginning of the centuries-old history of Chartreuse, medicinal aspects have played an important role.

The history of Chartreuse began with the future Marshal François Annibal d'Estrées. This great man, former bishop of Noyon, who exchanged his robe for a sword after the death on the battlefield of his older brother, was the brother of the beautiful Gabrielle, famous mistress of Henri IV. Later, d'Estrées was made Marshal by his son, Louis XIII. Meanwhile, in 1605, he handed over an ancient manuscript describing a skillful mixture of plants to the Carthusian Monks of Vauvert in Paris. The proportions seemed ideal for creating an elixir of life. At least, that is what the monks tried to decipher for several decades. Finally, the parchment ended up in a vault and would not reemerge until the turn of 1740 when it reached the Mother-House of the Order, the Grande Chartreuse monastery in Voiron.

To familiarize oneself with the origins of the order and the monastery, a visit to the Louvre is necessary, where a room – rarely visited – displays the twenty-two paintings which the painter Le Sueur painted between 1645 and 1648, showing the major episodes in the life of St. Bruno, founder of the Carthusian Order in 1084. The paintings adorned the small cloister of the Carthusian Convent in Paris. The Carthusians offered these works to King Louis XVI in 1776. They were added to the national collections. Furthermore, it was in 1762 that Brother Jérôme developed the Chartreuse Élixir. Two years later, Brother Antoine invented the Green Chartreuse and codified its manufacturing. We know little about its composition other than the 130 plants involved in its development.

The rise of the liqueur was short-lived as, in 1793, during the Reign of Terror, the Carthusians were expelled. They returned during the Restoration in 1816. Unoccupied since their departure, the monastery was practically in ruins. It was not until 1834 that the Carthusians were able to resume the liqueur's production. In 1840, Brother Bruno invented Yellow Chartreuse. Softer, weaker, it titrates 43°. It encountered great success upon production. From that point, the rise of Chartreuse happened very quickly. The monks had to protect their trademarks from countless counterfeits and created a new Chartreuse production unit – at the express request of Pope Pius IX – to preserve the rule of Saint Bruno, which governs their monastic existence. In 1880,

the Fourvoirie factory, near Voiron, a few kilometers from the monastery, was able to bottle 5,000 liters of Chartreuse per day, for it was a liqueur which followed an unchanged production process and aged two to three years before bottling. The huge revenues generated by this production allowed the monastic order to create a 100-bed hospital and Catholic schools and to participate in the financing of roads and tunnels in the region. They would help the surrounding populations in the wake of fires and floods, providing work. Even better, they would pay pensions to former employees in the amount of 400 gold francs after twenty-five years of work, or 40% of their annual salary and without a contribution requirement. The Carthusians scrupulously respect the vow of poverty and never receive the monetary fruit of their production.

From 1901, the promulgation of the Law on Associations paved the way for the separation of church and state. One of the most ardent promoters of this project was the parliamentarian Emile Combes, soon to be Council resident. He made, starting in 1902, every attempt to dismantle religious orders, particularly that of the Carthusians. In 1903, two years after the enactment of the Law of 1901, the Carthusians were again expelled from the monastery. One of the major reasons for the animosity against them was greed, motivated by the potential production of their liqueur. On April 20, 1903, despite protests from residents of neighboring villages who came in numbers, a division of dragoons commanded by Captain Colas des Francs was responsible for carrying out the eviction. As the monks passed by, the officer ordered his men to salute them with their swords drawn. The division then escorted the monks, who had opened their doors themselves, to the station of Saint-Laurent-du-Pont. This route was created to transport the raw materials needed for the development and shipment of the liqueurs. After saluting the Carthusian monks in a silence worthy of their way of life, the Captain broke his sword and handed his resignation to the general staff in order to cleanse his regiment of the shame of this sinister mission. There were many at the time who stood up against this expulsion, in vain, such as Léon Poncet, in *Le Drame de la Grande-Chartreuse*, published in 1931.

From 1904, some monks, refugees in the Carthusian Monastery of Tarragona, Spain, resumed production and shipment of Chartreuse to France. It was not, however, until 1932, along with countless twists and legal troubles, that they were able to return to Voiron and resume their production there. Meanwhile, they continued developing Chartreuse in Tarragona until 1988.

Since the creation of Chartreuse, counterfeits have always existed. The monks worked tirelessly to differentiate the labels, sanding the bottles and detailing the ruffs to make counterfeiting more difficult. These myriad variants are now the joy of collectors and especially help in dating the bottles, with a very significant margin of precision. Furthermore, how can the liqueur's perfection be counterfeited? Its production secret is one of the best kept in France. The plants composing it are partly known, but not the proportions. Among the plants that can be found therein include lemon balm, mugwort, lavender flowers, sage, marjoram, black currant leaves, wild thyme… And lesser-known plants: tansy, Hyssop flowers, sweet-clover, matricaria, betony…

Regarding the development of Chartreuse, it can briefly be described as follows:

– Weighing, assembly of plants and grinding by a monk in the secret herb room. These are prepared by family and distinct category. Each batch is then packaged in large jute sacks and handed over to an employee of the distillery, without contact between the latter and the monk.

– Maceration of plants according to predefined batches to extract sought-out fragrances and aromas, some in cold water, others in neutral alcohol (95°).

– Distillation of the result of the macerations in alcohol is produced in large stills. The "alcoholates" that result titrate around 80°. Multiple distillations are repeated. With each passing, the quality of the alcoholate increases.

– The processing of a syrup consisting of sugar and very pure distilled water is then carried out. The sugar content varies depending on whether the syrup is intended for green or yellow liqueur. Once completed, this syrup of plant alcoholates is assembled with infusions of plants macerated in water and then brought to a boil. These infusions are assembled to bring the liqueurs to the desired degree of alcohol.

– Depending on either green or yellow liqueur, the above operations will vary with each step. To color these sweetened alcoholates, a saffron decoction is used for yellow and chlorophyll for green liqueur.

– These liqueurs are then stored in *foudres*, very large-capacity barrels, to begin their long aging. The yellow liqueur will be aged in eighteen-month barrels. The green, around two years. A light filtration will then apply before bottling.

Note that the aging time in barrels is greatly increased for special cuvées such as VEP, which stands for "vieillissement exceptionnellement prolongé."

To go deeper into understanding the Carthusians and their lives today, you should view, on an autumn or winter evening, near a good fire, with a Partagas *Solomon* (dream a little!) and a Chartreuse VEP Jaune of antique appearance, an important film: *Le Grand Silence*, a documentary dedicated to the Carthusian monks of the Grande Chartreuse Monastery, released in theaters in 2006 and directed by Philip Gröning. The documentarian confided that he had sent the Father Prosecutor of the Grande Chartreuse a written request in 1984 describing his idea to capture, in images, evidence of their existence. He received a positive reply… in 1999.

**M**EMORIES
One of the most incredible events we organized as part of our association of wacky sommeliers, the Mad Wine Waiters of the World, was one that brought us together in Voiron on the distillery premises. It was in the spring of 1999.

Those present at the party:

– Olivier Poussier, from the Loire Valley, a fan of Chartreuse, dangerous limit. He is the Le Nôtre of wine, 2000 World's Best Sommelier.

– Gérard Basset, a native of the Loire but lives in the department. Quite frankly, he has all the titles, including those of Master of Wine and 2010 World's Best Sommelier.

– Éric Duret, Savoy, frontier wine merchant and, incidentally, 1998 Best Sommelier of Europe.

– Jean-Claude Ruet: At the time, Jean-Claude was still head sommelier at La Pyramide in Vienna. He then moved on to the Ritz before returning to Lyon, to Christian Têtedoie. He has won the Best Sommelier of Europe title twice.

– Henri Chapon, a French rooster, not as plump as that, but a traveler. Best Sommelier of Monaco and Britain and Vice Best Sommelier of Europe.

– Eric Boschman, gold star for his interstellar sommellerie humor and Best Sommelier of Belgium, as well as a semifinalist in the contests of Best Sommelier of Europe and the World.

– Yves Sauboua, founder and president of the Sommelier Club in London. Then a sommelier in Hong Kong, today in the United States. A smoker of cigars, which he keeps under wood.

– Édouard de Nazelle, one of the last great French ambassadors of Champagne. After him began the reign of marketing.

– Michèle Chantôme Aström: without her support and that of Roland de Calonne, what would have happened to our sommelier competitions from the years 1980-1990? Better not to think about it.

– André Cognard, our guest of honor. A patron of La Poularde in Montrond-les-Bains, with whom I have spent nights comparing the merits of Chartreuse. He is a great aikido master and received in 1998, upon the death of Master Kobayashi, the charge of directing the International Aikido Academy.

– Philippe Bonnard, the main contact between sommeliers and Chartreuse Diffusion. He has always supported us in every way!

– My faithful Thierry, and myself.

During the day, we attended a demonstration and some practical aikido exercises with André. It was, at least, vigorous, especially when we hit the ground without knowing how the teacher projected us there, even more so since everything happened so smoothly. An art. Following this fitness regimen, we were able to make it to the distillery of Voiron and visit all the facilities, under the direction of Philippe Bonnard. After this rare moment, we reached a reception room where the table had been set. In one corner, Henriroux Patrick, head of La Pyramide Fernand-Point in Vienna, managed to cook for us a fine dinner using makeshift means. Some gas heaters, two small ovens and a lot of resourcefulness and experience. His dishes, as good as could be, have faded in the meanderings of my memory. The wine also, for that matter! I still remember an airy Chartreuse soufflé with a Chartreuse Verte VEP, bottled in 1970.

The end of dinner was highly anticipated. In honor of the merry sommeliers participating, duly clad in evening dress and webbed black swim fins, the monks authorized Philippe Bonnard to serve us:
– a 1975 Chartreuse Tarragone, then a 1970.
– a 1941 Chartreuse Tarragone Jaune.
– a 1929 Chartreuse Fourvoirie.
– a 1910 Chartreuse Tarragone.

After taking the time to delve into each of these wonders, Yves took out a cigar box filled with Churchills: *Hoyo de Monterrey*, *Hoyo des Dieux*.

We returned to our hotel, hobbling along, around 4 o'clock in the morning. Rather than go to our rooms, however, totally bewitched by this evening and the bouquets of spices, plants and candied fruit, we decided to stay in the salon near the bar. There, we could continue tasting two of the half-finished Chartreuses, carefully transported thus far. We found a few glasses with the help of the night watchman and resumed (much to his chagrin) our delight, in coat and white socks, flippers strewn about us in joyful disarray. We all had our slippers on – a gift from the Carthusians who took care to fill each shoe with a half-bottle of Chartreuse VEP Verte. We looked pretty sharp.

I finally dozed off… when suddenly Thierry grabbed my arm: "It's 7:00, quick, let's go!" I immediately went upstairs to change, aided by Thierry, in this room where the bed wasn't even wrinkled. Ten minutes later, his Renault 25 Baccara was flying at high speed to Lyon, where I had a 9:00 train to Paris. That day, I had my interview with Didier Le Calvez… for the George V.

Hoping to at least sleep in the compartment, where I was still in slippers, I did not have time to even close an eye. Coming towards me, one of our good customers from Montrond recognized me. "So, Eric, on your way to Paris?" I was a goner. He talked to me for two hours. What a journey!

Oddly, the interview went well despite my air of fatigue "due to the evening service which dragged on," I said…

# Tasting at the George V, in January 2015

Among the characteristics of Chartreuse, there is one that is unique: their aging capacity.

**1605 Chartreuse Cuvée MOF Sommeliers – Santa Tecla** *(45% vol.). Lemon yellow color, bright, brilliant. The mouth is smooth, rich and sensual.*

**1605 Chartreuse Verte Épiscopale** *(56% vol.). Green khaki color, quite pale. Spicy nose, vegetal, a tad aggressive. The mouth is rather stretched, very peppery, licorice, refreshing finish, slightly sharp. The bitters are noticeable, the sensation in the mouth is numbing.*

**Chartreuse Jaune VEP** *(bottled in 2012, 42% vol.). Lemon yellow color, rich nose and generous. Notes of spiced honey, saffron, licorice, vanilla, calisson, lemon zest. Wooded. A complex nose, still very young. It needs some time. The mouth is soft, a little heavy, very round. Long finish. The sugar at this stage tends to cover the complexity.*

**Chartreuse Verte VEP** *(bottled in 2014, 54% vol.). Intense khaki green color. The nose is fine, discreet, powerful, a little closed. Notes of spices, bitter orange aroma. The smooth mouth is concentrated, hot, firm, peppered and fresh with a tannic impression. The finish is more stretched than the VEP jaune. Here, the liqueur is harmonious and delicate. A great success.*

**Chartreuse du 9ᵉ Centenaire** *(developed between 2001 and 2004, 47% vol.). Liqueur of a tender green, medium intensity. The nose is open, aromatic and fine. Notes of dry plant, peppermint, star anise and lemongrass. Notes recalling Sichuan berries and cloves. Forthright mouth, presence of refined liqueur but lacks complexity. It still needs to mature. Very nice finish.*

**Chartreuse Tarragone Jaune Période 1973-1985** *(40% vol.). Pale yellow color with emerald hues. Open nose, delicate and sensual. Notes of candy, calisson, candy sugar, spicy and resinous. Recalls Landes pine and dried hay. The mouth is very subtle, not aggressive, very good length, balanced. Needs to age to become more concentrated.*

**Chartreuse Tarragone Verte Période 1973-1985** *(55 % vol.). Light khaki color. Fresh and fine nose, discreet. Peppermint, licorice, camphor, artichoke hearts. A rich nose with a soothing sensation. Stretched mouth, airy, nice length. Very spicy and peppery. The whole is harmonious and fine.*

# CHÂTEAU HAUTEVILLE –
# ÉRIC BORDELET
## THE APPLE KNIGHT

I t is the dream of many sommeliers: to produce a vintage resembling *us*. In general, it is to wine that we turn to in order to give life to such a project. However, when you are born in the heart of a region covered with ancient apple and pear trees, a different path looms ahead. Here is a sommelier who has enriched the cider landscape of France and beyond, who helped the Sydres (apple ciders) and perries (pear ciders) of its orchards, fifteen years ago, make their debut on the wine lists of the greatest restaurants in the world: Éric Bordelet. Cider in a Michelin-starred restaurant? Never before seen! Éric Bordelet is a man of passion; tenacious, courageous and fearless, attached to his terroir and respectful of his family's legacy in the heart of Mayenne. His story begins in 1992, when he resumed his parents' operations. The man is, like his Sydres, a finely measured assemblage: a sommelier base enriched with the knowledge of a distinguished pomologist, on the path of one passionate for discovery and the sharing of knowledge.

Our first meeting took place in Bordeaux in 1989 during a Vinexpo with Didier Dagueneau – his friend and mentor – and through the mediation of an invaluable, exceptional man: the wine broker Raymond Garcia. Later, we met regularly during the tastings organized by a small group of passionate winemakers, gathered in an association under the self-proclaimed name, "Union des Gens de Métier." One of the axes was a desire to revolutionize the established order of recent decades regarding vine management. Biodynamics was also on equal footing in the debates. A real buzzing of ideas, projects and unbridled passions was led, among others, by the impressive and fiery Didier Dagueneau. These two found themselves and their involvement to be constantly growing. Among the participants, there were Marc Kreydenweiss, François Chidaine, Olivier Jullien and Éric Bordelet.

This association proved to be a stepping stone for him. Going from Head Sommelier at l'Arpège, with Alain Passard at the helm, to a pomologist, was a risky move to say the least – a complete career change. Our friend had a passion, a real vision of the potential of his terroir, the diversity of its varieties and the urgency of safeguarding this heritage. He also had the unconditional support of his wife.

Cider or rather, ciders, have suddenly gained acclaim. One of the secrets to its success is undoubtedly through the mastery of the developmental stages of its Sydres. The choice of apple and pear varieties is worthy of a classification by the Comte de Buffon. Bordelet has managed to preserve varieties grown on tall stock and identify geological areas particularly suited to certain varieties of ancient apple or pear trees. A mind completely identical to that of a winemaker. On less than 20 hectares were no fewer than thirty cider apple varieties with simply enchanting names: Kermerrien, Douce Coet Ligné, Carnette, Miclard, Rouge Duret, Fréquin vert... The names of the approximately fifteen varieties of perry pears did not lag behind. Oh, so many images: Rouge Vigny, Domfront, Plant de Blanc, De Cloche, Laurier, Belle Verge, Souris...

It begins with the harvest of apples, sweet, bitter, acidic. Each variety is harvested based on maturity, which ranges between September and December. Each variety is then coarsely crushed and gently squeezed, followed by settling and racking.

Fermentation will then begin, either in vats or barrels. After this, the cider is bottled with its content having more or less of its residual natural sugars, depending on the desired cuvée. The second fermentation and foam creation will unfold over several weeks, even months. This is an acquired, empirical skill, which Eric continues to perfect with every harvest.

His other great pursuit is perry pears. Quite simply, if such a title existed, Eric would deserve to be elevated to Knight of the Perry, as it was he who made us all rediscover this overlooked product. Before him, I never thought perries could reach such a level of elegance and purity. Eric has a clear vision of his domain's future, such as his rehabilitation project of the château's ruins, whose exterior will be preserved, and... the cellars! Besides, there's nothing else left standing after the fire, which ravaged this beautiful home in the late 1920s.

# CIDER
## Château Hauteville – Éric Bordelet

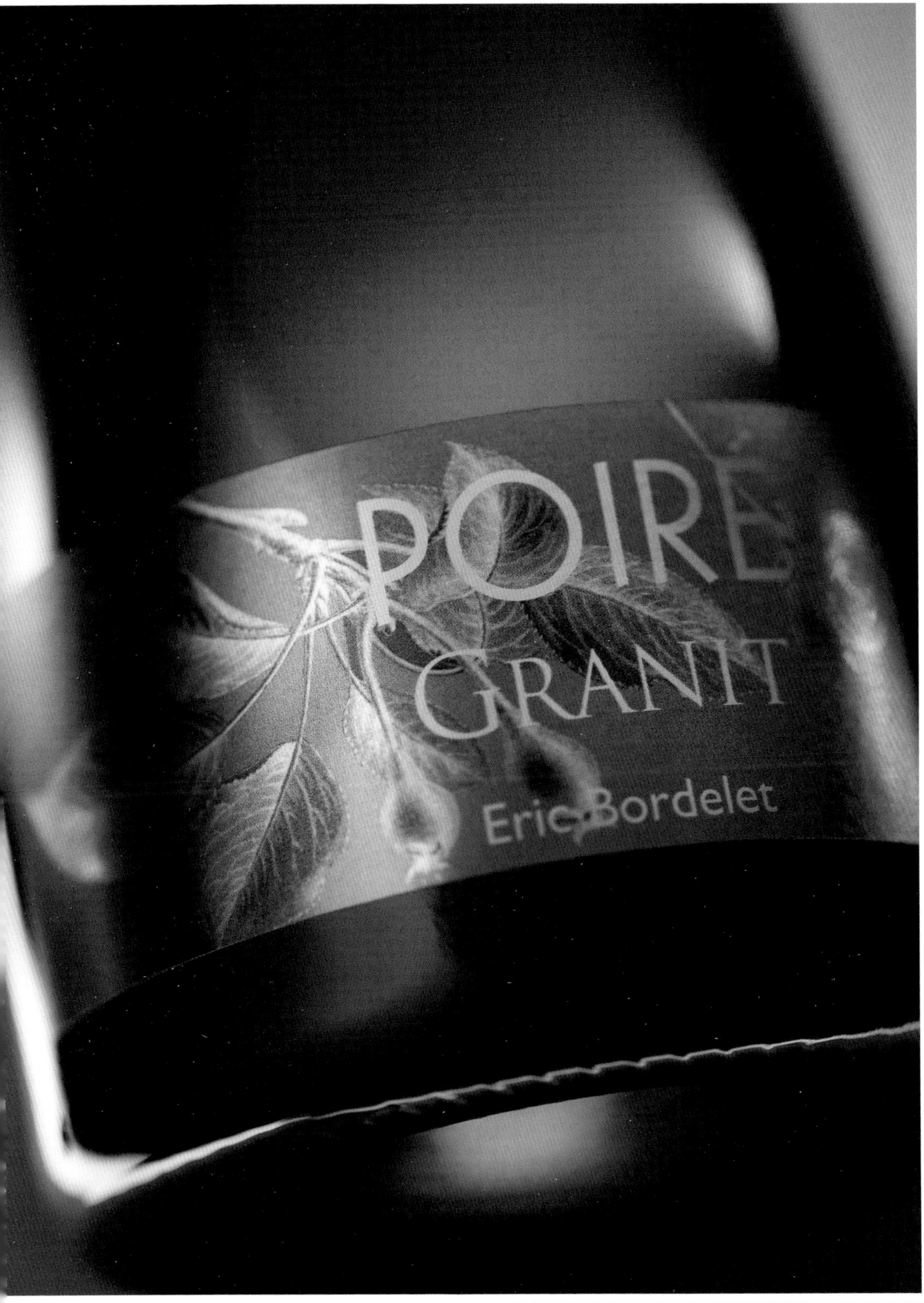
POIRE
GRANIT
Eric Bordelet

# MEMORIES

Among my last great pairings, I think back to that afternoon in September 2013, in the north of France, near Lille, with dear friends. Our host offered a welcoming snack on the teak table which overlooked an English garden speckled with hydrangeas, fruit trees and beds of aromatic herbs. The weather was mild, and the atmosphere was jovial.

The hostess cut an appetizing rhubarb *tarte sablée* (tart made with shortcrust pastry) – "It needs to cool down," she warned us – and to accompany this delicious moment, our host served a Granit (shortly followed by a second bottle), refreshing, joining the tangy tart with pleasure.

But the best was yet to come: a sublime *Kouign-amann* by Alex Croquet, of course, freshly baked, caramelized, just right, soft, melting… a dream. It should be noted that two big names came together for our enjoyment. This famous Breton dessert, rich with white sugar and fine butter, does not harmonize well with liqueur or sweet wines. It needs energy, freshness, in a word, a bubble that is at the same time refreshing, slightly dosed and low in alcohol. As our friend said, "As it is!"

# CIDER
## Château Hauteville – Éric Bordelet

# Éric's Recent Cider and Perry Cuvées

**2010. Poiré Granit.** *A great Grand Cru Perry whose strength comes from its granitic soil, upon which ancient pear varieties have been planted for nearly a century.*

*The Argelette is reminiscent of a great vintage in its category, since it ages beautifully, like the 2006 Sydre Argelette recently tasted in magnum, with fishermen friends in Cancale. Sensation of tarte Tatin, floral, a touch of bitter almond.*

**2013. Argelette.** *Clear and luminous topaz color. Very fine bubbles, open nose, fruity, intense. Revealing notes of baked apples and caramel, relatively cool and terribly seductive. The mouth is creamy, without heaviness. Tangy and slightly tannic finish.*

**2010.** *Clear, intense freshness in the aromas. Subtle sparkle.*

**2007.** *(In magnum). Very nice (continued over lunch). Good bitters, fine.*

**2001.** *(In magnum). Rich, Tatin finish, cinnamon.*

# BRASSERIE CANTILLON
## THE IRREDUCIBLE
## ANDERLECHT

Here we are in Brussels, or Brussel, depending on where you are in the kingdom. This little getaway seemed the least iconoclastic on the path we were following. And yet! This place is a reflection of the wealth of cultures, climates and terroirs of our continent. From north to south, consumption patterns also vary widely. If southern Europe is inseparable from the cultivation of the olive and its oil, the northern part is inconceivable without its butter. At Le Cinq, not wanting to favor one over the other but instead to serve the best of both, I would always present a great Jean-Yves Bordier butter and, at the same time, a Tuscan or Sicilian olive oil, specially selected for Le Cinq.

Similarly, there is a southern Europe strongly characterized by the growing and production of wine and a northern Europe with an immense brewing heritage. This Europe of beer, I discovered in Brussels, thanks to my friend Éric Boschman (a unique character in the world of wine; I recommend his books, you'll see!) We met at the Mondial du Vin de Bruxelles in 1989. Then, in the course of 1991, he introduced me to the Van Roys. After my first encounter with them, it occurred to me that while there are hundreds and thousands of beers produced in the world, the Cantillon is among the few to not divulge all their mysteries.

Beer, which follows a set recipe and is easily reproducible and reliable, usually offers no differences from one brew to another once the production has been established. The Van Roys, however, are an exception as the last irreducible brewers of Brussels, isolated in the middle of a neighborhood worthy of the Bronx circa 1960. A century ago, Brussels had 100 independent breweries. Today, Cantillon is the last one remaining (a second brewery, established three years ago, specializes in high fermentation). And again, it almost ended up a drugstore or supermarket of which Eddy Mitchell sang, defending small neighborhood cinemas. For that matter, Jean-Pierre Van Roy began his professional career in vinyl. Then, when the family was going to get rid of the brewery, he decided, against all odds, to take over alongside his stepfather – and it was to his credit! To do this, he had to redeem all respective shares. Over the next twenty years, from 1973 to 1993, he took, brew by brew, ownership of the walls.

Meanwhile, he created the Geuze Museum in 1978 so as to keep the ancient brewing traditions alive, preserving as much heritage linked to the Geuze as possible and multiplying openings for the public. It is through education, information and the sharing of knowledge that Jean-Pierre has also been able to stick around in the world of sharks, or that of international brewery group empires (I recommend reading about it the fabulous comic saga *Les Maîtres de l'orge* by Jean Van Hamme and Francis Vallès, Éditions Glénat). Later, in 1989, he began his imports to Japan, where friends from that country have found similarities with some of their sakés. A year later, Jean joined the brewery. The year 1990 also saw the birth of l'Union des Gens de Métier, to which Jean-Pierre will be linked, as well as several wineries in this book. Given the values conveyed by the Van Roys, like their roots in their brewery and the defense of their expertise, their presence within this group of enthusiasts was a given.

Since then, the pair has turned into a trio with a daughter of Jean-Pierre's joining the brewery's clan. At the George V, we put Cantillon on the menu early on at Le Cinq. It seemed iconoclastic. Then, however, we found that our most assiduous client was from a charming village a few steps from Lille. Imagine his surprise when, returning from some exhausting meeting, he opened the minibar of his suite at the George V and a Geuze or Kriek, whatever his fancy, sprang forth, infinitely cool and refreshing. For once, I can say, "*That's* a luxury hotel!" And as my friend and founder of Mad Wine Waiters of the World, Éric Boschman, whom I have already described, stated, "The Lambic is truly unique. The reason for its uniqueness lies in its development."

Since I've known the Van Roys, they have never ceased to improve upon the process without negotiating the quality. All from a mixture of malted barley flour (65%) and organic raw wheat (35%) mixed with water, brought to a temperature of around 50°C, stirred until obtaining a wort: warm, soft and protein-laden (surely close to the drinks already consumed by the Sumerians). We were able to taste a glass of it, hot, beside the wood-burning stove. This kind of liquid bread reminded us – we were three Bretons from Le Cinq that morning with Jean-Pierre – of the smell of our grandmothers' wheat crêpe batter. With a remarkable scent of buckwheat honey. A hot drink, soft, ephemeral. The wort is then lightly filtered and passed into a vat for cooking and hopping. It should be noted that the hop used (5 grams of hops per liter of finished product) is called a "suranné."

Then comes the wort cooling stage in a very flat copper tray located under the rooftops, amidst low walls and cleverly perforated skylights, closed off more or less based on the wind and outside temperatures. These brews take place during the winter, as temperatures and the atmospheric pressure are more favorable to better seeding, taking place through the wort's natural fertilization by bacteria and yeasts. These only proliferate in the Senne Valley and Pajottenland.

Once this wort is naturally reduced to about 18°C, it is "sung" in oak or chestnut barrels (no new oak, of course, but venerable containers in perfect condition). Spontaneous fermentation is very virulent at first and then slows down. It takes almost three years for the sugars to convert.

This beer, non-foaming, then becomes a "vin de grain." During fermentation the carbon dioxide goes flat through the wood. The Lambic is born! It is called "young" after a year of aging. At this stage, the Lambic contains natural sugars necessary for the second fermentation in bottles.

## BEER
### Brasserie Cantillon

This is the assembly for different beers of between one to three years of barrel aging, which will ensure the equilibrium and develop the complexity, finesse and bouquet of the future Gueuze.

Once the assembly is accomplished, the bottles (plugged with cork, plus a crown cap) will rest on slats for a year until the second fermentation occurs due to the presence of sugars, thereby creating the desired carbon dioxide. When Lambic becomes effervescent: it is a Gueuze. This beer deviates from the dictates of the brewing world, as acids and bitters are present in its balances.

Go on ahead without me! You will be warmly received. This is not folklore. It's not a matter of resetting an antique grandfather clock at a fair. Here, every object, every tool, is alive, playing a part in the development of a product born in the nineteenth century from the invention of a Brabant brewer, who had the idea of a Lambic bottling assembly. I always liked the idea that this order of ancient knowledge is still conveyed today. Here, there are no stainless steel vats, computers, cooling systems or white coats. Everything, however, is perfectly maintained, clean and neat. Only here, you will find more soul, smells that took me back nearly forty years to an ancient cellar – dark and disturbing for the child that I was – belonging to a friend of my grandfather, where there were old casks for the family wine (from Chenin grapes), next to the bins of elm where potatoes and Jerusalem artichokes were stored… these smells are like time machines.

# MEMORIES

No one will be surprised that after a beautiful morning tasting at Cantillon, we had developed an appetite. All the better, for a table had been reserved by Jean-Pierre at Les Brigittines, a traditional restaurant in Brussels where savory cuisine is enjoyed amidst ancient wooden decor, souvenirs collected in windows and dark green velvet, all next to a roaring fire. The staff is worthy of Robert Dalban's interpretation of the butler (the heyday of supporting film roles) in *Les Tontons flingueurs (Crooks in Clover)*. Charisma, repartee and life.

We began with shrimp croquettes and fried parsley. One of the great specialties of Brussels. Be careful not to immediately dive in as soon as the plate is put down – I did, unfortunately – and it was burning hot! However, it is ideal with a good Geuze, from last year, fresh, bouquet still fermenting. This meal, decidedly "light," was continued by a small serving of sauerkraut whelks and black pudding. A poem! But awfully good.

Then a rare dish: lamb brains, fried in brown butter with a crisp salad, without changing beer, only a Geuze of an older vintage.

Finally the said "plat de résistance" – and in this place, that would be… their famous veal cheeks braised in Cantillon Kriek. Of course, accompanied by a good Kriek from the previous season. Perfect harmony between the soft, melting flesh, revealed by the tone of the beer, softened by a parsnip mousseline.

By common consent, we bypassed the desserts, still accepting a coffee with some speculoos. Elsewhere, we stopped by the Maison Dandoy – "the" reference for this cookie – near the Grand Place, to stock up, and then continued a few meters away to the dispensary of Pierre Marcolini, where Thierry made a raid on chocolate bonbons and lemon meringue tarts (to nibble on in our compartment on the way back). They were the best I had ever known. Well done!

# Their Beers

The following tasting took place in winter 2014. This time, it was one of our young sommeliers, Alexandre Larvoir (from the illustrious restaurateur family of Sainte-Anne d'Auray), who accompanied us. I can never stress enough how important it is for our young people to meet winemakers and, here, great brewers! When we knocked on the brewery's door, the cold and the wind had chilled us up to the tip of our nose.

Also, after the outpouring of reunions, we were attracted like magnets by the view of the glowing stove. Moreover, Jean-Pierre's German shorthaired pointer, with a beautiful, single-colored brown coat, was sleeping in a halo of warmth. We sat around a table at the adjoining bistro. The serious business began.

**2010 Bruocsella.** *Made from Lambic of 3 years' barrel aging. Titrates at 5.5% vol. The nose is floral. The mouth is very honeyed, woody, powerful, with fragrances of bitter almond, dried hawthorn and hops. Slightly bitter finish. Refreshing.*

**2007 Bruocsella.** *Sapphire, oxidized "padparadscha" color, clear. Recalls the color of vintage Sauternes. Nose of aged hops, dried flowers, chamomile, slight reduction, with incredible notes of vegetable root broth (parsnips, chervil). Notes of parmesan. Soft mouth, no effervescence here. Pleasant, discreet bitterness. A real beer-wine.*

**2006 Gueuze.** *Amber, topaz color, luminous. Beautiful effervescence, rich nose, honeyed. With malted notes. Dried floral led by hops. Notes of aged champagne. Refreshing mouth. Slightly resinous. Recalls Vosges pine and honey in the finish. Discreet bitterness gives a lot of uniqueness. For a pairing, try a smoked herring on a bed of pickled radish, ambiance guaranteed!*

**1996 Gueuze.** *Very intense, stretched, with citrus notes and acidities masking the bitterness. Here again, there are aromatic resonances with aged champagnes, of cultivated mushrooms. Very nice flavor, fine, long. The bubble is maintained very well. Makes for a very refreshing beer. The finish recalls baked reinette apple.*

**Gueuze Rhubarbe.** *A cellar oddity. One of Jean's dearest experiments. The nose is impressively precise. The juice is of fresh rhubarb, slightly vegetal. The mouth is full, with beautiful bitters. The rhubarb flavor appears only at the end of the mouth. Saline finish, very persistent. I imagine it would go very well with a rhubarb* tarte sablée.

**2008 Rosé de Gambrinus.** *This is a raspberry Lambic, appearing in the early twentieth century. It debuted on the brewery records written by Paul Cantillon in the early 1910s, in larger numbers than Kriek. Between the 1930s and the early 1970s,* it disappeared for a better rebirth. The color offers a beautiful shade of rosé – hence its name. The nose is still of great aromatic purity. Everything is straightforward, longer, direct. Unlike the raspberry beer (usually flavored), here there is more uprightness and intensity. The most beautiful raspberry that I have tasted.

A few words about Kriek's conception (it is the Flemish and Brussels translation of "cherry"): it is prepared during the summer using fresh cherries; 150 kilos of fruit per pipe of 650 liters are measured. The cherries are then macerated in eighteen-month Lambic. After several days, the yeasts attach to the fruit skins; those ambient in the cellar will encounter the sugar of the cherries as well as those still active in the Lambic. And so begins the process of fermentation. Once completed, the plugs of the barrels are tightly closed and the acid Lambic begins its work, extracting the taste and color of the fruit until obtaining the characteristic ruby hue.

Finally, the beer is filtered and bottled. At this stage, the fermentation will again be triggered through ferments still present in the Lambic and in the natural fermentable sugars of the non-consumed cherries. After several months, it is ready for consumption.

2011 Kriek. The color is a poppy shade, blood orange. Open, terribly fruity nose, recalling cherry pits. The mouth is full. In the attack, lots of fruit, supported by a bitterness masking the acidity. The whole is very refreshing. Contrasts with a "classic" Kriek. Its originality: class in the unclassifiable. Like the Van Roys said, it should be eaten with a slice of country bread, spread with salted butter and a good layer of white cheese (with added salt, pepper and chopped chives, with slices of radishes on top). A tasty variation of our cervelle de canut.

Kriek Lou Pepe. Here are cherries of the endemic variety of Brabant, the Schaerbeek (little flesh, large pit and striking acidity), which are used, up to 300 grams of cherries per lambic liter (in comparison to the 'classic' Kriek where the proportion is 200 grams per liter). For the record, Lou Pepe is the name children use to call their grandfathers among the Van Roys' many friends. So, to Jean-Pierre's grandchildren, he is the "Lou Pepe" of Brussels! The result here is still pure. In fact, this version of Kriek matches what we can taste when a winemaker dares to plant non-grafted vines in a parcel. The resulting wine is purer, the rootstock acting as a filter. In a word, the pleasure here is tenfold. In a pairing, you can try more complex dishes such as breast of duck grilled over a wood fire, with fried cherries sautéed in a white balsamic.

*Other family beers bear evocative names worthy of cartoon characters: the Fou 'Foune (Lambic of Bergeron apricot), the Iris (no wheat here, the beer is brewed only with a type of pale ale malt, bringing more depth to the color. Also, both suranné and fresh hops are equally distributed), the Vigneronne (Lambic with white grapes) and the Saint Lamvinus (with red grapes). All names clearly illustrated in the "bubbles!"*

# Acknowledgements

*To my father and Maurice*

Between the moment when the idea for this book sprouted and the present release, nearly four years have passed. The principal reason lies in my desire to transmit, to witness and to share. Over the past thirty years of contact with the world of wine and beyond, I have learned that nothing can take flight alone. At the forefront of those who have always supported me is Marie, my wife, who has always followed me in my travels around the world. Such abnegation, such an incredible proof of love, for in marrying me she also married a profession: my devouring passion, the fire of which has been and remains constantly burning. We have witnessed the turning of many pages together.

These days spent on the road, to vineyards, have often distanced me from the family cocoon, thus adding to my number of absences from family meals. So many moments I couldn't spend with our children: Margot, Lisa and Baptiste. But wherever I am, at Le Cinq or around the world, every day, the phone brings us closer. As for our time together, the least I can say is that the Beaumards do not get bored. Today, I am very proud of their paths, their choices and their successes.

Marie and the children are inseparable from my equilibrium at Le Cinq, this great house, where, in the spring of 1999, Didier Le Calvez, then director general, placed his total confidence in me to create the cellar. And what a cellar! Later, Christopher W. Norton, while imprinting his style at the George V, renewed this confidence by developing close ties with our customers, lovers of exceptional bottles. On several occasions, he accompanied me to the vineyards with these brand hosts.

Chris, called to very important duties within the Four Seasons group, appointed Christian Clerc to continue the work in progress. This propelled me to Washington to spread the word of both wine and the George V. During the summer of 2014, José Silva became our director general. Through his intense involvement in Le Cinq, in the kitchens as well as the rooms, he helped project us towards exciting projects. This balance between work and family has allowed me, from the beginning, to further develop my relationship with the international wine industry. Starting with Raymond Garcia, who put an end to my journey through the desert from 1985 to 1987 by presenting me to Gilles Étéocle. It was he who gave me a chance, despite my disability.

This new beginning led me to Dominique Rézette, who opened up the Burgundian gates and helped me to understand each cru, thanks to his unparalleled knowledge. At La Poularde, I would like to thank our young people: Joëlle Marti-Baron, Philippe Emmanuelli, Tristan Ringenbach and Enrico Bernardo. In this house where I spent incomparable hours, one evening after a heated discussion with Monique Étéocle (because there is also, in this business, pesky quarters of an hour!), I remember saying to Thierry in the wine shop adjoining La Poularde: "I don't care about aches and words. They don't prevent a flower from blooming."

Then, helped by Virginia Morvan in November 1999, we were experimenting with a "dry run" at the George V. Very soon, I asked Enrico to join me in the Le Cinq adventure. I quickly sensed his firepower. With the help of the whole team, he climbed to the top in record time. For several years, we grew together in this great house, a unique case in sommellerie history where two of the best sommeliers in the world, gold and silver, would work together in the same restaurant. Of course, every day was not simple or easy. As Thierry has often said, "The sommelier is a solitary animal that, among us, is forced to live in packs."

Thierry. Since Montrond, he has been at my side. It all started in November 1994 when I was asked to sponsor his "Mention de Sommellerie" at Dinard. The following spring, he joined me at La Poularde. Since then, we've never left each other! Even when he was at Oxford! I called him and wrote to him. Nicolas, his companion, and Marie know, we are an "old married couple." He is the cornerstone of my success. He can be stubborn (Breton roots oblige!); he knew and knows how to support the team and to manage the cellars in my absence. He follows the journey of each sommelier passing through the George V and never forgets them. Over the years, I have looked out for him and he has looked out for me.

Just one look in the mirror reminds us that time passes too quickly. The era of our discussions in the shop at Montrond before services… seems so far away. Like those evenings in the spring of 1999, when we wrote the first drafts of what was to be the "Brigade du Cinq," creating a *dream team* with Olivier Roellinger in the kitchen and Christian Stevanin as deputy director of Le Cinq (furthermore, the same evening I called Dinard and offered him the job). Far away too, are the evenings' end, when we would read, dreaming, the *Mémoires de M. Hugo de Chez Maxim's, La Vie de César Ritz* by his wife Marie-Louise… an at-home viewing of *The Remains of the Day* with Anthony Hopkins and Emma Thompson, smoking *Sanchos* by Sancho Panza with a 1937 Colheita de Noval, near a roaring fire. That was in 1996.

We dreamed about professional futures that seemed inaccessible. Our passions, encounters and our destinies have led us here.

To all, I thank you.

**Éric Beaumard**
*Paris, September 2015*

# Index
## of domains
..........................

## Champagne

Diebolt-Vallois ~ 32
Veuve Clicquot Ponsardin ~ 38
Salon ~ 46
Dom Pérignon Dom Pérignon ~ 53
Krug ~ 62

## The Loire Valley

Domaine Luneau-Papin ~ 74
Le Clos Rougeard ~ 81
Domaine Lucien et
Gilles Crochet ~ 86
Domaine François Cota ~ 90
Domaine Edmond et
Anne Vatan ~ 96
Domaine Benjamin
   et Didier Dagueneau ~ 102
Domaine François Chidaine ~ 109
Domaine du Clos Naudin ~ 116

## Burgundy

Domaine Vincent Dauvissat ~ 126
Domaine François Raveneau ~ 133
Domaine Michel et
   Jean-Baptiste Bouzereau ~ 141
Domaine Roulot ~ 150
Domaine Jean-François
Coche-Dury ~ 158
Domaine Jean-Marc Boillot ~ 165
Domaine David Duband ~ 172
Domaine Georges Noëllat ~ 179
Domaine Méo-Camuzet ~ 186
Domaine de la Romanée-
Conti ~ 194
Château Thivin ~ 206

## Bordeaux

Château Haut-Bailly ~ 216
Châteaux Haut-Brion & La Mission
   Haut-Brion ~ 222
Château Rauzan Ségla ~ 229
Château Palmer ~ 234
Château Margaux ~ 240
Château Léoville Barton ~ 246
Château Batailley ~ 252
Château Lynch-Bages ~ 259
Château Mouton Rothschild ~ 264
Château Lafite Rothschild ~ 270
Château Latour ~ 276
Château Calon Ségur ~ 282
Château Soutard ~ 286
Château Figeac ~ 294
Château Ausone ~ 303
Château Cheval Blanc ~ 311
Pétrus ~ 320
Château Lafleur ~ 328
Château de Fargues ~ 334
Château d'Yquem ~ 341

## Rhone Valley

Domaine André Perret ~ 350
Château Grillet ~ 357
Domaine Jean-Louis Chave ~ 366
Domaine Jean-Paul Jamet ~ 376
Domaine Saint-Préfert ~ 389
Le Vieux Donjon ~ 395
Château Rayas ~ 402
Domaine Bonneau ~ 410

## Other Vineyards of France

Alsace
Domaine André Kientzler ~ 420
Domaine André Ostertag ~ 426
Jura
Domaine Michel Pichet ~ 432
Southwest
Domaine de Souch ~ 438
Les Jardins de Babylone ~ 443

## Europe and the World

Germany
Weingut Egon Müller ~ 450
Italy
Bruno Giacosa ~ 460
Giacomo Conterno ~ 466
Spain
Bodega Vega Sicilia ~ 482
Portugal
Quinta Do Noval ~ 492
Madeira Barbeito ~ 500
Hungary
Domaine Disznókö ~ 512
United States
Marciano Estate ~ 520
Harlan Estate ~ 526

## Spirits, Liqueurs, Ciders and Beer

Armagnac
Domaine Boingnères ~ 534
Calvados
Domaine de Semainville ~ 541
Liqueur
La Grande-Chartreuse ~ 548
Cider
Château Hauteville ~ 559
Éric Bordelet ~ 559
Beer
Brasserie Cantillon ~ 564

# Bibliography

*L'Accord parfait*
Philippe Bourguignon, Chêne,
2012.

*Atlas mondial du vin* – 7ᵉ édition
Hugh Johnson and Jancis
Robinson, Flammarion, 2014.

*Au Cheval Blanc. Une histoire
de millésimes*
Claude Fourcaud-Laussac,
Mollat, 1998.

*Bordeaux. Les Grands Crus classé*s
Jean-Charles Chapuzet
and Guy Charneau, Glénat, 2014.

*Bordeaux et ses vins* – 15ᵉ édition
Marc-Henry Lemay, Féret, 1995.

*Les Caves d'Ausone*
Damien Delanghe, Confluences
and Château Ausone, 2006.

*Chartreuse. Histoire d'une liqueur.
Guide de l'amateur*
Michel Steinmetz, Glénat, 2006.

*Châteaux*
Diane Biéville and Jean-Pierre
Godeaut (photos), Duchamp/
Chevalier, 1991.

*Le Chemin des vignes.
Vallée de la Loire*
Le Rouge & le Blanc,
Sang de la Terre, 2010.

*Climats du vignoble de Bourgogne.
Un patrimoine exceptionnel*
Under the direction of
l'Association pour l'inscription
des climats du vignoble de
Bourgogne au Patrimoine
mondial de l'Unesco, Glénat,
2013.

*Cyrano de Bergerac*
Edmond Rostand, Flammarion
Livre de Poche, 1996.

*Dictionnaire amoureux de la Loire*
Danièle Sallenave, Académie
française, Plon, March 2014.

*Éloges de la cuisine française*
Édouard Nignon, Inter-Livres,
1995.

*L'Esprit des vins. Crus classés
de Saint-Émilion*
Béatrice Massenet, Emmanuelle
Ponsan-Dantin and François
Querre, La Martinière, 2010.

*Le Goût des Belges* – tome 1
Éric Boschman, Racines, 2006.

*Le Guide des vins de Bordeaux*
Jacques Dupont, Grasset, 2011.

*Le Guide de la Champagne
2012-2013* Jean-Marie Curien, 2012.

*Château Latour*
Michel Dovaz, Assouline, 1998.

*Le Livre des cépages*
Jancis Robinson, Hachette, 1988.

*Le Livre des millésimes. Les grands
vins de France 1747 à 1990*
Michael Broadbent, Scala, 1993.

*La Loire. Les vignerons.
Leur histoire*
Frédéric Arlettaz and Gérard
Cloix, Frédéric Arlettaz
and Gérard Cloix, 2013.

*La Magie du 45ᵉ parallèle*
Olivier Bernard and Thierry
Dussard, Féret, 2014.

*Les Maîtres de l'orge*
BD in 8 volumes, Story Jean Van
Hamme, Illustrations Francis
Vallès, Glénat, 1992 to 2001.

*Château Margaux*
Nicholas Faith, Flammarion, 2004.

*La Morale d'Yquem*
Jean-Paul Kauffmann,
Grasset – Mollat, 1999

*L'Or du vin*
Pierre Casamayor, Michel Dovaz
and Jean-François Bazin, Hachette,
1994.

*Château Palmer*
René Pijassou, Stock, 1997.

*Château Pichon Longueville
Comtesse Lalande. La passion du vin*
David Haziot, La Martinière,
2007.

*Château Rauzan-Ségla.
La naissance d'un grand cru classé*
René Pijassou, La Martinière, 2004.

*La Cinquième République
aux fourneaux*
Joël Normand,
La Table ronde, 1999.

*Les Vins d'Alsace*
Serge Dubs, Robert Laffont
and Serpenoise, 1991.

*Vins feu. À la découverte
des terroirs des volcans célèbres*
Charles Frankel, Dunod, 2014.

*Le Vin d'hier. Vins historiques
et d'exception*
Pierre Chevrier, Slatkine, 2009.

*Les Vins d'hiver*
Philippe Bourguignon
and Jacques Dupont, Hatier, 1999.

*Vingt ans maître d'hôtel chez
Maxim's*
Hugo, Amiot-Dumont, 1951.

**Magazines**
All issues of the quarterly
magazine *Vigneron*

To Thierry, my friend.

He is, for me, an incredible figure in this business, constantly evolving. A tireless worker, a jack of all trades, he has a strong sense of duty and a real talent for teaching. He is integral to our success. His loyalty will forever remain in my heart.

Thierry, iconic Head Sommelier of the George V Hotel, is a friend, a confidant and my second brother. During the 20 years that we have worked together, we have learned to speak without saying anything. A large part of this work has been reviewed and adjusted by Thierry.

Gourmet and gourmand, he is one of the rare men in the industry with perfect taste, who breathes in the table and preserves, against all odds, a certain idea of France which is so dear to us.
Whenever we can, with his partner Nicolas, my wife Marie-France and our kids, we take advantage of good times together.

Thank you, Thierry, for maintaining your convictions and staying true to yourself. I'm proud to know you.

Finally, a thank you to Sylvain Charlois, owner of the Tonnellerie Berthomieu in Charité-sur-Loire. A longtime friend without whom this book would not have been possible.

**Éric Beaumard**

Graphic design and layout:
Olivier Fontvieille, Anne Ponscarme (offparis)
Photos: Fabrice Leseigneur
Editing: Francis Gramet
Copyediting and production: Nord Compo, Villeneuve-d'Ascq, France

Photo-engraving: APS Chromostyle
Printed in October 2016
by POLLINA printing presses
Legal deposit: November 2016

Printed in FRANCE